The Political Economy of Trade and Growth

To My Parents

The Political Economy of Trade and Growth

An Analytical Interpretation of Sir James Steuart's *Inquiry*

Hong-Seok Yang
Lecturer in Economics
Dongeui University

Edward Elgar

Published by
Edward Elgar Publishing Limited
Gower House
Croft Road
Aldershot
Hants GU11 3HR
England

Edward Elgar Publishing Company
Old Post Road
Brookfield
Vermont 05036
USA

British Library Cataloguing in Publication Data

Yang, Hong-Seok
Political Economy of Trade and Growth:
Analytical Interpretation of Sir James
Steuart's Inquiry
I. Title
330.1

Library of Congress Cataloguing in Publication Data

Yang, Hong-Seok, 1959–
The political economy of trade and growth : an analytical interpretation of Sir James Steuart's Inquiry / by Hong-Seok Yang.
336 p. 23 cm.
Includes bibliographical references.
1. Economics. 2. International trade. 3. Economic development. 4. Economics—Great Britain—History—18th century. 5. Steuart, James, Sir, 1712–1780. Inquiry into the principles of political economy. I. Title.
HB151.Y36 1994
330–dc20
94-12016
CIP

ISBN 1 85898 093 3

Printed and bound in Great Britain by
Hartnolls Limited, Bodmin, Cornwall

Acknowledgements

Without the help of Professor Denis O'Brien as my Ph.D. supervisor, this study would never have been completed. He took great pains not only to provide constructive criticisms and suggestions for the present work in particular, but also to orient my approach to the history of economic thought in general. I owe Hee-Seok Yahng and Nerio Naldi for their useful comments on various parts of the draft and their hearty encouragement, and Professor Ian Steedman for his sincere advice at the early stage of my research. I feel grateful to Professor Terence Hutchison and Dr. Rodney Wilson who examined rather thoroughly but supportively my thesis, which here becomes published. Thanks are also due to Sara Ridley, Bennett Palmer, Linden Townsley, Bruce Lorimer and others in Collingwood College, University of Durham, for correcting my English. I must be fortunate to find such an enthusiastic publisher as Edward Elgar and to hear that Professor Mark Blaug recommended the publication. Personally, I am indebted to all those good friends of mine, especially M-S Park, G-Y Ham, Rev. D-H Park, Rev. J-H Kim, S-H Lee, G-B Ko, Inok Baik, S-M Hong, Mr. and Mrs. Norton, Jacqueline Droguett, Francisco and Loudes Astorga, and Tracey West, and, above all, my family for their support and encouragement during my stay in England. Despite all this help, there surely remain many faults and errors, for which I am solely to blame.

H-S.Y.
July 1994

CONTENTS

List of Figures and Tables

Figures

Tables

1. Introduction

> The principal object of this science is to secure a fund of subsistence for all inhabitants, to obviate every circumstance which may render it precarious; to provide every thing necessary for supplying the wants of the society, and to employ the inhabitants (supposing them to be free-men) in such a manner as naturally to create reciprocal relations and dependencies between them to supply one another with their reciprocal wants.
>
> Sir James Steuart,
> *An Inquiry into the Principles of Political Oeconomy* (*Works*, vol.1, p.3)

I

The place of Sir James Steuart (1713-80)[1] in the history of economic thought must be re-assessed in consideration of his *true* contribution to the development of economic discipline. The contribution should be weighed in terms of his original thought as well as his influence on those who came after. There would not be any proportional relation between them. For Steuart, in fact, quite the opposite is true; that is, despite the insights of his original thought, his influence was limited. Apart from the question of why he exerted such limited influence,[2] many historians of the subject have not taken him seriously. His work has been so often exposed to wholesale treatments – mostly criticisms founded on commonplace sweeping judgements under the name of 'mercantilism'.[3] To do him justice, we must dig out his true meaning

---

[1] For some biographical accounts of Steuart, see Erskine (his nephew, 1792), General Sir James Steuart (his son, 1805), Campbell (1947; ch.1), Sen (1957; ch.2), Taylor (1957) and Skinner (1966; Biographical Sketch).

[2] There have been suggested many reasons for this in the literature. For instance, some focused on his being out of the *Zeitgeist* of his times (Sen (1957), Meek (1958), Akhtar (1978 and 1979) and Perlman (1990)); some on technical deficiencies of his analysis (Marx (1862-3), Feilbogen (1889) and Fraser (1937)); some on the prominence of Smith in his day (Johnson (1937) and Stettner (1945)); some on his non-utilitarian philosophical background (Vickers (1959)); some on his political inclination (Davie (1967)); some on his unfortunate writing style (Skinner (1966)); and others on some combinations of these (Schumpeter (1954) and Hutchison (1988)). For the relation between the two Scottish contemporary *Inquiries* – i.e., Steuart's (*into the Principles of Political Oeconomy*; 1767) and Smith's (*into the Nature and Causes of the Wealth of Nations*; 1776), see the appendix to Ch.5 below.

[3] Steuart's *Inquiry* was often bluntly dismissed as a typical out-of-date view of the state interventionism based on the mercantilist ideas. Among others, cf. Ingram (1888), Beer (1938), Roll (1942), Haney (1949) and Bell (1953). Meanwhile, an observation made by a well-known historian of general thought appears to reflect how Steuart's work had been received up until the end of the last century.

and cast new light upon his original thought. This is what the present interpretation of his major economic work, *An Inquiry into the Principles of Political Oeconomy*,[4] primarily aims at.

> ... his [Steuart's] style is awkward and his method intricate. He becomes hopelessly confused by the complexity of his subject-matter; and argues himself into elaborate blunders in attempting to refute Hume's lucid and satisfactory account of money and the balance of trade. ... instead of imitating their [the French writers'] logical simplicity, or adopting their conception of a fixed social order, he exaggerates the ordinary complexity of the mercantile theories, and believes implicitly in the indefinite modifiability of mankind. (Stephen (1876), vol.2, p.304; brackets added.)

He concluded that Steuart is 'amongst the most tiresome individuals of that most tiresome of all literary species – the inferior political economists' (*loc.cit.*; quoted by Hutchison (1988, p.350)). (Nevertheless, we shall see soon, among Steuart's other remarkable achievements, how successfully he refuted that sort of quantity theory of money shared by Locke, Montesquieu and Hume, and presented his own alternative theory; how his method is different from the French *systemes*; how far his theory of trade and growth reaches beyond the ordinary mercantilist theories; and what his discussion of the 'spirit of the people or the times' really implies.) On the other hand, occasionally, those emphasizing some historical and institutional aspects of economics spoke highly of Steuart: e.g., Grossman (1943) and Hasbach (1891). It is only in relatively recent years that some rigorous studies on Steuart have been carried out from various perspectives. Apart from a multitude of standard history books of economic thought, we may enumerate them as follows: for the whole of Steuart's political economy, Campbell (1947), Sen (1957) and Skinner (1966); and, for the particular subjects, Stettner (1945) on the public debt, Sen (1947) on the monetary analysis of output and employment, Meek (1958) on the economics of control, Vickers (1959; ch.12) on the theory of money, Eagly (1961) on the 'aspiration effect', Skinner (1962, 1963, 1967 and 1981) on the state interventionism, the international relations, the theory of money and the system, Chamley (1962, 1963 and 1965) on his relation to Keynes, his philosophical background and some relevant documents, Kobayashi (1967) on his relation to Smith and List, Akhtar (1978 and 1979) on the economic growth and an outline of macroeconomic model, Perelman (1983) on the primitive accumulation, Anderson and Tollison (1984) on his relation to Smith, Eltis (1986) on the corporate state, and Perlman (1990) on the balance of trade. Later on, we shall relate these studies to the present analysis in specific contexts.

[4] The full title is as follows:

An Inquiry into the Principles of Political Oeconomy: Being an Essay on the Science of Domestic Policy in Free Nations. In which are particularly considered Population, Agriculture, Trade, Industry, Money, Coin, Interest, Circulation, Banks, Exchange, Public Credit, and Taxes.

It was first published in 2 quarto vols., London, 1767; reprinted in 3 vols., Dublin, 1770; translated into German by J. Von Pauli, Hamburg, 1769-70 and C.F. Schott, Tubingen, 1769-72; and translated into French by M. de Senovert, Paris, 1789. A revised version was published in the first 4 vols. of *The Works, Political Metaphysical, and Chronological, of the late Sir James Steuart of Coltness, Bart. now first collected by General Sir James Steuart, Bart. his Son, from his Father's Corrected Copies. To which are Subjoined Anecdotes of the Author*, 6 vols., London, 1805. We use this version in the present interpretation. There is a reduced edition by Skinner, 1966. Meanwhile, Steuart's other economic writings are as follows:

1) *A Dissertation on the Policy of Grain, with a view to a Plan for preventing scarcity or exorbitant prices, in the Common Markets of England* (1759)
2) *A Dissertation upon the Doctrine and Principles of Money Applied to the German Coin* (1761)
3) *Notes to Memorial on Scottish Banks* (1764)
4) *Notes to Thoughts Concerning Banks, and the Paper Currency of Scotland* (1766)
5) *Considerations on the Interest of the County of Lanark in Scotland; which (in several respects) may be applied to that of Great Britain in General* (1769)
6) *The Principles of Money Applied to the Present State of the Coin in Bengal* (1772).

Except 3) and 4), which appear in *Caldwell Papers* (Item CVIII and CIX, respectively), all of them are contained in the *Works*. For a full list of Steuart's writings, both published and in manuscript, see Skinner (1966), Appendices D and E.

In conjunction with the rehabilitation of Steuart in particular, we may take note of a fundamental issue in the history of economic thought in general.[5] That is to say, how do we think economic ideas and theories have been developed so far? Could it be described as a linear progress of one, inferior and unsophisticated, to another, superior and sophisticated? Or has it simply reflected the economic reality of each different stage of development in the material world? Our assumption is that the evolution of economic ideas and theories in the past is to be seen as a sporadic and intermittent process, rather than a mere sequential and cumulative one. But it does not mean either that there is no linkage or common ground between different ideas and theories, or that there is any definite *vis-à-vis* correspondence between economic reality and theory. It rather implies the acceptance of both the diversity of analytical focus among different authors and the development of analytical tools through time. Therefore, as far as each individual author's economic doctrine is concerned, it should be understood in his own historical, ideological and methodological context. In our interpretation of Steuart, we will avoid as much as possible imposing on him anything that would have been alien to him.

II

We may further note a few characteristics of the present interpretation of Steuart's *Inquiry*. Above all, we will interpret the *Inquiry* mainly from an analytical rather than a comparative perspective. In the literature, there have been plenty of comparative studies – whether explicitly declared or not – without necessarily being based on any rigorous analysis of his work itself. We will thoroughly analyse both the logical structure and the actual contents of Steuart's *Inquiry*. In a theoretical view, the former might be more important; whereas, in a practical view, the latter might be more interesting. However, they both constitute integral parts of his political economy, being indispensable to each other. Therefore, we must take these two aspects evenly

[5] At the end of his extensive review of the 'pre-Adamite' economic thought and theories, Hutchison (1988) made a few concluding remarks on what has happened to them since 1776, as follows:

> Our first conclusion – perhaps barely worth drawing – is a total rejection of the view of J.B. Say, still to be met with today, that, before Smith, there was virtually no political economy. ... What may strike one next is that so many of the most important and central ideas, theories, or lines of thought, which have been alive and developing in the twentieth century, emerged in a clear form, or first underwent significant developments in this period. ... Jointly with this observation, or conclusion, what should also be remarked is the fate, or treatment, of some of the most important and fundamental of these ideas and lines of thought – still, of course, alive and widely defended more than two centuries later – in the approximately 100 years following 1776, when they were excluded, disregarded, seriously under-emphasized, or explicitly rejected as erroneous, by the classical orthodoxy which then prevailed. (pp.372-3.)

The present attempt to rehabilitate Steuart's political economy is largely inspired by Hutchison's stimulating account of the period concerned (1662-1776).

into account, in whatever way we analyse his *Inquiry*. As a matter of fact, this point partly explains why many commentators in the past failed to put him in the right place. Most of them did not pay due attention to the logical structure of his *Inquiry*, while they simply identified parts and pieces of its contents with some mercantilist ideas preceding him. Interpreting the work of an author should not be anything like painting with arbitrarily chosen colours. It may be interpreted from different angles, but its own logical structure should not be ignored or destroyed. In our interpretation of Steuart, we will try to understand the contents of his political economy according to its own logic.

One might ask whether Steuart's *Inquiry* was really written, from start to finish, coherently. If not, how can we interpret it in a consistent way? The answer to this question is that we merely assume that all its different parts and pieces are logically, more or less, coherent. Unless they are supposed to fit together, any attempt to interpret each of them would be prone to be at best piecemeal and fragmentary, or, at worst, serving one's own particular interest. Thus, upon the assumption of the logical coherence of his *Inquiry*, the task in hand might be seen as a *rational reconstruction* of Steuart's whole political economy.

We will reconstruct it *in modern guise*. That is to say, assuming Steuart's work to be logically consistent, we will re-present it in terms of modern economics. To some extent, thus, we have to make a compromise between the author's and our own way of presentation. Obviously, if we just follow his own, then we might simply reproduce his arguments. The best way to do this is to quote his work as often as we can. On the other hand, if we insist too much upon our own way, then it might lead us to establishing *our* arguments in *his* phrase. In that case, we would not particularly have to rely upon his authority. We will stay just in the middle. For instance, although we anatomize his *Inquiry* in terms of different areas of modern economics, e.g., the theory of value, that of output, etc., we will still keep pace with his own arrangement of the subject matter.

III

Finally, let us sketch how we will actually analyse Steuart's *Inquiry* in what follows. This book is composed of eight main chapters. Each chapter deals with Steuart's discussions of a different part or area of political economy. While the division itself is, by and large, corresponding to the usual practice of taxonomy in modern economics, the variety of subjects demonstratively shows us the comprehensiveness of his own political economy.[6] To almost

[6] Sen (1957) claimed that Steuart was the 'author of the first comprehensive treatise in English entitled Political Oeconomy, one of the first to induce a rigorous scientific methodology, deductive as well as inductive, into economic enquiries, and a pioneer theoretician who not only made

every chapter (except Ch.8), we append some additional discussions. In the appendices, we usually represent some others' view or theory of the subject concerned in comparison with Steuart's so that we may put the latter in its historical and disciplinary context after the actual analysis; otherwise, we give an account of some institutional background to his arguments within a particular subject (Appendix to Chs. 6 and 7) or discuss the methodological basis of his political economy as a whole (Appendix to Ch.9).

We will start with Steuart's basic conception of an exchange economy in Chapter 2. We will delineate a macroeconomic model of production, distribution and consumption in the economy, from his description of the circulation of money and commodities among the different economic sectors and social classes. It will serve as a basic framework of his economic analysis in later chapters. In the appendix, we will compare Steuart's model with Cantillon's and Quesnay's. Then, we will move on to his theory of value and distribution in Chapter 3. According to Steuart, the determination of the value of commodities is directly related to that of the distribution of income, in that the production of commodities in an exchange economy is primarily for marketing and their price determined in the markets becomes the source of income for those who participate in both production and exchange processes. In particular, we will discuss his distinction between the 'real value' of commodities and their 'current price', and his disentanglement of three different categories of income, i.e., the 'profit upon alienation', the wages of labour and the rent of land. In the appendix, we will discuss the cost-of-production theories of value in Petty, Cantillon, Quesnay, Steuart, and Smith.

As Steuart's definition of 'political oeconomy',[7] quoted above, implies, the determination of the level of output and employment in an exchange economy is one of the central themes of his *Inquiry*. The most conspicuous analytical device for this was the notion of 'effectual demand', derived from his recognition of the interdependence of different economic sectors and social classes in the economy. In Chapter 4, after scrutinizing the nature of his notion of 'effectual demand', we will examine Steuart's explanation of the determination of the level of output, the amount of employment and the volume of population, all, in terms of this notion. In the appendix, we will carry out a comparative study of Steuart's and Keynes's theory of output and employment. The dynamic aspect of Steuart's analysis of output, employment and population will be expanded in Chapter 5, dealing with his theory of economic growth and foreign trade. In his *Inquiry*, Steuart was chiefly concerned with a growing economy with ever-increasing labour force. He

---

considerable original contributions in the fields of population, exchange, money, public finance and agricultural economics but was one of the first to develop the economics of planning and the evolutionist and institutional approach in social enquiry' (p.2).

[7] For the origin of the term 'political economy', see Letwin (1963), p.217 ff.

linked the limits of growth to the benefits of trade. Their relation must be subject to the state or stage of development of the economy concerned. He aptly articulated it in terms of the three-stage theory of trade. His theory of growth and trade culminates in his analogy between the 'balance of wealth' of individuals and the 'balance of trade' of trading countries. With his unique concept of wealth, Steuart made out his case for economic growth by means of the favourable balance of trade. We will illustrate it in a simple model at the end of chapter. In the appendix, we will make a comparison between the concept of wealth in Steuart and that in Smith.

The topics discussed so far principally refer to the first two books of Steuart's *Inquiry*, i.e., 'Of Population and Agriculture' and 'Of Trade and Industry'. Those in the following chapters, except Ch.9, relate to the other three books of the *Inquiry*, i.e., 'Of Money and Coin', 'Of Credit and Debts' and 'Of Taxes, and the Proper Application of their Amount'. We may call the former part the analysis of the *real* economy, while the latter that of the *monetary* economy.[8] We will begin Steuart's monetary analysis with his theory of national money and interest in Chapter 6. First, we will sort out all the functions of money assumed in his analysis. This will provide us with a basic tool-kit for our later discussions. Next, we will examine his analysis of coin or metallic money, as a proxy for the ideal money with those functions. We will discuss his explanations of the imperfections of coin, and their consequences, and his suggestions of some remedies for them. We will also discuss how he saw the value of the money-unit of coin determined and the relative price of coin, bullion and commodities regulated. Meanwhile, Steuart considered paper or symbolical money as a sort of credit. In relation to this, thus, we will discuss his analysis of the interest of money. Essentially, according to him, the rate of interest is determined in the loans market, as the price of money. After discussing the relation between the interest of money and the 'profit of trade and industry', as envisaged in the *Inquiry*, we will formalize Steuart's analysis of the determination of the rate of interest in a

[8] Johnson (1937) regarded the first two books of the Inquiry as the '*corpus* of Steuart's work' (p.213); whereas Vickers (1970) observed that 'from the viewpoint of the history of analysis it is on his monetary theory that his permanent claim to fame will be found to rest' (p.1190). Meanwhile, Campbell (1947) noted,

> Steuart originally intended these [first] two books together to constitute a complete work – they were so dedicated and presented to Lady Mary Wortley Montagu in 1760. However, the additions made after Steuart's return to Britain greatly elaborated the monetary and fiscal analysis and are of the greatest significance in understanding the focus of his economics. (p.40; brackets added.)

The last of these is closest to our point of view: that is, in Steuart's *Inquiry*, both real and monetary analysis were in even balance. Indeed, it was carefully organized under a central theme, which seems to be regarded as the macroeconomic analysis of trade and growth in an exchange economy. We shall discuss the analytical structure of his political economy and its central theme and ultimate message later in our Conclusion (Ch.10), after going through the actual analysis of his *Inquiry*.

fixed-price macroeconomic model. This model could be used for his argument against a legal maximum for the rate of interest. At the end of the chapter, we will relax the assumption of a fixed price level and present a monetary general equilibrium model of his analysis of money, price and output in a closed economy. In Chapter 7, we will continue to examine Steuart's monetary analysis but this time in an open-economy setting. Premising some general concepts of foreign exchange in his analysis, we will discuss how, according to him, the rate of exchange between the different currencies of trading countries is determined, and what relation could be found between the rate of exchange and the balance of payments. After exploring Steuart's analysis of the effects of the balance of payments on the domestic circulation of money, we will extend our previous general equilibrium model of money, price and output, from a closed to an open economy. To Chapters 6 and 7, we will append a summary of Steuart's discussions of banking, as they constitute the institutional background to his theory of money, national and international.

In Chapter 8, we will discuss Steuart's theory of public finance. When we first examine his analysis of taxation, we will introduce what he called a 'fundamental principle of taxation', and look at his classification of various taxes. Then, we will scrutinize his detailed discussions of the nature of the two alternative taxes, i.e., 'proportional' and 'cumulative', and the consequences of their imposition in both microeconomic and macroeconomic contexts. Next, we will proceed to Steuart's analysis of public credit and debts, another means of procuring funds for government spending. We will examine his discussions of the nature of 'public credit', in comparison with 'private credit' and 'mercantile credit', and its social and economic consequences. After further going over his discussions of the various methods of repayment of public debts and of the public bankruptcy of the state, we will unravel some macroeconomic implications of his analysis. To this point, we will have discussed Steuart's macroeconomic analysis of taxation and that of public credit and debts on the implicit assumption that public spending immediately follows them. At the end of the chapter, we will eventually have an overall view of his theory of public finance, including public spending, and we will present an macroeconomic model incorporating it. The model is built up by way of expanding the previous monetary general equilibrium model for a closed economy without public sector in Chapter 6.

Chapter 9 contains a discussion of the analytical and methodological infrastructure of Steuart's *Inquiry*. It works at his understanding of some fundamental elements of political economy: i.e., human beings, society and the body politic. We will first examine some presumptions of human nature, which underlie the whole of his economic analysis. We will relate them particularly to some important ideas or notions in his analysis. Steuart also perceived human nature in its sociological and historical context. We will discuss it in terms of what he called the 'spirit of the times'. Next, we will deal with his concept of society. According to Steuart, who saw it in a historico-economic perspective, society has developed along with its economic conditions in three stages: i.e., the stage of gathering and hunting, that of agriculture and barter, and that of trade and industry. The three-stage theory of society would inevitably lead us to his view on the relation between the economy and the body politic. While all human relations could be explained in terms of 'subordination and dependence', their nature varies according to the stage of development of society. As far as the latest stage of society is concerned, the relation of 'subordination and dependence' is purely economic in its nature. Nevertheless, as his comparative account of alternative forms of government showed, the body politic of a 'free society' would definitely affect the workings of its economy. We will append to this chapter a brief note on Steuart's empirico-historical relativism in method.

In our Conclusion, we will discuss some significant implications of the present analytical interpretation of Steuart's *Inquiry*, focusing particularly on theoretical aspects of his political economy.

2. The Basic Conception of an Exchange Economy

As we launch into a thorough examination of Steuart's political economy, we shall discuss, in this chapter, his basic conception of the exchange economy, a particular form of economy with which he was primarily concerned. We will carry it out in two stages. In the first stage, we are going to have a close look into his description of both the class structure and the sectoral division in the economy. In the second, thereupon, we will delineate some macroeconomic model of the circulation of money and commodities among the different classes and sectors. The present discussion will serve as a basic framework of our later examination of Steuart's economic analysis. In the appendix, we shall further discuss R. Cantillon's and F. Quesnay's model of circulation in comparison with Steuart's. Despite some similarities in appearance among these three models, interestingly enough, the respective authors drew different theoretical implications from them as they laid emphasis on different aspects of the models.

1. THE CLASS STRUCTURE OF SOCIETY AND THE SECTORAL DIVISION OF ECONOMY

The society of which Steuart had a picture in his mind was economically interdependent among its members.[1] His discussion of the process of its advancement shows us how they have been getting more and more dependent upon each other in an economic sense. In this context, the meaning of the interdependence among the members of society is twofold in Steuart's conception. On the one hand, as society advances, both the scale and the extent of material production increase; therefore, the division of labour necessarily comes into existence and the process of exchange between products from different economic sectors becomes inevitable. Upon the ensuing enhancement of productivity, on the other hand, a certain relation of transferring economic products, particularly net products or 'surplus', comes about among different classes of people, subject to the institution or system of society, e.g., the private ownership of means of production. We may call the

[1] For Steuart's concept of society and his categorization of its advancement in history, see section 2, Ch.9 below.

one the sectoral division of economy and the other the class structure of society. Let us examine how Steuart actually conceived of them, one after the other.

According to Steuart, the social division of labour basically results from both the variety of human wants and the benefit of the specialization of occupations.

> I very readily agree, that any person, who would calculate his labour in agriculture, purely for his own subsistence, would find abundance of idle hours. But the question is, whether in good oeconomy such a person would not be better employed in providing *nourishment* for others, than in providing for any other want. When he provides food, he surely provides for a want; and experience shews, that it is better for a man to apply close to one trade, than to turn himself to several. Hence I conclude, that the best way of binding a free society together is by multiplying reciprocal obligations, and creating a general dependence between all its members. This cannot be better effected, than by appropriating a certain number of inhabitants, for the production of the quantity of food required for all, and by distributing the remainder into proper classes for supplying every other want. I say farther, that this distribution is not only the most rational, but that mankind fall naturally into it. (*Works*, vol.1, p.110; original italics.)

In the economy as a whole, the above division of labour between different occupations could be represented in terms of sectors. Throughout his analysis, in fact, Steuart assumed two economic sectors: agriculture and manufacturing industry.[2] The former was supposed to produce what he called 'physical necessaries [necessities]', composed of food and other subsistence goods, i.e., indispensable goods for living; whereas the latter was to produce what he called 'luxuries' including 'political necessaries [necessities]', composed of non-subsistence goods, i.e., dispensable goods for living.[3]

---

[2] Steuart called the manufacturing industry simply 'industry'.

[3] In a formal way, Steuart defined 'luxury' as follows:

> By luxury, I understand, the consumption of any thing produced by the labour or ingenuity of man, which flatters our senses or taste of living, and which is neither necessary for our being well fed, well clothed, well defended against the injuries of the weather, or for securing us against every thing which can hurt us. (*Works*, vol.1, p.41.)

Meanwhile, he distinguished between 'physical' and 'political necessary [necessity]' in the following way:

> *It is ample subsistence where no degree of superfluity is implied*, which communicates an idea of the *physical-necessary* as to food, when he is fully fed; if he is likewise sufficiently clothed, and well defended against every thing which may hurt him, he enjoys his full physical-necessary. ... this physical-necessary is not fixed to a point, but that it may vary like most other things. ... some desires relative to his wants ... proceed from the affections of his mind, are formed by habit and education, and when once *regularly established*, create another kind of necessary, which, for the sake of distinction, I shall call political. (*Works*, vol.1, pp.412-3; original italics.)

Thus, while he made no clear-cut distinction between 'physical necessary [necessity]' and 'luxury' by any means, he explained the ambiguity of the distinction in terms of what he called 'political necessary [necessity]'. That is to say, while he admitted that what is a luxury to one person might be a necessity to another, or *vice versa*, he ascribed this indefiniteness to the existence of 'political-

> ... we find the people distributed into two classes. The first is that of farmers who produce the subsistence, and who are necessarily employed in this branch of business; the other I shall call *free hands*; because their occupation being to procure themselves subsistence out of superfluity of the farmers, and by a labour adapted to the wants of the society, may vary according to the spirit of the times. (*Works*, vol.1, p.40; original italics.)

From this bisection of the economy, based on the division of labour, we may note that, while the production in each sector is dependent on the reciprocal demand, those employed in the manufacturing sector may be seen to 'live upon the surplus produced in the agricultural sector', in the sense that they can procure their subsistence only through the exchange of their manufactures (which are dispensable for living) for the agricultural products (which are indispensable).

Meanwhile, according to Steuart, there is another group of people who are employed in neither of those two sectors mentioned above, but who still 'live upon the surplus produced in the agricultural sector': the 'proprietors of land'.

> ... in countries where labour is required for feeding a society, ... all the surplus is consumed by people not employed in agriculture; ... the free hands who live upon the surplus produced by the farmers. These I must subdivide into two conditions. The first, those to whom this surplus directly belongs, or who, with a revenue in money already acquired, can purchase it. The second, those who purchase it with their daily labour or personal service. (*Works*, vol.1, pp.62-3.)

Thus, while Steuart called both the 'proprietors of land' and the 'industrious free hands', together, just 'free hands' as they commonly lived upon 'surplus' produced in agricultural sector, he actually assumed three classes or groups of people in the society whose economic sphere he portrayed as an exchange economy.[4] That is to say, they are the 'farmers' engaged in agriculture, some having their own land and some not; the 'industrious free hands' engaged in the manufacturing industry, including the merchants engaged in trade, both domestic and foreign; and the 'landlords' receiving rents from those 'farmers' who do not have their own land, either in kind or in money. From the discussions so far, we may summarize Steuart's conception of the sectoral division of an exchange economy and its social structure in a schematic diagram as Figure 2.1.[5]

---

necessary[necessity]'. In our analysis, however, we simply assume that the 'physical necessaries [necessities]' are equivalent to what we call subsistence goods, including some intermediate goods; whereas the 'luxuries' are equivalent to what we call non-subsistence goods, including some produced means of production. In Steuart's basic macroeconomic model, therefore, the agricultural sector is supposed to produce subsistence goods and the manufacturing sector to produce non-subsistence goods, while the subsistence and non-subsistence goods include some agricultural intermediate goods and some manufactured means of production, respectively.

[4] Steuart described this stage of society as that of 'trade and industry'. Cf. section 2, Ch.9 below.

[5] Steuart called the 'landlords' 'higher class', whereas both the 'industrious free hands' and the 'farmers', together, 'lower classes', in the sense that the one 'directly' acquire the surplus in agriculture through their rent revenue, whereas the other two should basically either offer 'their daily labour or personal service' or work for themselves, in order to procure their subsistence. On

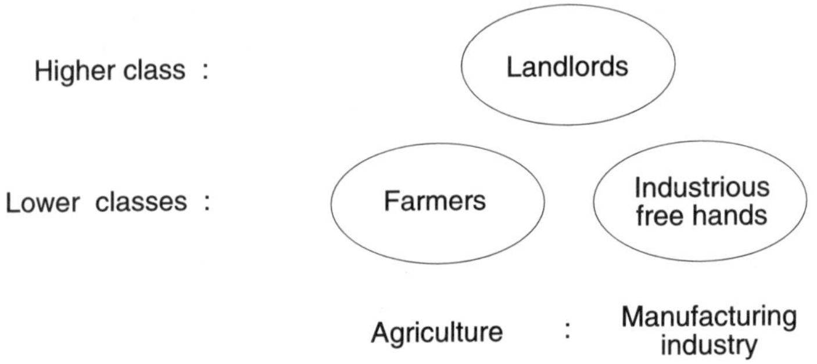

Figure 2.1 Social classes and economic sectors

Before we proceed further, we may note two things. One is that, in the present context, not only the division of economic sectors but also the conception of social classes is based on the economic relation among them. In particular, we cannot over-emphasize the significance of Steuart's recognition of their economic interdependence, i.e., their reciprocal wants or demand. It is from this that his notion of 'effectual demand' stems.[6] The other thing is Steuart's rather flexible definition of 'luxuries' and 'necessaries [necessities]', as he allowed the existence of 'political necessaries [necessities]', which must be subjective, depending on individuals.[7] In consequence, according to him, every class – higher or lower – consumes to some extent both 'necessaries [necessities]' and 'luxuries', i.e., both agricultural products and manufactures; the proportions between the consumption of each goods may however be quite different among classes.

2. THE CIRCULAR SYSTEM OF PRODUCTION, DISTRIBUTION AND CONSUMPTION

On the basis of our previous discussion of Steuart's understanding of the social structure and the sectoral division of an exchange economy, we shall examine in this section how he conceived of the circulation of goods and money both between the sectors and among the classes. The model of the

---

occasion, he referred to the 'higher class' as the 'idle', 'not-working part' or 'consumers', while the 'lower classes' as the 'industrious', 'working part' or 'producers'. See, for example, Steuart's discussion of the shifting and incidence of taxes of different nature in section 1, Ch 8 below. Also cf. note 9 in Ch.4 below.

[6] In this chapter of Steuart's basic conception of an exchange economy, suffice it to say that the 'effectual demand' is the very key notion in his macroeconomic model of the circulation of goods and money in that economy, as we shall fully discuss it in the chapter below (Ch.4) of his theory of output, employment and population.

[7] Cf. note 3 above.

circulation, derived here, underlies the whole of his macroeconomic analysis. We could gather it from his discussion of the relation between the rent of land and the bisection of the economy. That is to say, in discerning 'What Proportion of Inhabitants is necessary for Agriculture, and what Proportion may be usefully employed in every other Occupation',[8] Steuart pointed out how the rent of land might affect the proportion; this discussion, as such, shows us straightforwardly what picture of the circulation of goods and money he had in his mind, that could be applied to the rest of his macroeconomics. Let us carefully articulate this, step by step.

Concluding, from certain data, that 'the land-rents of England are to the gross produce, as nine is to twenty-one, or thereabout', he stated,[9]

> Now it is very certain, that all rents are in a pretty just proportion to the gross produce, after deducting three principal articles. First, The nourishment of the farmer, his family, and servants. Secondly, The necessary expences [expenses] of his family, for manufactures, and instruments for cultivating the ground. Thirdly, his reasonable profits, according to the custom of every country. ...
>
> Must not this [net produce or surplus] of necessity be employed in the nourishment, and for the use of those whom we have called the *free hands*; who may be employed in manufactures, trades, or in any other way, according to the taste of the times? Now the numbers of a people, I take to be very nearly in the proportion of the quantity of food they consume; especially when a society is taken thus, in such accumulative proportion, and when all are supposed to be under the same circumstances as to the plenty of the year. The whole gross produce of England we have said to be 21,000,000 *l.* sterling, of which 9 millions have remained for those not employed in agriculture; the farmers, therefore, and their attendants, must annually consume 12 millions; consequently the last class is to the first as 12 is to 9. If, therefore, according to Dr. Davenant, there be 5,545,000 people in that kingdom, there must be about 3,168,571 employed or dependent upon agriculture, and 2,376,429 free hands for every other occupation. (*Works*, vol.1, pp.55-7; original italics.)

From this, in the first place, we may note that the 'profits' for 'farmers', appearing in the first half of the quotation, were considered to be so indeterminate and precarious that they were actually out of Steuart's description of the circulation of goods and money in the last half.[10] Second, what he meant here by the 'free hands' was virtually the 'industrious free hands' who were engaged in the manufacturing industry, exclusive of 'landlords'. Taking these two points into account, we could delineate the circulation of goods in value terms on the ground of his calculation in the above quotation, as in Figure 2.2.[11] Note that, in this diagram, there are some

---

[8] The title of ch.VIII, book I of his *Inquiry*; *Works*, vol.1, pp.53-9.

[9] Steuart himself mentioned that he had recourse to the article *Political Arithmetic* of 'Mr. Chambers's Cyclopedia', for the data originally provided by Sir William Petty and Dr. Davenant, from which he drew the above conclusion. Cf. *Works*, vol.1, pp.55-7.

[10] We shall closely investigate the concept of capital and that of profit in Steuart, later in Ch.3 below.

[11] In the diagram, the rent of land is assumed to be paid in kind. Steuart sometimes assumed this simplified version of the model of circulation in his *Inquiry*, particularly in his analysis of output.

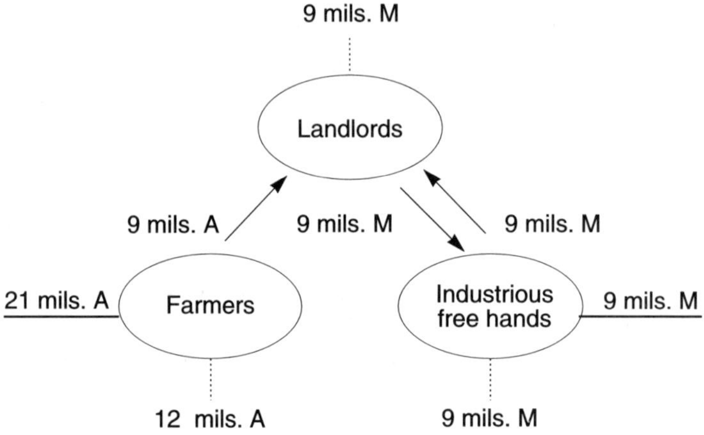

Proportion of pupulation - 12 : 0 : 9

where A: agricultural products, M: manufactures

—: production, ---: consumption, →: flow of goods

Figure 2.2 The circulation of goods: simplified

oversimplified assumptions which obviously conflict with what we said earlier in the previous section: that is, on the one hand, it is assumed here that the number of the 'higher class', i.e., 'landlords', is so small that the amount of 'physical necessaries [necessities]' which they consume would be negligible, but they still consume a great amount of 'luxuries' produced in the manufacturing sector. On the other hand, it is also assumed that the 'lower classes', i.e., 'farmers' and 'industrious free hands', consume only the 'physical necessaries [necessities]' produced in the agricultural sector. As for the second assumption, however, Steuart immediately relaxed it, as he corrected the proportion between the number of 'farmers' and that of 'industrious free hands', calculated above.

> But this proportion of farmers will be found far less, if we reflect, that we have reckoned for them the total amount of the three articles above mentioned, that is to say, the total consumption they make, as well in manufactures, profits upon their labour, &c. as for food and necessaries: whereas there has been nothing reckoned for the free hands, but the land-rent; consequently there should be added to the number of the latter as many as are employed in supplying with all sorts of manufactures the

---

Meanwhile, we shall discuss Steuart's analysis of the price of commodities and that of the level of output later in Chs. 3 and 4 below, respectively. We will also discuss Steuart's monetary general equilibrium model of both a closed and an open economy in Chs. 6 and 7 below, respectively.

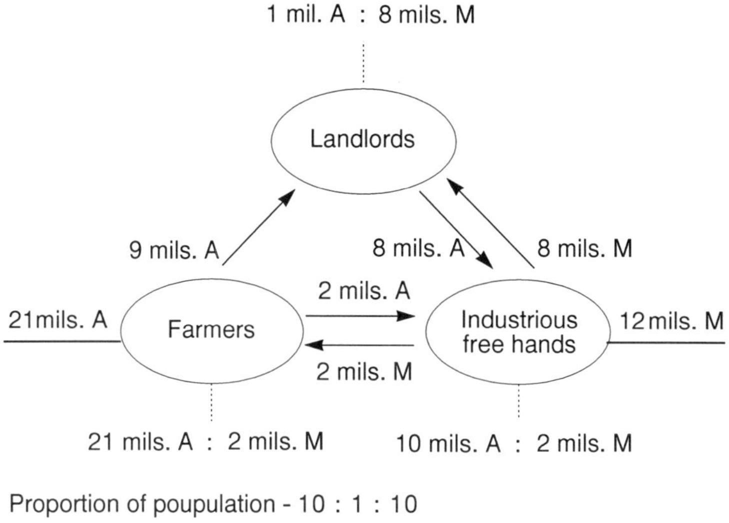

Figure 2.3 The circulation of goods: completed

> whole of the farmers of England, and all those depend upon them; and this number must be taken from one and added to the other class. (*Works*, vol.1, pp.57-8.)

Thus, it has to be admitted that the 'farmers' also consume manufactures, i.e., 'luxuries', and the 'profits upon their labour' should be regarded as one of their income sources, however indeterminate and precarious.[12] As far as the first of the above-mentioned assumptions is concerned, for the sake of generality, we may safely relax it. That is to say, in reference to the context of the rest of Steuart's analysis, the population of 'landlord' class would not be too small to be disregarded. Therefore, in our present delineation of Steuart's macroeconomic model of circulation based on his *Inquiry* as a whole, we shall suppose that the 'landlords' also consume agricultural products, i.e., 'physical necessaries [necessities]', and represent their number as proportional to the amount of the agricultural products they consume.

Making allowance for the above modifications to the previous simplified version, we shall assume here that the proportion between the amounts of consumption for each goods is the same for the 'farmers' and the 'industrious free hands', say 5:1, while the proportion for the 'landlords' is much smaller than that, say 1:8. If we further assume that the amount of manufactures consumed by the 'farmers' is 2 millions in value, we could give a diagrammatic description of the circulation of goods between sectors and

[12] In the same vein, we could allow that the 'industrious free hands' in the manufacturing sector also consume their own products, i.e., 'luxuries', and that some 'profits' would accrue to 'their labour'.

classes, presumed throughout Steuart's economic analysis, as in Figure 2.3.[13] In addition, in the this diagram, it seems not too difficult to imagine that money, as a medium of exchange, would circulate in the opposite direction to the flow of goods in all transactions between sectors and classes except the payment of rent by 'farmers' to 'landlords', which we assume to be made in money.

From our discussions so far, after all, we could surmise that the whole process of production, distribution and consumption in an exchange economy was described as a circular system in Steuart's analysis. That is to say, in each period, the 'farmers' and the 'industrious free hands' in the respective sectors of the economy produce certain amounts of their own goods, consume some part of them, and exchange some for each other, while those 'farmers' not having their own land ought to pay rent to the 'landlords', who in their turn spend it on their consumption of both goods. We may depict the system of production, distribution and consumption, underlying Steuart's *Inquiry*, in Figure 2.4, with slight changes to the previous diagram for emphasizing its circularity.[14]

Finally, let us discuss some first-hand implications of the above macroeconomic model of circulation, leaving in later chapters its further applications for some particular aspects of his economic analysis. What could we immediately say, or rather what did he actually say, in terms of such a model? Apparently, it could be summed up in two respects – apart from the interdependence of economic sectors and social classes and the circularity of all their economic activities and processes: Steuart's notion of 'effectual demand' and his concept of 'surplus'.

As far as the former notion is concerned, we could observe from Steuart's model of circulation that the mutual dependence for their respective production between the two sectors, i.e., agriculture and manufacturing industry, was to materialize mostly through the demand of 'landlords', who get

[13] Figure 2.3 is drawn in value terms. In his discussion related to the above quotations, Steuart took 400,000 from the number of 'farmers', surmised in the previous model of circulation, and added it to that of 'free hands', on account of the amount of manufactures consumed by the 'farmers', which is equivalent to 1,514,878.2 *l.* in value according to his calculation. That is, as he supposed that 5,545,000 people in England at that time consumed 21,000,000 *l.* of its agricultural products, we might say that 400,000 people would consume 1,514,878.2 *l.* Meanwhile, the same amount of manufactures in value should be in exchange for that. Therefore, if the 'farmers' are said to consume 1,514,878.2 *l.* of manufactures, then the same amount of agricultural products in value should additionally go to the manufacturing sector in exchange for that. This means that 400,000 more people should be engaged in that sector. In our model, however, we assume that the amount is 2,000,000 *l.* rather than 1,514,878.2 *l.* (and thus the number of people 528,095 rather than 400,000), for the sake of simplicity. Cf. *Works*, vol.1, p.58.

[14] In Figure 2.4, expressed in value terms, the transaction of 10 millions between 'farmers' and the 'industrious free hands' represents the latter's purchase for agricultural products; whereas that of 2 millions the former's for manufactures. In the meantime, we may assume the amount of money circulating in the economy to be given in any fixed sum, as long as its velocity of circulation could vary.

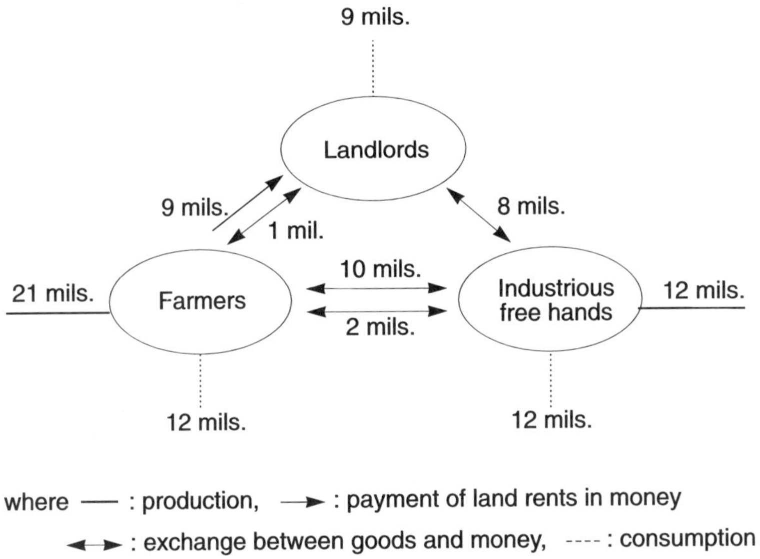

Figure 2.4 The circular system of production, distribution and consumption

get rent revenues from 'farmers', for manufactures, i.e., 'luxuries'; however it also partly relies on the two 'lower classes'' own demand for the products of the other sector. In consequence, the landlords' demand for 'luxuries' would take a great part in determining the level of output in the whole economy, so far as the demand is 'effectual'.[15] From his discussion of the proportion of population among classes, quoted previously, Steuart himself drew some conclusions in connection with the amount of land rent to the same effect. It reads as follows:

> From these matters of fact (so far as they are so) we may conclude: First, That the raising of the rents of lands shews the increase of industry, as it swells the fund of subsistence consumed by the industrious; that is, by those who buy it. Secondly, That it may denote either an increase of inhabitants, or the depopulation of the land, in order to assemble the superfluous mouths in villages, town, &c. where they may exercise their industry with greater convenience. While the land-rents of Europe were very low, numbers of the inhabitants appeared to be employed in agriculture; but were really no more than idle consumers of the produce of it. This shall be farther illustrated in the subsequent chapters. (*Works*, vol.1, p.58.)

Thus, if the amount of land rent could be raised through the enhancement of productivity in agriculture, and if therefore the 'effectual demand' for

[15] Steuart described the role of demand for 'luxuries', in general, in the determination of the level of output in the economy as the 'political effects of luxury'. Cf. section 2, Ch.4 below.

manufactures could be augmented, then the level of output in manufacturing industry would increase, together with that in agriculture.

On the other hand, as to the concept of surplus, we may say that, in Steuart's model of circulation, both agriculture and manufacturing industry are commonly assumed to produce some *economic* surplus, in the sense that both the 'farmers' in the former sector and the 'industrious free hands' in the latter are supposed to consume not only 'necessaries [necessities]' but also 'luxuries' which cannot be said to constitute, at least directly, what they spend in their production; let alone the land rent which is paid by the 'farmers' to the 'landlords'. It appears, however, that it was not such a matter of concern for Steuart, as it was for the Physiocrats, whether or not the manufacturing sector, as well as the agricultural sector, produces the surplus.[16] In his part, rather, emphasis was laid on the very nature of the mutual dependence of economic sectors, as such, and its ramifications for the rest of his economic analysis. In other words, according to Steuart, both agricultural and manufacturing sectors take their own parts in the economy, being actually indispensable to each other: the former sector provides subsistence for all the classes of people in the economy and determines the size of its population, whereas the latter supply various wants of people, other than 'necessaries [necessities]', and promotes the division of labour. While the equivalents for exchanging each other's goods are produced in both sectors, the 'effectual demand' for them is realized either through the medium of 'landlord' class, mostly, or on their own, partly. In any case, as regards the concept of surplus in Steuart, we may still note that it is the agricultural sector only which produces *social* surplus, in that the rent revenues of 'landlord' class are assumed to be transferred from the 'farmers' of that sector in his model of the circular system of production, distribution and consumption.[17] In this context, Steuart clearly pointed out,

> ... this net produce or surplus of the quantity of food and necessaries remaining over and above the nourishment, consumption, and expence [expense], of the inhabitants employed in agriculture ... we have observed ... to be equal to the land-rents of England ... (*Works*, vol.1, p.57.)

To conclude, from our analysis in this chapter, it is evident that while the key notion of the basic macroeconomic model of an exchange economy, assumed in Steuart's *Inquiry*, is the 'effectual demand' of each class in the economy, the most important parameter of the model is the productivity in the agricultural sector, which is supposed to materialize into either the rent of land or the consumption of 'farmers' in that sector. Most of the transferred rent

---

16 By way of making a comparison between Steuart's model of circulation and that of the Physiocrats, we shall attempt to derive one assumed in F. Quesnay's *Tableau Economique*, in the appendix to this chapter. And it seems also interesting to compare both of them with the model of circulation, assumed in R. Cantillon's *Essai*, which we shall present as well in the same place, as they all three were contemporaries.

17 Cf. Ch.3 below.

revenue of 'landlords' goes to the consumption of 'luxuries', i.e., manufactures, and thus provides some fund for 'industrious free hands' in the manufacturing sector to consume both 'necessaries [necessities]', i.e., agricultural products, and 'luxuries'. And the 'farmers' also provide some fund for the 'industrious free hands' through their own consumption of 'luxuries'. Therefore, the more productive the agriculture becomes, the more 'luxuries' the 'landlords' and 'farmers' consume, and the higher level of output the economy as a whole produces. In the meantime, the interdependence of economic sectors and social classes, on the one hand, and the circular process of production, distribution and consumption among those sectors and classes, on the other hand, are two main pillars of the basic conception of an exchange economy in Steuart.

APPENDIX: Cantillon's and Quesnay's Model of Circulation

In this appendix, we shall make an attempt to present the macroeconomic models of production, distribution and consumption in the works of two of Steuart's contemporaries, that is, those in R. Cantillon's *Essai sur la Nature de Commerce en Général* and F. Quesnay's *Tableau Economique*, and comparing them with the one assumed in his *Inquiry*.[1]

I

In Cantillon's conception, in the first place, there are two economic sectors and four groups or classes of people in the economy concerned. That is to say, throughout his *Essai*, Cantillon assumed two sectors, i.e., agriculture in the country and manufacture in the city; whereas he classified the whole population of a country into four, by and large, i.e., 'farmers', 'labourers' (or 'husbandmen'), the 'proprietors of land' (or 'landlords'), and 'mechanicks' ('artisans' or 'handicraftsmen'). The 'labourers', the only class which is absent in Steuart's model, are those who are employed by the 'farmers' in the agricultural sector. Meanwhile, these 'labourers' and the 'mechanicks' in the manufacturing sector are supposed to consume only agricultural products and the 'proprietors of land' consume only manufactures, as in the simplified version of Steuart's model; whereas the 'farmers' in the agricultural sector consume both agricultural products and manufactures.[2]

Let us see how Cantillon actually described the circulation of goods between those sectors and classes.

[1] We refer to the *Essai* edited by Higgs (1931); whereas we use Meek (1962), Kuczynski and Meek (1972), and Groenewegen (1983), for the translations of Quesnay's works.

[2] As we may notice in the following quotation, in Cantillon, agricultural products are, by definition, subsistence goods, i.e., 'necessities', including some intermediate goods; whereas manufactures are non-subsistence goods, i.e., 'luxuries', including some produced means of production, as is the case in Steuart. But in the former the distinction between 'necessities' and 'luxuries' is stricter than in the latter. That is to say, as Steuart allowed the existence of 'political necessary [necessity]', his distinction is rather flexible. In effect, in Steuart's model, every class in the economy is supposed to consume 'luxuries', i.e., manufactures, to a certain extent; whereas, in Cantillon's, some classes, 'labourers' and 'mechanicks', are supposed not to consume them at all. Cf. note 3 in Ch.2 above.

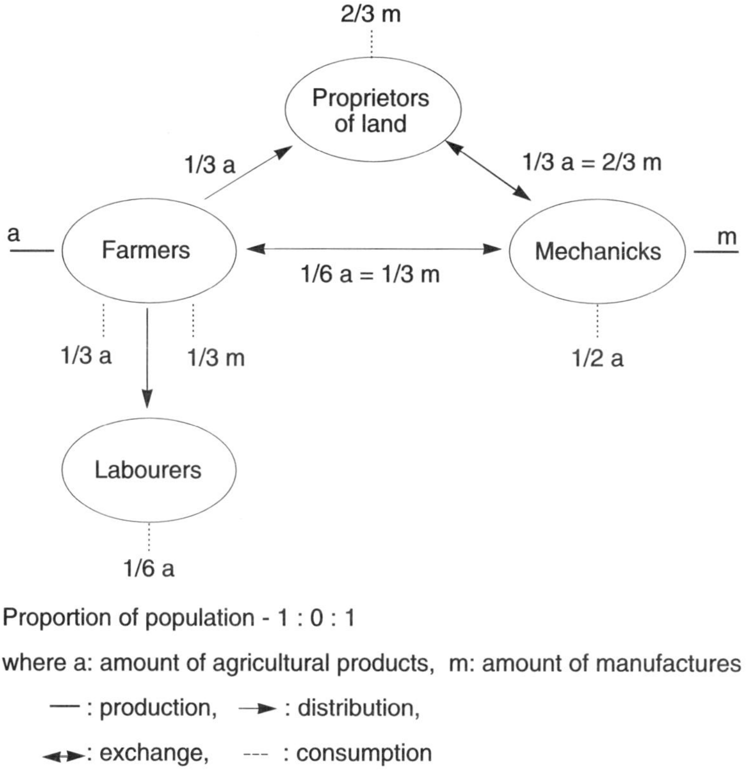

Figure 2.5 The circular system of production, distribution and consumption in Cantillon's Essai

> The Farmers have generally two thirds of the Produce of Land, one for their costs and the support of their Assistants [Labourers], the other for the Profit of their Undertaking: on these two thirds the Farmer provides generally directly and indirectly subsistence for all those who live in the Country, and also several Mechanicks or Undertakers in the City in respect of the Merchandise of the City consumed in the Country. The Proprietor has usually one third of the produce of his Land and on this third he maintains all the Mechanicks and others whom he employs in the City as well, frequently, as the Carriers who bring the Produce of the Country to the City. It is generally calculated that one half of the Inhabitants of a kingdom subsist and make their Abode in Cities, and the other half live in the Country; on this supposition the Farmers who has two thirds or four sixths of the Produce of the Land, pays either directly or indirectly one sixth to the Citizens in exchange for the Merchandise which he takes from them. This sixth with one third or two sixths which the Proprietor spends in the City makes three sixths or one Half of the Produce of the Land. (*Essai*, in Higgs (1931), pp.43-5; brackets added.)

Being based on Cantillon's description above of the circulation of goods, we could depict the process of production, distribution and consumption in the exchange economy, in terms of physical goods, as shown in Figure 2.5.[3]

Now, we may note some similarities and differences between Steuart's and Cantillon's macroeconomic model of circulation. First of all, the interdependence between sectors and classes in the economy, and the circularity of their economic activities and processes, are explicitly shown in the latter as they are in the former. In both models, it is obvious that the circular process of production is represented implicitly as that of stationary state, as all that is produced in each period is to be consumed in the same period. In Cantillon's model, however, the 'farmers' are the only other class which consume manufactures, i.e., 'luxuries', apart from the 'proprietors of land' who receive land rents from them as a transferred income. It virtually amounts to being that only the agricultural sector produces some *economic* as well as *social* surplus, in the sense that the 'farmers' in that sector not only pay both rents to the 'proprietors of land' and wages to the 'labourers' employed in their production process, but also can still afford those goods which could not be said to be necessary, at least directly, for their production.[4] This is one of the distinctive points in Cantillon's model, compared with Steuart's.

What did Cantillon actually express in terms of his model of circulation? He asserted,

> All Classes and Inhabitants in a State subsist or are enriched at the Expense of the Proprietors of land. (*Essai*, in Higgs (1931), p.43; title of chapter XII, part I.)

To prove this proposition, i.e., the primacy of agriculture, Cantillon went through an examination of the circular process of production, distribution and consumption in an exchange economy. Cantillon seemed to succeed in this, as he showed that, though the 'proprietors', totally, and the 'farmers', partly, were not supposed to *directly* 'live upon the produce of land',[5] their incomes as the source of their expenditure still came from the agricultural sector, and that, therefore, all the classes in the economy could be said to either *directly* or *indirectly* 'live upon the produce of land'. That is,

---

[3] We may note that, in the above quotation, Cantillon actually regarded the number of 'proprietors' as so small that the amount of agricultural products they consumed could be negligible. Meanwhile, we assume that the 'costs' incurred to the 'farmers' during their production process amount to one half of what remains to them after paying the land rents to the 'proprietors of land', i.e., one sixth of the whole 'produce of land', so that the 'labourers' consume one sixth of the whole 'produce'. As they also spend one half of the 'profit of their undertaking' on agricultural products, the 'farmers' are therefore supposed to consume, altogether, one third of the agricultural products.

[4] Of course, we now let aside some manufactured means of production, employed in the production process of agriculture.

[5] As we notice from the above description, the entire income of 'labourers', that of 'mechanicks' and two thirds of that of 'farmers' are spent on agricultural products, whereas the entire income of the 'proprietors of land' and one third of the income of 'farmers' are spent on manufactures.

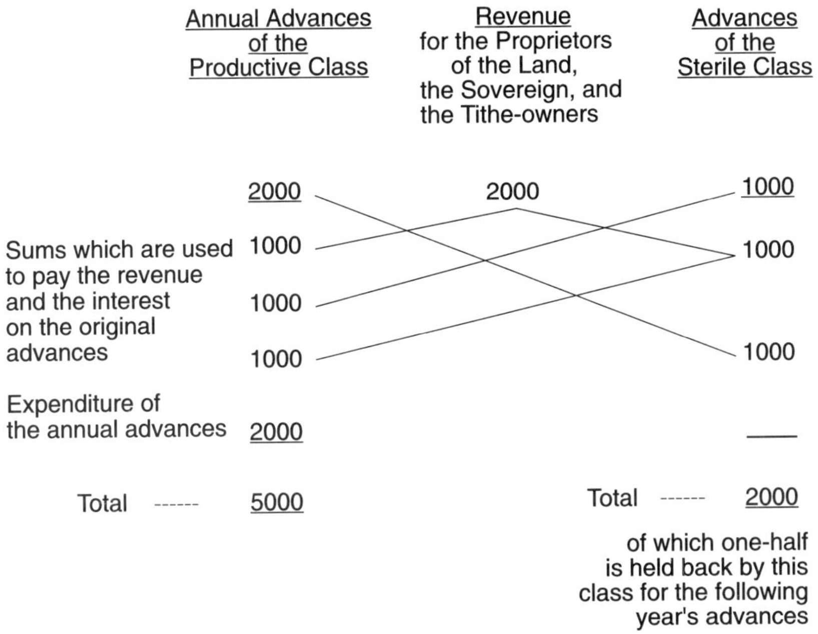

Figure 2.6 Quesnay's Tableau Economique: 'formule' *in his* Analysis

> ... if we examine the Means by which an Inhabitant is supported it will always appear in returning back to the Fountain-Head, that these Means arise from the Land of the Proprietor either in the Two thirds reserved by the farmers, or the one third which remains to the Landlord. (*Essai*, in Higgs (1931), P.45)

This result is rather natural, in that it simply reflects a basic presumption of his model of circulation, i.e., that agriculture is the only sector which produces surplus, *economic* as well as *social*, in the economy. In any case, Cantillon's emphasis on the primacy of land or agriculture might be deemed to be one of the significant influences he exerted on the later Physiocrats, together with his view on economic phenomena as a circular process.[6]

II

Let us move on to the model of circulation in Quesnay, the father of Physiocracy. In particular, from the various diagrammatic forms of Quesnay's *Tableau Economique*, we shall here reproduce the one called '*formule*', which appeared in his *Analysis*, as it seems to be the most complete as well as the

[6] We shall further investigate this point, in connection with the cost-of-production theory of value in Cantillon and in Quesnay, in the appendix to Ch.3 below.

most concise version (see Figure 2.6).[7] We will carefully look at the *Tableau* so that we can derive the macroeconomic model of circulation in Quesnay.

First, we may note that, as shown explicitly or implicitly in the diagram itself, there are three classes and two sectors in the economy concerned: i.e., the 'proprietors of land', the 'productive class' in agriculture, and the 'sterile class' in the non-agricultural sector, including manufacture and commerce.[8] Second, the total of 5000 for the 'productive class' represents the sum of the monetary income (3000), which they receive from the other two classes, and their 'annual advances' (2000); whereas the total, in turn, is used for either the reproduction of capital, i.e., 'annual advances' (2000) and 'interest on original advances' (1000), or the payment of land rents to the 'proprietors' (2000).[9] Third, meanwhile, the total of 2000 for the 'sterile class' represents just the monetary income which they receive from the other two classes; whereas the total, in turn, is used for either the reproduction of capital, i.e., 'annual advances' (1000), or the purchase of what they consume during the production process, e.g., raw materials and subsistence goods, from the 'productive class' (1000).[10] Lastly, the 'proprietor' class, having initially received their annual 'revenue' (2000) from land rents, spend each half of it on agricultural products and on manufactures, etc.

From the above observations, we may depict the flow of money between sectors and classes in the economy in a different way from the *Tableau*, giving emphasis on its circularity, as in Figure 2.7. At the beginning of each period, the 'productive class' have 2000 units of money which are to go to the 'proprietors' for the payment of land rents (1). The 'proprietors', in turn, spend this 'revenue' on both agricultural products and manufactures in equal amounts (2). In the meantime, the 'sterile class' also have 1000 units of money at the beginning of each period. Together with this initially possessed money, they spend their income, received from the 'proprietors' for the sale of the manufactures, on agricultural products (3). Finally, the 'productive class'

[7] It is known that there exist three editions of original *Tableau Economique* of Quesnay, brought out during between 1758 and 1759. They are virtually identical to one another, except some minor respects. Subsequently, he changed the diagrammatic form of the original *Tableau*, called 'zigzag', into relatively more simplified but more self-contained forms, known as '*precis*' and '*formule*', as he tried to make it less confusing and to add more explanatory details to it. The former was introduced in the *Rural Philosophy* (1763), co-written with Mirabeau, one of his laudable disciples; whereas the latter first appeared in his *Analysis* (1766), being adopted later both in the *First Economic Problem* (1766) and the *Second Economic Problem* (1767). Figure 2.6 is taken from Meek's (1962) translation of the *Analysis*, p.158.

[8] Each of the three editions of the original *Tableau* has more or less the same long-listed 'maxims', which in fact amount to the assumptions underlying the *Tableau*.

[9] We may further note that the 'productive class' are supposed to spend half of their 'annual advances' (1000) in buying manufactures, etc. from the 'sterile class'.

[10] As we could notice from Figure 2.6, since the 'sterile class' are to consume another 1000 of agricultural products as either raw materials or subsistence goods, during the production process, by means of the 'annual advances' held back in the previous year, they are actually supposed to consume agricultural products to the amount of 2000, altogether, in a year.

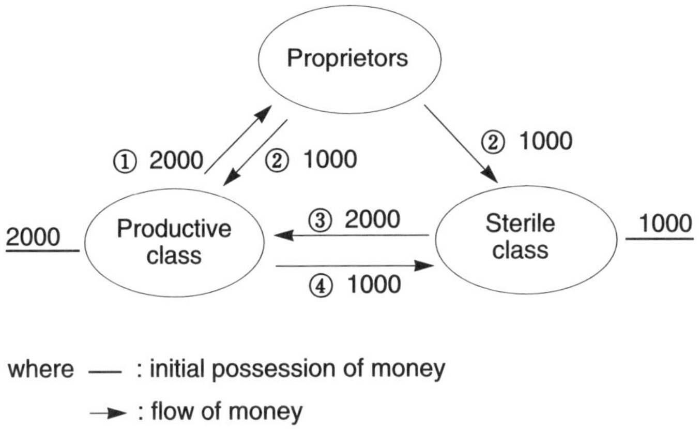

Figure 2.7 The circulation of money in Quesnay's Tableau Economique

spend 1000 units of money on manufactures (4). So, apart from the initially possessed 2000 units of money which come out to the 'proprietors' for the payment of land rents, the 'productive class' receive 3000 units and spend 1000 units, and thus in the end they restore 2000 units, which would be paid for the rents at the beginning of the next period; whereas the 'sterile class', initially possessing 1000 units, receive 2000 units and spend 2000 units, and thus in the end they keep 1000 units as the 'advances' for the next period. Meanwhile, the 'proprietors' receive and spend 2000 units of money.

Eventually, if we trace the flow of physical goods in the direction opposite to that of money in the above diagram, we can derive the circular system of production, distribution and consumption between sectors and classes, assumed in Quesnay's *Tableau Economique*, in value terms, as shown in Figure 2.8.[11] So to speak, while the 'productive class' and the 'sterile class' produce 5000 of agricultural products and 2000 of manufactures, respectively, the former consume 2000 of the agricultural products and 1000 of the manufactures whereas the latter consume 2000 of the agricultural products only. The 'proprietors', receiving the rent of land from the 'productive class', consume 1000 of agricultural products and 1000 of manufactures.

[11] In Figure 2.8, the transaction of 2000 between the 'productive class' and the 'sterile class' represents the latter's purchase for agricultural products; whereas that of 1000 the former's for manufactures. In the meantime, it is implicitly assumed in the diagram that the amount of money circulating in the economy is given as 3000 units, the sum of the amount of money possessed initially by both 'productive' and 'sterile class': as it were, at the beginning of each period, the 'productive class' possess 2000 units and the 'sterile class' 1000 units, respectively. (Although this is rather obvious from the above *Tableau* itself, most commentators, e.g., Marx (1862-3; part 1) and Meek (1960), have supposed only 2000 units of circulating money in the economy; Woog (1950) is an exception.) Each period is supposed to start with the payment of land rents by the 'productive class' to the 'proprietors' with their initial balance of money, i.e., 2000 units, as we noted earlier.

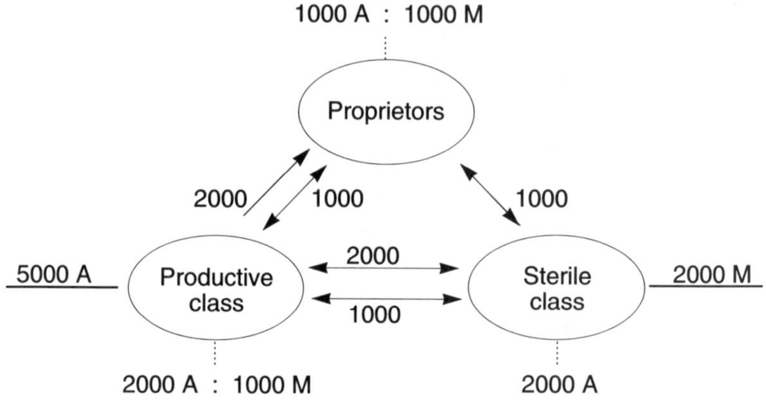

where A: agricultural products, M: manufactures

—: production, →: payment of land rents in money

↔: exchange between goods and money, ---- : consumption

Figure 2.8 The circular system of production, distribution and consumption in Quesnay's Tableau Economique

To conclude, let us examine some characteristic features of the macroeconomic model of circulation assumed in Quesnay's *Tableau*, in comparison with the one in Steuart's *Inquiry* and the one in Cantillon 's *Essai*. First, here in Quesnay's model, we can fully recognize the interdependence between sectors and classes in the economy and the circularity of their economic activities and processes as in Steuart's and Cantillon's. Second, as in the latter two, it is assumed in the former that the circular process of production is implicitly represented as that of stationary state, since all that produced in each period is to be consumed in the same period. Third, however, despite some resemblance in appearance with Steuart's model, Quesnay's model is rather akin to Cantillon's, in that it is assumed in both models that the 'productive class' or 'farmers' are the only other class which consume manufactures, i.e., 'luxuries' or non-subsistence goods, including some produced means of production, apart from the 'proprietors of land' who receive land rents from them as a transferred income, whereas in Steuart's model every class in the economy is supposed to consume, to some extent, those goods. In consequence, according to both Cantillon and Quesnay, it is only land or agriculture which produces some *economic* as well as *social* surplus, whereas according to Steuart any sector in the economy may produce some *economic* surplus.[12] Hence, Quesnay called those who engaged in agriculture 'productive class' and those in other than that 'sterile class'. Finally, it is worth while noting the concept of capital in their respective models of circulation. In describing the circular system of production, distribution and consumption, it is Quesnay who most explicitly paid his attention to the advancement of capital in the production process and its restoration afterwards, though the other two also seems to have taken account of these.[13] In his *Tableau Economique* itself, particularly in the '*formule*' version quoted above, Quesnay plainly made explicit reference to two sorts of 'advances': 'annual' and 'original'.[14] Moreover, in that particular diagrammatic form of *Tableau*, the process of the reproduction of capital, i.e., the restoration of both kinds of 'advances', is clearly delineated.[15] While the production process requires both 'annual' and 'original advances' in the agricultural sector and only 'annual advances' in the manufacturing sector, all these 'advances ' are to be restored at the end of each period so that the economy may repeat the same process in the next period.[16] In virtue of this

---

[12] We have already explained in what sense this is the case when we discussed both Steuart's and Cantillon's model. And we also noted that, as far as Steuart is concerned, agriculture could be said to be the only sector which produces some *social* surplus, in our usage of the term. Meanwhile, Quesnay did not explicitly mention in his *Tableau* that the manufactures are classified as 'luxuries' whereas the agricultural products as 'necessities'. We may just assume that those manufactures consumed by the 'productive class' are used as the means of production in agriculture. Even in this case, we could still say that, according to Quesnay, agriculture is the only sector which produce some surplus, in that the proprietors' revenue is transferred from the very sector in terms of the rent of land. This is what we mean by *social* surplus.

[13] The latter fact is evident in our previous quotations from Steuart's *Inquiry* and Cantillon's *Essai*, which describe the circulation of goods between sectors and classes in the economy, respectively. That is, when Steuart calculated the amount of 'net produce or surplus' in agriculture, he deducted both the 'necessary expences [expenses] of 'farmers' for manufactures and instruments for cultivating the ground' and their subsistence, which had to be advanced before the completion of the production process, from the 'gross produce' in that sector, apart from their 'reasonable profits'. (Cf. *Works*, vol.1, pp.55-6.) In fact, it would become obvious in Steuart's theory of money (cf. Ch.6 below) that he was actually assuming the advancement of capital in the production process. See our next chapter and its appendix, for Steuart's concept of capital and his notion of 'profit upon alienation'. Meanwhile, regarding the 'farmers' in agriculture as 'undertakers', Cantillon also took into account both the 'costs' incurred and some funds for supporting the 'labourers' who assist them during the production process, in determining the amount of the 'produce of land' which remains in their hands. (Cf. *Essai*, in Higgs(1931), pp.43-5.) Also see the appendix to Ch.3 below.

[14] While we might note that the two types of capital, i.e., '*avances annuelles* (annual advances)' and '*avances primitives* (primitive or original advances)' are roughly equivalent to 'circulating' and 'fixed capital', respectively, in modern terminology, the notion of capital in Quesnay has been regarded as one of his major contributions to the subsequent development of political economy, particularly by K. Marx among others. The latter remarked that it is the analysis of capital that makes the Physiocrats the 'true fathers of modern political economy'. Cf. Marx (1962-3; part 1), pp.44-68.

[15] In other forms of *Tableau*, i.e., in either 'zigzag' or '*precis*', there is no explicit reference to the 'original advances' and even the 'annual advances' which appear on the top of each form are not actually related to any transaction.

[16] We may note, from the above-quoted *Tableau*, that the total 'annual reproduction' of the agricultural sector should be 5000 to restore its 'annual advances' (2000) and to pay the 'interest on original advances' (1000) and the rent of land (2000), whereas that of the manufacturing sector could be any amount greater than 1000 which is the minimum 'reproduction' to restore its 'annual advances', depending on the demand of the other classes for manufactures. In the meantime, in the

last point, it is appreciated that Quesnay developed the concept of capital and acknowledged its role in production process and circulation far more than his predecessors and contemporaries, although he did not actually consider the profit upon capital advanced to constitute a distinct income of its own.[17]

---

course of the determination of the total 'annual reproduction, we might conceive some asymmetry between the two sectors in the economy envisaged by Quesnay. That is to say, in the agricultural sector, the 'annual reproduction' depends on the process of production and distribution as well as on the other classes' demand for its products; whereas, in the manufacturing industry, it depends for the most part on the other classes' demand for its products. Not only the demand for manufactures of the 'productive class' but also that of the 'proprietors', in its turn, relies on the process of production and distribution in the agricultural sector, in that the latter' revenue directly comes from this sector as its net products. Therefore, we might say that the total 'annual reproduction' of the manufacturing sector ultimately depends on the process of production and distribution in the agricultural sector. Hence, the primacy of agriculture: i.e., all classes and sectors in the economy depend on agriculture. It appears, then, that this Physiocratic doctrine is rather a natural corollary of the assumptions of his macroeconomic model of circulation.

[17] Nevertheless, it is believed that it was A.J.R. Turgot in his *Réflexions* (1766; published 1769), who first generalized the concept of capital for all sectors of the economy and clearly grasped the notion of profit upon capital advanced in the production process. Cf. Meek's (1973a) introduction and Groenewegen's (1977) introduction. Meanwhile, for Quesnay's notion of 'profit', see the appendix to our next chapter.

3. The Value of Commodities and the Distribution of Income

In Steuart's conception of an exchange economy, as we noted in the previous chapter, the economic processes of production, distribution and consumption constitute a circular system. This is expressly represented in his description of the circulation of money and goods between economic sectors and among social classes. Meanwhile, in the macroeconomic model of circulation which we established to illustrate this, all the magnitudes appearing were counted in terms of monetary value. Although we allow, in this case, that money could be regarded as a mere medium of exchange,[1] a question still arises: that is, how are the exchange ratios between different goods, i.e., their exchange value, supposed to be determined in Steuart's analysis? On the other hand, while the production of goods in an exchange economy is carried out chiefly for marketing, the income originating from the price of goods is distributed, one way or another, among those who participate in their production and exchange processes. Thus, in parallel with the above question, there is yet another one: how are the participants in the production and exchange of commodities supposed to be remunerated for their contributions in Steuart's analysis? In this chapter, we shall therefore examine Steuart's theory of the value of commodities and the distribution of income, in connection with our previous discussion of his circular system of production, distribution and consumption.

We shall first discuss two different notions of value or price, appearing in Steuart's *Inquiry*, and then examine one of them, which is fully compatible with his basic model of circulation, further in relation to the rest of his political economy. Thereon, we shall look into his analysis of income distribution, disentangling each category of income, inferred from his analysis of value, one by one. Meanwhile, we shall separately deal with some threads of a certain tradition running through the subject in question ever since the birth of modern economics. As in the appendix, they are the cost-of-production theories of value in W. Petty, R. Cantillon, F. Quesnay, and A. Smith, as well as Steuart.

[1] When we discuss Steuart's theory of money in Ch.6, we shall introduce other functions of money, assumed in his *Inquiry*, and relate them to the rest of his economic analysis.

1. 'REAL VALUE' AND 'CURRENT PRICE'

Throughout Steuart's *Inquiry*, there were two kinds of notions of the value or price of commodities: the 'current' or 'ordinary price' and the 'real value' or 'fundamental price'. One is the actual price of commodities, determined according to their supply and demand conditions in the markets, and the other is composed of the prime cost incurred directly or indirectly in their production process. The difference between the two amounts to what he called the 'profit upon alienation'. Steuart succinctly summarized the relation between these two notions of price as follows:[2]

> In the price of goods, I consider two things as really existing, and quite different from one another; to wit; the real value of the commodity, and the profit upon alienation. ... to establish this distinction, and to shew how the operation of trade severally influences the standard of the one and the other ... I. The first thing to be known of any manufacture when it comes to be sold, is, how much of it a person can perform in a day, a week, a month, according to the nature of the work, which may require more or less time to bring it to perfection ... upon an average ... II. The second thing to be known, is the value of the workman's subsistence and necessary expence [expense], both for supplying his personal wants, and all providing the instruments belonging to his profession, which must be taken upon an average as above ... III. The third and last thing to be known, is the value of the materials, that is the first matter employed by the workman; and if the object of his industry be the manufacture of another, the same process of inquiry must be gone through with regard to the first, as regard to the second: and thus the most complex manufactures may be at last reduced to the greatest simplicity. These three articles being known, the price of manufacture is determined. It cannot be lower than the amount of all the three, that is, than the real value; whatever it is higher, is the manufacturers profit. This will ever be in proportion to demand, and therefore will fluctuate according to circumstances. (*Works*, vol.1, pp.244-5.)

Did Steuart give each of these notions of value or price its *own* analytical role in his theory of value and distribution? Or was one of them merely a secondary parameter to the other? In answering this question, we may get to the kernel of his theory. Let us have a close look at the two notions of value or price. First, his notion of the 'real value' of commodities.

1.1 The 'Real Value' of Commodities as their Prime Cost

As clearly shown in the above quotation, according to Steuart, the 'real value' of a commodity depends on three factors: i.e., the amount of labour (time) employed, the (value) amount of the producer's necessary expenses incurred, including his subsistence, and the (value) amount of raw materials and

[2] Although, in the following quotation, Steuart was apparently talking about only the price of manufactures, the same point of argument could be applied to the other sorts of commodities, i.e., agricultural products, as there is no particular reason for thinking otherwise. For his conception of economic sectors in relation to the classification of commodities, see Ch.2 above.

intermediate goods used, in its production. If we assume that land is the only raw material existing in the economy (assumption 1), then we may put these three factors into three component parts of the 'real value' of commodities: i.e., the wages of the producer's labour, given for his subsistence, the price of intermediate goods, and the rent of land. Thus, if we further assume that the wages of labour are given as a certain bundle of physical goods (assumption 2) and that the rent of land is given at a certain rate uniformly throughout the economy (assumption 3), then we may represent the 'real value' of commodities in the economy as a whole in a simple algebraic equation system, as follows:[3]

$$\begin{aligned} \mathbf{p} &= \mathrm{w}\,\mathbf{l} + \mathbf{A}\,\mathbf{p} + \mathrm{e}\,\mathbf{L} \\ &= \mathbf{l}\,\mathbf{d}\,\mathbf{p} + \mathbf{A}\,\mathbf{p} + \mathrm{e}\,\mathbf{L} \\ &= \mathbf{B}\,\mathbf{p} + \mathrm{e}\,\mathbf{L}, \end{aligned}$$

where $\mathbf{p}$: price (column) vector
w: subsistence wages of labour
$\mathbf{l}$: labour-coefficient (column) vector
$\mathbf{d}$: row vector of subsistence wage bundle
$\mathbf{A}$: input-coefficient matrix
e: rate of rent
$\mathbf{L}$: land-coefficient (column) vector
$\mathbf{B}$: socio-technical input-coefficient matrix, i.e., $\mathbf{l}\,\mathbf{d} + \mathbf{A}$.

From this price equation system, we could obtain the (relative) 'real value' of commodities and the (uniform) rate of rent in the economy.[4] To see what the equation system actually means, let us rearrange it in the following way:

$$\mathbf{p} = \mathrm{e}\,(\mathbf{I} - \mathbf{B})^{-1}\,\mathbf{L}.$$

As $(\mathbf{I} - \mathbf{B})^{-1}\,\mathbf{L}$ in the above equation represents no more than a vector of the 'vertically integrated' land-coefficients, it might be said that, according to Steuart, the 'real value' of a commodity is proportional to the physical quantity of land 'embodied' in that commodity.[5] The *land* theory of value!

[3] As we assume n commodities produced in n industries, the dimensions of those vectors and matrices appearing in the above equations are $(n \times 1)$ or $(1 \times n)$ and $(n \times n)$, respectively.
[4] Since there are n equations and n unknowns, i.e., $(n - 1)$ relative prices and the rate of rent, we may solve the above simultaneous equations. In fact, we can safely assume the non-singularity of matrices to obtain significant rather than trivial solutions, if we secure general rather than incidental cases. That is to say, in our model, the singularity of matrices might happen only incidentally, in that the coefficient vectors and matrices are determined by the state of technology, i.e., methods of production, in the economy and, therefore, the columns and rows of each matrix can be linearly dependent on each other only by chance.
[5] As *i*th row of $(\mathbf{I} - \mathbf{B})^{-1}$ represents the (physical) quantities of commodities required, directly and indirectly, to produce one (physical) unit of *i*th commodity as final goods, we obtain the (physical) quantity of land used, directly and indirectly, in the production of one (physical) unit of that commodity as final goods, by multiplying it with the land-coefficient vector ($\mathbf{L}$).

While this result seems to be rather in common with his predecessors' and contemporaries' cost-of-production theories of value, or at least not peculiar to Steuart,[6] it is none other than a logical *dénouement* of our formalization of his notion of the 'real value' of commodities under those assumptions mentioned above.[7]

Apart from those strong assumptions which it was necessary to make for the above model, however, Steuart's intention of the argument seems rather different from what we have just concluded. He continued, from the passages quoted above,

> Hence appears the necessity of a great demand in order to promote flourishing manufactures. By the extensive dealings of merchants, and their constant application to the study of the balance of work and demand, all the above circumstances are made known to them, and are made known to the industrious, who regulate their living and expence [expense] according to their certain profit. I call it certain, because under these circumstances they seldom overvalue their work, and by not overvaluing it, they are sure of a sale: a proof of this may be had from daily experience. (*Works*, vol.1, p.245.)

From this we may observe that in terms of his notion of the 'current price' of commodities, rather than their 'real value', Steuart was trying to express the importance of maintaining demand for enhancing the level of output in the economy as a whole. In other words, while he just denoted the 'real value' of commodities as their prime cost, his main concern was with their 'current price ', determined by the supply and demand in the markets, as far as it has to do with the level of output in the economy.[8] Moreover, his particular emphasis was on the existence of 'profit upon alienation'. The point becomes clear, if we ask which one of the two notions of the value or price, i.e., the 'real value' and the 'current price', of commodities is compatible with his basic model of circulation, as described in the previous chapter. It is the 'current price' which includes the 'profit upon alienation', for Steuart considered the gross produce of both sectors, i.e., agriculture and manufacturing industry, to contain some profits accruing to the 'farmers' and the 'industrious free hands', respectively, in that model. This is evident from the fact that, according to him, both the 'farmers' in the one and the 'industrious free hands' in the other are supposed to consume, to some extent,

---

[6] We may draw a more or less similar conclusion, i.e., the land theory of value, from W. Petty's 'natural price', R. Cantillon's 'intrinsic value' and F. Quesnay's 'fundamental price', respectively. We shall discuss in detail some affinities and differences between them in the appendix.

[7] It is true that the formalization of Steuart's notion of the 'real value' of commodities in this way is a simple 'caricature' of his general equilibrium system. It is the case, particularly, in that the model falls within the 'linear world', as long as we assume the fixed coefficients of labour, land and the produced means of production. However, it is another question whether or not this model assumes the constant returns to scale in production. It only assumes that the state of technology in the economy concerned is given from outside.

[8] We shall retain his analysis of demand with reference to the level of output in the economy, for the next chapter.

the 'luxuries' which are by definition non-subsistence goods.[9] Having made this point clear, let us next move on to examine Steuart's notion of the 'current price' of commodities and its determination.

1.2 The 'Current Price' of Commodities

First, some distinctive features of Steuart's concept of competition. He explained the fluctuation of the 'current price' of commodities in terms of his own notions of competition, as follows:

> When *competition* is much stronger on one side of the contract than on the other, I shall call it *simple*. ... This is the species of competition which is implied in the term *high demand*, or when it is said, that *demand raises prices*. *Double competition* is, when, in a certain degree, it takes place on both sides of the contract at once, or vibrates alternately from one to the other. This is what restrains prices to the adequate value of the merchandize. (*Works*, vol.1, p.263; original italics.)

Thus, according to him, there are two sorts of competition: 'simple' and 'double'.[10] While it is the former competition which 'overturns the balance of work [supply] and demand' and thus causes a further fluctuation of the 'current price' of commodities, it is the latter which eventually determines it so that the price is 'adequate'.[11] He illustrated how the 'double competition'

---

[9] Nevertheless, here arises a question: how could a distinction between two different categories of income, the wages of labour and the 'profit upon alienation', be made in Steuart's analysis? We shall discuss this later in section 3 of his analysis of the distribution of income. Meanwhile, for Steuart's discussion of 'luxuries' and 'necessaries [necessities]', see Ch.2 above and sub-section 1.2, Ch.9 below.

[10] According to Steuart, the 'simple competition' in the supply side would bring down prices, in contrast with that in the demand side.

> Simple competition ... may equally take place among sellers, ... and then it works a contrary effect: it makes prices sink, and is synonymous with low demand. (*Works*, vol.1, p.264.)

[11] Of course, there are some circumstances in which the 'simple competition' only exists either in the supply side or in the demand side. Steuart allowed for this.

> Can there be no case formed, where the competition upon one side may subsist, without a possibility of its taking place on the other, although there should be separate interests upon both? I answer. The case is hardly supposable among merchants who buy and sell with a view to profit; but it is absolutely supposable, and that is all, when the direct consumers are the buyers; when the circumstances of one of the parties is perfectly known; and when the competition is so strong upon one side, as to prevent a possibility of its becoming double, before the whole provision is sold off, or the demand satisfied. (*Works*, vol.1, p.270)

In these exceptions, the 'current price' of commodities must either soar or sink 'excessively'. Steuart took the case of the shortage of grain as an example of the 'simple competition' among buyers and the case of an uncommon and unexpected draught of fish as an example of that among sellers. Cf. *Works*, vol.1, pp.270-1. However, in most other cases, the 'double competition' among the sellers and the buyers would secure the 'balance of work and demand' so that the price could stay within 'reasonable' bounds.

> *Double competition* is what is understood to take place in almost every operation of trade; it is this which prevents the excessive rise of prices; it is this which prevents their excessive fall. While *Double competition* prevails, the balance [of work and demand] is perfect, trade and industry flourish. (*Works*, vol.1, p.264; original italics but brackets added.)

actually operates in most transactions between the sellers and the buyers of commodities, as follows:

> You come to a fair where you find a great variety of every kind of merchandize, in the possession of different merchants. These, by offering their goods to sale, constitute a tacit competition; every one of them wishes to sell in preference to another, and at the same time with the best advantage to himself. The buyers begin, by cheapening at every shop. The first asked marks the covetousness of the seller; the first price offered, that of the buyer. From this operation, I say, competition begins to work its effects on both sides, and so becomes double. (*Works*, vol.1, p.265.)

As long as competition takes place among both the sellers and the buyers of commodities at the same time, the fluctuation of their 'current price' should be confined within certain limits. Indeed, in reference to the *tâtonnement* process of the 'current price', Steuart gave a dynamic account of his notion of 'double competition' in the following way:

> Sometimes it [competition] is found strongest on the side of the buyers, and in proportion as this grows, the competition between the sellers diminishes. When the competition between the former has raised prices to a certain standard, it comes to stop; then the competition changes sides, and takes place among the sellers, eager to profit of the highest price. This makes prices fall, and according as they fall, the competition among the buyers diminishes. They still wait for the lowest period. (*Works*, vol.1, p.267.)

That is to say, while changing the sides between the sellers and the buyers of commodities, the 'double competition' eventually makes their 'current price' converge to a certain point at its level.[12]

Meanwhile, we might note that the 'current price' of commodities, determined thereby in the markets, is *necessarily* high enough to include some 'profit upon alienation' – though its amount may vary according to circumstances, so far as all the producers or sellers of commodities in the economy are supposed to consume some 'luxuries', as well as certain 'necessaries [necessities]' for their subsistence, as assumed in Steuart's macroeconomic model of circulation.[13] Furthermore, if we allow for the

---

[12] On the contrary, therefore, we may say that without 'double competition', there would be no definite 'current price' of any commodity, as is the case of 'simple competition', mentioned in note 11 above; or *vice versa*, that is, if the price of some commodity either soars or sinks 'excessively', there would be no 'double competition' for that commodity.

> In proportion therefore as the rising of prices can stop demand, or the sinking of prices can increase it, in the same proportion will competition prevent either the rise or the fall from being carried beyond a certain length; and if such a case can be put, where the rising of prices cannot stop demand, nor the lowering of prices augment it, in such cases double competition does not subsist; because these circumstances unite the most separate interests of buyers and sellers in the mercantile contract, and when upon one side there is no separate interest, there can then be no competition. (*Works*, vol.1, pp.271-2.)

From this discussion, we may realize that there was not only the notion of demand schedule but also the concept of *tâtonnement* in Steuart's analysis of 'current price'.

[13] Cf. section 2 of Ch.2 above.

intermediation of 'merchants' between production and consumption process in the exchange economy, those profits accruing to them should be superadded to the 'real value' of commodities. Indeed, this also partly accounts for what Steuart called the 'profit upon alienation'. Alluding to the uniformity of the 'profit upon alienation' within the same 'trade' or 'industry' in the economy, Steuart elucidated the relation between the 'current price' of commodities and the 'profit upon alienation' in terms of the 'double competition', as follows:

> This [double competition] is what confines the fluctuation of prices within limits which are compatible with the reasonable profits of both buyers and sellers; for, as has been said, in treating of trade, we must constantly suppose the whole operation of buying and selling to be performed by merchants; the buyer cannot be supposed to give so high a price as that which he expects to receive, when he distributes to the consumers, nor can the seller be supposed to accept of one so low as that which he paid to the manufacturer. This competition is properly called double, because of the difficulty to determine upon which side it stands; the same merchant may have it in his favour upon certain articles, and against him upon others; it is continually in vibration. ... In every transaction between merchants, the profit resulting from the sale must be exactly distinguished from the value of the merchandize. The first *may* vary, the last never *can*. It is this profit alone can be influenced by competition; and it is for this reason we find such uniformity every where in the prices of goods of the same quality. (*Works*, vol.1, p.266; original italics.)

Thus, according to Steuart, while the 'current price' of commodities comprises two parts, i.e., 'real value' and 'profit upon alienation', as we already noted earlier; the latter is dependent on the conditions of competition in their markets, whereas the former, as their prime cost, could not be affected by those conditions. So, when the 'current price' of commodities is actually determined in their markets, it is the proportion of 'profit upon alienation' in it, which is subject to the various degrees of competition in those markets.[14]

The role of demand in Steuart's theory of value is clear. As we have seen so far, it is one of the two forces which actually determine the 'current price' of commodities, the other being what he called 'work', i.e., supply. Leaving for the next section the implications of the determination of the 'current price' of commodities in terms of the 'balance between work and demand' on the rest of his economic analysis, we shall merely remark here on the nature of demand, which Steuart conceived of in relation to both the 'real value ' and the 'current price' of commodities. In his conception, demand is, by its very nature, reciprocal.[15]

---

[14] In this sense, the 'profit upon alienation' might be seen as a contingent and indeterminate source of income. We shall discuss in detail Steuart's notion of the 'profit upon alienation', in connection with his analysis of income distribution, later in section 3 below.

[15] Steuart gave a detailed account of the nature of demand in relation to the 'current price' of commodities in ch.II 'Of Demand', book II of his *Inquiry*. Apart from the discussion of the 'reciprocity' of demand, he distinguished between 'simple' and 'compound demand' according to whether different interests produce competition or not; and between 'great (or small)' and 'high (or low) demand' according to whether it is concerned with the quantity demanded or the competition

> Whether this term [demand] be applied to bartering or to trade, it must constantly appear reciprocal. If I demand a pair of shoes, the shoemaker either demands money, or something else for his own. (*Works*, vol.1, p.232; brackets added.)

While the production of commodities in an exchange economy necessarily presupposes the existence of demand, the latter in its turn requires the former as its precondition. If the 'current value' of commodities is less than their 'real value', i.e., their prime cost, there would be no production. Therefore, the 'real value' is a sort of minimum price which makes the production possible; whereas the 'current price', or to be exact, the positive 'profit upon alienation' in it, secures the production to keep going. Meanwhile, if there is no demand, then the competition among the buyers diminishes and the 'current price' might be less than the 'real value'; and thus there is no production because the 'profit upon alienation' becomes negative. On the contrary, if demand advances the 'current price' of commodities by increasing the competition among the buyers, then it raises the amount of 'profit upon alienation' accruing to the sellers and producers and thus there might be more production.[16] Steuart pointed out this vital role of demand in the determination of the 'current price' of commodities and the proportion of 'profit upon alienation' in it, in particular, as follows:

> ... profits may rise and fall, in the proportion of quantity to demand; that is to say, if the provision is less than demand, the competition among the demanders, or the rise of the price, will be in the compound proportion of the falling short of the commodity, and of the prospect of selling again with profit. It is this proportion which regulates the competition, and keeps it within bounds. It can affect profits only upon the transaction; the intrinsic value of the commodity stands immoveable [immovable]: nothing is ever sold below the real value; nothing is ever bought for more than it may probably bring. I mean in general. (*Works*, vol.1, p.272.)

Thus, we may note that as his full recognition of the role of demand in determining the exchange value of commodities in the markets eventually led him to make a clear-cut separation of the 'profit upon alienation ' from the 'real value' of commodities, Steuart's analysis of value seems to be far from any version, whatsoever, of the cost-of-production theory. To put it another way, in Steuart, as long as the demand for commodities ensures a *positive* 'profit upon alienation', it should be a distinct category of income, like the wages of labour and the rent of land; and as long as it never constitutes the cost of production, the price of commodities could not be explained in terms of their cost by any means. On the other hand, it was this very notion of the

---

among the buyers. That is to say, the more 'compound' and the 'higher' the demand, the higher the 'current price'. Cf. *Works*, vol.1, pp.231-5.

16 While the production of a particular commodity may go on, in so far as the proportion of the 'profit upon alienation' in its 'current price' is high enough, compared to other commodities, its level of output would ultimately be determined by the amount of the 'effectual demand' for it. We shall examine Steuart's analysis of the determination of the level of output in the economy as a whole, in the next chapter.

'current price' of commodities, coupled with that of the 'profit upon alienation', that made Steuart's theory of value and distribution dispense with any concept of the profit upon capital as a necessary component part of what was called the 'natural price' of commodities in later literature.[17] This uniqueness of his notion of the 'profit upon alienation' will stand out in relief as we discuss further in the next sections his analysis of the 'balance of work and demand' and that of the distribution of income.

Before closing our discussion of the two notions of value or price of commodities, i.e., 'real value' and 'current price', in Steuart's analysis, we have two more things to deal with: his treatment of the price of subsistence goods and also that of the measure of value. For the one, it appears to be rather exceptional to his analysis of the 'current price' of commodities in general and has some implications for his analysis of income distribution to be discussed later in this chapter; whereas the other relates to his theory of money, which we shall discuss in a separate chapter afterwards. We shall first examine his treatment of the price of subsistence goods.

1.3 The Price of Subsistence

Steuart distinguished subsistence goods from others, observing that they are the 'articles of the first necessity' and thus their price does necessarily influence that of others. The price of subsistence goods might be seen to be too high for the growth of manufacturing industry and yet they also might be too low for the interests of agriculture. Steuart gave an account of the determination of the price of subsistence goods, as follows:

> The standard price of subsistence is determined from two considerations. ... The *number* of the buyers of subsistence, nearly determines the *quantity* to be sold: because it is a necessary article, and must be provided in a determinate proportion for every one: and the more the sale is frequent, the more the price is determinate. Next as to the standard: this, I apprehend, must depend upon the faculties of the buyers; and these again must be determined by the extent of those of the greatest numbers of them; that is to say, by the extent of the faculties of the lower classes of the people. This is the reason why bread, in the greatest famine, never can rise above a certain price; for did it exceed the faculties of the great classes of a people, their demand would be withdrawn, which would leave the market overstocked for the consumption of the rich; consequently, such persons, who in times of scarcity are forced to starve, can be such only whose faculties fall, unfortunately, below the standard of those of the great class. (*Works*, vol.2, pp.82-3; original italics.)

Thus, according to Steuart, the price of subsistence (goods) is subject to the restriction of the 'faculties' of the 'great classes'. In other words, the level of

---

[17] In contrast, some of his contemporaries, Cantillon in particular, inevitably faced some analytical discrepancy between the actual market price of commodities and their normal price, based on the cost of production, as they lacked any equivalence to Steuart's 'profit upon alienation' or Smith's the 'profit upon stock'. Cf. our appendix below.

income or the budget constraint of the most numerous 'lower classes' of people in purchasing subsistence goods would put a ceiling on their price; whereas, within or below that ceiling, it is determined according to the supply and demand conditions of the markets. Apart from the fact that the demand for subsistence goods is a function of both their price and the income of those who demand, as is the case with other sorts of goods, we may confirm from this discussion an important aspect of Steuart's analysis of value and distribution, which we have already alluded to: that is, the wages of labour, of which the income of the 'great classes' mainly consists, are not supposed to be fixed at a subsistence level, although they would *apparently* stay at that level whenever the price of subsistence might reach its upper ceiling. As they are supposed to vary independently of the price or the level of subsistence, the question of how then the rate of wages is determined is to be further pursued in his analysis of the distribution of income, which we will discuss later on.[18]

1.4 The Measure of Value

Let us move on to Steuart's treatment of the measure of value. Above all, of what use did he think the measure of value is?

> The value of commodities therefore, depending upon circumstances relative to themselves and to the fancies of men, the value ought to be considered as changing with respect to one another only: consequently, any thing which troubles or perplexes the ascertaining these changes of proportion by the means of a general, determinate and invariable scale, must be hurtful to trade, and a clog upon alienation. This trouble and perplexity is the infallible consequence of every vice in the policy of money or of coin. (*Works*, vol.2, p.273.)

As far as Steuart was concerned, the use of an invariable measure of value is to grasp changes in the relative proportion between the amount of commodities produced and that of commodities wanted in the economy, so as to keep the exact 'balance of work and demand' and thereby promote 'trade and industry'. He described the nature of the 'ideal money' that could serve this use, as follows:

> That money, therefore, which constantly preserves an equal value, which poises itself, as it were, in a just equilibrium between the fluctuating proportion of the value of things, is the only permanent and equal scale, by which value can be measured. ... Money of account, therefore, cannot be fixed to any material substance, the value of which may vary with respect to other things. (*Works*, vol.2, pp.276-7.)

Thus, apart from the fact that Steuart could not find any 'artificial or material money' of such nature after all, we can ascertain, from the above discussion of the function assigned to the invariable measure of value, which one of the two

[18] Cf. section 2 below in this chapter.

notions of value or price he was mainly concerned with.[19] That is to say, it was the 'current price' of commodities, determined by the 'relative proportion between the commodities supplied and the fancies of men for them'; rather than their 'real value' or prime cost, which represents just a sort of minimum price to make the production possible. This point will become even clearer from his discussion of the 'balance of work and demand' in terms of the 'current price' of commodities.

2. THE 'BALANCE OF WORK AND DEMAND'

In his *Inquiry*, ch.I, book III, Steuart concisely recapitulated some principles regarding the determination of the 'value of things', i.e., the 'current price' of commodities, in connection with the function of money as a measure of value, as follows:

> The value of things depends upon many circumstances, which however may be reduced to four principal heads: Firstly, The abundance of the things to be valued. Secondly, The demand which mankind make for them. Thirdly, The competition between the demanders; and Fourthly, The extent of the faculties of the demanders. The function therefore of money is to publish and make known the value of things, as it is regulated by the combination of all these circumstances. (*Works*, vol.2, pp.271-2.)

In the previous section, we saw that Steuart explained the fluctuation of the 'current price' of commodities in terms of some different notions of competition. As summarized in the above quotation, those circumstances which influence the 'current price' of commodities are none other than the supply and demand conditions of their markets. In other words, according to Steuart, the 'current price' of commodities is ultimately determined by their supply or 'work' and demand in the markets. In what follows, we shall examine some implications of the determination of 'current price' for the rest of his economic analysis.

First of all, Steuart put great emphasis on the role of the 'current price' of commodities, actually determined in the markets, as a signal for the proper allocation of resources in the economy. This point is clearly expressed in the following passage.

> From the current prices, the manufacturers are as well informed as if they kept the correspondence themselves: the statesman feels perfectly where hands are wanting, and young people destined to industry, obey, in a manner, the call of the public, and fall naturally in to supply the demand. (*Works*, vol.1, p.242.)

[19] Cf. *Works*, vol.2, pp.270-8. In his analysis of money, Steuart gave a detailed explanation of what he called the 'moral and physical incapacities' of such metals as gold and silver, which prevent them from performing the above mentioned function of a scale. We shall fully discuss this point later in Ch.6; particularly for his discussion of 'invariable standard', see sub-section 1.1 in the same chapter.

To do this job in an efficient way, Steuart accentuated, the 'current price' of commodities should be the one '*adequately*' determined according to their supply and demand in the markets.

> ... wants are easily supplied, for the adequate value of the thing wanted. (*Works*, vol.1, p.247.)
>
> ... when we say that the balance between work and demand is to be sustained in equilibrio, as far as possible, we mean that the quantity supplied should be in proportion to the quantity *demanded*, that is, *wanted*. While the balance stands justly poised, prices are found in the adequate proportion of the real expence [expense] of making the goods, with a small addition for profit to the manufacturer and merchant. (*Works*, vol.1, p.289; original italics.)

As long as the 'current price' of commodities is the 'equilibrium price' determined by way of the 'balance between work and demand' in the markets, it would be seen to be 'adequate' in the sense that it allows some *reasonable* 'profit upon alienation' for both the producers and the middlemen between production and consumption in the economy.[20]

As we noted in the previous section, in most cases, the 'current price' of commodities is determined through the 'double competition' of both their sellers and buyers, which secures the 'balance of work and demand' and thus ensures the price to be 'adequate'. In some cases, nevertheless, there only exists the 'simple competition', either in the supply side or in the demand side, which 'overturns' the 'balance' and thus makes the price either soar or sink *excessively*.[21]

> Whenever, therefore, this perfect balance of work and demand is overturned by the force of a simple competition, or by one of the scales preponderating, one of two

[20] Steuart himself explained why he chose to use the term 'work' rather than 'supply', in the recapitulation of book II of his *Inquiry*, as follows:

> ... for better understanding my ideas, I have considered them [the proportions between *demand* and *supply*] as two quantities suspended in the scales of a political balance, which I call that *of work and demand*; preferring the word *work* to that of *supply*, because the interests of the workmen are those which chiefly come under our consideration. (*Works*, vol.2, p.222; original italics but brackets added.)

[21] Cf. note 12 in the previous section, and section 2 of the previous chapter. In the above context, we should take notice of the distinction, made by Steuart, between the 'overturning' or 'subversion' of the 'balance of work and demand' and its moderate 'vibration'. According to him, the latter simply represents some alternation of the 'balance' during the 'groping' or *tâtonnement* process of the 'current price' of commodities till reaching an equilibrium through the 'double competition'; whereas the former denotes an actual break of the 'balance' due to the 'preponderance' of the 'simple competition' in one side, either demand or supply, over the other. We may realize this point clearly from Steuart's description of 'a perfect balance of work and demand', in contrast with that of the 'subversion' of the balance, quoted above.

> As long as any market is fully supplied with this sort work, and no more; those who are employed in it live by their trade, and gain no unreasonable profit: because there is then no violent competition upon one side only, neither between the workmen, nor between those who buy from them, and the balance *gently vibrates under the influence of a double competition.* (*Works*, vol.1, p.290; italics added.)

> things must happen; either a part of demand is not answered, or a part of the goods is not sold. (*Works*, vol.1, pp.291-2.)

In so far as the 'overturning' or 'subversion' of the 'balance of work and demand', occasioned by the 'simple competition', results in either soaring (or sinking) the price of commodities to an 'unadequate [inadequate]' extent or failing to make the amount of production and that of consumption meet, as its immediate effects, the 'current price', thereby determined in the markets, must be far from signalling the efficient allocation of resources in the economy.

What is more, according to Steuart, as the 'subversion' of the 'balance of work and demand' may still further exert a harmful influence on both an individual industry and the economy as a whole, the 'current price' of commodities in this case really marks no less than a market failure. That is to say, if the market could not regulate itself to restore the 'balance of work and demand', the 'subversion' of the 'balance' would end up with either the decline of industry or the prevalence of cost-push inflation in the economy. Let us turn to Steuart's discussion of these further effects of the 'subversion of the balance of work and demand' so as to expose another implication of the determination of the 'current price' of commodities for his political economy.

We shall first look into the situation where the demand for commodities falls short of their supply or 'work'.[22] According to Steuart,

> ... it might happen, that workmen will keep upon hand that part of their goods which exceeds the demand, until necessity forces them to enter into competition with one another, and sell for what they can get. Now this competition is hurtful, because it is all on one side, and because we have supposed the preponderating of the scale of work to be an overturning of a perfect balance, which can by no means be set right ... but by the scale of demand becoming heavier, and re-establishing a double competition. Were this happen before the workmen come in competition, then the balance would again be even, after what I call *a short vibration*, which is no *subversion*; but when the scale of work remains too long in the same position, and occasions a strong, hurtful, and lasting competition, upon one side only, then I say, the balance is *overturned*; because this diminishes the reasonable profits, or perhaps, indeed, obliges the workmen to sell below prime cost. The effect of this is, that the workmen fall into distress, and that industry suffers a discouragement; and this effect is certain. (*Works*, vol.1, p.293; original italics.)

Thus, as long as competition remains 'simple' in the supply side only, the 'balance of work and demand' is 'overturned' and the market mechanism cannot restore the 'balance' for itself. Consequently, as the 'current price' of

---

[22] Steuart enumerated four different ways in which the 'balance of work and demand' may be 'overturned': that is, in 'positive' terms, either the demand diminishes, and the work remains the same; the work diminishes, and the demand remains; the demand increases, and the work remains; or the work increases, and the demand remains. Later he summarized the above four ways into two, as he describes them in 'relative' terms: that is, either the demand diminishes or increases 'relatively' to the work. Cf. *Works*, vol.1, pp.290-2.

commodities sinks indefinitely, the very production is no longer sustainable and in due course the industry must decline.[23]

According to Steuart, on the other hand, if the scale of demand preponderates over that of supply or 'work', competition would take place among the demanders only, which raises the 'profit upon alienation' for the suppliers, i.e., producers and middlemen.[24] If the 'work' comes to be subsequently increased, competition would changes sides and, after a 'short vibration', bring down the 'profit'. Otherwise, the 'balance of work and demand' would be 'overturned', and the long-sustained 'profit upon alienation' due to the excess demand would allow both the producers and the middlemen to elevate their level of consumption for the 'political necessaries [necessities]' until they become embodied in the 'real value' of commodities like other necessary expenses for the production.[25]

> But if the scale of demand remains preponderating, and so keeps profits high, the consequence will be, that, in a little time, not only the immediate seller of the goods, but also every one who has contributed to the manufacture, will insist upon sharing these new profits. ... in consequence of this wide repartition, by such profits subsisting for a long time, they insensibly become *consolidated*, or, as it were, transformed into the intrinsic value of the goods. ... When therefore it happens, that large profits have been made for a considerable time, and that they have had the effects of forming a taste for a more expensive way of living among the industrious, it will not be the cessation of the demand, nor the swelling of the supply, which will engage them to part with their gains. ... these profits become, by long habits, virtually *consolidated* with the real value of the merchandize. These are the consequences of a neglected simple competition, which raises the profits upon industry, and keeps the balance overturned for a considerable time. (*Works*, vol.1, pp.295-6; original italics.)

As Steuart himself summarized nicely in the above quotation, the 'subversion of the balance of work and demand', occasioned by the 'simple competition' from the demand side only, would result in the 'consolidation' of the 'profit upon alienation' with the 'real value' of commodities. It would eventually perpetuate the rise in the 'current price' of commodities, unless the excess

---

[23] In fact, Steuart questioned whether there is any possibility that the fall in the 'current price' of commodities, due to their oversupply, might induce more demand so that the market could be cleared.

> But it may be asked, Whether, by this fall of prices, demand will not be increased? That is to say, will not the whole of the goods be sold off? I answer, That this may, or may not, be the effect of the fall, according to circumstances: it is a contingent consequence of the simple, but not the certain effect of the double competition: but the distress of the workmen is a certain and unavoidable consequence of the simple competition. (*Works*, vol.1, p.294.)

Thus, by its nature, the 'simple competition' in the supply side cannot guarantee any increase of demand, even though it makes the price of commodities fall down.

[24] Steuart allowed that the 'preponderance' of demand over supply or 'work' might not always occasion competition among the demanders to raise the 'profit upon alienation' consequently, as he considered some commodities of no great necessity or use, for which the buyers are not expected to pay more than usual. Cf. *Works*, vol.1, p.296.

[25] For Steuart's discussion of 'luxuries' and 'necessaries [necessities]', cf. Ch.2 above; particularly, for his notion of 'political necessaries [necessities]', see note 3 in that chapter.

demand is removed. Steuart particularly exemplified some causes for this sort of 'subversion'. For instance, he pointed out the diminishing returns in agriculture.[26]

> ... so soon as the progress of agriculture demands an expence [expense], which the natural return, at the stated prices of subsistence, will not defray, agriculture comes to a stop, and so would numbers, did not the consequences of industry push them forward, in spite of small difficulties. The industrious then, I say, continue to multiply, and the consequence is, that food becomes scarce, and that the inhabitants enter into competition for it. This is no contingent consequence, it is an infallible one; because food is an article of the first necessity, and here the provision is supposed to fall short of the demand. (*Works*, vol.1, p.301.)

As the price of agricultural products rises because of diminishing returns and the 'profit upon alienation' for the suppliers is 'consolidated' with their 'real value', the price of all other commodities would necessarily rise, too, since the former constitute the subsistence goods for the producers of latter and any change in the price of the former is bound to influence the 'real value' of the latter, i.e., their prime cost.[27] There would then ensue a cost-push inflation in the economy as a whole, which might affect its foreign trade adversely.

The above discussion of the market failure in the case of 'simple competition' naturally leads us to another implication of the determination of the 'current price' of commodities in terms of the supply and demand conditions of the markets for Steuart's political economy: i.e., the role of the state.[28] That is to say, according to him, whenever there prevails 'simple competition' either in the demand or the supply side only, then government intervention is inevitable to ensure a 'perfect balance of work and demand' or, at least, its gentle 'vibrations'.

> When it [the balance of work and demand] vibrates in moderation, and by short alternate risings and sinkings, then industry and trade go on prosperously, and are in harmony with each other; because both parties gain. The industrious man is

---

[26] Apart from the diminishing returns in agriculture, Steuart also took the case of the increase of population, the augmentation of the wages of labour as a result of the industrialization, and the government's imposition of heavy taxes on commodities. (The latter two cases, however, seem to be related to some consequences, rather than causes, of the 'simple competition'.) Cf. ch.XI 'Why in Time this Balance is destroyed', book II, *Inquiry*; *Works*, vol.1, pp.300-8.

[27] In Steuart's own words,

> This augmentation on the value of subsistence must necessarily raise the price of all work, because we are here speaking of an industrious people fully employed, and because subsistence is one of the three articles which compose the intrinsic value of their work, as has been said. (*Works*, vol.1, p.302.)

Cf. the previous section, for his discussion of three factors or component parts of the 'real value' of commodities. Meanwhile, we may note that the increase of population could have exactly the same effects on the price of agricultural products and therefore on that of manufactures, as the diminishing returns in agriculture.

[28] As a matter of fact, it seems rather well known that the active role of the state in guiding a market economy and adjusting its mechanism assumes a character of Steuart's political economy. For a general discussion of Steuart's interventionist view on the role of the state, see Ch.10 below.

> recompenced [recompensed] in proportion to his ingenuity; the intrinsic value of goods does not vary, nor deceive the merchant; profits on both sides fluctuate according to demand, but never get time to consolidate with, and swell the real value, and never altogether disappear, and starve the workman. This happy state cannot be supported but by the care of the statesman; and when he is found negligent in the discharge of this part of his duty, the consequence is, that either the spirit of industry, which, it is supposed, has cost him much pains to cultivate, is extinguished, or the produce of it rises to so high a value, as to be out of the reach of a multitude of purchasers. (*Works*, vol.1, p.298; brackets added.)

Thus, the duty of 'statesman' is to promote the 'double competition' in every industry of the economy, permitting only gentle alternate vibrations of the two scales, supply and demand, in the markets, as a 'groping' process for the 'current price' of commodities to reach an 'adequate' level, i.e., to ensure an 'adequate' proportion between the 'real value' and the 'profit upon alienation' in it. The role of government in securing the 'balance of work and demand' is, according to Steuart, of great importance for the balanced growth between industries in the economy and for its favourable balance of trade, since without it the 'current price' of commodities might be either so low or so high that some industries would either decline or lose their foreign markets, as mentioned above.[29]

From the above discussions of Steuart's notions of the 'current price' of commodities, 'simple' and 'double competition' and the 'balance of work and demand', and his analysis of the 'subversions' of the 'balance', including his

---

[29] Regarding actual practices of government intervention in the market economy, Steuart gave an example in which the diminishing returns in agriculture render the price of subsistence too high as the economy grows.

> When the progress of industry has augmented numbers, and made subsistence scarce, he [the statesman] must estimate to what height it is expedient that the price of subsistence should rise. If he finds, that, in order to encourage the breaking up of new lands, the price of it must rise too high and stand high too long, to preserve the intrinsic value of goods at the same standard as formerly; then he must assist agriculture with his purse, in order to that exportation may not be discouraged. This will have the effect of increasing subsistence, according to the true proportion of the augmentation required, without raising the price of it too high. And if this operation be the work of time, and the demand for the augmentation be pressing, he must continue to assist his agriculture and have subsistence imported, or brought from abroad, during that interval. This supply he may cut off whenever he pleases, that is, whenever it ceases to be necessary. ... If this step be neglected, the consequence may be, that the foreign supply will go on increasing every year, and will extinguish the agriculture already established in the country, instead of supplying a temporary exigency, which is within the power of the country itself to furnish. These, I suppose, were the principles attended to by the government of England, upon opening their ports for the importation of provisions from Ireland. (*Works*, vol.1, pp.306-7; brackets added.)

Thus, according to Steuart, whenever competition stands too long upon one side only, either 'work' or demand, and the balance between them is 'overturned', the government should intervene in the market and induce competition upon the other side as well. This would prevent the 'current price' of commodities from sinking or soaring to too great an extent, and thereby achieve the well-balanced growth of industries and keep the balance of trade favourable. For Steuart's discussion of the relation between economic growth and foreign trade, particular in terms of the sectoral division of economy, cf. Ch.5 below.

emphasis on the role of the state in preventing them, we might arrive at rather a plain question: why is not there supposed to be any vigorous movement, either inflow or outflow, of entrepreneurs to and from different industries, which may help the autonomy of the market mechanism in the economy? Does it represent a limitation of Steuart's analysis, originating from the absence of the concept of capital, the notion of profit upon capital advanced, and a due account of the role of capitalist entrepreneurs pursuing the profit, in his analysis? Apparently not. As far as the concept of capital is concerned, it is clear from some evidence in his *Inquiry* that Steuart must have conceived of it as advances for production. As we noted in our previous analysis of his basic model of the circulation of goods and money in the exchange economy, on the one hand, Steuart took account of some 'necessary expences [expenses]' of 'farmers', including their subsistence, which must be advanced before the completion of production, in counting the amount of 'net produce or surplus' from that of 'gross produce' in the agricultural sector.[30] On the other hand, again as we discussed in our analysis of his two notions of price or value, the 'current price' and the 'real value' of commodities, Steuart included, in the three factors determining the 'real value' of manufactures, the (value) amount of the workman's subsistence and other necessary expenses incurred and the (value) amount of raw materials and intermediate goods used in its production, both of which were implicitly supposed to be advanced during the production process.[31] Moreover, the concept of capital as advances for production is more explicitly presented in his analysis of money. For example, he assumed that there are two sorts of demand for money, i.e., for the purpose of production and for the purpose of consumption, and that those who demand money for the former purpose are seeking the gains from the difference between the 'profit upon alienation' and the interest of money, no matter whether they may own or borrow the money.[32]

Now, is Steuart's notion of the 'profit upon alienation' equivalent to that of the profit upon capital advanced, appearing in later literature, as a distinct category of income like the wages of labour and the rent of land? Retaining a detailed discussion of this question for the next section, suffice it to say here that, according to Steuart, those who organize the production by means of the advancement of capital are more or less expecting the 'profit upon alienation', as this is obvious enough from our examination of his notion of the 'current price' of commodities so far.[33] If so, there must be vigorous and continuous

[30] Cf. Ch.2 above; particularly, see note 13 in its appendix.
[31] Cf. section 1 of this chapter.
[32] Cf. Ch.6 below, particularly section 3.
[33] In the above context, we mean by the term 'production' all sorts of 'trade and industry', including agriculture: that is, not only the production of physical goods but also the performance of incorporeal service and mercantile business. In parallel, all these goods and services are commonly called 'commodities' in what follows.

movements of the profit-seeking capitalist entrepreneurs from less to more lucrative industries in the market economy, according to the signalling of the 'current price' of commodities. Supposedly, this would prove to be a rather natural course for the efficient allocation of resources in the economy in terms of so-called *Pareto* optimality. Then, why was Steuart, in his discussion of the 'balance of work and demand', so emphatic on the role of 'public-spirited statesman'; instead of that of 'self-interested free people' which could be a self-adjusting force for the market mechanism? Apart from what he called the 'natural stop', e.g., the diminishing returns in agriculture, as a general cause for the 'subversion of the balance', which the market mechanism cannot help, there seems to be a fundamental character to Steuart's political economy, which might explain his emphasis on the intervention of government in restoring the 'balance of work and demand'. That is to say, its analytical focus was on the interdependence of economic sectors and the dynamic process of balanced growth among them, rather than on any static criterion for the efficient allocation of economic resources.[34] To put it another way, according to Steuart, although the market could carry out the allocation of economic resources among industries efficiently *in a static sense* with the help of the 'current price' of commodities as a signal to the movement of capital, it might fail to do so *in a dynamic sense* as the possible imbalance between the industries impedes directly, or indirectly through the decline of foreign trade, the growth of the economy as a whole, owing to the very interdependence among different industries in the economy.[35] Hence, government's active role in securing the 'balance of work and demand' in every industry of the economy. To sum up, Steuart's interventionist view on the 'balance of work and demand' in the market economy seems to have very little to do with a certain analytical limitation of his *Inquiry*, e.g., the lack of the concept of capital, the absence of the notion of profit upon it or an undue account of the role of profit-seeking capitalist entrepreneurs. On the contrary, it reflects his dynamic vision of the market mechanism, i.e., the role of the state in complementing its autonomy so as to lead the economy to the well-balanced growth with a favourable balance of trade.[36] Next, let us move on to Steuart's

---

[34] Steuart's conception of an exchange economy, as such, seems to reflect this point to some extent. That is to say, as we have already seen in the previous chapter, his discussion of the sectoral division of the economy is essentially based on the interdependence between different sectors.

[35] We shall closely examine Steuart's analysis of economic growth and foreign trade, founded on a full recognition of the interdependence of economic sectors, later in Ch.5. In the meantime, we may note that his analysis of the level of output, employment and population, which we shall deal with next in Ch.4, was also firmly built on his conception of the mutual dependence among economic sectors.

[36] One might observe that Steuart's dynamism in this context came from his vast knowledge of historical and institutional backgrounds of the exchange or market economy across many different countries. For some distinctive features of government interventionism in Steuart's political economy as a whole, see Ch.10 below.

analysis of income distribution, including the nature of his notion of the 'profit upon alienation'.

3. THE 'PROFIT UPON ALIENATION', WAGES AND RENT

In the market economy, where production is carried out for the most part in order to exchange, the distribution of income is inseparably related to the value of commodities determined in the markets. As we consider the three component parts of the 'current price' of commodities, expounded in the previous sections, we might logically infer that there are three categories of income in Steuart's analysis: that is, the wages of labour, the rent of land, and the 'profit upon alienation'. In conjunction with our previous discussion of his analysis of the value of commodities, we shall examine in this section how these three categories of income are supposed to be determined, respectively – if distinguishable from each other, and how they are related to one another, according to Steuart. Let us, first of all, look into the determination of the 'profit upon alienation' and its nature.

3.1 The 'Profit upon Alienation'

As we have already noted in our discussion of Steuart's notions of value or price, the 'profit upon alienation', or what Steuart sometimes called the 'profit of trade and industry', represents the difference between the 'current price' of commodities, actually determined in the markets, and their 'real value', i.e., their prime cost.[37] Thus, unlike the other two categories of income, it might be said to be determined in the process of exchange rather than in that of production. And in so far as its determination depends on the circumstances of the markets, i.e., the competition among the sellers and buyers of commodities, the 'profit upon alienation' might be seen to be, in its nature, a precarious source of income.

Nevertheless, the 'profit upon alienation' seems to remain as a distinct category of income from the other two, as long as, in Steuart's own words, it is a 'positive profit' rather than a 'relative' one. That is, according to Steuart, there are three kinds of 'profit' in its general sense: 'positive', 'relative' and 'compound'.[38]

> *Positive profit*, implies no loss to any body; it results from an augmentation of labour, industry, or ingenuity, and has the effect of swelling or augmenting the public good.

[37] Cf. section 1 in this chapter.

[38] Symmetrically, Steuart also classified 'loss' into three kinds, as the counterparts of those of 'profit': 'positive', 'relative' and 'compound'. Cf. *Works*, vol.1, pp.275-6.

> ... *Relative profit*, is what implies a loss to somebody; it marks a vibration of the balance of wealth between parties, but implies no addition to the general stock. ... The *compound* is easily understood; it is that species of profit ... which is partly *relative*, and partly *positive*. I call it compound, because both kinds may subsist inseparably in the same transaction. (*Works*, vol.1, pp.275-6; original italics.)

As its proportion in the 'current price' of commodities might be indeterminate in certain circumstances of the markets and contingent on the competition among the sellers and the buyers, the 'profit upon alienation' could be of any kind of these three. However, if it is of 'relative' kind, the 'profit upon alienation' must leave the scene in the macroeconomic analysis of income distribution, for the 'relative profit' and the 'relative loss' would counterbalance each other and disappear in the macroeconomic level. Therefore, only when it is 'positive', the 'profit upon alienation' would become its own category of income. Now, we need to pursue this point further to understand fully Steuart's notion of the 'profit upon alienation'. In fact, here arise two basic questions. That is, on the one hand, under what circumstances could we regard the 'profit upon alienation' as 'positive' rather than 'relative'? On the other hand, how could we distinguish it from the wages of labour, if it is also supposed to come from the 'augmentation of labour, industry, or ingenuity'?

As we have previously seen in his discussion of the 'balance of work and demand', according to Steuart, the 'perfect balance' – or a 'moderate vibration' around it – attained through the 'double competition' among both the sellers and the buyers of commodities, only could guarantee the 'adequate' proportion between the 'real value' and the 'profit upon alienation' in their 'current price'. When the 'current price' begets an 'adequate' amount of 'profit upon alienation' in it, the 'profit' might be seen to be 'positive', in that it implies no 'loss' to any party, either the sellers or the buyers. To put it another way, according to Steuart, if, and only if, the 'current price' of commodities is determined through the 'perfect balance of work and demand', allowing 'gentle vibrations', the 'profit upon alienation' is of 'positive' nature and thus it becomes a distinct category of income.

> Here is the criterion of a perfect balance: A positive moderate profit must balance a positive moderate profit; the balance must vibrate, and no loss must be found on either side. (*Works*, vol.1, p.294; original italics.)

From this, we may realize another reason why Steuart laid so great stress on keeping the 'balance between work and demand' in every industry of the economy; apart from the dynamic efficiency for the allocation of resources in the economy, discussed in the previous section. That is to say, the maintenance of the 'balance between work and demand' is of great importance in securing the stability of the 'current price' of commodities and thereon ensuring an 'adequate' proportion of the 'profit upon alienation' in it, so as to procreate a 'positive profit' and to further enhance 'trade and industry' in the economy.[39]

Meanwhile, although it could be ascertained from the above discussion that Steuart's notion of the 'profit upon alienation' should be regarded as a distinct category of income, like the wages of labour and the rent of land, there is still some ambiguity, in his analysis of income distribution, of the exact distinction between them; particularly between the 'profit upon alienation' and the wages of labour.[40] As a matter of fact, the term 'profit' was used on some occasions other than the 'profit upon alienation' in his *Inquiry*: sometimes it was accompanied with 'of (upon) trade and industry' and sometimes 'upon labour'. As far as the former usage is concerned, it seems to be no more than an alternative way of expressing the 'profit upon alienation', as noted before. That is, the one is used to emphasize that the 'profit' *originally* comes from 'trade and industry', i.e., the production process; whereas the other to describe that, nevertheless, its amount is *conventionally* to be determined through 'alienation', i.e., the exchange process.[41] On the other hand, the latter usage, i.e., the 'profit upon labour', seems to represent the root of the ambiguity in question, because it implies a source of income which is in its essence related to 'labour' but in its appearance akin to any other sort of 'profit'. Steuart's notion of the 'profit upon labour' basically has to do with the heterogeneity of labour.[42] The ambiguity comes from the fact that while he clearly distinguished between the 'profit upon alienation' and the wages of labour on the supposition that the one does not constitute the 'real value' of commodities

---

39 In this light, Steuart held that anything which prevents the 'double competition' among buyers and sellers from operating to bring forth a 'perfect balance of work and demand' and thereby to make the 'profit upon alienation' 'adequately' proportioned to the 'real value' of commodities, is undesirable for the prosperity of trade and industry. For example, he was strongly opposed to the forestalling of markets.

> From these principles of competition, the forestalling of markets is made a crime, because it diminishes the competition which ought to take place between different people, who have the same merchandize to offer to sale. The forestaller buys all up, with an intention to sell with more profit, as he has by that means taken other competitors out of way, and appears with a single interest on one side of the contract, in the face of many competitors on the other. This person is punished by the state, because he has prevented the price of the merchandize from becoming justly proportioned to the real value; he has robbed the public, and enriched himself; and in the punishment, he makes restitution. (*Works*, vol.1, p.268.)

Thus, unless the 'current price' of commodities is 'justly' proportioned to its 'real value' via the 'double competition', the 'profit upon alienation' might be either of 'relative' or 'compound' nature. In that case, according to Steuart, the government should intervene to check any monopolistic power in the market.

40 We shall discuss, later in this section, the ambiguity in the distinction between the 'profit upon alienation' and the rent of land in Steuart's analysis.

41 Although, here, we suppose that 'trade and industry' and 'alienation', respectively, mean the process of production and that of exchange, Steuart sometimes considered these two terms to be synonymous, presuming that commodities are produced to exchange each other.

42 We shall examine in detail the matter of heterogeneous labour in connection with his notion of the 'profit upon labour' shortly when we discuss Steuart's analysis of the wages of labour.

whereas the other does, *at the same time* he generalized that any 'positive profit', including the 'profit upon alienation', results from an 'augmentation of labour, industry, or ingenuity'. Thus, as it is obvious that the 'profit upon alienation' is not merely a sort of 'profit upon labour', i.e., part of the wages of labour, how could the former be distinguished from the latter in spite of some affinities between them? This question seems to point to a crucial feature which characterizes Steuart's analysis of value and distribution, as far as his own notion of the 'profit upon alienation' stands out.[43]

As indicated in Steuart's alternative ways of describing it, the 'profit upon alienation' has a double-sided nature. That is, while its amount is actually determined in the exchange process so that it is excluded from the 'real value' of commodities, it is still supposed to originate in the production process, in that those who organize the production by means of the advancement of capital should be remunerated in one way or another. Thus, the 'profit upon alienation' contained in the 'current price' of commodities is not only the reward for a special sort of labour exerted in the production process, as is the case of the 'profit upon labour', but also the return on the capital advanced in that process, as is the case of the profit upon capital in the later literature; both of which are not yet separable. This does not mean, in Steuart's analysis, that there is no concept of capital or that capital and labour themselves are inseparable, but that the returns for them are inseparable as they are determined in the exchange process rather than in the production process.[44] Nevertheless, not all the wages of labour employed in the production are inseparable from the return on the capital advanced; only those of a certain special sort of labour used in organizing the production itself by means of the advancement of capital. Steuart called this inseparable but still distinct category of income, the 'profit upon alienation' or the 'profit of (upon) trade and industry'. So far, so much for the 'profit upon alienation'. Next, let us examine Steuart's discussion of the wages of labour.

---

[43] In fact, Steuart's notion of the 'profit upon alienation' seems to represent one of the features which differentiate his analysis of value and distribution from those of both some of his predecessors and successors. As far as his predecessors, such as W. Petty and R. Cantillon, are concerned, there is no equivalent of the notion of the 'profit upon alienation' which could fill up the analytical discrepancy between the actual market price and the normal or natural price of commodities. As far as his successors, such as A. Smith, are concerned, the notion of the profit upon capital advanced in the production replaces that of the 'profit upon alienation', as the actual market price of commodities is supposed to tend in the long run to be equal to their normal or natural price which includes the profit upon capital. We shall further discuss these authors' theories of value and distribution, particularly their cost-of-production theory of value, in comparison with Steuart's, in the appendix below.

[44] One might hold that the economy which concerned Steuart was based on what Marx called 'petty commodity production', where there is no clear distinction between labour and capital employed in the production and thus no separation between wages of labour and profit upon capital. But this is not the case, in that, as we discussed in the last section, Steuart evidently conceived the capital, either as the physical means of production or the money advanced in the production process, in his *Inquiry*.

3.2 The Wages of Labour

According to Steuart, as already alluded to in his notion of 'profit upon labour', the wages of labour are basically determined by its supply and demand conditions of the market, as its price. He concisely summarized it as follows:

> ... where every one lives by his own industry, a competition comes, and he who works cheapest gains the preferences. (*Works*, vol.1, pp.92-3.)

Therefore, in Steuart's analysis, the rate of wages does not depend on the price (or the level) of subsistence for those who supply labour.[45]

> The price of subsistence ... does not determine the price of labour. This is regulated by the demand for the work, and the competition among the workmen to be employed in producing it. (*Works*, vol.4, p.206.)

Instead, it is constantly regulated by the productivity of labour and the competition among the labourers.

> ... the value of a workman's labour is determined from the quantity performed, in general, by those of his profession, neither supposing them the best or the worst, or as having any advantage or disadvantage, from the place of their abode. A workman therefore, who, to an extraordinary dexterity, joins the advantages of place, must gain more than another. ... [On the other hand,] competition between workmen of the same profession, diminishes the profits upon their labour. (*Works*, vol.1, p.420; brackets added.)

As far as the notion of competition is concerned, the determination of the rate of wages as the 'price of labour' is exactly analogous to that of the 'current price' of commodities in Steuart's analysis, in the sense that they in common depend upon the different degrees of competition in both demand and supply side of the market.

---

[45] In this context, Steuart gave a historical account of the level of wages before and after the industrialization of an economy.

> While the land remained loaded with a number of superfluous mouths, while numbers were found in every province employed in agriculture, for the sake of subsistence, merely, such people were always ready to employ their idle hours and days, for a very small consideration from those who hired them. They did not then depend upon this employment for their subsistence; and a penny in their pocket purchased some superfluity for them. But when modern policy has by degrees drawn numbers into towns, the few that remain in the country find sufficient employment; and he who demands them must feed them, clothe them, and provide for all their other wants. No wonder, then, if labour be dearer: there is a palpable reason for the augmentation. The price of all necessaries has risen, no doubt, partly for the same reason, (to wit, the additional demand for them,) and this circumstance certainly enters into the account; but work, in the country especially, has risen far beyond the proportion of the price of necessaries, and will rise still more either as the lands become better purged of superfluous mouths, or as the demand for labourers shall increase. (*Works*, vol.1, pp.197-8.)

Thus, while the price of subsistence may rise after the industrialization, as its demand increases; the level of wages would also rise, not because of that but because of the increase of the demand for labour in the economy.

Now, while the differences in productivity among various sorts of labour ultimately refer to the heterogeneity of labour, the measure of its productivity could not be independent of the value of commodities. Let us further examine this point, i.e., the heterogeneity of labour in terms of its (value) productivity, as it has a certain bearing on the relation between the wages of labour, the 'current price' of commodities, and the price or the level of subsistence. From these we may grasp the gist of Steuart's analysis of the wages of labour. Above all, Steuart's notion of the 'profit upon labour' seems to be the key to this matter. As we could deduce from the above-quoted passage, the 'profit upon labour' essentially amounts to that part of the 'price of labour' which is over and above the subsistence of a labourer on account of his 'ingenuity'.[46] In Steuart's own words,

> The physical-necessary, therefore, ought to be the reward of labour and industry; whatever any workman gains above this standard, ought to be in consequence of his superior ingenuity. It is not at all necessary to ascertain the limits between these two classes; they will sufficiently distinguish themselves by the simple operation of competition. Let a particular person fall upon an ingenious invention, he will profit by it, and rise above the lower classes which are confined to the physical-necessary; but if the invention be such as may be easily copied, he will quickly be rivalled to such a degree as to reduce his profits within the bounds of the *physical-necessary*; so soon as this comes to be the case, his *ingenuity* disappears, because it ceases to be *peculiar* to him. (*Works*, vol.1, p.419; original italics.)

Thus, while the 'profit upon labour' is by its nature subject to competition among the same profession, at the same time it depends on the value of the work performed by the labourer, i.e., the (value) productivity of labour, which in turn could not be determined until the 'current price' of the commodities produced is determined according to their supply and demand in the markets. Steuart was actually pointing to this dependence of the 'profit upon labour' on the 'current price' of commodities, when he explained the rate of wages in terms of the productivity of labour without regard to either the price or the level of 'physical necessary [necessity]', i.e., subsistence.[47]

---

[46] Sometimes Steuart meant by the 'profit upon labour' the differential price of labour itself, which is usually marked up beyond the 'physical necessary [necessity]' of the labourer, particularly when he is self-employed. Meanwhile, Steuart enumerated several circumstances which might beget relatively more 'profits upon labour'. That is to say, (1) when the work requires extraordinary dexterity; (2) when it is difficult, e.g., it takes time or expense, to acquire the dexterity requisite; (3) when the work requires expensive facilities or apparatus; (4) when masters increase their profits greatly by sharing those of their journeymen; and (5) when the workmen make a parsimonious living with great economy. On the whole, according to Steuart, 'in such arts where the least competition is found, there must be the largest profits'. Cf. *Works*, vol.1, pp.420-2.

[47] In Steuart's own phases, the 'current price' of commodities always 'regulates' the rate of wages, whereas the price of subsistence may sometimes 'influence' it and thus the 'current price' of other commodities.

> The price of the market at all times *regulates* the price of work; because it regularly makes it fluctuate, in proportion to its own fluctuations. The price, again, of subsistence *influences* it only; because two circumstances may destroy its effect. A high demand for work will raise the

> ... people who labour hard, and those who added to their diligence, have also a share of ingenuity in their several professions, constantly receives wages proportionally higher. ... the demand for their labour will constantly regulate [the rate of wages], independently of the price of subsistence. ... [On the other hand] the rate of wages is in proportion to the value of work performed, relatively to the person who employs the workman, and not in proportion to the price of subsistence. ... When the rate of market for goods or labour is therefore raised upon any branch of industry; whether in consequence of a rise in the price of subsistence, or in consequence of a higher demand; then wages will rise, in spight [spite] of all attempts to circumscribe them. If, on the other hand, the rate of the market for goods and labour shall either stand the same, even diminish, the employer will give no augmentation of wages, let provisions be ever so dear. (*Works*, vol.2, pp.201-2; brackets added.)

Therefore, it might be said that the 'profit upon labour' is still to materialize as a part of the differential price of heterogeneous labour through the determination of the 'current price' of commodities.[48] Steuart himself summarized it as follows:

> Let the demand of the market fall, the prices of labour will fall, in spite of all the reasons which ought naturally to make them rise. ... Let the demand of the market

---

> price of wages in years of plenty: a low demand will sink the price of wages in years of scarcity. When therefore it is said, that the price of subsistence *influences* the rate of markets, we only mean, that the average price of subsistence, when good and bad years are taken together, have a certain influence in regulating prices. But this average price of subsistence cannot everywhere *regulate* the value of work, as the average price of a ship's cargo can regulate the price of every part of it; because the variations in the price of subsistence have not efficacy sufficient to overbalance the variations in the state of demand. (*Works*, vol.4, p.208; original italics.)

Thus, as far as the demand and supply conditions of the commodity market preponderates over that of the labour market, neither the price nor the level of subsistence for labourers could be a decisive factor in the determination of the rate of wages. Meanwhile, Steuart allowed for the fact that the preponderance is the other way round on some special occasions. That is, if the competition among the labourers is relatively stronger than that among the demanders for commodities, the rate of wages might be fixed to its subsistence level.

> In every industrious society, the lowest class is frequently found reduced to the barely necessary. The competition among themselves to obtain employment at any rate, produces this effect; and competition must be allowed its free course. (*Works*, vol.2, p.202.)

According to Steuart, nevertheless, this result must be seen to be rather exceptional in two senses. That is, on the one hand, the very standard of the subsistence level should be arbitrary.

> ... in industrious nations, who on the average of years are subsisted on their own growth, the difference of crops [between in years of plenty and in years of scarcity] is not greater than the difference between ample and bare subsistence. (*Works*, vol.2, p.203; brackets added.)

And, on the other hand, there still exists the differentiation in the rate of wages, due to the homogeneity of labour.

> ... the deficiency [of subsistence] will be found to affect the *portion of him only* who comes last to be served. (*Works*, vol.2, p.207; original italics but brackets added.)

The relation between the rate of wages and the price of subsistence, discussed here, is applied in Steuart's analysis of taxation, particularly in his discussion of the shifting of the 'proportional taxes' on subsistence goods. Cf. section 1, Ch.8 below.

[48] In this respect, the 'profit upon labour' resembles the 'profit upon alienation'. However, as we noted earlier, the one is just a part of, or a different name for, the wages of labour as its price, whereas the other is of double-sided nature, i.e., as a reward for labour and as a return on capital.

rise, manufacturers may raise their wages in proportion to the rise of the market. (*Works*, vol.4, pp.204-5.)

Thus, we may conclude that, in Steuart's analysis, while wages of labour are determined as its price by the demand and supply in the market, the demand for commodities plays a crucial role in their determination as the demand for labour in turn depends on the 'current price' of commodities.

3.3 The Rent of Land

Having discussed so far the 'profit upon alienation' and the wages of labour, we have another distinct category of income, in Steuart analysis, to be dealt with: the rent of land. Let us begin by examining how Steuart actually conceived of it in his *Inquiry*.

> ... all rents are in a pretty just proportion to the gross produce, after deducting three principal articles. First, The nourishment of the farmer, his family, and servants. Secondly, The necessary expences [expenses] of his family, for manufactures, and instruments for cultivating the ground. Thirdly, His reasonable profits, according to the custom of every country. Of these three articles, let us distinguish what part implies the direct consumption of the pure produce, from what does not. Of the first sort are the nourishment of men and cattle, wool and flax for clothing, firing, and other smaller articles. Of the second are all manufactures bought, servants' wages, the hire of labourers occasionally, and profits, either spent in luxury, (that is, superfluity,) lent, or laid up. The three articles above mentioned (which we have distributed under two heads) being deducted from the gross produce, the remaining *value* shews the land-rent. (*Works*, vol.1, p.55; italic added.)

Thus, according to him, the rent of land represents that part of gross output in agriculture, which remains after all the necessary expenses incurred in the production process – including those for the remuneration for labour employed and those for the intermediate goods used – and the 'profit upon alienation' are deducted.[49] In this conception of the rent of land, two things must be pointed out. One is the concept of surplus in Steuart. The amount of land rents in the economy as a whole must be equivalent to, in his own words, 'net produce or surplus of the quantity of food and necessaries [necessities] remaining over and above the nourishment, consumption, and expence [expense], of the inhabitants employed in agriculture'.[50] This is nothing more than the whole amount of the revenues of 'landlord' class, transferred from the 'farmers' in that sector. Meanwhile, not only the 'farmers' in the agricultural sector but also the 'industrious free hands' in the manufacturing sector are supposed to consume 'luxuries' to some extent with their income from either

---

[49] In this context, the remuneration of labour comprehends the wages of labour, including the 'profit upon labour', for both the farmer and the labourers, employed by him.
[50] Cf. *Works*, vol.1, p.57.

the 'profit upon labour' or the 'profit upon alienation'.[51] Therefore, in Steuart's analysis, while every sector in the economy is supposed to produce 'economic surplus', it is only the agricultural sector which produces 'social surplus', which is the rent of land.[52]

The other thing to be mentioned about Steuart's conception of the rent of land is that it is expressed in value terms, as explicitly indicated in the above quotation. As a result, unless the 'current price' of commodities is determined in their markets, it is impossible to deduct the 'profit upon alienation' and all the necessary expenses incurred in the production process from the gross output so as to determine the rent of land, as a residual. This is because both the 'profit upon alienation' and the wages of labour could not be determined independently of the 'current price' of the commodities produced, as we have already examined, and because both input and output of the production are composed of different commodities, as Steuart himself clearly remarked in the above quotation. What does this all mean? From his illustration of the 'difference between agriculture exercised as a trade and a direct means of subsisting', we might take the following hint.

> By the supposition, we imply, that the bit of land is sufficient for maintaining the man and his family, and nothing more; he has no grain to sell, no food can by him be supplied to any other person whatever; but the state of the other lands capable of yielding a surplus, such as the vineyard, produces a demand for his labour. This labour, considered with respect to the vine-dresser, is a fund for providing all his wants in manufactures, salt, &c. and what is over must be considered as his profits, out of which he pays the royal impositions. The same labour, considered with regard to the proprietors of the vineyard, enters into that necessary deduction out of the fruits, which, when deducted, leaves the remainder, which we call surplus, or what answers to the land-rent. This belongs to the proprietor, and becomes a fund for supplying all his wants. Here we have an idea of society. The vine-dresser depends upon the proprietor for the price of his labour; the proprietor upon the vine-dresser for his surplus. (*Works*, vol.1, p.115.)

In this example, the additional products from the vineyard, relative to what the present vine-dresser used to produce, are to be distributed partly to himself as the 'profit upon labour' and partly to its proprietor as the land rent. Thus, the gross produce of the vineyard is eventually divided into two categories of income: the wages of labour as its price and the rent of land as a surplus.[53] How, then, is it supposed to be divided? Is there any analytical or hypothetical mechanism to answer this question in Steuart's analysis of income distribution? In fact, we could only refer to one possible cause for this

---

[51] Cf. our previous analysis of Steuart's basic macroeconomic model of production, distribution and consumption in the last chapter and our discussion of his notions of the 'profit upon alienation' and the 'profit upon labour' earlier in this section.

[52] Cf. section 2, Ch.2 above.

[53] In the above example, Steuart ruled out another category of income, i.e., the 'profit upon alienation', as he did not *explicitly* take into account either any other labour to organize the production process and any advances for that process or the exchange process, i.e., 'alienation', as such.

throughout his *Inquiry*: that is, the (value) productivity of labour in determining the its wages. In other words, while the wages of labour are to be determined as its price in the market in terms of its (value) productivity, the rent of land remains as a residual of the gross produce. Now, since the productivity, in its turn, depends on the value of commodities, the distribution of income between the wages of labour and the rent of land in this example could be ascertained only after the 'current price' of commodities is determined in their markets. Therefore, as the 'profit upon alienation', excluded in this example, is also ascertained through the determination of the 'current price' of commodities as we already discussed, we may observe that all three categories of income are necessarily dependent on the 'current price' of commodities determined in the markets. That is to say, in Steuart's analysis, both the value of commodities, directly, and the distribution of income, indirectly, depend on the supply and demand conditions of the commodity market.[54]

Now, while the wages of labour are determined according to its supply and demand in the market, they are taken out of the (value) gross produce of the agricultural sector, together with the (value) amount of intermediate goods used in the production, so that the remainder may be distributed between the 'profit upon alienation' and the rent of land. As long as the 'profit upon alienation' is entirely dependent on the exchange process and thus excluded in the 'real value' of commodities, as their prime cost, the rent of land must be determined *logically or analytically* prior to the 'profit upon alienation'; though it may be regarded, *ex post*, as a residual of the gross produce. Otherwise, there would be no clear distinction between the 'real value' and the 'profit upon alienation' in the 'current price' of commodities. Therefore, our next task is to examine the actual determination of the rate of land rent in Steuart's analysis.

Although, in the above example, Steuart apparently alluded to the inner workings of differential rent, it is not clear whether the different amounts of gross produce from the respective modes of production, i.e., agriculture exercised as a direct means of subsisting and that of a trade, result from the different degrees of fertility of land or the different degrees of productivity of labour.[55] Let us explore this point further in his following discussion of the different rates of land rent among different methods of production in

[54] In this respect, it seems that Steuart's analysis of value and distribution is far from those of some other economists before and after him, in which the relative price of commodities is understood in terms of their supply price and thus the distribution of income is explained independently of the demand conditions of the commodity market. Cf. the appendix to this chapter.

[55] In the passage quoted above, Steuart explicitly assumed, on the one hand, that some lands are 'capable of yielding a surplus' and others are not; whereas, on the other hand, he implicitly supposed the wages of the vine-dresser, including his 'profit upon labour', to be determined by the productivity of his labour, which is obviously different between the different modes of agriculture.

agriculture, so that we may get to the gist of Steuart's analysis of the rent of land.

> ... the land-rents of England are to the gross produce, as nine to twenty-one, or thereabouts. Let me now examine some other proportions. The rents of the corn-lands are to the gross produce of them, as two is to nine; those of pasture, as seven to twelve. ... This difference must proceed from the greater proportion of labouring and other inhabitants employed in consequence of tillage; which makes the expence [expense] of it far greater than that of pasture. ... in the one and the other, every article of necessary expence [expense] or consumption ought naturally to be proportionally equal among those concerned in both, that is, proportional to the number of labouring inhabitants. (*Works*, vol.1, p.55-6.)

Above all, in this discussion, the rate of land rent is reckoned in terms of the ratio of the (value) amount of rent, as net produce, and that of gross produce. Consequently, the different rates of rent between tillage and pasture are attributed to the greater or lesser necessary expenses incurred in producing the same (value) amount of gross produce by the respective methods of production. Since, as Steuart explicitly assumed, the expenses, particularly the amount of the wages of labour, are proportional to the number of those employed in the production process, the rate of rent should be in inverse relation to the labour-output ratio of each method. That is, the pasture which requires relatively less labour begets a higher rate of rent than the tillage which requires relatively more labour. Therefore, in Steuart's analysis, the rate of land rent seems to be related to the method of production itself rather than the fertility or the scarcity of land. To put it another way, while he neither particularly ascribed its existence to any productivity of land nor described its rate to be determined by the supply and demand conditions in the 'land' market, he simply understood the rate of land rent to be regulated instead by the technological conditions in agriculture. Thus, in parallel with his conception of the rent of land as social surplus, Steuart's explanation of the determination of its rate as the ratio between the net and the gross produce of agriculture in terms of the method of production is characteristic of his analysis of rent.

Now, the analytical corollary of the above discussion of Steuart's analysis of the rent of land for the rest of his theory of value and distribution is straightforward. That is, if the rates of land rent, *vis-à-vis* various methods of production in agriculture, are found out, then the (value) amount of the rent of land could be deducted from the (value) gross produce less the (value) amount of the wages of labour determined in the labour market, and the remainder would be the (value) amount of the 'profit upon alienation'. Therefore, once the technology in agriculture of the economy is known, the distribution of its national income among the 'profit upon alienation', the wages of labour and the rent of land can all be discerned as soon as the 'current price' of both agricultural products and manufactures and the rate of wages, as the price of heterogeneous labour, are determined in the commodity and the labour market, respectively. At the same time, we could distinguish exactly between the 'real value' and the 'profit upon alienation' in the 'current price' of commodities.

Generally, nevertheless, how could we define a particular method of production in agriculture in terms of the ratio between its (value) net and gross produce, before the proportion of the 'profit upon alienation' in the 'current price' of commodities is known? Without such a strong assumption, as Steuart himself made in the above quotation, that all the necessary expenses incurred are proportional to the number of those employed in the production process, his analysis of income distribution might be seen to be exposed to the problem of circular reasoning. That is, unless we assume some restricting conditions of the technology in agriculture, we must simply presuppose the determination of the 'profit upon alienation' through valuation of commodities so as to obtain the rates of land rent, *vis-à-vis* methods of production; or *vice versa*. Otherwise, the two categories of income would remain indeterminate in Steuart's analysis. This result apparently originates from the very nature of his notion of the 'profit upon alienation', i.e., its precariousness and uncertainty, as is the case with his ambiguous distinction between the wages of labour and the 'profit upon alienation', as we have already seen. Meanwhile, it reflects a significant aspect of Steuart's political economy as a whole. Although we may say that there is no determinate theory of returns for the factors of production in his economics, except that of the wages of labour as its market price, it might have been natural, on his part, not to pay much attention to the theory of income distribution as such, since he was so preoccupied with the 'alienation', circulation, consumption and employment. As a matter of fact, what he really tried to say by means of his analysis of unequal rates of land rent among various methods of production seems to lie in another area of economic theory, i.e., that of the relative proportion of employment between different economic sectors. Retaining it for a full-dress discussion of Steuart's analysis of the level of output, employment and population in the next chapter, we shall close the present section by discussing an apparent ramification of his analysis of the different rates of land rent among the different methods of production in agriculture, examined above.

On the basis of the data of the different rates of land rent between tillage and pasture, quoted above, Steuart calculated their relative population in England at the time, in the following way.

> Now as the consumption upon corn-farms is 7/9, and that upon pasture 5/12, the proportion of these two fractions must mark the ratio between the populousness of pasture-lands, and those in tillage; that is to say, tillage-lands in England were, at that time, peopled in proportion to pasture-lands, as 84 is to 45, or as 28 to 15. (*Works*, vol.1, p.56.)

As the rate of rent for tillage is 2/9 and that for pasture is 7/12, the (value) amount of consumption in the tillage is 7/9 of its gross produce and that in the pasture is 5/12. Therefore, as the numbers of those employed in the respective production processes, by assumption, should be in proportion to the amounts of consumption, the ratio between them must be 28 : 15 (= 7/9 : 5/12). Likewise, we might get the ratio between the numbers of the 'free hands', both 'landlords' and the 'industrious free hands', who are sustained by the respective methods of production in agriculture, as 8 : 21 (= 2/9 : 7/12).[56] From these calculations, Steuart draw the following conclusion.

> The *more* a country is in tillage, the more it is inhabited, the smaller is the proportion of *free hands* for all the services of the state. The more a country is in pasture, the *less* it is inhabited, but the greater is the proportion of *free hands*. (*Works*, vol.1, pp.58-9; original italics.)

Thus, he explained the relative size of employment between economic sectors in terms of the different rates of land rent between different methods of production in agriculture. That is to say, the higher rate of land rent a method of production begets, the more employment in the non-agricultural sector and the less in the agricultural sector it creates; the more the agricultural sector adopts the method begetting a higher rate of land rent, the more employment and thus the higher level of output in the non-agricultural sector the economy has. From this, it seems that Steuart's analysis of diverse rates of land rent among different methods of production ends in proving that the rent of land, which depends on the *total* productivity of each method of production –rather than the *partial* productivity of land or labour, is one of the most vital parameters in the determination of both employment and output in the economy.

To sum up, Steuart's analysis of the distribution of income is so closely related not only to that of the value of commodities but also to that of employment and output, that it appears rather to be a by-product of the latter two in his *Inquiry*. While this very nature of his analysis might account for some ambiguity in distinguishing different categories of income, it plainly mirrors the main concerns in his political economy.

---

[56] For the social classes and the economic sectors in Steuart's conception of an exchange economy, see section 1, Ch.2 above.

APPENDIX: The Cost-of-production Theories of Value in Petty, Cantillon, Quesnay, Steuart and Smith

Ever since the period of classical philosophers, such as Plato and Aristotle, and throughout the scholastic era, it has been evident that the exchange ratio between different goods can be explained by the 'use' and 'scarcity' of those goods, i.e., their demand and supply in the markets. At the same time, it is also true that there existed the concept of 'customary' or 'just price', which was supposed to reflect certain ethical criteria of justice in the exchange process.[1] These criteria often related to the legitimate or just remuneration for those who participated in the production process; let alone the question of whether or not they were paid sufficiently to maintain a certain standard of living.[2] In other words, to define the 'customary' or 'just price' of commodities, it was quite natural then to turn attention to their cost of production. Obviously, the notion of the price of commodities in terms of their cost of production would not be plausible unless the cost itself could be made known. As far as the concept of 'customary' or 'just price' was concerned, it was simply presupposed that the cost of production could be known for each and every kind of commodity on the basis of some common agreement or estimation, which had to do with certain ethical criteria, e.g., contractual or distributive justice. When the range of economic activities was relatively limited, it might have been possible to take into account in such a way all the items of the cost incurred in the production. But as both domestic and foreign trade were expanding and as both the price of inputs and that of outputs of production were to be determined simultaneously in the markets, the cost of production of commodities became unknown or, at least, uncertain in either value or physical terms.[3]

---

[1] Cf. O'Brien (1920), pp.102-20; Gordon (1975), pp.174-9.

[2] Even in those days, it was not generally believed that the cost or remuneration of the labour of those engaged in the production should be the only factor in the determination of the value of commodities, i.e., their 'just price'. Moreover, the concept of 'just price' did not seem to necessarily depend on the need to allow those participating in the production process to maintain their station in society. Cf. O'Brien (1920), pp.109-36.

[3] Meek (1973b) explained this point in its historical perspective, as follows:

> The Mediaeval concept of the just price gradually lost its power over men's minds as the impersonal and unconscious market took over the task of regulating prices. But the habit of thinking of "value" in terms of producers' cost remained firmly rooted in the consciousness of

The subjective theory of value, according to which the value of commodities ultimately depends on their utility to individual consumers, dominated the 'inadequate' cost-of-production theory of value during the so-called mercantilist period of the 16th and early 17th centuries. It was thought then that as long as the actual market price of commodities, determined by their demand and supply, could secure some 'reasonable' profits for the merchants engaged in commerce, it must represent their value as such. Interestingly enough, if we look at the historical evolution of economic thought – that of the theory of value and distribution, in particular – from the late 17th century, we may realize that the analytical focus or emphasis was gradually switching again from the process of exchange to that of production.[4] In this appendix, an attempt will be made to sort out a few strands in the transition of the subject matter at the time of the birth of modern economics in terms of the cost-of-production theories of value appearing in the works of some conspicuous authors in those days, including Steuart.[5]

Petty's 'Natural Price'

Among others, W. Petty (1623-87) might be regarded as the forerunner of the impending theoretical change, although it is hard to find the concept proper of

---

> the direct producers themselves, and was later to prove itself one of the most influential of all the economic legacies left by the Schoolmen. (p.14.)

[4] According to Meek (1973b), in those days, as the 'industrial capital' was emerging and increasingly replacing the 'merchant capital' as a dominant factor of economic life, there appeared, in both economic reality and theory, the growing recognition of the 'profit upon capital' in the production process rather the 'profit upon alienation' in the exchange process. (Cf. pp.11-44.) Apart from his 'reflection' approach to the history of economic thought, of which a detailed treatment obviously lies beyond the scope of this appendix, his concept of the 'profit upon alienation' in the above context seems to be quite different from what the originator of the term, Steuart, himself meant by that. We shall clarify this point later on in the present appendix.

[5] In a similar vein, Bowley (1973) gave a detailed account of the transition of the subject matter in the theory of value between the 17th and 18th centuries, with a number of interesting insights into the contemporary literature. For instance,

> ... the seventeenth-century discussions of the theory of value concentrated on market price. In contrast the most important novelties in the discussions of price in the eighteenth century related to long-run price or supply price with interest centred on the significance of the difference between it and market price as the stimulus to the allocation of resources between uses – in short, the nature and functions of the price mechanism. It is symptomatic of this change of emphasis that the term 'natural' was used by Adam Smith and his classical successors to describe this long-run price, while English seventeenth-century writers used it to describe the price in any market that was freely competitive. ... Petty was an exception to these generalizations about the seventeenth-century English writers' interest, while Pufendorf on the continent provided a striking example of the continued scholastic type of interest in legal or long-run customary price to which he applied, like Adam Smith after him, the term 'natural'. (pp.91-2.)

Thus, according to her, the transition itself was expected to be diversified in its content, as presaged by the different uses of the term 'natural' by Petty and Pufendorf, respectively.

capital or that of profit on it in his economic writings.[6] He identified such important concepts as normal price and surplus, both of which would underlie the subsequent development of economic theory.[7]

In order to analyse how commodities are produced and exchanged with each other and how the net products, i.e., the gross products less the intermediate products, are distributed among the participants of production in an exchange economy, it is necessary to conceptualize the exchange value of commodities, whether it is their market price or normal price – however defined. As for Petty, it appears that the latter is more relevant than the former for the theoretical structure of some particular areas of his analysis.[8] For instance, he tried to calculate the national wealth of a country – particularly the value of land – as such or as the source of public revenue, especially in connection with the problem of taxation and foreign policy of his time. As he carried out the calculation of the value of land in terms of the capitalization of the rent of land, his theory of value and distribution was inseparable from the actual course of the calculation.[9] In what follows, we shall first examine how he defined the normal price of commodities and then discuss how it was related to his calculation of the value of land, so that eventually we may find out the nature of the cost-of-production theory of value in Petty.

---

[6] Among Petty's economic writings, *A Treatise of Taxes and Contributions* (written and published anonymously in 1662), might be seen to be the most important and systematic, in the sense that the subsequent ones – such as *Verbum Sapienti* (written in 1665), *The Political Anatomy of Ireland* (written in 1671-2), *Political Arithmetick* (written in 1672-6) and *Quantulumcunque concerning Money* (written in 1682) – were devoted to relatively minor details of his economic analysis, which had already appeared in the first one. For all of these works, here we refer to Hull's edition published in 1899. After classifying Petty's economic writings into three chronological groups, Hull (1900) examined some common characteristics within each group in terms of their method and content.

Meanwhile, although we come across the terms 'stock' and 'profit' in the above writings, they were not used in the same meanings as in the subsequent literature or at least in modern economic theories.

[7] In his *Treatise*, Petty was dealing with some practical problems in the taxation and fiscal system after Interregnum (1649-60) and Restoration (1660) in England, and suggesting some solutions for them. Obviously, this intention relates to the direct need of his time, while the same thing is true, more or less, for most of his other works. From the angle of the evolution of economic theory, nevertheless, it seems that it is one thing to treat economic matters for practical purposes and another to adopt a certain analytical method and to employ a certain conceptual framework in theorizing them. As far as Petty was concerned, although he overtly dealt with some economic problems of his own days, he alluded to some embryonic patterns of economic analysis and several important concepts, which were to be used and further developed by those after him. We shall examine some of them in the present discussion.

[8] After discussing the relative price of corn in terms of silver, Petty remarked,

> This, I say, to be the foundation of equallizing and ballancing of values; yet in the superstructures and practices hereupon, I confess there is much variety, and intricacy; of which hereafter. (*Treatise*, in Hull (1899), vol.1, p.44.)

Thus, although he was well aware of the enormous development of domestic and foreign trade in his time and fully recognized the importance of the supply-and-demand price of commodities in the workings of a real economy, Petty chose another notion of price, i.e., normal price, for his particular analysis.

[9] In this context, Johnson (1937) described that Petty's inquiry yielded an important by-product: his experimental analysis of the 'mysterious nature of rent' (p.102).

Apart from the market price of commodities, actually determined according to both their supply and demand conditions, Petty put forward three different categories of their supply price, as follows:

> ... natural dearness and cheapness depends on the few or more hands requisite to necessaries of Nature: As corn is cheaper where one man produces Corn for ten, then where he can do the like but for six; and withall, according as the Climate disposes men to a necessity of spending more or less. But Political Cheapness depends upon the paucity of Supernumerary Interlopers into any Trade over and above all that are necessary, *viz.* Corn will be twice as dear where are two hundred Husbandmen to do with the same work which an hundred could perform: the proportion thereof being compounded with the proportion of superfluous expence [expense], (*viz.* if to the cause of dearness abovementioned be added to the double Expence [expense] to what is necessary) then the natural price will appear quadrupled; and this quadruple Price is the true Political Price computed upon naturall grounds. And this again proportioned to the common artificiall Standard Silver gives what was sought; that is, the true Price Currant [Current]. (*Treatise*, in Hull (1899), vol.1, p.90; brackets added.)

The 'natural price' of commodities is the one which can be attained under *normal* circumstances of the present state of technology in the economy without any short-run disturbance, whereas the 'political price' refers to the supply price of commodities which takes into account all the factors which might affect the normal state of technology available at a certain point of time. The 'price currant [current]' seems to represent simply the monetary value of the latter. Depending further on the demand conditions of the markets, the actual price of commodities would oscillate around their 'price currant [current]'.[10] Thus, we may note here that Petty's notion of 'natural price' is equivalent to what was called normal or natural price in later literature.[11]

---

[10] As a matter of fact, Petty continued to explain the actual determination of the market price of commodities, in the following way.

> But forasmuch as almost all Commodities have their Substitutes or Succedanea, and that almost all uses may be answered several wayes; and for that novelty, surprise, example of Superiours, and opinion of unexaminable effects do adde or take away from the price of things, we must adde these contingent Causes to the permanent Causes abovementioned, in the judicious foresight and computation whereof lies the excellency of a Merchant. (*Treatise*, in Hull (1899), vol.1, p.90.)

Thus, considering some demand-side elements, he pointed out that the actual market price of commodities would be determined by both their supply and demand conditions.

[11] Roncaglia (1985) seems to have rather a different view on the difference between 'natural price' and 'political price' in Petty's conceptualization of the price of commodities. According to him,

> Petty's "natural price " thus has the meaning of a target, or of an optimal price, a meaning which would later disappear in the use of the term by the economists of the Classical school. In Petty's writings it is the price corresponding to the best technology available (at least in principle) on the basis of the state of technology, and corresponding to the most efficient possible operation of the "body politick". In fact, the Classical idea of "natural price" corresponds to Petty's "political price", which regulates the behavior of the market and depends on the actual conditions of production prevailing in the economic system (Marx would subsequently refer to these conditions with the expression "socially necessary labour"). (p.77.)

Thus, in Roncaglia's interpretation, all the above three notions of price, i.e., 'natural price' , 'political price' and even 'price currant [current]', are related to the long-run normal price in one way or

While it seems to be based on a quantitative method of the Baconian 'scientific approach' of his days, rather than on any ethical criteria of the mediaeval Scholasticism, it almost exactly parallels the classical tradition, a hundred years or so after him, of the normal or natural price of commodities, which was supposed to be dependent only upon the technological conditions of their production without any reference to the supply and demand conditions of their markets.

Now let us look in detail at how Petty's 'natural price' of commodities was to be determined. As mentioned above, basically, the explanatory mechanism is seen as a by-product of the technical procedure of his calculation of the value of land. It is related to two occasions, when Petty tried to capitalize the rent of land for the value of land: that is, his expression of the rent of land directly in terms of money and his 'par between land and labour'. Let us examine one after the other. In the former, after defining the rent of land as net product or surplus, Petty appeared to consider two 'sub-systems', i.e., those of corn and silver, to explain the determination of their relative price by comparing the amounts of net product produced in the respective 'sub-systems' during the same labour time.[12] Because of the very nature of 'sub-

---

another: that is, the first being its 'optimal target', the second being itself, and the last being its monetary expression. To go a step further, he attributed Petty's distinction between the 'natural' and 'political price' to the historical background of his time, i.e., 'predominantly one of transition from feudalism to capitalism rather than fully developed capitalism', as, according to him, Petty might try 'to emphasize the higher costs attached to then still backward level of social organization'. Now, however, there arises a simple question: on what basis could Petty count the 'natural price' of commodities? In other words, how could he conceive the 'most efficient possible operation of the "body politick"', which was supposed to be far different from the 'actual conditions of production prevailing in the economic system'? Since this point is not clear in Petty's own analysis, Roncaglia's argument seems to have no firm basis. Instead, as those factors – appearing in the above quotation from Petty's *Treatise* – which might make the 'political price' different from the 'natural price' could be regarded as some of short-run disturbances for the supply price of commodities to become their normal price attained in the long-run normal state of technology in the economy, the real ground for the distinction between the two notions of price seems to lie rather in the analytical period of each price. It might become obvious, in addition, from the fact that the current price could hardly be seen to be identified with the normal price expressed in terms of money. Cf. Roncaglia (1985), pp.76-79.

[12] Petty defined the 'natural' rent of land as an excess of the gross product over the expenses of its production paid in corn, as follows:

> Suppose a man could with his own hands plant a certain scope of Land with Corn, that is, could Digg, or Plough, Harrow, Weed, Reap, Carry home, Tresh, and Winnow so much as the Husbandry of this Land requires; and had withal Seed wherewith to sowe the same. I say, that when this man hath subducted his seed out of the proceed of his Harvest, and also, what himself hath both eaten and given to others in exchange for Clothes, and other Natural necessaries; that the remainder of Corn is the natural and true Rent of the Land for that year. (*Treatise*, in Hull (1899), vol.1, p.43.)

Thus, here we could note that, while Petty identified the rent of land with the agricultural surplus remaining after seed and subsistence have been subtracted from the total yield, all the amounts were expressed in terms of one and the same physical unit, corn. Therefore, although the concept of surplus in Petty, whether it might be interpreted as 'surplus-value' or 'physical surplus', could be attributed to one of his most significant contributions to the subsequent development of economic theory, it was defined without any problem of the determination of the relative price of commodities, both input and output.

system', however, the supposed relative price of corn and silver could not be determined in terms of the relative amount of physical surplus from the two industries unless they were assumed to be the only industries in the economy, which is obviously not the case in the present context.[13] This result comes from the fact that even though in his analysis the rent of land was defined as net product or surplus, and the wages of labour were supposed to be at subsistence level,[14] the determination of the amount of (physical) surplus as such still have recourse to the determination of the relative price of commodities. A contradiction in determining the relative price of commodities by means of itself![15] After all, Petty's above discussion of the

---

On the other hand, Petty continued to consider the two 'sub-systems', that of corn and that of silver, to explain how to express the rent of land in money, as follows:

> But a further, through collaterall question may be how much English money this Corn or Rent is worth? I answer, so much as the money, which another single man can save, within the same time, over and above his expence [expense], if he imployed himself wholly to produce and make it; *viz.* Let another man go travel into a Countrey where is Silver, there Dig it, Refine it, bring it to the same place where the other man planted his Corn; Coyne it, &c. the same person, all the while of his working for Silver, gathering also food for his necessary livelihood, and procuring himself covering, &c. I sat, the Silver of the one, must be esteemed of equal value with the Corn of the other: the one being perhaps twenty Ounces and the other twenty Bushels. From whence it follows, that the price if a Bushel of this Corn to be an Ounce of Silver. (*Treatise*, in Hull (1899), vol.1, p.43.)

Thus, according to Petty, the relative price of commodities could be represented by the relative amount of land rent, i.e., net product.

[13] According to Sraffa (1960), a 'sub-system' is defined as 'a self-replacing system the net product of which consists of only one kind of commodity', obtained by 'subdividing each of the industries of the original system into parts of such size as will ensure self-replacement for each sub-system' (p.89). Although, on account of one of its important characteristics, the commodity forming the net product of each 'sub-system' should be equal to the rent of land, as the net product in this context does not include the wages of labour employed in the production process, the relative price, as such, ought to be either given from outside the model or determined in the whole or 'original' system covering all the sectors of the economy, together with the relative prices of other commodities, including those of wage goods. Therefore, Petty's discussion of the relative price of commodities, quoted in note 12 above, seemed to be far from the cost-of-production theory of value of Sraffian sort. Cf. Sraffa (1960), p.89.

[14] As a matter of fact, Petty was not consistent in his treatment of wages. Sometimes, he regarded the wages of labour as fixed at the level of subsistence which depends on not only physiological but also socio-historical conditions. Cf., for example, our previous quotation concerning his definition of land rent in note 12 above. See also Hull (1899), vol.1, p.52, pp.89-90 and pp.274-5. Sometimes, he thought that the wages of labour could be regulated by law. Cf., for example, Hull (1899), vol.1, p.87. Sometimes, he considered the wages of labour to be determined according to its productivity. Cf., for example, Hull (1899), vol.1, p.181.

[15] On the contrary, some historians held that Petty anticipated a Ricardian theory of rent, i.e., one price-determined rather than price-determining. Hull (1900), arguing that in Petty there was no explanation of why the cultivator must pay rent rather than of how he can pay, maintained that the 'so-called Ricardian theory of rent supplies this gap by means of the law of diminishing returns' (p.327). See also pp.328-9 and Marx (1862-3; part 1), pp.359-60. Indeed, Petty hinted, in several places, of the concept of 'differential rent' based on both the different fertility of land and its different location from the market. For example, see Hull (1899), vol.1, p.89 and p.48, respectively; and also pp.51-3 and p.286. Roncaglia (1985, pp.69-70) also strongly supported this view, quoting the same passages from Petty as Marx did. Although he conceded that 'Petty does not recognize the possibility, which would be later be exploited by Ricardo, of eliminating rent from the price of the product by concentrating on the conditions of production on the marginal land', he seemed to go too far when he stated that 'Petty's use of physical costs of production gave an objective formulation to his analysis'

value of corn in terms of silver appears to leave only a possibility that it can be interpreted as a sort of labour theory of absolute value – rather than a theory of exchange value or relative price of commodities in terms of their cost of production.[16]

The second occasion, on which Petty seemed to discuss the determination of the normal price of commodities in terms of their cost of production, relates to his 'natural par and equation between land and labour'. While the problem was still how to quantify the normal price without recourse to any ethical criteria, it was to be resolved by means of reducing it into its components. Therefore, as a first step, the cost incurred in the production of commodities should be decomposed in one way or another. As Petty emphasized the wealth of a nation in terms of its physical sources, so he directed his attention to the physical inputs of commodities in relation to their value.[17] Then, as a second step, any sort(s) of common denominator(s) should be found, since those physical inputs as well as outputs must be heterogeneous among different commodities. As far as Petty was concerned, land and labour were conceived as the 'two natural denominations' of value, i.e., two primal physical inputs of the commodity in general. And, as a final step, as long as the proportions between the common denominators still vary among different commodities, there must be found such a relation between them that the value of commodities may be expressed in those terms commensurable with one another. All these steps ultimately account for Petty's attempt to seek a 'par and equation between land and labour'.[18] However, his attempt as what he

---

(p.82), in that he tried to find this 'formulation' in the determination of the relative price of commodities in terms of their cost of production in Petty. We shall discuss this point soon.

[16] In this context, Marx (1862-3; part 1) asserted that it just represents Petty's explanation of expressing the rent of land in money (p.357). In fact, he argued that germs of his labour theory of value could be found in Petty. Quoting the same passages, as we did in note 12 above, he remarked,

> ... for Petty, therefore, since the value of corn is determined by the labour-time contained in it, and that rent is equal to the total product minus wages and seed, rent is equal to the surplus-produce in which the surplus-labour is materialised. Rent here includes profit; the latter is not yet separated from rent. ... The difference in the kind of labour, Petty expressively notes, is here quite immaterial; all that matters is the *labour-time*. (Marx (1862-3; part 1), p.357; original italics.)

See also Marx (1862-3; part 1), pp. 355-9 and pp.180-1, and Petty's *Treatise*, in Hull (1899), vol.1, p.43, pp.50-1, p.87, p.89, and p.90.

[17] Cf. Petty (1927), pp.190-2.

[18] Petty himself summarized the final two steps, as follows:

> ... all things ought to be valued by two natural Denominations, which is Land and Labour; that is, we ought to say, a Ship or garment is worth such a measure of Land, with such another measure of Labour; forasmuch as both Ships and Garments were the creatures of Lands and mens Labours thereupon: This being true, we should be glad to finde out a natural Par between Land and Labour, so as we might express the value by either of them alone as well or better then by both, and reduce one into the other as easily and certainly as we reduce pence into pounds. (*Treatise*, in Petty (1899), vol.1, pp.44-5.)

However, from the above quotation, it is not clear whether his theory of value was concerned with the absolute value of commodities, like Marx's labour theory of value, or with its relative price, like

called 'the most important consideration in political oeconomy' appears to have ended in failure since he found no more than a common unit for the products of various sectors, i.e., 'days' food', which already presupposes the prior determination of their relative price; unless the various sectors (?) would produce one and the same commodity, i.e., (composite) wage goods.[19] Therefore, it seems that if Petty was really concerned with the determination of the relative price of commodities in terms of their cost of production, then he must have faced the same contradiction on this occasion of his 'par between land and labour' as on the other occasion discussed earlier: that is, the determination of relative price by means of relative price.[20]

From the viewpoint of the cost-of-production theory of value, so far, we have examined some relevant concepts which appeared in Petty's economic writings and have made a mosaic analysis based on them. Although we might

---

Sraffa's physical-cost-of-production theory of value. Roncaglia (1985; pp.80-2) concluded that the latter is the case, on the supposition that it 'should be interpreted as a simplification with respect to a more complex theory based on labor and land, and that Petty is implicitly presuming the hypothesis of proportionality between the quantities of land and the quantities of labor used in the production of the various commodities' (p.81). Nevertheless, for, as he himself emphasized, 'the problem of the equivalence between land and labor is a central subject of discussion' (*loc.cit.*), the conclusion must depend on how Petty's 'par between labour and labour' actually works.

[19] According to Petty,

> ... I would hope to come to the knowledge of the Value of the said Commodities, and consequently the Value of the Land, by deducting the hire of Working-People in it. And this brings me to the most important Consideration on Political Oeconomies, *viz.* how to make a *Par* and *Equation* between Lands and Labour, so as to express the Value of anything by either alone. To which purpose, suppose two Acres of Pasture-land inclosed, and put thereinto a wean'd Calf, which I suppose in twelve Months will become 1 *C.* heavier in eatable Flesh; then 1 *C.* weight of such Flesh, which I suppose fifty days Food, and the Interest of the Value of the Calfe, is the value or years Rent of the Land. But if a mans labour for a year can make the said Land to yield more than sixty days Food of the same, or of any other kind, then that overplus of days food is the Wages of the Man; both being expressed by the number of days food. (*Political Anatomy*, in Hull (1899), vol.1, pp.180-1.)

In his procedure of finding a 'par between land and labour', first of all, the net product of each sector is supposed to consist of the rent of land and the wages of labour, with the latter depending on the productivity of labour. The 'par' represents the proportion between them, measured in a homogeneous magnitude, i.e., 'days' food'. Therefore, unless the 'par' determined in the (composite) wage-goods industry by comparing the amounts of output with and without employing labour could be applied to all the other industries in the economy, the relative prices of commodities, including wage-goods, should be pre-determined to obtain the 'par' in each industry. This is exactly analogous to the Sraffa's so-called 'corn-model' for the determination of the rate of profit in Ricardo's early works, in which the rate of profit determined in the subsistence-goods industry, whose input and output are the same (corn), is supposed to 'regulate' the rate of profit in the whole economy. Cf. Sraffa (1951), pp.xxx-xxxvii. We shall discuss Petty's 'par' further in comparison with Cantillon's.

[20] Rather, as the title of the chapter in *The Political Anatomy of Ireland*, where the above discussion of his 'par' appeared, i.e., '*Of the Proportion in value, which the several Counties in* Ireland *do bear to each other*', suggests, it seems that Petty simply sought a common measure to compare the value of land in different parts of a country for certain practical purposes, mentioned earlier, by way of establishing 'pars' not only 'between lands and labour' but also 'between art and simple labour', etc. Cf. *Political Anatomy*, in Hull (1899), vol.1, pp.176-83. Then, as to the question we raised in note 18 above, i.e., whether his theory of value was concerned with the absolute value of commodities or with their relative price in terms of the physical cost of production, we may conclude that none of them sound pertinent to this case.

appreciate that he identified some important concepts, such as normal or 'natural price' and surplus or net produce, which were to underlie the subsequent development of the subject, we could hardly see any self-contained analysis of the relative price of commodities in terms of their cost of production in Petty's economic writings. While, nevertheless, his legacy – not only those concepts but also his analytical framework itself in many respects – was bequeathed to some of those after him, R. Cantillon (1680?-1734) stood out distinctly from others. In the cost-of-production theory of value, in particular, we may regard Cantillon as the direct successor to Petty, aside from the respective authors' various other contributions to the progress of economic discipline.[21] Thus, our next task ought to be to examine Cantillon's analysis of the normal price of commodities and related analysis of the distribution of income.

Cantillon's 'Intrinsic Value'

Let us start with Cantillon's definition of the 'intrinsic value' of commodities in his *Essai*.[22]

---

[21] In this tenor, Bowley (1973) observed,

> Petty's emphasis on the physical sources of wealth, land and labour, and his statement that the value of goods ought to be measured by the land and labour used in their production emphasised the importance of physical inputs in relation to value. ... he found himself involved in finding a par between land and labour. He left unresolved the problem of the relationship between market values and values calculated on the basis of land and labour inputs. This problem seems to be that which Cantillon set out to resolve in his analysis of the price mechanism. (p.93.)

Moreover, in a more general sense, making the analogy that 'Cantillon was to Quesnay, and Petty was to Cantillon, what Ricardo was to Marx', Schumpeter (1954) stated,

> What Petty failed to accomplish – but for what he had offered almost all the essential ideas – lies accomplished before us in Cantillon's *Essai*. True, it was not accomplished in the style of a pupil who at every step looks back over his shoulder for the master's guidance, but in the style of an intellectual peer who strides along confidently according to his own lights. Likewise, Quesnay strode on according to his own lights and was no more a mere pupil of Cantillon than Cantillon was of Petty. Nevertheless, few sequences in the history of economic analysis are so important for us to see, to understand, and to fix in our minds, as is the sequence: Petty - Cantillon - Quesnay. (p.218.)

While he held, thus, that Cantillon could be seen to be indebted to Petty for his general theoretical 'set-up', Schumpeter particularly emphasized that 'it was Petty's problem – mainly the "par" between land and labour – and Petty's methods which inspired him'. Cf. Schumpeter (1954), pp.215-23. Meanwhile, in a comprehensive treatment of pre-Smithian era, Hutchison (1988) observed that what Cantillon owed to Petty was vital, and additionally pointed to his indebtedness, whether positive or negative, to Locke; King, Davenant, Halley; Sir Isaac Newton; Vauban, Jean Boizard, Boisguilbert, the work of the Rouen master; and John Law. (Cf. pp. 163-5.)

[22] Jevons (1881) once praised Cantillon's *Essai sur de Nature de Commerce en General* (written in the 1720s but published in 1755) as the 'first systematic Treatise on Economics' and even as the 'Cradle of Political Economy' in that it covered in a concise manner nearly the whole field of economics, with the exception of taxation. Though appreciating Jevons's 'rediscovery' of Cantillon, Schumpeter (1954) dismissed his estimate as an overestimation. He remarked that 'in particular nothing could be more infelicitous than to call the *Essai* the "cradle" of Economics: this is precisely

> ... the Price or intrinsic value of a thing is the measure of the quantity of Land and of Labour entering into its production, having regard to the fertility or produce of the Land and to the quality of the Labour. (*Essai*, in Higgs (1931), p.29.)

His notion of 'intrinsic value', as the normal price of commodities, was defined in terms of their physical inputs, i.e., land and labour.[23] Like Petty before him, Cantillon also sought the 'par between land and labour'. How then could he achieve it for his part?

> Land is the matter and Labour the form of all produce and Merchandise, and as those who labour must subsist on the produce of the Land it seems that some relation might be found between the value of Labour and that of the produce of the Land. (*Essai*, in Higgs (1931), p.31.)
>
> ... it is seen that the value of the day's work has a relation to the produce of the soil, and that the intrinsic value of any thing may be measured by the quantity of Land used in its production and the quantity of Labour which enters into it, in other words by the quantity of Land of which the produce is allotted to those who have worked upon it. (*Ibid.*, p.41.)

Unlike his predecessor, Cantillon found the 'par' by calculating the quantity of land required to produce that amount of the 'produce of land', i.e., necessary goods for subsistence, which might be regarded as the value of labour.[24] That is to say, on the one hand, Petty's 'par' was just a result of having found a common unit (days' food) with which to compare the value of different commodities. This virtually presupposes the prior determination of their relative price, unless the wage goods were assumed to be composed of a single

---

what it was not' (p.217 n). Nevertheless, Cantillon's *Essai* still rates as the 'most systematic, lucid and original of all the statements of economic principles before the *Wealth of Nations*' (Blaug (1985), p.20). Claiming the *Essai* to represent the 'state of the art of economics before Adam Smith' (p.77), Ekelund and Hebért (1990) provide a fairly detailed bibliography of Cantillon (pp.91-2). There is an interesting biography of Cantillon, whose life has long been veiled in mystery, by Murphy (1986). Here we refer to the *Essai* edited by Higgs (1931).

23 Meanwhile, in ch.II, part II of the *Essai*, Cantillon was explaining the actual market price of commodities in terms of their demand and supply in the markets at any point in time. (Cf. Higgs (1931), pp.117-21.) Cantillon did not fail to mention the relationship between the 'intrinsic value' and the actual market price of commodities. It reads as follows:

> But it often happens that many things which have actually this intrinsic value are not sold in the Market according to that value. ... There is never a variation in intrinsic values, but the impossibility of proportioning the production of merchandise and produce in a State to their consumption causes a daily variation, and a perpetual ebb and flow in the Market Prices. However in well organised Societies the Market Prices of articles whose consumption is tolerably constant and uniform do not vary much from the intrinsic value. (*Essai*, in Higgs (1931), pp.29-31.)

Thus, according to Cantillon, while the 'intrinsic value' of commodities is determined by the prevailing technology of production and never varies without any change in the state of technology, their actual market price oscillates around this normal price, depending on the demand and supply conditions of their markets.

24 As in this calculation Cantillon actually took into account the heterogeneity of labour, he discussed the wage differentials due to it, particularly, in chs. VII and VIII, part I of his *Essai*; Higgs (1931), pp.43-57. Cantillon further emphasized the variety of the modes of living, which were supposed to determine the levels of subsistence, and the diversity of the methods of producing the necessary goods. Cf. *Essai*; in Higgs (1931), pp.31-43.

(composite) commodity produced from one and the same industry. On the other hand, Cantillon established the 'par' by measuring that quantity of land which could produce necessary goods for the subsistence of those who worked upon it.

As far as the necessary goods, i.e., subsistence wage goods, are composed of more than one (composite) commodity,[25] the 'par' is no longer invariable to the changes in the relative price of those necessary goods. This is a crucial point which differentiates Cantillon's from Petty's 'par'. While the latter had reached an impasse, the former broke a path. As Cantillon himself asserted, his 'par' related to the 'causes' of the value of commodities, whereas Petty's 'par' to its 'effects'.[26] In fact, it is in the course of his search for the 'par' that Cantillon found the 'causes' of the value of commodities. In other words, while Cantillon's 'par', as such, represents the subsistence wages of labour, calculated in the quantity of land, which must vary depending on the relative

---

[25] This is evident from here and there in Cantillon's *Essai*. He stated, for instance,

> I have caused some figures to be drawn up which will be found in the Supplement, to determine the amount of Land of which one man can consume the produce under the head of Food, Clothing, and other necessaries of life in a single year, according to the mode of living in Europe. (*Essai*, in Higgs (1931), pp.37-9.)

Thus, although it seems that the Supplement, mentioned in the above quotation, has not been found yet, it is obvious that he assumed the 'produce of land' to include more than one necessary or subsistence goods.

[26] Cantillon criticized his predecessor's 'par' in the following way:

> Sir Wm. Petty, in a little manuscript of the year 1685, considers this Par, or Equation between Land and Labour, as the most important consideration in Political Arithmetic, but the research which he has made into it in passing is fanciful and remote from natural laws, because he has attached himself *not to causes and principles but only to effects*, as Mr Locke, Mr Davenant and all the other English authors who have written on this subject have done after him. (*Essai*, in Higgs (1931), p.43; italics added.)

From our previous analysis of Petty's 'par', it may be confirmed that this criticism was precise and to the point.

Meanwhile, in the case of the single (composite) wage goods, which we may call either 'days' food' or 'corn', both Petty's and Cantillon's 'par' amount to the same thing if it is assumed that the 'par' determined in the wage-goods industry should be the same as those in all the other industries in the economy. Petty determined the 'par' by comparing the 'days' food' produced in a certain quantity of land without employing labour and that with employing labour (the difference between them represented no more than the wages of labour); whereas Cantillon determined it by measuring the quantity of land which could provide 'corn' as subsistence for a labourer working upon it (that amount of 'corn' represented no more than the wages of his labour). By means of the 'par' thereof calculated in either way, we may convert the quantity of labour employed in the production of each commodity, to that of land; or *vice versa*. The value of commodities can then be expressed in terms of the quantity of land, or that of labour, alone. This argument could be summarized in the following value equation system:

$$\mathbf{v} = w\,\mathbf{l} + \mathbf{L}$$

where $\mathbf{v}$: value (column) vector
w: 'par' between land and labour in the wage-goods industry
$\mathbf{l}$: labour-coefficient (column) vector
$\mathbf{L}$: land-coefficient (column) vector.

Thus, from the above n equations, we can get the 'par' (w) and (n – 1) relative values of commodities.

price of subsistence goods, his analysis ultimately points to the explanation of the value of commodities in terms of their component parts; no matter whether it would be expressed in land or any other *numéraire*. Thus, in order to formalize Cantillon's version of the cost-of-production theory of value, we should articulate these component parts of the value of commodities on the basis of our previous discussion of his macroeconomic model of circulation.[27]

As we already noted, when Cantillon examined the circular process of production, distribution and consumption in an exchange economy, he actually anticipated the Physiocratic doctrine – that is, 'agriculture is the only productive sector'. The argument could be summarized in the following system of equations:[28]

$$\mathbf{q} = \mathbf{v}_w + \mathbf{q}\,\mathbf{A} + \mathbf{v}_r = \mathbf{q}\,\mathbf{l}\,\mathbf{d} + \mathbf{q}\,\mathbf{A} + \mathbf{v}_r$$

where $\mathbf{q}$: row vector of gross output
$\mathbf{v}_w$: row vector of farmers', labourers' and mechanicks' consumption
$\mathbf{A}$: input-coefficient matrix
$\mathbf{v}_r$: row vector of proprietors' consumption
$\mathbf{l}$: labour-coefficient (column) vector
$\mathbf{d}$: row vector of subsistence wage bundle.

Therefore,

$$\mathbf{v}_r = \mathbf{q}\,(\mathbf{I} - \mathbf{l}\,\mathbf{d} - \mathbf{A}) = \mathbf{q}\,(\mathbf{I} - \mathbf{B})$$

where $\mathbf{B}$: socio-technical input-coefficient matrix, i.e., $\mathbf{l}\,\mathbf{d} + \mathbf{A}$.

That is, the proprietors' consumption is equal to the net products, i.e., surplus, of the economy. In value terms, the proprietors' consumption should be equal to their income, i.e., the total amount of land rents in the economy. Thus,

$$\mathbf{v}_r\,\mathbf{p} = \mathbf{q}\,(\mathbf{I} - \mathbf{B})\,\mathbf{p} = \mathrm{e}\,\mathbf{q}\,\mathbf{L}$$

where e: rate of rent.

From this, we could note that while the social (value) net products in the economy accrue to the hands of the 'proprietors of land', they come from that sector which uses land in its production, i.e., agriculture.

Now we may derive the price equation system as *dual* to the above equation system of physical quantities. That is,[29]

---

[27] Cf. the appendix to Ch.2.

[28] In this context, the 'farmers' who were supposed to organize the production in agriculture were also assumed to get only subsistence wages, like 'labourers' and 'mechanicks'. We shall shortly discuss the 'profit of their undertaking', which Cantillon obviously took into account when he described the circulation of the goods between sectors and classes in the economy. Meanwhile, as we assume n commodities produced in n industries, the dimensions of vectors and matrices are (1 × n) or (n × 1) and (n × n), respectively.

[29] The original price equation system is, therefore, as follows:

$$\mathbf{p} = \mathbf{B}\,\mathbf{p} + \mathrm{e}\,\mathbf{L} = \mathbf{l}\,\mathbf{d}\,\mathbf{p} + \mathbf{A}\,\mathbf{p} + \mathrm{e}\,\mathbf{L}.$$

$$\mathbf{p} = e\,(\mathbf{I} - \mathbf{B})^{-1}\,\mathbf{L}.$$

Hence, a land theory of value.[30] Starting with emphasis on the physical inputs of production, i.e., land and labour as two component parts of the 'intrinsic value' of commodities, Cantillon established the 'par between land and labour' in terms of subsistence wages of labour, and finally arrived at a land theory of value as his version of the cost-of-production theory of value.

From this equation system, we could obtain the (relative) 'intrinsic value' of commodities and the (uniform) rate of rent in the economy, as we have n equations and variables, respectively, under the assumption of non-singularity of matrices. Cf. our formalization of Steuart's 'real value' of commodities in sub-section 1.1 in this chapter.

[30] As we have already seen in the previous discussion of Steuart's land theory of value, the section $(\mathbf{I} - \mathbf{B})^{-1}\,\mathbf{L}$ from the above equation represents a vector of the physical quantities of land 'embodied' in commodities.

Meanwhile, even if we introduce the wage differentials due to the heterogeneity of labour, which Cantillon explicitly took into account (cf. our note 24 above), it makes no difference to his land theory of value. For instance, if we consider two sorts of labour of different quality ($\mathbf{l}_1$, $\mathbf{d}_1$; $\mathbf{l}_2$, $\mathbf{d}_2$), the price equation system could be expressed as follows:

$$\mathbf{p} = e\,\{\mathbf{I} - (\mathbf{l}_1\,\mathbf{d}_1 + \mathbf{l}_2\,\mathbf{d}_2) - \mathbf{A}\}^{-1}\,\mathbf{L}.$$

So, we have the same interpretation as above.

However, if we introduce the rent differentials due to the different quality of land, which Cantillon also expressly emphasized, his land theory of value becomes no longer safe, unless the 'land structure' is the same in all industries. For example, if we consider two sorts of land of different quality ($\mathbf{L}_1$, e_1; $\mathbf{L}_2$, e_2), the price equation system could be expressed as follows:

$$\mathbf{p} = e_1\,(\mathbf{I} - \mathbf{B})^{-1}\,\mathbf{L}_1 + e_2\,(\mathbf{I} - \mathbf{B})^{-1}\,\mathbf{L}_2.$$

So, no more land theory of value, unless the ratio of two different land-coefficients is assumed to be the same in all industries, i.e., $\mathbf{L}_1/\mathbf{L}_2$ = constant.

The difficulty which Cantillon was faced with in his land theory of value seems to be exactly analogous to that which Ricardo was faced with in his labour theory of value, in the sense that the assumption of the same 'land structure' and that of the same 'capital structure', in all industries, were crucial to their respective theories. Obviously, the following passage, from his *Essai*, pointed to this difficulty.

> ... the real value of everything used by man is proportionable to the quantity of Land used for its production and for the upkeep of those who have fashioned it. ... after summing up the different degrees of fertility of the Land in several Countries and the different kinds of produce it can bring forth with greater abundance according to its intrinsic quality, and assuming the establishment of Towns and Markets to facilitate the sale of these products, it will be shown ... that it was impossible to fix their respective intrinsic value. (*Essai*, in Higgs (1931), p.115.)

Thus, according to him, the difference in the quality of land chiefly depends on its fertility and its distance from the market for products. Likewise, as Ricardo sought the 'invariable measure of value' as an ideal medium to 'sieve' only that price change, occasioned by changes in the quantity of labour 'embodied' in a commodity, from the other, occasioned by changes in the rate of profit, so might Cantillon have done the same thing to 'sieve' only that price change only, occasioned by changes in the quantity of land 'embodied' in a commodity, from the other, occasioned by changes in the rate of rent. In fact, alluding to this point, he continued,

> Thence arose the choice of Gold and Silver for large business and of Copper for small traffick. These metals are not only durable and easily transported but correspond to the employment of a large area of land for their production, which give them the real value desirable in exchange. (*Essai*, in Higgs (1931), pp.115-7; italics added.)

Although Cantillon recognized the need for a sort of 'invariable measure of value' to resolve the problem of the different quality of land, he did not try any further to portray its nature, i.e., its production by the average proportion of land and labour in all industries in the economy, as Ricardo did. Cf. Ricardo (1951-73), ch.1, pp.10-51.

Meanwhile, there appeared another, though rather rudimentary, version of the cost-of-production theory of value in Cantillon's *Essai*: that is, an embryonic Smithian 'adding-up' theory of value in his analysis of the 'intrinsic value' of commodities. As a matter of fact, his emphasis on the role of 'undertakers' as capitalist entrepreneurs in every sphere of the economy, gave a clue to this interpretation.

From Cantillon's description of the risk-taking and profit-seeking economic activities of 'undertakers' in his *Essai*, two things become obvious. On the one hand, their activities were not envisaged as necessarily involving the advancement of capital in the production process, and thus they could not be exactly identified with the capitalists appearing in later literature. On the other hand, their income, i.e., the 'profit of undertaking', was not conceived of as being distinct, in its nature, from the wages of labour, and thus it could not be the same notion as the profit upon capital again found in later literature.[31]

---

[31] In ch.XIII, part I of the *Essai*, Cantillon detailed the characteristics and roles of the 'undertakers'. For instance, he described the farmer in the agricultural sector, one of the most typical 'undertakers', as follows:

> The Farmer is an undertaker who promises to pay the Landowner, for his Farm or Land, a fixed sum of money (generally supposed to be equal in value to the third of the produce) *without assurance of the profit he will derive from his enterprise.* He employs part of the land to feed stocks, produce corn, wine, hay, etc. according to his judgment without being able to foresee which of these will best. The price of these products will depend partly on the weather, partly on the demand ... And yet the price of the Farmer's produce depends naturally upon these unforeseen circumstances, and consequently he conducts the enterprise of his farm at an uncertainty. (*Essai*, in Higgs (1931), pp.47-9; italics added.)

In the subsequent pages, Cantillon gave some other examples of 'undertakers', such as carriers, merchants, manufacturers, etc.

Here, the questions are whether the 'undertaker' in Cantillon's analysis is identical with the capitalist in later literature, who is supposed to organize the process of production with his capital and get some profit upon it, and whether the 'profit of undertaking' is the same category of income as the profit upon capital, distinct from the wages of labour and the rent of land. First of all, as we note from the above description of the farmer as an 'undertaker', Cantillon plainly assumed that some profit would accrue to the farmer for his 'undertaking', though its amount was uncertain. Indeed, he explicitly called it the 'profit of undertaking'.

> The Farmers have generally two thirds of the Produce of the Land, one for their costs and the support of their Assistants, the other for the *Profits of their undertaking.* (*Essai*, in Higgs (1931), p.43; italics added.)

Second, however, Cantillon's 'undertakers' actually included not only the capitalist entrepreneurs but also those independent workers who produce commodities from their own labour, without capital.

> ... except the Prince and the Proprietors of Land, all the Inhabitants of a State ... can be divided into two classes, Undertakers and Hired people; ... all the Undertakers are as it were on unfixed wages and the others on wages fixed so long as they receive them though their functions and ranks may be very unequal. The General who has his pay, the Courtier his pension and the Domestic servants who has wages all fall into this last class. *All the rest are Undertakers, whether they set up with a capital to conduct their enterprise, or are Undertakers of their own labour without capital,* they may be regarded as living at uncertainty; the Beggars even and the Robbers are Undertakers of this class. (*Essai*, in Higgs (1931), p.55; italics added.)

Third, therefore, his notion of the 'profit of undertaking' seems apparently to refer to the wages of some particular kind of labour, i.e., the 'wages of superintendence', rather than the profit upon capital, as it did not necessarily presuppose the involvement of capital. Like others, these sorts of wages are

Nevertheless, all these imply neither that there was no concept of capital itself in Cantillon, nor that his notion of the 'profit of undertaking' was simply another name for the 'wages of superintendence'. Throughout his *Essai*, on the contrary, it is evident that Cantillon had a proper concept of capital as advances for production process and that his 'profit of undertaking' includes some profit upon those advances.[32]

> ... a master Hatter who has capital to carry on his manufacture of Hats, either to rent a house, buy beaver, wool, dye, etc. or to pay for the subsistence of his workmen every week, ought not only to find his upkeep in his enterprise, but also a profit like that of the Farmer who has his third part for himself. This upkeep and the profit should come from the sale of the Hats whose price ought to cover not only the materials but also the profit in question. (*Essai*, in Higgs (1931), p.203.)

---

supposed to be spent on the subsistence. (Cantillon explicitly assumed the different levels of subsistence within and without the class of 'undertakers'. Cf. note 24 above.)

Finally, the economy, depicted in Cantillon's *Essai*, was basically one in a stationary state, in that any and every part of all the categories of income were supposed to go to the consumption for either subsistence or luxury, not to the investment for the further accumulation of capital, which might be ascribed to the dynamic nature of the profit upon capital.

From the above points, at least, we may conclude that the 'profit of undertaking' in Cantillon is not the same notion as that of the profit upon capital in Smith.

32 As far as the concept of capital is concerned, it is self-evident from the discussions so far, particularly from the fact that Cantillon was talking about two sorts of 'undertakers', with or without capital as advances in the production process. Cf. note 31 above. For his notion of the 'profit of undertaking', we may grasp what he really meant by it from his discussion of its relation to the interest of money, in which his concept of capital also clearly presented itself. Regarding the origin of the interest for money loan, he remarked,

> A man who lends his money on good security or on mortgage runs at least the risk of the illwill of the Borrower, or of expenses, lawsuits and losses. But when he lends without security he runs the risk of losing everything. For this reason needy men must in the beginning have tempted Lenders by the bait of a profit. And this profit must have been proportionate to the needs of the Borrowers and the fear and avarice of the Lenders. This seems to me the origin of Interest. But its constant usage in States seems based upon the Profits which the Undertakers can make out of it. (*Essai*, in Higgs (1931), pp.199-201.)

Thus, while Cantillon explained the origin of interest in terms of the risks being accompanied with money loans, at the same time he related it to the 'profit of undertaking'; that is, the one ultimately depends on the other. He continued to expose further their relationship, as follows:

> The Farmer who conducts the working of it [Land] has generally two thirds of the produce, one third pays his expenses and upkeep, the other remains for the profit of his enterprise. If the Farmer have enough capital to carry on his enterprise, if he have the needful tools and instruments, horses for ploughing, cattle to make the Land pay, etc. he will take for himself after paying all expenses a third of the produce of his Farm. But if a competent Labourer who lives from day to day on his wages and has no capital, can find some one willing to lend him land or money to buy some, he will be able to give the Lender all the third rent, or third part of the produce of a Farm of which he will become the Farmer or Undertaker. However he will think his position improved since he will find his upkeep in the second rent and will become Master instead of Man. If by great oeconomy and pinching himself somewhat of his necessities he can gradually accumulate some little capital, he will have every year less to borrow, and will at last arrive at keeping the whole of his third rent. (*Essai*, in Higgs (1931), p.201.)

Now, it becomes clear that the 'profit of undertaking or enterprise' in this context refers to some profit upon capital advanced during the production process, from which some interest would be paid for the money borrowed, if any.

According to Cantillon, apart from their 'upkeep', comprising the wages of labour and some expenses for the intermediate goods and for the depreciation of produced means of production, the 'undertakers' were supposed to get some profits upon the capital advanced for their production.[33] Thus, in every production, the net output was to be distributed among the wages of labour, the 'profit of undertaking', and the rent of land, if applicable. From this observation, Cantillon proceeded to what might be called a Smithian distributive cost-of-production theory of value, in which the normal price of commodities was determined by the component parts of the distribution of net products, i.e., the wages of labour, the 'profit of undertaking' and the rent of land, rather than the physical inputs of the production, i.e., subsistence goods for labourers, produced means of production and land.[34]

As soon as the 'profit of undertaking' entered into the cost of production of commodities, in addition to the wages of labour and the rent of land, Cantillon's 'intrinsic value' of commodities should have been expressed as a mere aggregate of these three distributive variables, since the 'profit of undertaking' was supposed to be determined in the exchange process. That is, although the 'profit of undertaking' *originally* comes from the production process, i.e., the risking-taking activities of 'undertakers' and their advancement of capital in that process, its amount *ultimately* materializes in the exchange process. Therefore, the 'intrinsic value' of commodities, as their cost of production, could not be determined purely on the basis of the socio-technical conditions of production without reference to the supply and demand conditions of the markets; otherwise, any attempt to determine the 'intrinsic value' of commodities would fall into a circular reasoning – i.e., the determination of value by means of value.[35] As a result, despite the fact that

---

[33] Cantillon observed,

> ... if a water-carrier in Paris sets up as the Undertaker of his own work, all the capital he needs will be the price of two buckets which he can buy for an ounce of silver and then all his gains are profit. If by his labour he gains 50 ounces of silver a year, the amount of his capital or borrowing will be to that of his profit as 1 to 50. That is he will gain 5000 per cent. while the Hatter will gain only 50 per cent. ... It might well be that a Water-carrier gains 5000 per cent. of the value of the buckets which serve as his capital, even 10,000 per cent. if by hard work he gains 100 ounces of silver a year. But as he may spend on his living 100 ounces just as well as 50, *it is only by knowing what he devotes to his upkeep that we can find how much he has of clear profit.* The subsistence and upkeep of Undertakers must always be deducted before arriving at their profit. (*Essai*, in Higgs (1931), pp.205-7; italics added.)

Thus, it is obvious that, while the 'profit of undertaking' in this context includes both the 'undertaker's upkeep' and what Cantillon called 'clear profit', i.e., the profit on his capital advanced, the latter is clearly distinguished from the former.

[34] We shall discuss Smith's own version of the cost-of-production theory of value in terms of his 'natural price ' of commodities, later on in this appendix.

[35] In fact, this logical contradiction might account for his other attempt to explain the 'intrinsic value' of commodities in terms of physical inputs, which, as we have already seen, led to a land theory of value. As he considered the 'profit of undertaking' to be determined in the exchange process, he sometimes ruled it out from the components of 'intrinsic value' of commodities, as their prime cost.

Cantillon fully recognized the role of capital in the production process and clearly discerned the profit upon capital from other categories of income, his analysis of the relative price of commodities in terms of their cost of production, based on his notion of the 'profit of undertaking', seems to end up with an anticipation of Smith's 'adding-up' theory of value.[36]

As thus far we have examined Cantillon's *Essai*, we could detect therein some threads of the two different versions of the cost-of-production theory of value: physical-cost and distributive-cost theory. In the former, succeeding Petty, Cantillon considered the two physical inputs, land and labour, as fundamental constituents of the 'intrinsic value' of commodities, and, in search of his own 'par' between them, he arrived at a land theory of value. In the latter, he anticipated Smith's 'adding-up theory of value on the basis of due appreciation of the role of 'undertakers' in organizing the production process. It seems that, although Cantillon had a clear concept of capital and his own

[36] In this light, Cantillon and Smith assumed exactly the same role of demand in their respective analyses of the 'intrinsic value' and the 'natural price' of commodities. That is, they explained the tendency of the actual market price of commodities to gravitate toward the normal price of commodities in terms of their own notion of demand. Above all, as Smith (1776) defined his notion of 'effectual demand' as the 'demand of those who are willing to pay the natural price of commodity' (p.63), it represents a single price-quantity point, rather than a continuous curve as a definite schedule. If the quantity supplied falls short of 'effectual demand', (or *vice versa*,) the actual market price would rise above (or fall below) the 'natural price'. Consequently, the increasing quantity supplied gradually brings the actual market price down (or up) to the 'natural level'. From this notion of 'effectual demand', Smith could gain an analytical ground for the 'natural price' of commodities, and accomplish his own version of the cost-of-production theory of value. Meanwhile, Cantillon, for his part, also seemed to have a similar notion of demand.

> ... if some of the Farmers sowed more corn than usual they must feed fewer Sheep, and have less Wool and Mutton to sell. Then there will be too much Corn and too little Wool for the consumption of the Inhabitants. Wool will therefore be dear, which will force the Inhabitants to wear their clothes longer than usual, and there will be too much Corn and a surplus for next year. As we suppose that the Landowner has stipulated for the payment in silver of the third of the produce of the Farm to be paid to him, the Farmers who have too much Corn and too little Wool, will not be able to pay him his Rent. If he excuses them they will take care the next year to have less corn and more Wool, for Farmers always take care to use their land for the production of those things which they think will fetch the best price at Market. If, however, next year they have too much Wool and too little Corn for the demand, they will not fail to change from year to year the use of land till they arrive at proportioning their production pretty well to the consumption of the Inhabitants. So a farmer who has arrived at about the proportion of consumption ... will not change his plan unless he sees some considerable change in the demand. (*Essai*, in Higgs (1931), pp.61-3.)

Thus, according to Cantillon, if the quantity of commodities supplied fails to meet the given demand, their market price will change, and as the quantity supplied adjusts itself to the demand, the market price will oscillate around a certain stable level. While this stable level represents the normal price of commodities, it in turn reflects the normal rates of component distributive variables, i.e., the rent of land, the wages labour, and the 'profit of undertaking'. This is precisely what Smith was talking about later, as regards the 'natural price' of commodities at the 'natural rates of rent, wages and profit'. (We shall shortly deal with Smith's notion of 'natural price'.) As far as both Cantillon and Smith were concerned, nevertheless, it was one thing to discuss the actual market price of commodities in terms of their supply and demand conditions in the markets, and another to explain the relative price of commodities in terms of their cost of production, based on the normal condition of its demand in the above context.

notion of 'profit of undertaking', he was still facing an analytical limit, as his distributive cost-of-production theory of value turns out to be a mere theoretical abstraction of the normal price of commodities and the normal rates of distributive variables under the assumption of the normal condition of demand in the markets, however defined.

Quesnay's 'Average Fundamental Price'

As we mentioned before, Cantillon seemed to directly influence the French Physiocrats in many respects, particularly the view of economic phenomena as a circular process and the emphasis on the land as the only source of surplus.[37] Of the Physiocrats, F. Quesnay (1694-1774) was the originator and leader.[38] On the basis of the previous analysis of his basic macroeconomic model of the circular process of production, distribution and consumption, we shall discuss Quesnay's theory of value and distribution, particularly his version of the cost-of-production theory of value, in comparison with those of other authors before and after him.[39]

---

[37] Cf. the appendix to the previous chapter. Hutchison (1988), emphasizing some influences of both Boisguilbert and Cantillon on Quesnay, remarked,

> As regards Cantillon, though it would be misleading to describe him as the first physiocrat (because he was so much more than a physiocrat), he certainly provided, as we have seen, the two main pillars on which Quesnay built his system, the primacy of agriculture, and the circular flow of payments. (p.274.)

[38] Quesnay's economic writings were chiefly concerned with some practical issues of his day, e.g., the problem of stagnation of the then French economy, involving debates on free trade, taxation and methods of cultivation in agriculture. Since he inquired into the causes of the stagnation and some means to cure it, his early economic writings, such as *Farmers* (1756), *Corn* (1757), *Men* (1757; published in 1908), and *Taxation* (1757; appearing in 1902), were written mainly for this purpose. In consequence, it might seen quite natural that he needed some sort of norm with which he could compare the real situation of the French economy in those days. In fact, the celebrated *Tableau Economique* (1st ed., 1758; 2nd and 3rd eds., 1759), with its long-listed assumptions, was designed to provide this norm. (The assumptions called 'maxims' in the *Tableau* surely describe certain ideal conditions for the economy. We shall discuss it later on.) While he further developed its diagrammatic form, he actually made some comparisons between the real situation of the economy, where many undesirable impediments to its prosperity existed, and the ideal one where certain proper government policies were to be adopted. (Cf. note 7 in the appendix to the previous chapter, for details of the changes in the diagrammatic form of *Tableau.*) He carried out them in his later economic writings, such as *Rural Philosophy* (1763; co-written with Mirabeau), *Analysis* (1766), the *First Economic Problem* (1766) and the *Second Economic Problem* (1767). Meanwhile, in the present appendix, we refer to those of Quesnay's works, translated by Meek (1962), Kuczynski and Meek (1972), and Groenewegen (1983).

[39] For Quesnay's model of circulation, envisaged in his *Tableau*, see the appendix to the previous chapter. His theory of value and distribution seems to deserve due attention from historians of economic thought. Especially, despite the fact that his *Tableau* actually underlay the whole of his economic doctrine and in itself implies a particular theory of value, it has been believed that there is no theory of value at all in the *Tableau* or, at least, it plays no significant role in it. Nevertheless, the theory of value, implied in the *Tableau*, is linked to the gist of his whole economics. It is notable in this light that Vaggi (1983, 1985 and 1987) turned his special attention to the role of value in Quesnay's whole system. It appears, however, that while his work helps us to link the theory of value to the major features of Quesnay's economics, it is not directly related to the *Tableau* itself, which is the core of Quesnay's system.

Above all, although the previously discussed basic model of circulation seems to relate to certain normative conditions which Quesnay visualized as the ideal situation of the French economy of his time, it still could be seen to provide a refined framework for his economics as a whole. In that model, all the magnitudes were expressed in terms of monetary value. The question is whether or not the model was based on a particular theory of value, which may in turn comply with the rest of his economic doctrine.

Let us begin by examining some different notions of the value or price of commodities, appearing in Quesnay's economic writings. Like Smith after him, he made a distinction between the exchange value and the use value of commodities, and he understood the wealth of a nation in terms of the former.[40] He was talking about three different kinds of exchange value of commodities throughout his economic analysis: i.e., 'good price' (*bon prix*), 'fundamental price' (*valeur fondamentale*) and 'market price' (*valeur venale*).[41]

According to him, the 'good price' of commodities is the one which is 'constantly maintained by means of proper cultivation, large consumption and external trade', and at the same time 'high enough to yield a gain sufficient to encourage people to maintain or increase their production'.[42] As it represents

---

[40] Quesnay remarked,

> *The price represents the market value of exchangeable wealth.* Thus we should not confuse the price of items of exchangeable wealth with their use value, for these two values rarely have any connection with one another. The use value is always the same, and is always a matter of greater or lesser concern to men according to the relation it bears to their needs and their desire to enjoy it. But the price on the contrary varies, and is dependent upon different causes which are inconstant as they are independent of men's will. This means that the price is not regulated at all by men's needs, is far from being an arbitrary value or a value which is established by agreement between the contracting parties. (*Men*, in Meek (1962), p.90; original italics.)

Thus, according to him, the wealth of a nation consists in the exchange value of commodities, rather than in their use value, on the supposition that the former does not depend on the latter. In the meantime, Quesnay allowed for the case of extreme scarcity, in which the use value of a commodity might exert a decisive influence on the determination of its exchange value. Cf. *Men*, in Meek (1962), *passim*.

[41] Particularly in his early economic writings, before the first edition of *Tableau Economique* (published in 1758), Quesnay had advocated certain government economic policies based on the hypothesis of exclusive productivity of agriculture: that is, the 'large-scale cultivation' of agriculture in *Farmers* (1756), free trade in *Corn* (1757) and *Men* (written in 1757), and the direct taxation on the rent revenue of 'proprietors' in *Taxation* (written in 1757). All these were closely related to his theory of value, based on the above three notions of price.

[42] Cf. *Corn*, in Meek (1962), p.84, and *Men*, in Meek (1962), p.93. We may observe some characteristics of the 'good price' of commodities from the following passage. (Meek translated *bon prix* as 'proper price'.)

> ... not only is the proper [good] price favourable to the progress of agriculture, but it is also in the proper [good] price itself that the wealth which agriculture procures consists. The value of a *setier* of corn, regarded as wealth, consists only in its price. Thus the dearer and more abundant are corn, wine, wool, and live-stock, the more wealth there will be in the state. *Valuelessness plus abundance does not at all equal wealth. Dearness plus dearth equals poverty. Abundance plus dearness equals opulence.* (*Corn*, in Meek (1962), p.84; original italics.)

a *profitable price* resulting from favourable conditions of production and consumption, the 'good price' might become general and common among trading nations if the trade is unobstructed and competitive. Meanwhile, Quesnay defined the 'fundamental price' of commodities as the one which is 'determined by the expenses or costs which have to be incurred in their production or preparation'.[43] This 'fundamental price' could be better understood, in its relation to the 'good price'. According to Quesnay,

> If as a result of scarcity their price rises to a level which is burdensome to the people, then this price is excessively high. If such a price, in spite of the fact that it greatly exceeded the fundamental price, were not in fact burdensome to the people, it would then simply be a high price, and a very advantageous one. (*Men*, in Meek (1962), p.93.)

Thus, the 'fundamental price' of commodities seems to represent simply their prime cost, whatever the cost is composed of; whereas the 'good price' is the one which allows the producers to continue production, at least without loss, and thus it is equal or higher than the 'fundamental price'.

As far as the 'market price' of commodities was concerned, Quesnay considered it in two different situations: free trade and non-free trade. In the case of free trade, according to him, the 'market price' is regulated by the comparative conditions of production and consumption among the trading nations; whereas, in the case of non-free trade, it is ultimately determined by the demand and supply conditions of the domestic market.[44] Is there then any

---

Thus, the 'good price' does not simply represent that sort of high price, occasioned by the excess of demand over supply; rather, it has to do with Quesnay's concept of wealth as exchange value rather than as use value. Given that he was particularly concerned with free trade between nations, this implies that he was talking about the international comparative price which was supposed to reflect the technical conditions of production in each nation, as well as the demand and supply conditions of its domestic market. We shall further discuss this point as we examine his other notions of price and the relationship between them.

[43] Cf. *Men*, in Meek (1962), p.93.

[44] As mentioned in note 41 above, while Quesnay's free-trade argument was particularly well presented in his *Corn* and *Men*, it was closely related to his theory of value. From the respective essays, we may quote some passages for his discussions of the determination of the 'market price' of commodities, in which he made a good comparison between the case of free trade and that of non-free trade.

> When trade is free, the dearness of produce has necessary limits which are determined by the prices of the produce of other nations which have extended their trade to all parts of the world. The same cannot be said of the valuelessness of dearness of produce caused by the absence of free trade. These follow one another in turn and irregularly. Both are extremely harmful, and are almost always due to unsound government policy. (*Corn*, in Meek (1962), p.86.)

> The revenue of a kingdom is regulated by the price of its produce; and the price of produce is maintained and regulated by the foreign trade. For in a state which has no external trade at all, either of export or import, the price of produce cannot be subject to any rule or any order. It necessarily follows the variations of scarcity and abundance in the country, and the state has put up with excessively low or excessively high prices, both of which are equally disastrous and inevitable. (*Men*, in Meek (1962), p.93.)

relation between the 'market price' of commodities and their 'fundamental price' or their 'good price'? In fact, it is through the relationship between these different notions of price that we may grasp some significant aspects of the theory of value which the basic model of circulation in his *Tableau Economique* might have been based on.

According to Quesnay, if an economy is engaged in foreign trade which is mutual and free, the 'market price' of commodities would remain stable at their 'average fundamental price' among trading nations, as the 'mutual alterations of abundance and scarcity' among trading nations would keep the supply and demand of commodities steady and the 'general intercommunication' among them would secure competition in the international market.[45] Consequently, while the 'average fundamental price' among trading nations becomes a general and common price both in the international market and each nation's domestic market, it may be a 'good price' to some nations whose state of technology is more advanced than the average of the trading nations; whereas it could be a 'fundamental price', or worse, to others whose state of technology is at the average level, or below that. These relations among the three notions of price, i.e., 'market', 'fundamental' and 'good price', seems to be quite peculiar to Quesnay's theory of value. That is, in Quesnay, the cost-of-production price of commodities, if any, was conceived as their 'average fundamental price' which would prevail in free-trading nations; whereas, in some of those before and after him, it was regarded as their long-run normal price. In other words, while Quesnay's 'average fundamental price' might be seen to be equivalent to the long-run normal price of others, the tendency of the actual market price

---

From these, we may conclude that Quesnay's free-trade argument was firmly based on his theory of value. According to him, in particular, the determination of the 'market price' of commodities in a trading nation must be subject to its foreign trade.

[45] When he built up his argument in favour of free trade, Quesnay observed,

> Prices, as we have said, are never subject to big variations in a kingdom with an import and export trade with other nations which is mutual, unobstructed, and perfectly free: because prices in such a kingdom are equal to the common prices which are current in the other countries. For then the poor harvests and abundant harvests which this kingdom may experience do not normally bring about any change at all in prices, because in one and the same year there are abundant harvests in some countries and poor harvests in others, and by means of free and unobstructed trade between these different countries those which in a particular year are suffering from a scarcity are supplied by those which have an abundance, while in another year the latter, who are now in their turn suffering from a scarcity, are supplied by the former. Thus, as a result of this general intercommunication and these successive and mutual alterations of abundance and scarcity, prices always remain at an international level, determined by the average fundamental price in these countries which are joined together by trade. (*Men*, in Meek (1962), pp.94-5.)

Thus, as long as free trade is established between nations and the abundance of commodities in one nation offsets their scarcity in another, the supply and demand of commodities in each nation can be kept steady so that their 'market price' may remain stable. As long as the trading nations intercommunicate and the international market is competitive, the 'market price' would converge to the 'average fundamental price' among trading nations.

to gravitate towards the cost of production was differently described in each case: i.e., in terms of international trade in the former and in terms of long-run equilibrium in the latter.

As mentioned above, the circular process of production, distribution and consumption, envisaged in Quesnay's *Tableau*, assumed some ideal, rather than real, conditions of the French economy of his day, including the government policy of free trade; some of them were not so explicitly related to the circular process itself, though.[46] Whether or not it was supposed to be 'good price', the price of commodities, in terms of which all the magnitudes in the *Tableau* were expressed, could be seen as their 'average fundamental price' among the trading nations, as far as it is certain that the *Tableau* was concerned with an open economy rather than a closed one – i.e., that it was designed to describe the circulation of money and commodities within this open economy. Apparently it might still be said that Quesnay's *Tableau Economique* was based on a variant of the cost-of-production theory of value, in the sense that the 'average fundamental price' referred to some 'intermediate level' of the various costs of production among trading nations. As long as the cost of production in one nation was supposed to be different from that of another on account of their different states of technology, one could not say that the value of commodities was determined by their cost of production unless the state of technology in the economy concerned might incidentally be the 'intermediate level' among the trading nations.[47]

[46] As we sometimes confuse the assumptions of a model with its logical conclusions, or *vice versa*, (and this is particularly true in interpreting Quesnay,) it is quite necessary for us to articulate the assumptions underlying his *Tableau*. Interestingly enough, as the diagrammatic forms of the *Tableau* were getting more and more self-explanatory, i.e., from the original 'zigzag' via '*precis*' in the *Rural Philosophy* to '*formule*' in the *Analysis*, certain additional assumptions were subsequently introduced. Nevertheless, from the very beginning, those of normative character were patently presented in the 'maxims' of *Tableau*. Some of them could be summarized as follows:

1) In agriculture, the production is carried out in the best of prevailing methods, i.e., the large-scale cultivation' which is more capital-intensive than the others.
2) The fertility of soil is kept in good condition all the time.
3) There is no barrier in both internal and external trades, that is, free trade prevails within the economy and between the trading nations.
4) Taxes are imposed directly on the revenue of 'proprietors', not on products or advances. Thus, it makes no difference to the circular process whether it is with and without taxes, as long as the government's expenditure pattern is the same as that of the 'proprietors of land'.
5) There is no shortage of labour in both 'productive' and 'sterile' sectors, that is, there is a continuous supply of labour without any scarcity.

Cf. 'Remarks on the Variations in the Distribution of the Annual Revenue of a Nation' in the first edition of the *Tableau*, in Meek (1962), pp.109-14; 'Extract from the Royal Economic Maxims of M. De Sully' in the second edition, in Meek (1962), pp.120-5; and some notes to the maxims of the third edition, made by Meek himself, in Meek (1962), pp.136-7. Meanwhile, some additional assumptions, made subsequently, appear to be mostly concerned with the 'advances', 'annual' and 'original'.

[47] Therefore, according to Quesnay, the 'fundamental price' of commodities in an individual nation simply represents their prime cost, which does not include any profit, either upon capital advanced or upon anything else. In relation to this, it seems that Vaggi (1983, 1985 and 1987) went too far. Although he admitted that 'the fundamental price is a sort of lower limit of the current one' and that

Now, we know that the determination of the price of commodities in Quesnay's *Tableau Economique* should be explained in terms of their 'average fundamental price' among trading nations, which would be subject to the competition among them. Let us move on to examine how this theory of value based on international trade could go together with the actual description of the circulation of money and commodities in the *Tableau*, so that we may further understand its nature. As far as an individual trading nation is concerned, the domestic 'fundamental price' of commodities as their prime cost, should be lower than, or at worst, equal to the 'average fundamental price' determined in the international market; otherwise, the production itself would not be possible. Having premised this, we need to specify what, according to Quesnay, is supposed to constitute the 'fundamental price' of commodities within each trading nation, and to find out how his model of circulation works if the state of technology in the economy concerned might bear some 'good price' of commodities, which is apparently the case as envisaged in his *Tableau*.[48] While the question may ultimately go down to Quesnay's analysis of the distribution of income, we will concentrate instead on that which was assumed in the *Tableau*. First of all, the 'fundamental price' of commodities can be decomposed into three parts: i.e., the wages of labour, the rent of land, and other expenses including those for raw materials and produced means of production. It was assumed, in his *Tableau*, that the

---

'Quesnay does not include the profits of the cultivator in the fundamental price of primary products', he alleged that 'the notion of fundamental price appears as an intermediate step between the price theories of the seventeenth and the eighteenth centuries and the analysis of price determination of Turgot and Smith; in particular it shows a strong similarity with the concept of natural price' (1987, p.93). In fact, the latter allegation plainly contradicted his other assertion that 'Quesnay's analysis of prices shows that a purely cost-of-production theory of value is inadequate to describe a situation where the distribution of surplus among classes is increasingly regulated via the market' (1987, pp.91-2). All this confusion seems to reveal that his discussions of Quesnay's theory of value were not based on his economics as a whole, but rather just on fragments. Particularly, as far as Quesnay was concerned, there was no logical or analytical inconsistency between the Physiocratic doctrine of the supremacy of agriculture and the theory of value based on international trade, which could be seen as two of the principal ingredients of his *Tableau Economique*. Let us turn to this last point.

48 As we have already noted in the analysis of Quesnay's model of circulation in the appendix to the previous chapter, it was actually assumed in his *Tableau* that the 'productive class' also consumed some non-subsistence goods, including produced means of production, apart from the 'proprietors of land' who received land rents from them as a transferred income; whereas the 'sterile class' did not. Therefore, the *Tableau* itself should be interpreted as being open to accommodate any profit which might accrue to the 'productive class'. That is, the price of commodities implied in it could not be seen to be based on any theory which rules out the possible existence of profit as a distinct category of income.

Meanwhile, if the state of technology in the economy concerned coincidentally bears the 'fundamental price' at the same level as the 'average fundamental price' among the trading nations, then no profit, whatsoever, would accrue to the 'productive class'. Given the subsistence level of wages, this situation would be exactly analogous to the one which Cantillon presupposed when he talked about the 'par between land and labour' and which led to the land theory of value and the exclusive productivity of agriculture. (Cf. our previous discussions on this.) As we have discussed, however, this is a special rather than a general case in Quesnay. (Even for Cantillon, the case proved to be a simplified version of his theory of value, as we have already noted.)

wages were fixed at subsistence level and paid in advance while only agricultural products comprised the subsistence goods. The rents of land were also predetermined in the aggregate and paid in advance. Each sector was supposed to employ some of the other sector's products, as necessary produced means of production and raw materials.

As far as the profits resulting from the 'good price' of commodities were concerned, it is evident, from his exclusion of them from the component parts of the 'fundamental price' of commodities, that Quesnay did not perceive them to accrue upon the capital advanced in the production, although he did refer to the 'large-scale cultivation' in agriculture which was carried out by the 'farmers' who employed labourers on their account and with their own advances and even emphasized the further diffusion of 'large-scale cultivation' and thereupon the growth of agriculture and the economy as a whole.[49] Meanwhile, as long as the 'large-scale cultivation' prevailed in agriculture and

---

[49] As for Quesnay's notion of profit, first, it is evident throughout his economic writings that he was emphatic on the existence of profits, particularly in agriculture, and their important role for economic growth. Regarding the nature of his notion of profit, Vaggi (1987) refuted Meek's (1959 and 1962) view that it is 'essentially temporary in character', arguing that 'the physiocrats regarded farmers' profits as part of the net product, because this is the only element of the annual surplus which can ensure an increase in means of production in agriculture' (p.121). Although these two views apparently seem contradictory to each other, they may actually be complementary. That is to say, Meek grasped the essential character of the notion of profit in Quesnay, i.e., its being no more than the difference between the 'good price' of commodities and their 'fundamental price' or their prime cost; whereas, Vaggi emphasized its significant part assigned in the dynamic aspect of Quesnay's economics. Nevertheless, from our discussion so far, it must be clear that Quesnay's theory of value could not be identified with any pure 'physical' or 'distributive' cost-of-production theory of value, in which the 'profit of farmers' may or may not be included in the component parts of price. In other words, the notion of profit in Quesnay should be regarded as a distinct category of income as a share of net products, whether 'temporary' or not.

As far as the role of the 'profit of farmers' is concerned, it could be better understood in conjunction with the general dynamic process of economic growth, envisaged in Quesnay's whole works. That is, although it is true that the macroeconomic model of circulation depicted in the *Tableau* was concerned with an economy in stationary state in which the same reproduction occurs every year, he actually alluded in all his other economic writings to the crucial role of the 'profit of farmers' in securing their advances for adopting a better method of cultivation. For, according to him, there must be some or other means found within the economy for the further progress of agriculture and thereon the prosperity of the French economy of his time. For instance, Quesnay explicitly stated,

> ... the farmers of landed property profit up the renewal of their leases from the constant increase in the prices of products which occurs during the terms of these leases. And this gain is most fruitful, most profitable, and most necessary in a nation whose agriculture is in need of extension and improvement. For farmers, if they are not oppressed, never leave their occupation; *the profits which they make increase the wealth which they employ in cultivation, which is greatly to the advantage of agriculture.* And these profits, which increase the number of wealthy farmers, promote at the of the renewal of the leases a great degree of competition
>
> between them, which then assures to the proprietors and the sovereign the full return of the net product. (*First Economic Problem*, in Meek (1962), pp.180-1; italics added.)

In the same tenor, also in *Taxation* and *Rural Philosophy*, Quesnay considered the 'profit of farmers' to be an important source of fund which could be used for additional advances in agriculture so as to increase the 'revenue' of the 'proprietors of land' and, therefore, to enhance the level of output in the economy (see note 51 below). Cf. some extracts in Meek (1962), pp.102-7 and pp.138-49, respectively.

the resulting price of agricultural products begot some profits for 'farmers', these profits, together with the rents of land, must have been regarded as the net products in agriculture. They were defined as the difference of the value of outputs and that of inputs in that sector.[50]

Although this concept of net products, based on the notion of 'fundamental price', might be one of the distinctive features of Quesnay's economics, it was the revenue of land rents, rather than the whole net products, that played a pivotal role in the circulation of money and goods in the economy, as depicted in his *Tableau.* In other words, Quesnay's *Tableau Economique* – particularly its original 'zigzag' version – seemed to be designed mainly to illustrate the sequential process which would follow the initial expenditure of rent revenue of the 'proprietors of land', abstaining from detailed complementary explanations.[51] Therefore, while the Physiocratic doctrine of the supremacy of

[50] In this context, it might be noteworthy that, unlike Cantillon's model of circulation, Quesnay's in his *Tableau* was expressed in terms of monetary value.

[51] As a result, it might be seen that, in Quesnay's *Tableau*, the level of output – both its scale and composition – in the economy depends on the initial expenditure of proprietors' rent revenue, i.e., what is known as 'base'.

Table 3.1 Transactions in Quesnay's Tableau

Demand \ Supply		Commodities A	Commodities M	Revenue	Total supply
Sectors	A	2000	1000	2000	5000
Sectors	M	2000	0	0	2000
Proprietors		1000	1000		
Total demand		5000	2000		

In fact, on the basis of his model of circulation, discussed in the appendix to the previous chapter, we could demonstrate the analysis of the determination of the level of output that he implied in the *Tableau*. First of all, we may summarize all the transactions appearing in the model into Table 3.1. While we should note that all the amounts in Table 3.1 were expressed in value terms, we may transform the table in a simple algebraic equation as follows:

$$\mathbf{y} = \mathbf{y}\,\mathbf{C} + \mathbf{b}$$

where $\mathbf{y}$: row vector of (value) gross output, i.e., (5000, 2000)

$\mathbf{C}$: (value) input-coefficient matrix, i.e., $\begin{bmatrix} 2/5 & 1/5 \\ 1 & 0 \end{bmatrix}$

$\mathbf{b}$: row vector of (value) proprietors' expenditure of rent revenue, i.e., (1000, 1000).

Thus,

$$\mathbf{y} = \mathbf{b}\,(\mathbf{I} - \mathbf{C})^{-1}.$$

Therefore, as long as the price of commodities was determined by their 'average fundamental price' among the trading nations and thereon the (value) input-coefficient matrix ($\mathbf{C}$) was given with the model, both the scale and the composition of output in the economy ($\mathbf{y}$) depended on the 'base' of *Tableau*, i.e., the amount of proprietors' revenue and their propensity to consume between agricultural

agriculture has a twofold meaning, i.e., its exclusive productivity and its role in the determination of both the scale and the composition of output in the economy, the two aspects do not seem to depend upon each other in Quesnay. This is because obviously his *Tableau* does not exclude the possibility of the price of agricultural products becoming a 'good price' – i.e., an 'average fundamental price' among the trading nations which is higher than its domestic 'fundamental price' – and thus allows the existence of the 'profit of farmers'.[52]

After all, we may come to the conclusion that as Quesnay tried to demonstrate the Physiocratic doctrine in his *Tableau* without any recourse to a pure physical or distributive cost-of-production theory of value, he found a way out via his own notion of the 'average fundamental price' of commodities, based on international trade. This seems to be the natural course for his analysis, in the sense that Quesnay's economics as a whole had to do with certain development strategies of the French economy of his time in terms of the 'large-scale cultivation' in agriculture, free trade, and the direct taxation on the rent revenue of the 'proprietors of land'.[53]

---

products and manufactures. For example, if the 'base' was changed from (1000, 1000) to (1200, 800) for some reason, i.e., the same amount of revenue but a different propensity to consume, then the level of output would become

$$\mathbf{y} = (1200,\ 800)\begin{bmatrix} 3/5 & -1/5 \\ -1 & 1 \end{bmatrix}^{-1} = (5000,\ 1800).$$

That is, the production of agricultural products would remain the same but that of manufactures would decrease in the economy, and consequently not only the composition of output would change but its scale would also contract.

[52] On the contrary, in Cantillon, these two aspects of the supremacy of agriculture represented different sides of the same coin. That is, according to him, the level of output in an economy depended on the proprietors' expenditure of rent revenue because only the revenue was the net products of the economy, and *vice versa*. As we might have already noticed, this point originally comes from the very duality of his system of the 'intrinsic value' of commodities, i.e., the land theory of value. (Compare the equation $\mathbf{q} = \mathbf{v}_r\,(\mathbf{I} - \mathbf{B})^{-1}$ in Cantillon and $\mathbf{y} = \mathbf{b}\,(\mathbf{I} - \mathbf{C})^{-1}$ in Quesnay, and note that the one is in physical terms and the other in value terms.)

In this context, as mentioned previously in the appendix to the previous chapter, the asymmetry between the two sectors in Quesnay, i.e., the supremacy of agriculture over manufacturing sector, was a direct corollary of the assumptions of his model of circulation (or itself one of those assumptions), rather than a logical conclusion based on any inductive or deductive analysis, in that it did not need to presuppose a land theory of value, as was the case with Cantillon's physical cost-of-production theory of value. Meanwhile, focusing on Quesnay's asymmetrical conception of competition between in agriculture and in manufacturing sector, Vaggi (1987) considered the hypothesis of the supremacy of agriculture as a part of Quesnay's theory of value (pp.94-120).

[53] As mentioned earlier, Quesnay's *Tableau* was actually based on some normative conditions of the French economy of his time. Above all, the assumptions of the prevalence of 'large-scale cultivation', free trade and the direct taxation on rent revenue were far from its reality. Conversely speaking, his whole economics was indeed aimed at advocating those normative conditions and to support certain government policies to achieve them. In his first economic writing, *Farmers*, Quesnay made some comparison between two kinds of methods of production in agriculture, i.e., 'small-scale' and 'large-scale cultivation', and gave a detailed explanation of the advantages of the latter over the former. In *Corn*, he proposed a proper tax system and endorsed free international trade, in association with the

Steuart's 'Real Value'

So far in this appendix, we have discussed a few strands of the cost-of-production theory of value in some authors before Steuart, and realized that each of them had his own version. We had also discussed Steuart's own version in the preceding chapter. Although we do not need to repeat it here, nevertheless, we shall examine further Steuart's notion of the 'real value' of commodities in association with Petty's 'natural price', Cantillon's 'intrinsic value' and Quesnay's 'average fundamental price', so that we may find out some affinities or links among them, as well as some individual differences.

On the basis of the previous discussions, first of all, we may note that all these notions commonly related to the exchange value of commodities rather than their use value, as implicitly or explicitly proclaimed by the respective authors. Second, as the relative price of commodities, they all referred to the real value rather than the nominal or monetary value of commodities. Third, as the normal price of commodities, they were also distinguished from their actual market price determined by the demand and supply conditions. Thus, while the subjective and monetary factors in the determination of the value of commodities were gradually eliminated by the process of theoretical abstraction, a certain hypothetical ground must have been provided, one way or another, to the very normality of those notions of value. They found it in either in some analytical time horizon, e.g., the long-run competitive conditions of the markets, or in some analytical space setting, e.g., a small country engaged in international trade, both of which were supposed to already offset those subjective and monetary factors; except Steuart who never saw the normality of price phenomena in such conceptual manner. Finally, as they

---

discussions of the above methods of cultivation and the price of corn. In *Men*, he elaborated the free-trade argument on the basis of a full analysis of the three notions of the exchange value of commodities, i.e., 'market price', 'fundamental price' and 'good price'. The *Taxation* was particularly devoted to specifying some merits of the direct imposition of tax on rent revenue, compared to the indirect imposition on the 'profit of farmers' or their means of production, or on the products themselves. After bringing out the three editions of *Tableau Economique*, Quesnay tried to expose more precisely and mechanically the results of the deviation of reality from the normative conditions. He carried out sorts of comparative statics with the help of the *Tableau* as an essential tool, utilizing one or another diagrammatic form of it. Thus, in *Rural Philosophy*, written together with Mirabeau, he gave detailed numerical examples for the comparison between the situations before and after the adoption of free-trade policy and that of direct taxation, while using what was called the '*precis*' form of *Tableau*. Thereafter, in the *First Economic Problem*, he performed a more accurate comparative statics of 'full freedom and immunity of external trade' than in the *Rural Philosophy*, while using this time what was called the '*formule*' form of *Tableau*. In the *Second Economic Problem*, he made a closer examination of the detrimental effects of the indirect taxation upon agriculture and the economy as a whole than in the *Rural Philosophy*, while again using the '*formule*'. To sum up, we may note from all his economic writings that, beyond the stationary state of an economy, assumed in his *Tableau* as a norm, Quesnay really had in his mind a dynamic view of how the economy could grow further. Thus, it cannot be emphasized too much that the analytical system of his economics was originally designed to diagnose and prescribe for the French economy of his day.

Meanwhile, though Quesnay himself had done those comparative-static analyses rather thoroughly, Eltis (1975a, 1975b and 1984) revised them in a more concise and consistent manner.

conceptualised the competition among the producers in the supply side, they formalised the cost-of-production theories of value in terms of their respective notions of the normal price of commodities.

As we have already seen, nevertheless, they all differed in their conception of component parts of the cost of production; therefore, they varied in the determination of the cost-of-production price of commodities. Petty perceived the two physical inputs of production, i.e., land and labour, as the fundamental constituents of value, and tried to find a 'par or equation' between them so as to express the 'natural price' of commodities in a commensurable measure. It turned out, however, to be a contradiction, as it were, unless the wages of labour, as well as other produced means of production, were still to be decomposed into the physical inputs. His direct successor, Cantillon, did that job on his behalf and accomplished the land theory of value. At the same time, Cantillon, in his turn, confronted another problem: that is, how to explain the 'profit of undertaking'. Could it be regarded simply as a temporary market phenomenon of 'relative' nature (one's profit is another's loss)? It was this question which eventually led Cantillon to a sort of 'adding-up' theory of value, according to which the 'intrinsic value' of commodities was determined by the 'distributive' variables of net products of the economy – i.e., the wages of labour, the 'profit of undertaking' and the rent of land, rather than the physical inputs of the production – i.e., subsistence goods for labourers, produced means of production and land. Although his economics seemingly exerted a great influence on some major aspects of the Physiocracy after him, his land theory of value was not directly bequeathed to Quesnay, the father of the school. Upon a rather hypothetical assumption, that is, the exclusive productivity of agriculture, Quesnay built up his own theory of value. In fact, avoiding any *pure* physical or distributive cost-of-production theory of value, he was able to comprehend the 'profit of farmers' in his notion of the 'average fundamental price' of commodities among free-trading nations.

Unlike his predecessors, Steuart separated, rather decisively, the 'profit upon alienation' from the 'real value' of commodities as their prime cost, and put analytical emphasis on the very relationship between them, instead of trying to comprehend the former in the latter. Thus, despite its appearance, his notion of 'profit upon alienation' actually played a totally different role in his analysis of value from Cantillon's 'profit of undertaking' and Quesnay's 'profit of farmers'. That is to say, on the one hand, as Cantillon supposed the 'profit of undertaking' to constitute the 'intrinsic value' of commodities, he alluded to a distributive cost-of-production theory of value. Also as Quesnay described the 'profit of farmers' to originate from the international 'average fundamental price' of agricultural products, which is higher than their domestic 'fundamental price' in a trading nation, he suggested a *sort* of distributive cost-of-production theory of value, based on international trade.

On the other hand, in Steuart, as he simply defined the 'profit upon alienation' as the difference between the actual market price of commodities ('current price'), and their prime cost ('real value'), he indeed abandoned any version of cost-of-production theory of value.[54]

As long as any 'profit' still remains of 'positive' nature, i.e., one's profit without incurring any loss to another at the same time, it should be as distinct a category of income as others. While both Cantillon and Quesnay tried to fill the analytical discrepancy between the actual market price and the normal price, which resulted from the existence of 'profit' in the market phenomena, they must have found another component part of the cost of production, apart from the wages of labour, the rent of land, and other expenses covering raw materials and produced means of production. Without a proper notion of the profit upon capital advanced in the production process, they simply added up those component parts of the cost of production, including the 'profit'. As for Steuart, in contrast, his notion of the 'profit upon alienation' seems even to obviate this analytical discrepancy, since it already links the two notions of price, i.e., 'current price' and 'real value', in terms of the 'balance of work and demand'. That is to say, in his analysis, as the 'balance of work and demand' assures the 'profit upon alienation' of being a distinct category of its own, the 'current price' of commodities could be explained as the sum of their 'real value' and the 'profit upon alienation', or the 'real value' as the 'current price' less the 'profit upon alienation'.

After all, we could observe that, while all three had no notion of the profit upon capital, or at least no proper notion of the uniform rate of profit, unlike in Cantillon and in Quesnay, there was no theoretical dichotomy, in Steuart, between the value of commodities and the distribution of income. In other words, whereas in the former the value of commodities should have been determined independently of the distribution of income; in the latter both the value of commodities and the distribution of income were dependent on each other. Not only the wages of labour but also the 'profit upon alienation' were supposed to depend on the price of commodities, or *vice versa*; with the rent of land being determined as a residual.

Smith's 'Natural Price'

Just nine years after the publication of Steuart's *Inquiry* (1767), there appeared another *Inquiry* by a fellow countryman who did know of his predecessor's work but did not even mention it in his own work: A. Smith (1723-90).[55] He

[54] This point is evidently true, unless we impose some of *our own* assumptions on his notion of the 'real value' of commodities, as we have seen earlier in section 4.

[55] Despite no *formal and explicit* relation between them, the theoretical approaches and the ideological views in the respective *Inquiries* form a singular contrast. For the relation between Steuart and Smith, *inter alia*, between the two Scottish contemporary *Inquiries* – i.e., Steuart's (*into the Principles of*

has long been regarded as the system builder of so-called classical political economy by the majority of historians. Among other remarkable achievements, he has a claim to be the first who methodically shaped up the concept of the uniform rate of profit upon capital advanced in various production processes, in line with his notion of the 'natural price' of commodities.

Presenting his own version of the cost-of-production theory of value, Smith exactly followed in his predecessors' footsteps. In his *Wealth of Nations*, first, Smith explicitly distinguished between the exchange value and the use value of commodities as follows:

> The word VALUE, it is to be observed, has two different meanings, and sometimes expresses the utility of some particular object, and sometimes the power of purchasing other goods which the possession of that object conveys. The one may be called 'value in use;' the other 'value in exchange.' (Smith (1776), p.32)

Of course, Smith's concern was with the 'principles which regulate the exchangeable value of commodities'.[56] Second, as he set out to explain the 'exchangeable value' of commodities, Smith also drew a distinction between the real and the nominal price of commodities.[57] According to him,

> The same real price is always the same value; but on account of the variations in the value of gold and silver, the same nominal price is sometimes of very different values. (Smith (1776), p.38.)

Third, Smith conceptualised the normal price of commodities in terms of his own notion of 'natural price', as follows:

> The natural price, therefore, is, as it were, the central price, to which the prices of all the commodities are continually gravitating. Different accidents may sometimes keep them suspended a good deal above it, and sometimes force them down even somewhat below it. But whatever may be the obstacles which hinder them from settling in this center of repose and continuance, they are constantly tending towards it. (Smith (1776), p.65.)

His notion of 'effectual demand' serves as a conceptual tool for his explanation of the tendency of actual market price of commodities to gravitate toward their 'natural price'. Smith defined it as the 'demand of those who are willing to pay the natural price of the commodity'; it is 'effectual' since 'it may be sufficient to effectuate the bringing of the commodity to market'.[58]

Political Oeconomy) and Smith's (*into the Nature and Causes of the Wealth of Nations*), see the appendix to ch.5 below.

[56] Smith (1776), p.33.

[57] Cf. Smith (1776), book 1, ch.V.

[58] Smith (1776) explained the gravitation of the actual market price of a commodity to its 'natural price' in terms of the notion of 'effectual demand', as follows:

> The market price of every particular commodity is regulated by the proportion between the quantity which is actually brought to market, and the demand of those who are willing to pay the natural price of the commodity, or the whole value of the rent, labour, and profit, which must be paid in order to bring it thither. Such people may be called the effectual demanders,

Finally, according to Smith, in the long run under competitive conditions, the price of commodities tends to be equal to their cost of production which would include the profit upon capital at its 'natural' rate. In his *Wealth of Nations*, Smith gave a typical description of his 'natural price' of commodities, as follows:

> When the price of any commodity is neither more nor less than what is sufficient to pay the rent of the land, the wages of the labour, and the profits of the stock employed in raising, preparing, and bring it to market, according to their natural rates, the commodity is than sold for what may be called its natural price. (Smith (1776), p.62.)

Thus, Smith's 'natural price' of commodities, as their long-run normal price, represents no more than the sum of the rent of land, the wages of labour and the 'profits of stock', all employed in the production process, at their 'natural rates'.

> and their demand the effectual demand; since it may be sufficient to effectuate the bringing of the commodity to market. ... When the quantity of any commodity which is brought to market falls short of the effectual demand, all those who are willing to pay the whole value of rent, wages, and profit, which must be paid in order to bring it thither, cannot be supplied with the quantity which they want. Rather than want it altogether, some of them will be willing to give more. A competition will immediately begin among them, and the market price will rise more or less above the natural price, according as either the greatness of the deficiency, or the wealth and wanton luxury of the competitors. ... When the quantity brought to market exceeds the effectual demand, it cannot be sold to those who are willing to pay the whole value of rent, wages and profit, which must be paid in order to bring it thither. Some part must be sold to those who are willing to pay less, and the low price which they give for it must reduce the price of the whole. The market price will sink more or less below the natural price, according as the greatness of the excess increases more or less the competition of sellers, or according as it happens to be more or less important to them to get immediately rid of the commodity. ... The quantity of every commodity brought to market naturally suits itself to the effectual demand. It is the interest of all those who employ their land, labour, or stock, in bringing any commodity to market, that the quantity never should exceed the effectual demand; and it is the interest of all other people that it never should fall short of that demand. ... The natural price, therefore, is, as it were, the central price, to which the prices of all commodities are continually gravitating. (pp.63-5.)

As the 'effectual demand' denotes the amount of demand for a commodity at its 'natural price', it could be represented as a single point, rather than a continuous schedule, in the price-quantity co-ordinates. Its relation to the amount of supply is supposed to determine the actual market price of the commodity. In the long run, as the supply would not fail to adjust itself to the 'effectual demand', the actual market price is to be constantly tending toward the 'natural price'. Thus, the notion of 'effectual demand' serves as an analytical device for linking the actual market price of a commodity and its 'natural price' in his version of the cost-of-production of theory of value.

Meanwhile, Steuart had already employed exactly the same term, i.e., 'effectual demand', in his *Inquiry*. His notion of 'effectual demand' presents a contrast to Smith's. In Smith, as discussed above, it relates to the value of commodities; whereas, in Steuart, it refers to the operation of the economy as a whole, rather than that of a single industry in it. Steuart derived his own notion of 'effectual demand' from the reciprocity of individuals' wants and their efforts to have some equivalents to gratify them in the macroeconomic level. Based on the idea that those who demand must have some proper equivalents to give those who supply, therefore, it underlies his analysis of the level of output in an exchange economy rather than that of the value of individual commodities. For a detailed discussion of Steuart's notion of 'effectual demand', see section 1, ch.4 below. See also note 36 above, for a discussion of the role of demand in Cantillon's analysis of the 'intrinsic value' of commodities.

What was then supposed to determine the 'natural rates' of rent, wages and profits? While Smith spared detailed explanations for this, the main idea could be summarised in his own words, as follows:[59]

> There is in every society or neighbourhood an ordinary or average rate both of wages and profit in every different employment of labour and stock. This rate is naturally regulated, as I shall show hereafter, partly by the general circumstances of the society, their riches or poverty, their advancing, stationary, or declining condition; and partly by the particular nature of employment. There is likewise in every society or neighbourhood an ordinary or average rate of rent, which is regulated too, as I shall show hereafter, partly by the general circumstances of the society or neighbourhood in which the land is situated, and partly the natural or improved fertility of the land. These ordinary or average rates may be called the natural rates of wages, profit, and rent, at the time and place in which they commonly prevail. (Smith (1776), p.62.)

Now, it becomes obvious from the quotation above that the three 'natural rates', as component parts of the 'natural price' of commodities, were simply assumed to be given by the social and natural circumstances of the economy. To put it another way, in Smith, while the distributive variables are to be determined independently of the value of commodities, the one eventually regulate the other. This is a crucial point. Although Smith deserves full credit for recognising the uniform rate of profit upon capital and thereby terminating the analytical discrepancy between the actual market price of commodities and their normal price, his analysis of 'natural price' is still falling into a distributive cost-of-production theory of value, similar to Cantillon's: i.e., an 'adding-up' theory.[60] It ignores not only the interdependence among the components parts of the 'natural price' of commodities but also the very dependence of the component parts themselves on the 'natural price'. In this light, it might be said that while Smith's notion of the profit upon capital so aptly replaced Steuart's notion of the 'profit upon alienation', the former's cost-of-production theory of value did not completely displace the latter's 'work-and-demand' theory of value, in the sense that a theoretical dichotomy

---

[59] Cf. Smith (1776), book I, chs.VII-XI.

[60] In this context, Sraffa (1951) observed,

> This latter theory [Adam Smith's theory of value], in brief, was that 'as soon as stock has accumulated in the hands of particular persons' and 'as soon as the land of any country as all become private property', the price of commodities is arrived at by a process of *adding up* the wages, profit and rent: 'in every improved society, all the three enter more or less, as component parts, into the price of the far greater part of commodities.' In other words, 'wages, profit, and rent, are the three original sources ... of all exchangeable value.' Adam Smith speaks also of the natural price varying 'with the natural rate of each of its component parts, of wages, profit, and rent'. (pp.xxxv-xxxvi; original quotations and italics, but brackets added.)

However, we may add that, in a dynamic context, Smith's 'natural price' and the 'natural rates' of its three component parts might be seen as being determined endogenously, rather than exogenously, as they change along with economic growth.

between the value of commodities and the distribution of income still existed in the former.

4. The Level of Output, Employment and Population

At the very outset of his *Inquiry*, Steuart proclaimed that the principal object of 'political oeconomy' is to secure subsistence and other necessities for all the members of the society and to maintain their employment by means of creating 'reciprocal relations and dependencies' among them.[1] While this view reflected what he was really interested in and what his economics was chiefly about, it demonstratively indicated how he actually conceived of the mechanism of an exchange economy. That is, Steuart's main concern was with the level of output and employment in the economy, and his analytical focus was on the interdependence between economic sectors and social classes therein. In fact, his discussions of population, economic growth and foreign trade in the *Inquiry*, all seemed intimately related to those of the level of output and employment in terms of his notion of 'effectual demand', coined to signify the interdependence of sectors and classes in the economy. Highlighting this analytical device in Steuart, we shall examine his analysis of the level of output, employment and population in the present chapter, and continue to study that of economic growth and foreign trade in the next chapter.[2]

In this chapter, we shall first examine the nature of Steuart's notion of 'effectual demand'. We may find that it is totally different from what Smith, after him, meant by the same term. Rather, it resembles Keynes's 'effective demand' in a sense or relates to the 'capacity utilization' of a growing economy in another. After grasping some implications of the 'effectual demand' in Steuart's economics as a whole, we shall scrutinize how, in terms of the very notion, the determination of the level of output in an exchange economy was actually explained in his *Inquiry*. Naturally, this will lead us to his discussions of the level of employment in the economy and the related

[1] *Works*, vol.1, p.3. Cf. the quotation from Steuart's *Inquiry* in the first page of Ch.1 above.

[2] In these two chapters, we shall neglect money and credit for a while. After we go through Steuart's detailed explanations of their nature and functions, we shall gradually take account of money and credit, and make an attempt to set up a macroeconomic model, focusing particularly on his monetary analysis of the determination of price level and the level of output in a closed economy in Ch.6 below. Having dealt with his discussions of foreign exchange and the balance of payments, we will extend the previous macroeconomic model to an open economy in Ch.7 below. Further, we shall develop the macroeconomic model of money, price and the level of output in Steuart, as we bring in his treatment of public finance to our analysis in Ch.8 below. In fact, all this procedure accords with how Steuart himself built up his argument in the *Inquiry*.

problem of unemployment. Finally, as we look into Steuart's treatment of population, we will realize again how significant an analytical role the notion of 'effectual demand' played in his economics. In our appendix to this chapter, we shall make a close comparison between our author and Keynes with regard to their respective analyses of output and employment, based on the notion of 'effectual demand' in the one and that of 'effective demand' in the other.

1. 'EFFECTUAL DEMAND'

Throughout his *Inquiry*, Steuart assumed, implicitly or explicitly, that the economic activities of individuals abide by the 'principle of self-interest'.[3] At the same time, he put great emphasis on the fact that, in an exchange economy, these activities must be mutually dependent. According to him, this mutual dependence among individuals in their economic activities originates from the reciprocity of their wants or demand. In this regard, Steuart described, rather dramatically, the characteristic feature of an exchange economy in comparison with a slave economy, as follows:[4]

> Men were then forced to labour because they were slaves to others; men are now forced to labour because they are slaves to their own wants. (*Works*, vol.1, p.52.)

In Steuart's conception, as discussed in the previous chapter, all the economic sectors and social classes in the exchange economy were envisaged as depending on each other for their production and consumption. While the transactions between sectors and classes, appearing in his basic macroeconomic model of circulation, particularly well illustrated the point, they represented just the results of the economic activities of individuals for securing their means of subsistence and other necessities, i.e., their wants or demand.

From this observation of the reciprocal wants or demand of individuals and their efforts to have some equivalents to gratify them or to meet it in the exchange economy, Steuart derived his own notion of 'effectual demand'.

> Every person who is hungry will make a demand, but every such demand will not be answered, and will consequently have no effect. The demand must have an equivalent to give: it is this equivalent which is the spring of the whole machine; for without *this* the farmer will not produce any surplus, and consequently he will dwindle down to the

[3] We shall examine some presumptions on human nature underlying the whole of Steuart's political economy, including that of self-interest, in section 1, Ch.9 below; particularly, see sub-section 1.1, for his discussion of the 'principle of self-interest' in the economic activities of individuals in contrast with the 'public spirit of statesman' in guiding and adjusting them.

[4] For detailed discussions of Steuart's conception of an exchange economy, see Ch.2 above; and particularly for those of the nature and consequence of the mutual dependence among individuals in the exchange economy, see section 1 therein. Also cf. his three-stage theory of society in section 2, Ch.9 below.

> class of those who labour for actual subsistence. ... it is the *effectual* demand, as I may call it, which makes the husbandman labour for the sake of the equivalent. (*Works*, vol.1, pp.153-4; original italics.)

Steuart's notion of 'effectual demand' basically conveys the idea that those who demand or consume must have some proper equivalents to give those who supply or produce. Thus, it seems to relate to the operation of the economy as a whole, rather than that of a single sector or industry in it. In other words, in Steuart, the notion of 'effectual demand' underlies his analysis of the level of output in an exchange economy rather than that of the value of an individual commodity.[5]

To understand further the nature of Steuart's notion of 'effectual demand', let us examine whether there is any relation premised, in his *Inquiry*, between the level of output, the amount of employment and the size of population in the economy. The following quotation may give us a general idea on this question.

> If he [the statesman] acts consistently with that spirit of liberty, which we have supposed to animate his subjects, he has no method left, but to contrive different employments for the hands of the necessitous, that, by their labour, they may produce an equivalent which may be acceptable to the farmers, in lieu of this superfluity; for these last certainly will not raise it, if they cannot dispose of it; nor will they dispose of it, but for a proper equivalent. This is the only method (in a free society) of procuring additional food, and of distributing it through the society, as the price of those hours which before were spent in idleness: and, as this will prove a more certain and more extensive fund of subsistence, than the precarious production of spontaneous fruits, which cannot be increased at discretion, and in proportion to demand, it will greatly increase numbers; but, on the other hand, it must evidently destroy that simplicity of manners which naturally reigns among nations who do not labour. (*Works*, vol.1, p.35.)

Apart from his emphasis on the active role of the state,[6] we could notice from this that, according to Steuart, as the reciprocal wants among individuals materialize into the 'effectual demand', the level of output, the amount of employment and the size of population in the economy, altogether, would be determined correspondingly. Indeed, in his analysis, they are so closely

---

[5] In this respect, though both used exactly the same term, Smith's notion of 'effectual demand' was in contrast with Steuart's. In Smith, it relates to a single sector or industry as it serves for explaining the relation between the actual market price of commodities and their 'natural price'. (Cf. note 58 in the appendix to Ch.3 above.) On the other hand, as discussed above, Steuart's 'effectual demand' rather has an affinity with Keynes's 'effective demand', in that both notions have some bearing on the level of output in the economy as a whole. (We shall further discuss some similarities and dissimilarities between their respective analyses of the determination of the level of output or national income in the appendix to the present chapter.)

[6] We shall discuss the role of the state in the operation of an exchange economy, in general, in Ch.10 below where we appraise Steuart's political economy as a whole in terms of the state interventionism; and its role in the determination of the level of output, in particular, in Ch.8 below where we examine his analysis of public finance in terms of its functional application.

related to each other that they go together from start to finish.[7] This point seems to reflect the fact that the economy concerned in his *Inquiry* is basically the one in growth, where both labour and natural resources, such as land, become fully utilized and thereupon the multiplication of population further accelerates the increase of the level of output. In other words, for Steuart, the determination of the level of output, along with that of both the amount of employment and the size of population, is an integral part of his dynamic analysis of economic growth, based on the 'capacity utilization' of economic resources. In this dynamic analysis, labour is supposed to be the only input which could be augmented for the further expansion of production in the economy while land and other natural resources have 'physical' limitations and both the composition and the scale of various produced means of production are determined by the technology of the economy. Thus, the growth of population is essential to that of output. This explains why he constantly endorsed the increment of population. In any case, it is this dynamism in the simultaneous determination of the level of output, the amount of employment and the size of population in a growing economy, which Steuart's notion of 'effectual demand' primarily concerns.[8]

Bearing in mind the above characteristics of Steuart's notion of 'effectual demand', let us move on to examine in detail how Steuart actually carried out his analysis of the level of output, the amount of employment and the size of population, in terms of the notion.

2. THE LEVEL OF OUTPUT

As we explained in the previous chapter, Steuart conceived of an exchange economy as being composed of two economic sectors and three social classes. It was assumed, in his basic macroeconomic model of the circulation of goods and money in the economy, that two different goods are produced in the two sectors, i.e., agriculture and manufacturing industry; whereas, including some intermediate goods employed in the production process, they are consumed by the three classes, i.e., 'farmers', the 'industrious free hands' and 'landlords'. Thus, there are supposed to be three kinds of transactions in the whole economy: intrasectoral, intersectoral and non-sectoral. Those transactions of

---

7 Actually, the main theme of Book I of Steuart's *Inquiry* is how the level of output, the amount of employment and the size of population in an exchange economy are determined simultaneously.

8 In this context, we might observe that Steuart's analysis of the level of output, based on his notion of 'effectual demand', originally started at a different point from Keynes's, based on his notion of 'effective demand'. So to speak, the one was in a more dynamic setting than the other, as it allowed an important factor of economic growth, i.e., population, to be determined within the model. Cf. the appendix to this chapter. Meanwhile, we shall further pursue the dynamic aspect of Steuart's economics in the next chapter where we will discuss his theory of economic growth in connection with foreign trade.

Table 4.1 Transactions (I)

Demand \ Supply		Commodities A	Commodities M	Revenue	Total supply
Sectors	A	10	2	9	21
	M	10	2	0	12
Landlords		1	8		
Total demand		21	12		

the first two kinds are to take place on the basis of the social division of labour within and without each sector, involving both production and consumption. Those of the last kind, occurring between 'landlords' and either 'farmers' or the 'industrious free hands', are to be based on the transfer of income from the 'farmers' to the 'landlords' in terms of land rent, involving the latter's consumption only.[9] While all these transactions eventually underlie the circular process of production, consumption and distribution in the economy as a whole, each of them represent the realization of 'effectual demand' of the sectors and classes concerned. In what follows, scrutinizing the transactions appearing in his macroeconomic model of circulation, we shall closely examine how the 'effectual demand' of each sector and class is realized and how, as a result, the level of output, i.e., both the scale and the composition of gross output in the economy, is determined in Steuart's analysis.[10]

2.1 An Input-output Model

First of all, let us summarize all the transactions among sectors and classes, described in Steuart's model of circulation, into a table (see Table 4.1).[11]

[9] In association with the different natures of all these transactions, Steuart sometimes called both 'farmers' and the 'industrious free hands' the 'producers', i.e., 'those who are constantly employed in acquiring one by supplying the wants of the other', whereas 'landlords' the 'consumers', i.e., 'those who live upon a revenue already acquired'. Cf. *Works*, vol.2, p.17. In other words, 'the consumers live without employment, the producers cannot' (*Works*, vol.1, p.350). This division between the 'consumers' and the 'producers', in turn, seemed to correspond to that between the 'not-working part' and the 'working part' of a society, on other occasions, in his *Inquiry*. That is, 'the not-working part is given to excesses in all kinds of consumption, and the working-part to labour and ingenuity, in order to supply them' (*Works*, vol.1, p.354).

[10] For the detailed description of Steuart's basic macroeconomic model of the circulation of goods and money, see Ch.2 above.

[11] In this table, all the magnitudes are expressed in value terms; and while the rent revenue of 'landlords', transferred from 'farmers', is counted in the supply side, their expenditure is counted in the demand side. In the meantime, we might observe that this transactions table looks quite similar to the one derived from Quesnay's *Tableau Economique*. (Cf. the appendix to Ch.3 above.) Despite their apparent resemblance, nevertheless, there is one thing significantly different between Steuart's and Quesnay's table, i.e.,, the fact that in the former every class in the economy was supposed to

Through the table below, we may grasp the interdependence among the sectors and classes in the economy, in terms of the demand and supply conditions of each commodity. Nevertheless, there seem to be two important but latent elements of Steuart's basic conception of an exchange economy, missing in this table: i.e., his distinction between the 'physical necessaries [necessities]' and 'luxuries', and his identification of the 'profit upon alienation' in the value of commodities. As far as the former is concerned, on the one hand, although he alluded to no definite dividing line between 'physical necessaries [necessities]' and 'luxuries' as such, Steuart broadly classified commodities into these two sorts: the one consisting of subsistence goods and some intermediate goods, produced in the agricultural sector, and the other of non-subsistence goods and some produced means of production, produced in the manufacturing sector.[12] On the other hand, as for the latter, he clearly distinguished the 'profit upon alienation' from the 'real value' of commodities, as their prime cost, and regarded it as a distinct category of income like the wages of labour and the rent of land.[13] After all, mainly on account of the existence of the 'profit upon alienation' in the value of commodities, not only the 'farmers' in the agricultural sector but also the 'industrious free hands' in the manufacturing sector are supposed to consume 'luxuries' as well as 'physical necessaries [necessities]', apart from the 'landlords' receiving the rent of land from the 'farmers'.[14]

To take these points into consideration, we may modify the previous transactions table for Steuart's macroeconomic model of circulation, as in Table 4.2.[15] From this table, we may formalize Steuart's discussions of the

---

consume some manufactures or 'luxuries', whereas in the latter only the 'proprietors of land' and the 'productive class' were to consume them. As already discussed, it has to do with their divergent conceptions of economic sectors in relation to productivity or the production of surplus. That is, for Steuart, every sector in the economy could produce some *economic* surplus; whereas, for Quesnay, only agriculture could. (Cf. the appendix to Ch.2 above.) This divergence in their conception of economic sectors eventually led them to different analytical focuses on their respective analyses of the level of output. As we have already seen (in the appendix to Ch.3 above), in Quesnay who premised the supremacy of agriculture over manufacturing industry, the focus was on the agricultural surplus, i.e., the rent revenue of the 'proprietors of land', and he traced out the effects of their expenditure on the scale and composition of gross output, by means of his *Tableau*; whereas, as we shall see later on, in Steuart who did not admit the asymmetry between the two sectors, the focus was on their mutual dependence, and he emphasized the effects of the consumption of 'luxuries' on the general output level in the economy, on the basis of his notion of 'effectual demand'.

[12] Cf. Ch.2, particularly section 1, above.

[13] Cf. Ch.3, particularly sub-section 3.1, above.

[14] This point seemed to be one of the characteristics of Steuart's model of circulation, compared with Cantillon's and Quesnay's. (Cf. Ch.2, particularly its appendix, above.) Meanwhile, in Steuart, the wages of labour were not fixed at a subsistence level, but determined by its productivity. Thus, part of the wages also contribute to the consumption of 'luxuries'. Cf. section 3, Ch.3 above.

[15] In Table 4.2, we further distinguish, in the demand side, between the intermediate goods and the 'physical necessaries [necessities]' in the agricultural products and between the produced means of production and the 'luxuries' in the manufactures, respectively. Meanwhile, we simply assume those amounts of intermediate goods and produced means of production in each sector and those of 'physical necessaries [necessities]' and 'luxuries' in each class, appearing in the table, in an arbitrary

Table 4.2 Transactions (II)

Supply / Demand		Real value				Profit upon alienation	Total supply
		Commodities		Wages of labour	Rent of land		
		A	M				
Sectors	A	2	1	8	9	1	21
	M	2	1	8	0	1	12
Classes	Farmers	8	1				
	Industrious free hands	8	1				
	Landlords	1	8				
Total demand		21	12				

determination of the level of output – both its scale and composition – in an exchange economy. Assuming that the value of commodities is given as their 'current price' determined in the markets, we can represent the table in a simple algebraic equation, as follows:[16]

$$\begin{aligned}\mathbf{y} &= \mathbf{y}\,\mathbf{C} + \mathbf{f}_1 + \mathbf{f}_2 + \mathbf{f}_3 \\ &= \mathbf{y}\,\mathbf{C} + \mathbf{f} \\ &= \mathbf{y}\,\mathbf{C} + \mathbf{f}_n + \mathbf{f}_x\end{aligned}$$

where $\mathbf{y}$: row vector of (value) gross output

$\mathbf{C}$: (value) input-coefficient matrix, i.e., $\begin{bmatrix} 2/21 & 1/21 \\ 2/12 & 1/12 \end{bmatrix}$

$\mathbf{f}_1$: row vector of (value) farmers' consumption

$\mathbf{f}_2$: row vector of (value) the industrious free hands' consumption

$\mathbf{f}_3$: row vector of (value) landlords' consumption

$\mathbf{f}$: row vector of the (value) total consumption in the economy, i.e., $\mathbf{f}_1 + \mathbf{f}_2 + \mathbf{f}_3$

way. Correspondingly, in the supply side, we make separate entries for both the wages of labour and the 'profit upon alienation' in each sector, and again arbitrarily assume their amounts in the table. Of course, all these amounts are in aggregate terms.

16 As all the amounts in Table 4.2 were expressed in terms of monetary value, we assume further, here, that money was just supposed to serve as a mere medium of exchange. In fact, if we relax this assumption, we might see that the value of commodities and the level of output were actually determined simultaneously in Steuart's analysis. Cf. Ch.6 below.

$\mathbf{f}_n$: row vector of the (value) total consumption of 'physical necessaries [necessities]' in the economy, i.e., $\mathbf{f}\begin{bmatrix}1 & 0\\0 & 0\end{bmatrix}$

$\mathbf{f}_x$: row vector of the (value) total consumption of 'luxuries' in the economy, i.e., $\mathbf{f}\begin{bmatrix}0 & 0\\0 & 1\end{bmatrix}$.

Thus,

$$\mathbf{y} = (\mathbf{f}_n + \mathbf{f}_x)(\mathbf{I} - \mathbf{C})^{-1} = \mathbf{f}_n (\mathbf{I} - \mathbf{C})^{-1} + \mathbf{f}_x (\mathbf{I} - \mathbf{C})^{-1}.$$

Therefore, as long as the technology of production (**C**) and the total amount of the consumption of 'physical necessaries [necessities]' ($\mathbf{f}_n$) are given from outside of the model, the level of output in the economy (**y**) is to be dependent upon the total amount of the consumption of 'luxuries' ($\mathbf{f}_x$).[17]

2.2 The 'Political Effects of Luxury'

The above result seems to come rather directly from Steuart's notion of 'effectual demand' in his analysis of production and consumption in an exchange economy. In other words, as the very notion implies that those who demand and consume should have some equivalents to give those who produce and supply, the consumption of some goods must logically precondition the production of other goods to exchange. Therefore, as far as the production methods of all the goods are to be predetermined, the determination of the level of output in the economy could be explained in terms of the consumption of final goods; and, moreover, as far as the consumption of 'physical necessaries [necessities]' are, more or less, stable at a certain point in time, the level of output could be described as depending on the consumption of 'luxuries'. Without doubt, Steuart had in mind this analytical mechanism of the determination of the level of output in terms of the 'effectual demand' for the very final goods, i.e., 'luxuries', when he referred to the 'political effects of luxury or the consumption of superfluity'.[18] Let us explore further this point.

---

[17] Apparently, the model itself simply tells us that, on the basis of the equilibrium condition of supply and demand for all the commodities in the economy, we could derive both the scale and the composition of its gross output from such data as the technology of each economic sector and the consumption of 'physical necessaries [necessities]' and 'luxuries' by each social class. However, the emphasis of Steuart's analysis was rather on the effects of the consumption of 'luxuries' on the gross output, than on the equilibrium as such. In other words, he wanted to show us how the level of output changes in an economy as its total amount of the consumption of 'luxuries' changes, *ceteris paribus*.

[18] Cf. *Works*, vol.1, p.350.

According to Steuart, the interdependence among individuals in an exchange economy could be reduced to the mutual relation between the producers or suppliers and the consumers or demanders of commodities. This mutual relation, in turn, is based on their 'effectual demand' for either 'physical necessaries [necessities]' or 'luxuries'. In the meantime, there is some asymmetry between the 'effectual demand' for 'physical necessaries [necessities]' and that for 'luxuries', stemming from the nature of the respective kinds of commodities. That is to say, the demand for 'physical necessaries [necessities]' basically depends on the number of people or the population in the economy, whereas that for 'luxuries' usually depends on the 'spirit' or the 'taste of superfluity' which prevails among the people. Moreover, the demand for 'physical necessaries [necessities]', mostly made by 'farmers' and the 'industrious free hands', is related to both consumption and production, whereas the demand for 'luxuries', mostly made by 'landlords', is related to consumption only. Therefore, in so far as the 'physical necessaries [necessities]' of the producers could be regarded as sorts of inputs for their production, the demand for 'physical necessaries [necessities]' must be regulated by the level of output. On the other hand, as long as the 'spirit' of the people affects their consumption of 'luxuries' and only the 'effectual demand' makes the consumption possible, it is the 'effectual demand' for 'luxuries' which ultimately determines the level of output in the economy. Steuart pointed to this 'political effects of luxury', when he remarked,

> ... the use of dependences, I have said, is to form a band of society, capable of making the necessitous subsist out of the superfluity of the rich, and to keep mankind in peace and harmony with one another. (*Works*, vol.1, p.352.)

As we might have already alluded to, there are two fundamental things presupposed in Steuart's discussion of the 'political effects of luxury'. One of the presumptions underpinning his analysis of the level of output is about the productivity of each sector in the economy. As already explained, according to him, both *economic* and *social* surplus or net product are produced in the agricultural sector and distributed to 'farmers', either as their 'profit upon alienation' or as part of their wages of labour, and to 'landlords', as their land rent, respectively; whereas, in the manufacturing sector, only *economic* surplus is produced, going to the 'industrious free hands', either as their 'profit upon alienation' or as part of their wages of labour.[19] In consequence, the agricultural surplus is supposed to be what sustains the consumption of 'luxuries' by both the 'landlords' and the 'farmers', and the manufacturing

[19] Cf. Ch.2 above. It should be noted here that, apart from the 'profit upon alienation', accruing to 'farmers' and the 'industrious free hands', and the land rent, transferred to 'landlords', part of the wages of labour might be regarded as surplus and being spent on 'luxuries', as they are determined by its productivity, rather than fixed at a subsistence level, according to Steuart. Cf. section 3, Ch.2 above.

surplus is to be what enables the 'industrious free hands' to consume their 'luxuries'. Therefore, the 'effectual demand' for 'luxuries' could be augmented only through the enhancement of productivity of each sector. The more productive the agriculture, the more the land rent transferred to 'landlords' and the more the 'profit upon alienation' and the wages of labour accruing to 'farmers'; as a result, the more the 'effectual demand' for 'luxuries', the higher the level of output in the economy. The more productive the manufacturing industry, the more the 'profit upon alienation' and the wages of labour accruing to the 'industrious free hands'; as a result, the more the 'effectual demand' for 'luxuries', the higher the level of output in the economy. The productivity of economic sectors might be, then, a most crucial determinant or parameter in Steuart's analysis of the level of output in terms of the 'political effects of luxury'. This point is self-evident in the following statement, in which Steuart argued for the increase in the rent of land with a view to boosting the level of output in the economy.

> ... the raising of the rents of lands shews the increase of industry, as it swells the fund of subsistence consumed by the industrious; that is, by those who buy it. (*Works*, vol.1, p.58.)

That is, while the landlords' demand for 'luxuries', i.e., manufactures, promotes the production in the manufacturing sector so far as the demand is 'effectual'; this 'effectual demand' for 'luxuries' could be augmented, whenever the productivity of agriculture increases their rent revenue.

Another significant presumption in Steuart's analysis of the level of output is about what ultimately decides the degree or level of consumption of 'luxuries' in an exchange economy. Regarding the development of trade in general, he observed,

> The next thing to be examined, is ... how trade comes to be extended among men; how manufactures, more ornamental than useful, come to be established; and how men come to submit to labour, in order to acquire what is not absolutely necessary for them. This, in a free society, I take to be chiefly owing to the introduction of money, and a taste for superfluities in those who possess it. (*Works*, vol.1, p.237.)

Thus, Steuart suggested two major circumstances which would exert a great influence on people's consumption of 'luxuries': i.e., the existence of money and the 'standard of taste' of the people. That is to say, whilst money as 'imaginary wealth' stimulates 'farmers' and the 'industrious free hands' to further produce and 'alienate' subsistence and 'luxuries', respectively, with a view to supplying more and more wants, it is the very 'taste for superfluities' in those who have equivalents to give for them, including 'landlords', that actually determines the level of consumption of 'luxuries' in the economy.[20]

---

[20] Steuart described how the introduction of money had been spurring people on to more production and 'alienation', as follows:

After all these fundamental suppositions and postulates premised, it might be said that, according to Steuart, the level of output in a monetary economy is determined by the 'effectual demand' for 'luxuries', which depends not only on the productivity of each economic sector – as it should be *effectual* – but also on the 'standard of taste' of each social class – as it is the demand for *luxuries*. Indeed, to this effect, Steuart himself succinctly laid down a desirable 'plan of political oeconomy' in terms of the following two principles.

> A ruling principle ... is to keep the husbandman closely employed, that their surplus may be carried as high as possible; because this *surplus is the main spring of all alienation and industry*. The next thing is *to make this surplus circulate*; no man must eat of it for nothing. (*Works*, vol.2, p.175; italics added.)

As long as the productivity of each sector is ultimately decided by the technological conditions of the economy, its level of output might be seen as being determined by the very consumption of 'luxuries'. That is, the more the consumption of 'luxuries', the higher the level of output.[21]

> So soon as money is introduced into a country it becomes ... *an universal object of want* to all the inhabitants. The consequence is, that the free hands of the state, who before stopped workings, because all their wants were provided for, having this new object of ambition before their eyes, endeavour, by refinements upon their labour, to remove the smaller inconveniences which result from a simplicity of manners. (*Works*, vol.1., p.239; italics added.)

Want is the mother of industry! Nevertheless, the existence of money is rather a necessary than a sufficient condition, for the enhancement of consumption of 'luxuries' in the exchange economy.

> In ancient times, money was not wanting; but the taste for superfluities not being in proportion to it, the specie was locked up. This was the case in Europe four hundred years ago. A new taste for superfluity has drawn, perhaps, more money into circulation, from our own treasures, than from the mines of the new world. ... It is more, therefore, through the taste for superfluity, than in consequence of the quantity of coin, trade comes to be established; and it is in consequence of trade only what we see industry carry things in our days to so high a pitch of refinement and delicacy. (*Works*, vol.1, pp.237-8.)

Thus, according to Steuart, it is the 'taste for superfluities' which eventually determines the level of consumption of 'luxuries' in a monetary economy. Also see *Works*, vol.1, pp.41-6. Meanwhile, in association with the various functions of money assumed in Steuart's economics as a whole, we shall discuss the overall picture of his analysis of consumption, output, money and price, in Chs. 6 and 7 below.

21 In the same tenor, Steuart remarked,

> The misapplier, or dissipator, is punished by the loss of his money; the industrious man is rewarded by the acquisition of it. ... vice is not more essentially connected with superfluity, than virtue with industry and frugality. (*Works*, vol.1, p.199.)

It is well known that the argument of this sort, i.e., the fallacy of composition with regard to the consumption of 'luxuries', was rather common among some mercantilist authors in the seventeenth and eighteenth centuries. Among others, Bernard Mandeville, in his *Fable of the Bees: or Private Vices, Public Benefits* (first edition, 1714), typified the doctrine of the economic beneficence of luxury spending in those authors. Cf. Hutchison (1988), pp.115-26, and also Keynes (1936), pp.358-71. Meanwhile, Steuart placed great emphasis on maintaining an adequate proportion between the amount of consumption and that of 'circulating equivalents', i.e., money, in the economy.

> ... a statesman who intends to increase industry and domestic consumption, should set out by providing a circulating fund of one kind or other, which ought always to be ready, and

> Now in the question before us, the only abuse I can find in these habits of extraordinary consumption, appears to be relative to the character of the consumers, and seems in no way to proceed from the *effects of the consumption*. The vices of men may no doubt prove the cause of their making a superfluous consumption; but the consumption they make can hardly ever be the cause of this vice. (*Works*, vol.1, p.190; italics added.)

In sum, while Steuart apparently seemed to inherit some of his predecessors' views of the utility of luxury, as he was so emphatic on the consumption of 'luxuries' in his analysis of the level of output; his argument was rather based on his unique notion of 'effectual demand', in terms of which he firmly grasped the interrelation of economic sectors and social classes and, thereupon, systematically analysed the determination of the level of output in an exchange economy.[22] So much about Steuart's analysis of output, so far. Let us move on to his discussions of the related subject of employment.

3. EMPLOYMENT AND UNEMPLOYMENT

No sooner has the level of output been determined in an exchange economy, than the amount of employment is to be known correspondingly, in Steuart's analysis. In other words, the level of output and the amount of employment are so closely related to each other that they would be determined together at the same time, in proportion as the 'effectual demand' of individuals in the economy becomes realized. Apparently, it might then be the insufficiency of this 'effectual demand' which accounts for the existence of unemployment in the economy. In this section, we shall first examine how the actual amount of employment in an exchange economy would be determined, along with its level of output, and how it might fall short of the potential capacity of the economy, according to Steuart. We shall then move on to discuss how he understood the problem of unemployment and what he prescribed for it.

3.1 The Determination of the Amount of Employment

According to Steuart, the actual amount of employment in an economy is to be determined rather straightforwardly in association with the level of output.

> constantly at the command of those who have any sort of real equivalent to give for the consumption they incline to make: for as specie may oftentimes be scarce, a contrivance must be fallen upon immediately to supply the want of it. (*Works*, vol.2, pp.59-60.)

Thus, in addition, we may note that, according to Steuart, there is no difference between paper money and one made of some precious metal, such as gold or silver, in so far as they in common serve as 'circulating equivalents'. Cf. Ch.6 below.

[22] When he discussed the respective development strategies for an exchange economy, corresponding to its different stages of trade, Steuart was still consistently utilizing his own notion of 'effectual demand'. For an open economy, however, he did not consider the domestic consumption of 'luxuries' to be always preferable. Cf. Ch. 5 below.

> The more the necessities of man increase, *caeteris paribus*, the more free hands are required to supply them; and the more free hands are required, the more surplus food must be produced by additional labour, to supply their demand. (*Works*, vol.1, p.236.)

Given the technological conditions of production and the mutual relation of economic sectors, both the level of output and the amount of employment in the economy depend on the 'effectual demand' for 'luxuries'. As we have seen in the previous section, the 'effectual demand', as the 'main spring of the whole operation', in its turn is determined by two factors: i.e., the productivity of each economic sector and the 'spirit of the people'. Let us articulate these factors in relation to his discussion of employment and unemployment.

Taking agriculture as an example, Steuart stressed the importance of the productivity of each sector, particularly its extent of the production of 'surplus' or 'net produce', for the enhancement of the level of output and employment in the economy as a whole.[23]

> ... in proportion to the culture of the soil, and to the number of crops it is made to produce, a greater or less number will be required; and in proportion to the surplus of food above what is necessary to maintain the labourers, will a number of free hands be provided for. If therefore a species of agriculture can be found established, which produces little or no surplus, *there* will little or no industry can be exercised; few wants can be supplied: this will produce a wonderful simplicity of manners, will ruin the system of modern policy, produce what I must call an abuse. (*Works*, vol.1, p.114.)

Thus, the more the net product produced in each economic sector, the more the 'effectual demand' made between the sectors, the greater the amount of employment created in the economy as a whole. Promoting productivity in each sector through technological improvement is the first precondition for enhancing employment in the economy. Together with the production of 'surplus' in economic sectors, the 'spirit of the people' or the 'taste for superfluity' in social classes is another determinant or parameter of the level of output and employment in the exchange economy.

> The spirit therefore of the principal people of a country determines the employment of the lower classes; the employment of these determines their usefulness to the state, and their usefulness, their multiplication. The more they are useful, the more they gain, according to our definition of the contract of society; the more they gain, the more they can feed. (*Works*, vol.1, p.138.)

As the 'spirit of the people', particularly, the inclination for 'luxuries' in those who acquire the 'surplus' or 'net produce' of the economy, affects their consumption of 'luxuries', it should be encouraged so as to maintain a certain level of 'effectual demand' and thereby that of output and employment in the economy.

---

[23] In this context, Steuart considered both the over-extension of agriculture and the subdivision of lands to be 'abuses' and to occasion 'over-multiplications' of 'farmers', as they commonly would render agriculture producing little or no surplus. Cf. *Works*, vol.1, pp.107-24.

In the meantime, Steuart emphasized that the above two factors which determine the amount of 'effectual demand' in an exchange economy, i.e., the productivity of economic sectors and the luxury spending of social classes, should be concurrent.

> ... *no one can become luxurious*, in our acceptation of the word, without giving bread to the industrious, without encouraging emulation, industry, and agriculture; and *without producing the circulation of an adequate equivalent for every service*. This last is the palladium of liberty, the fountain of gentle dependence, and the agreeable band of union among free societies. (*Works*, vol.1, p.410; italics added.)

What does this mean in the present context of our discussion of Steuart's analysis of employment? In fact, it is the very crux which characterizes what his analysis was about. It basically implies that in an exchange economy production and consumption would go together, as the one actually presupposes the other and *vice versa*. (Any demand should be 'effectual', so far as it is to be realized.) If then supply and demand are equilibrated at all times, what is the matter with employment in the economy? That is, notwithstanding that the equilibrium of the commodity market might seemingly ensure that of the labour market in which the wages of labour are determined, as its price, by the supply and demand, why is there any problem of unemployment at all?[24] In Steuart's analysis of employment, the matter lies in the composition of production and consumption, rather than the equilibrium of their total amounts, itself. In other words, although all that is produced would be consumed, there might still exist unemployment in the economy, because of the disproportion between the amount of 'physical necessaries [necessities]' and that of 'luxuries', produced and consumed. *Whereas the former, alone, accounts for the population of the economy;*[25] *it is both the former and the latter that its employment counts on.* Therefore, whenever population outgrows employment in consequence of the imbalance between economic sectors, there must ensue unemployment in the economy.[26] We could thus observe that Steuart's analysis of employment is about a *dynamic* process of the determination of its amount in association with the size of population in an exchange economy.

---

[24] Cf. our previous discussion of Steuart's analysis of the wages of labour in sub-section 3.2, Ch.3 above.

[25] As we are going to fully discuss Steuart's analysis of population in the next section, suffice it here to say, in his own words, that 'what gives food gives numbers' (*Works*, vol.1, p.118).

[26] If the employment outgrows the population, there must be a shortage of labour force in the economy. This might be the case, when people spend too much on 'luxuries'. But, on the whole, Steuart seemed to be more concerned about relatively too little consumption, rather than relatively too much consumption, of 'luxuries', as implied in his discussion of the 'political effects of luxury'.

To sum up, as soon as the level of output in an economy is determined, not only the amount of employment but also the size of population are to be determined. While population ultimately has to do with the 'physical necessaries [necessities]' produced in the agricultural sector, no matter how they are allocated among the different social classes; employment basically depends on the scale and the composition of the whole gross output of the economy in association with the productivity of labour. Therefore, the amount of employment is determined regardless of the size of population in the economy. From this, according to Steuart, stems the problem of the 'abuse' or 'overcharge' of population, that is unemployment.

3.2 The Problem of Unemployment

Steuart's idea of society in general seems to be founded on the give-and-take relation among its members.[27]

> The political oeconomy of government is brought to perfection, when every class in general, and every individual in particular, is made to be aiding and assisting to the community, in proportion to the assistance he receives from it. This conveys my idea of a free and perfect society, which is, *a general tacit contract, from which reciprocal and proportional services result universally between all those who compose it.* (*Works*, vol.1, p.109; original italics.)

He regarded unemployment in an exchange economy as a breach of the 'general tacit contract of society', which ends in an 'abuse' or 'overcharge' of its population.

> Whenever therefore any one is found, upon whom nobody depends, and who depends upon every one, as is the case with him who is willing to work for bread, but who can find no employment, there is a breach of the contract, and an abuse. (*Works*, vol.1, p.109.)

As Steuart duly recognized this problem of unemployment to be more than common in the real economy, he constantly emphasized that 'inhabitants require to be well employed than increased in numbers'.[28] He remarked,

> Wants promote industry, industry gives food, food increases numbers: the next question is, how numbers are to be well employed? (*Works*, vol.1, p.77.)

> We shall always have a numerous and free common people, and shall constantly have the same inconveniences to struggle with, as long as the lowest classes remain in such depression as not to be able to support their own numbers. (*Op.cit.*, vol.1, p.92.)

As a matter of fact, in the previous discussion of Steuart's analysis the determination of the amount of employment, we have already seen where the

---

27 For a detailed discussion of Steuart's conception of society, see section 2, Ch.9 below.

28 *Works*, vol.1, p.79. Indeed, throughout the first book of his *Inquiry*, 'Of Population and Agriculture', Steuart kept making this point. Cf., particularly, chs. XI and XII; *Works*, vol.1, pp.76-98.

fundamental cause of the problem lies. In line with that, we shall discuss his diagnosis of some symptoms of unemployment and his prescription for them, in what follows.

The following passage from his *Inquiry* may give us a clue to where we should start our discussion.

> ... there can be no determinate number of rich idle consumers necessary to employ a determinate number of industrious people, no more than of masters to employ a fixed number of menial servants. (*Works*, vol.1, pp.80-1.)

That is, according to Steuart, unemployment essentially results from the indeterminate relation between the consumption and the actual employment created through the 'political effects' of the very consumption. In other words, *the number of those who consume must be related to the population of the economy and the relative proportion between its social classes, whereas that of those who produce depends on the technological conditions of its economic sectors, respectively*; therefore, basically, the difference between the number of consumers and that of producers accounts for the existence of unemployment. As long as those who consume are different from those who produce, or, at least, their respective economic activities are separated from each other, a general symptom of unemployment is the insufficiency of 'effectual demand' in the economy, apart from some partial friction between demand and supply in the labour market. Even though consumption would always meet production in the economy – that is, there is no actual under-consumption, there might be still some shortage of 'effectual demand' and, thereupon, the problem of unemployment due to the unbalanced capacity utilization between economic sectors. In this context, we may note that Steuart's notion of 'effectual demand' refers to what relates to the capacity utilization of economic resources in a *growing* economy rather than in a *stationary* one.[29]

In consequence, while it is necessary to create 'effectual demand' in order to reduce unemployment in the economy, the creation of 'effectual demand' has a twofold meaning: that is, the enhancement of productivity in each economic sector, being accompanied with a corresponding increment of spending, and at the same time the balanced growth between different sectors. While it is the former which would raise the absolute levels of output and employment in the economy, it is the latter which would eventually resolve the problem of unemployment. To this effect, Steuart remarked,

> Let it therefore never be said, that there are too many manufacturers employed in a country; it is the same as if it were said, there are too few idle persons, too few beggars, and too many husbandmen. We have more than once endeavoured to shew, that these manufacturers never can be fed but out of the superfluity of the farmers. It

[29] Cf. the appendix to this chapter.

> is a contradiction, I think, to say, that those who are fed upon the surplus of those who cultivate the soil are necessary for producing a sufficiency to themselves. For if even this surplus were to diminish, the manufacturers, not the labourers, would be the first to be extinguished for want of nourishment. (*Works*, vol.1, p.46.)

While all economic sectors in an exchange economy are dependent on each other, it is the output level of the agricultural sector which determines its population or labour force. Unless the other economic sectors grow proportionally in parallel with the agricultural sector, there must be either some unemployment or an overall stagnation in the economy.[30]

We shall close this section by additionally looking into Steuart's treatment of the unemployment of a frictional sort. There seem to be two categories of frictional unemployment, discussed in his *Inquiry*: one occasioned by the 'subversion' of the 'balance of work and demand' and the other by the introduction of machines which supposedly replace the labour and industry of people. The first category is actually related to the fundamental cause of unemployment in general, i.e., the imbalance between different sectors in the economy. For, as we have already seen in his discussion of the 'balance of work and demand', Steuart saw its 'subversion' result from the unbalanced growth between economic sectors as well as the 'natural stop' like the diminishing returns in agriculture, rather than from a mere temporary disequilibrium of supply and demand in the market.[31] In any case, upon the 'subversion' of the 'balance of work and demand', some frictional unemployment might ensue. As long as the self-adjusting market mechanism, driven by profit-seeking capitalist entrepreneurs, cannot prevent the 'balance' from overturning, the role of 'public-spirited statesman' must be called for in restoring the 'balance' and obviating the harmful consequences of its 'subversion', e.g., unemployment. Stressing the importance of full employment, Steuart pointed to the duty of the state in guiding and adjusting the market mechanism to remove this sort of frictional unemployment.

> Upon the proper employment of the free hands, the prosperity of every state must depend: consequently the principal care of a statesman should be, to keep all employed, and for this purpose he must acquire an exact knowledge of the state of every denomination, in order to prevent any one from rising above, or sinking below that standard which is best proportioned to the demand made for their industry. As the bad consequences resulting from the loss of this exact balance are not immediate, a moderate attention, with the help of the proper recapitulations, will be sufficient to direct him. (*Works*, vol.1, p.106.)

---

[30] This conclusion seems to follow directly as a logical inference from Steuart's basic conception of an exchange economy, e.g., his division of its economic sectors, based on the classification of commodities into 'physical necessaries [necessities]' and 'luxuries'. In the meantime, as we shall see in the next chapter, it is not always the case, if the economy is engaged in foreign trade.

[31] Cf. section 2, Ch.3 above.

Whenever the imbalance of economic sectors, which the market virtually fails to correct for itself, gives rise to either the population overgrowing or the 'balance of work and demand' overturning and, as a result, unemployment spreads in the economy, the state must actively intervene in the market and restore the balance between the sectors with direct or indirect measures.[32]

Meanwhile, Steuart also perceived some frictional unemployment which might occur upon the introduction of machines into the production process, i.e., upon the labour-saving innovation in technology.

> As agriculture, exercised as a trade, purges the land of idle mouths, and pushes them to a new industry which the state may turn to her own advantage; so does a machine introduced into a manufacture, purge off hands which then become superfluous *in that branch*, and which may quickly be employed in another. If therefore the machine proves hurtful, it can only be because it presents the state with an additional number of hands bred to labour; consequently, if these are afterwards found without bread, it must proceed from a want of attention in the statesman: for an industrious man, made idle, may constantly be employed to advantage, and with profit to him who employs him. (*Works*, vol.1, p.164; original italics.)

As regards Steuart's treatment of this kind of frictional unemployment, two things could be noticed from the above quotation: i.e., its transitory nature and the government's preventive act against it. Upon the whole, Steuart considered it to be a passing phenomenon and rather appreciated the advantage and improvement which the machines would eventually bring to the state of technology in the economy.

> Let the inconveniences complained of ever so sensibly felt, let a statesman be ever so careless in relieving those who are forced to be idle, all these inconveniences are only temporary; the advantage is permanent, and the necessity of introducing every method of abridging labour and expence [expense], in order to supply the wants of luxurious mankind, is absolutely indispensable, according to modern policy, and according to reason. (*Works*, vol.1, p.166.)

Nevertheless, Steuart entrusted the state for the prevention of certain classes of people from being out of employment immediately after the introduction of machines, as he did not simply suppose that their *particular* loss would be compensated with any *general* welfare which might augment thanks to the progress of technology.

> It is hardly possible *suddenly* to introduce the smallest innovation into the political oeconomy of a state, let it be ever so reasonable, nay ever so profitable, without incurring some inconveniences. A room cannot be swept without raising dust, one cannot walk abroad without dirtying one's shoes; neither can a machine, which abridges the labour of men, be introduced *all at once* into an extensive manufacture,

---

[32] Here, we have a characteristic feature of Steuart's political economy: the state interventionism. In the present context, the argument is based on his supposition that the market alone cannot help the imbalance between different sectors in the economy. As we discussed earlier, according to him, it comes from the very nature of the exchange economy, where production and consumption are 'alienated'. Cf. Ch.10 below.

without throwing many people into idleness. ... if a number of machines are all at once introduces into the manufactures of an industrious nation, (in consequence of that freedom which must necessarily be indulged to all sorts of improvement, and without which a state cannot thrive,) it becomes the business of the statesman to interest himself so far in the consequences, as to from the sudden alteration. It is farther his duty to make every exercise even of liberty and refinement an object of government and administration; not so as to discourage or to check them, but to prevent the revolution from affecting the interests of different classes of the people, whose welfare he is particularly bound to take care of. (*Works*, vol.1, pp.160-1; original italics and parentheses.)

Thus, while the innovation of technology is essential to the economic growth, the state must make sure of its gradual introduction into the economy, lest it should be accompanied with some frictional unemployment.[33]

4. THE 'EFFECTUAL DEMAND' THEORY OF POPULATION

As we noted, Steuart's discussion of population, *per se*, is an integral part of his dynamic analysis of the determination of the three macroeconomic magnitudes, i.e., the level of output, the amount of employment and the size of population in an exchange economy. In fact, on some occasions in the previous sections, we have already alluded to what it is like. It seemed apparently to amount to a Malthusian sort, as it could be summarized in the following few words of Steuart's own: 'what gives food gives numbers'. It was also seen to be based on his notion of 'effectual demand'. In what follows, we shall examine how these two aspects of Steuart's analysis of population cohabit or interact.

Basically, according to him, the population of a country must be in proportion to the amount of food or 'physical necessaries [necessities]' produced in agriculture.[34]

... the generative faculty resembles a spring loaded with a weight, which always exerts itself in proportion to the diminution of resistance: when food has remained some time without augmentation, generation will carry numbers as high as possible; if then food come to be diminished, the spring is overpowered; the force of it becomes less than nothing. Inhabitants will diminish, at least, in proportion to the overcharge. If,

---

[33] We will take up Steuart's discussion of the introduction of machines again, shortly, in relation to his analysis of population.

[34] Also in Cantillon's *Essai*, we may come across the same sort of view on population.

Men multiply like Mice in a barn if they have unlimited Means of Subsistence; and the English in the Colonies will become more numerous in proportion in three generations than they would be in thirty in England, because in the Colonies they find for cultivation new tracts of land from which they drive the Savages. (*Essai*, in Higgs (1931), p.83.)

As we shall see later on, in fact, both Cantillon and Steuart seems to have anticipated the so-called Malthusian theory of population.

> upon the other hand, food be increased, the spring which stood at 0, will began to exert itself in proportion as the resistance diminishes; people will began to be better fed; they will multiply, and, in proportion as they increase in numbers, the food will become scarce again. (*Works*, vol.1, pp.25-6.)

The increment of agricultural products is therefore the most essential requisite for the increase of population in any country. That is, 'agriculture is the foundation of multiplication of people', as the 'multiplication never can stop but for want of food'.

On what ground, then, is the agriculture set up in a 'free' exchange economy? Unlike a 'slave' economy, according to Steuart, both the 'farmers' in the agricultural sector and the 'industrious free hands' in the manufacturing sector must exercise their labour and industry to procure their own subsistence, except those who appropriate land and get some revenue from it. While the 'farmers' exert themselves directly on the soil to produce the 'physical necessaries [necessities]' and pay land rents to the 'landlords', the 'industrious free hands' are engaged in providing the other two classes with goods other than the 'physical necessaries [necessities]' in exchange for them. In Steuart's conception of an exchange economy, therefore, agriculture must be founded on both the sectoral division of labour and the class ownership of land.[35] In terms of this interdependence between the economic sectors and among the social classes, Steuart explained the cause-and-effect relation between agriculture and population in the exchange economy.[36]

> ... when I employed the term agriculture in treating of modern policy, I always consider it to be exercised as a trade, and producing a surplus, and not as the direct means of subsisting, where all is consumed by the husbandman. ... it is the surplus produced from it, which proves a fund for multiplying inhabitants. Now there must be a demand for this surplus. ... The demander must have an equivalent to give. ... The poor, who produce children, make an ineffectual demand, and when they cannot increase the equivalent, they divide the food they have with the new comers, and prove no encouragement to agriculture. By dividing, the whole become ill fed, miserable, and thus extinguished. Now because it is the effectual demand, as I may call it, which makes the husbandman labour for the sake of the equivalent, and because this demand increases, by the multiplication of those who have an equivalent to give, therefore I say that multiplication is the cause, and agriculture the effect. (*Works*, vol.1, pp.153-4.)

While the net products produced in the agricultural sector is the very source for the further multiplication of population in the economy, they would only increase as the 'effectual demand' for them does. Thus, as long as the amount of demand for the agricultural products as 'physical necessaries [necessities]' is in turn determined by the size of population, the multiplication of population

---

[35] Cf. Ch.2 above.

[36] On the other hand, Steuart allowed that, 'in the infancy of society, the spontaneous fruits of the earth, which are free to all, are the efficient cause of a multiplication, which may rise to the exact proportion of them' (*Works*, vol.1, p.153.).

might be said to be the origin of agriculture. In short, the multiplication of population and the development of agriculture depend on each other.

From the above argument, we may clearly realize how significant a role the notion of 'effectual demand' plays again in Steuart's analysis of population, as well as in his analysis of output and employment. The 'effectual demand' for agricultural products, i.e., 'physical necessaries [necessities]', and that for manufactures, i.e., 'luxuries', eventually turn out to be different sides of the same coin in the sense that both goods are the equivalents in exchange for each other. No sooner the latter determines the level of output in the economy as a whole, than the former is determined by the very level of output. The actual production in agriculture, thereby determined, eventually regulates the size of population in the economy. As a result, the 'effectual demand' for 'luxuries' would play a crucial role in the determination of the size of population. In this light, Steuart remarked,[37]

> ... the human species will multiply pretty much in proportion to their industry; their industry will increase according to their wants, and these again will diversified according to the spirit of the times. (*Works*, vol.1, p.47.)

As far as the demand for 'luxuries' is 'effectual', it determines not only the actual production in the manufacturing sector but also that in the agricultural sector, and, consequently, the multiplication of population in the economy.

The 'effectual demand' for 'luxuries', based on the productivity of economic sectors and the 'taste for superfluity' among people, is to be seen as the main spring of the whole operation of the determination of the level of output, the amount of employment and the size of population in an exchange economy, in Steuart's analysis. The whole operation may be summarized as follows. It starts with the 'effectual demand' for 'luxuries', which determines the level of production and, accordingly, the amount of employment in the manufacturing sector. With the equivalents thus given to them either in money or in kind, the 'industrious free hands' make their own demand for 'physical necessaries [necessities]', depending on the population in that sector. On the other hand, apart from their demand for 'luxuries', the 'landlords' also make their demand for 'physical necessaries [necessities]', depending on their population. The 'effectual demand' for 'physical necessaries [necessities]' of these two classes, together with that of farmers' intrasectoral demand, determines the level of production and, accordingly, the amount of employment in the agricultural sector. The 'farmers', who acquire the

---

[37] In the same tenor, Steuart noted,

> What is it that encourages agriculture, but a great demand for its productions? What encourages multiplication, but a great demand for people; that is, for their work? (*Works*, vol.1, p.191.)

Thus, the demand for 'luxuries' determines the demand for labour in the manufacturing sector, which could be supplied by the multiplication of people. Also, see *Works*, vol.1, p.138 and pp.142-3.

equivalents thereupon, spend them partly on paying the land rents to the 'landlords' and partly on 'luxuries'. In the meantime, the 'landlords', who obtain the rent revenue from the 'farmers', spend it partly on 'luxuries' and partly on 'physical necessaries [necessities]', as described above. Both the landlords' and the farmers' spending on 'luxuries', together with the intrasectoral demand of the 'industrious free hands', constitute the 'effectual demand' for 'luxuries' in the economy as a whole. The circular process of production, distribution and consumption is then completed. Through this process, the 'effectual demand' for 'luxuries' determines the level of output and the amount of employment in the economy, while the actual production in the agricultural sector regulates the size of its population which in turn determines the demand for 'physical necessaries [necessities]'. In short, Steuart ascribed the determination of population in an exchange economy, as well as that of output and employment, to the 'political effects of luxury'.[38]

Finally, we shall deal with Steuart's discussion of the impact of the introduction of machines into the production process on the population of an economy. According to him, above all, machines are of great utility in enhancing the productivity of the industry concerned, since they 'augment the produce or assist the labour and ingenuity of man'. Thus, only if appropriately accompanied by an increment in demand, would their introduction increase the level of output in the economy and, thereby, augment its population 'without the expence [expense] of feeding the additional people'.[39]

---

[38] In connection with the 'political effects of luxury' upon the population, Steuart was talking about 'moral incapacity (or impossibility)'. According to him, a nation is in a 'moral incapacity' of multiplying people, when its population stands still for want of subsistence, even though it is abundantly able to produce more of it in a physical sense.

> Such nations, whose statesmen have not the talent to engage the husbandmen to wish for the equivalent, which the labour of their fellow-citizens can produce; or, in other words, who cannot create reciprocal wants and dependences among their subjects, must stand in a moral incapacity of augmenting in numbers. (*Works*, vol.1, pp.155-6.)

Thus, the 'moral incapacity' of the multiplication would basically result from the lack of 'effectual demand' for 'luxuries'. On the other hand, according to Steuart, the 'incapacity' would be 'physical', if there is an 'actual impossibility of procuring an augmentation of food by any means whatsoever'. That is, this is the case when 'the soil in its actual state of fertility refuses to supply a sufficient quantity of such food as the inhabitants incline to live upon'. Cf. *Works*, vol.1, pp.38-9 and p.157; also p.237 and pp.152-3, in conjunction with his discussion of money and that of foreign trade, respectively. We shall discuss more about these 'incapacities', later when we examine his analysis of economic growth and foreign trade in the next chapter.

[39] Cf. *Works*, vol.1, pp.160-6. Meanwhile, according to Steuart, as there might ensue some frictional unemployment upon the sudden introduction of machines, the state must keep watch on the market economy to make sure of the re-employment of those who would be laid off in an industry, owing to the machines, in another, as we noted in our previous section.

> We have shewn how population must go on, in proportion to subsistence, and in proportion to industry: now the machine eats nothing, therefore does not diminish subsistence: and industry (in our age at least) is in no danger of being overstocked in any well-governed state. (*Works*, vol.1, p.165.)

As long as the production of subsistence rises in proportion to the increase of the production of any industry into which machines are introduced, the population would be augmented accordingly. Therefore, despite the temporary presence of some unemployment due to the technical change, the labour-saving innovation in any production process in the economy would eventually prove to be a 'method of augmenting the number of people', as far as it enhances the productivity of the economic sector and creates the 'effectual demand' for subsistence. This argument for the introduction of machines seems to illustrate the whole of Steuart's analysis of output, employment and population, examined so far. So to speak, anything which augments 'effectual demand' would raise the level of output in an exchange economy. In addition, the amount of employment in the economy might also increase, subject to the technological conditions of production and the government's active role in guiding and adjusting the market; whereas, in so far as the production of subsistence rises consequently, the size of population would definitely expand.

To conclude the whole of this chapter, it could be said that, according to Steuart, the level of output, the amount of employment and the size of population in an exchange economy are so closely related to each other that they are to be determined concurrently. The key analytical device in his explanation is the notion of 'effectual demand'. Steuart derived it from the firm recognition of interdependence between different economic sectors and among different social classes in the exchange economy.[40] In particular, the level of output is determined through the 'political effects of luxury', subject to both the productivity of the economic sectors and the 'taste for superfluity' in the social classes. Thereon, the amount of employment is to be known from the level of output, as the one is a function of the other, given the technological conditions of the economy; whereas the problem of unemployment is viewed as a result of the imbalance between the economic sectors, i.e., between the one producing subsistence and the other producing non-subsistence goods. If the market cannot help it, the state must intervene. Meanwhile, so soon as the production of subsistence in agriculture is determined, the size of population is ascertained accordingly, since the former ultimately regulates the latter. The size of population in turn affects the determination of the level of output in the economy. After all, the 'effectual

---

[40] We have already seen in Ch.1 how Steuart conceived of economic sectors and social classes of the modern exchange economy and how he assumed in his *Inquiry* commodities and money to circulate between the economic sectors and the social classes. In that context, we also noted the significance of his recognition of the economic interdependence, particularly the reciprocal demand, among them.

demand' for 'luxuries' may be seen as the 'main spring of the whole operation', as it directly or indirectly determines the level of output, the amount of employment and the size of population in the economy, upon the dynamic relation between them.

APPENDIX: Steuart and Keynes

One of the issues which have been constantly debated in the history of economic thought is whether or not the market would ensure, of itself, full employment for the labour force in an exchange economy. Steuart was one of the earliest of those who advanced a systematic analysis which questioned the market mechanism in this particular respect. A century and half or so later, J. M. Keynes (1883-1946) proclaimed a doctrine to the same effect in the midst of the Great Depression. The 'principle of effective demand' expounded in his *General Theory of Employment, Interest and Money* threw serious doubt upon the then widely accepted approaches to the theory of output and employment. In contrast with the latter, it was basically intended to show that the equilibrium position of the market economy might not always be one of full employment; though there have been numerous interpretations of it, based on divergent arguments, ever since its first appearance. The debate is still going on to this day. As many attempts have been made to accommodate the messages of the *General Theory* to the existing theories, in fact, its 'initial novelty' seems to be getting vaguer.[1] Here in what follows, another attempt is made to cast a new light upon Keynes's contribution to the development of the theory of output and employment, with emphasis on its distinctive feature. In the present context, this would involve two specific tasks before us: on the one hand, to scrutinize his 'principle of effective demand' in terms of the prototype actually presented in the *General Theory* and its implications, and, on the other hand, to trace one of its cognates in Steuart's *Inquiry* as making a close comparison between them.[2] Having done so, we might not only better understand their respective theories of output and employment but also grasp

[1] Hutchison (1977) explained the process of decline of a once successful system of theory in economics, in general, in terms of three different 'sources of weakness and inadequacy': that is, (i) its original internal logical or empirical weakness, (ii) changes in historical conditions and institutions, and (iii) the hardening into dogma and mystique of the original doctrines. As regards Keynesian economics, in particular, while observing that it has not only undergone interminable examinations and re-examinations over last few decades in terms of the first source but also been subject to the second source of historical-institutional obsolescence, he concentrated mainly on the third source of weakness, i.e., 'the way it has come to be adapted or altered by disciples, successors, or popularizers'. In relation to this, we might note that the process of decline of Keynesian economics, if any, could be seen as that of rising-again of its antithesis or that of synthesizing the two, in the sense that it has come to be 'adapted and altered' by opponents, rather than proponents.

[2] As a matter of fact, the aim of this appendix primarily consists in the latter task, while the former is indispensable as a preliminary step. For this reason, the present account of Keynes's theory must be schematic but not necessarily oversimplified.

those views of the market economy, which are contrary to theirs. We shall start with Keynes's theory.

Keynes's 'Principle of Effective Demand'

It is not too much to say that the 'principle of effective demand' is the gist of Keynes's economics and, at the same time, one of the most significant contributions made by him to the development of economic thought. Broadly speaking, it refers to the proposition that, given the productive capacity of an economy, there must exist an appropriate amount of 'effective demand' so as to actually utilize the whole capacity. That is, it ultimately amounts to an explanation of the determination of the actual *vis-à-vis* potential level of output in the economy, in terms of his notion of 'effective demand'.

Let us begin our examination of Keynes's 'principle of effective demand' with his definition of the 'effective demand'.

> ... the *effective demand* is simply the aggregate income (or proceeds) which the entrepreneurs expect to receive, inclusive of the incomes which they will hand on to the other factors of production, from the amount of current employment which they decide to give. The aggregate demand function relates various hypothetical quantities of employment to the proceeds which their outputs are expected to yield; and the effective demand is the point on the aggregate demand function which becomes effective because, taken in conjunction with the conditions of supply, it corresponds to the level of employment which maximises the entrepreneur's expectation of profit. (*General Theory*, p.55; original italics and parentheses.)

Thus, according to him, the aggregate demand for output becomes 'effective', as far as the production goes on until the aggregate expected 'proceeds' from the production would be equal to the aggregate 'supply price' of output, given the methods of production and the amount of resources in the economy. In other words, the 'effective demand' is that amount of the aggregate demand for output in the economy, which would be equilibrated with its aggregate supply in consequence of the entrepreneurs' maximization of their expected profits from the production.[3] While it is firmly grounded on the recognition

[3] In a given state of technique, resources and costs, according to Keynes, the production process involves an entrepreneur in two kinds of expenses: the 'factor cost' and the 'user cost' of production. The one refers to the 'amounts which he pays out to the factors of production (exclusive of other entrepreneurs) for their current services'; whereas the other the 'amounts which he pays out to other entrepreneurs for what he has to purchase from them together with the sacrifice which he incurs by employing the equipment instead of leaving it idle'. Then, after defining the 'profit or income' of the entrepreneur as the 'excess of the value of the resulting output over the sum of its factor cost and its user cost', Keynes assumed the entrepreneur to endeavour to maximize it in deciding what amount to produce. Meanwhile, the aggregate 'income' or 'proceeds' of production in the economy, as a whole, comprise all those expenses and profits resulting from the production. On the other hand, what was called the 'aggregate supply price' of the output of production is the 'expectation of proceeds' which will just make it worth the while of the entrepreneurs to carry out the production. Given the production techniques and the economic resources in an economy, the entrepreneurs' expectation of profits will be maximized at the point where the 'aggregate income or proceeds', expected to receive from their production, is equal to its 'aggregate supply price'; for if the 'expected proceeds' are

of the circularity of income in the economy as a whole, the notion itself presupposes the equilibrium of supply and demand of output in the aggregate. This does not imply that 'supply creates its own demand' at any level of output. Rather, it points to the fact that the proposition involves an additional, *ad hoc*, assumption as to the relationship between the 'aggregate expected proceeds' and the 'aggregate supply price' of output in the economy, i.e., that they are equal for all levels of output.[4] On the other hand, *in general*, the 'effective demand' has a 'unique equilibrium value', rather than an 'infinite range of values'. Conversely speaking, in Keynes's analysis, the level of output and the amount of employment are determined exactly in the same amount as the 'effective demand' in the economy, as a result of the equilibrium of aggregate demand and aggregate supply.[5] Of what then is the 'effective demand' composed?

In Keynes's analysis, while income is generated by the 'effective demand' in the economy, the latter, in its turn, consists of two sorts of demand: the demand for consumption goods and the demand for investment goods. Hence, his theory of consumption and that of investment. According to Keynes, on the one hand, the amount of consumption in the economy depends on its level of income.[6] On the other hand, the amount of investment depends both on the expected profitability of all possible investment projects and on the rate of interest in the economy.[7] While both the consumption function ('propensity to consume') and the expected profitability of projects (the 'schedule of the

---

greater than the 'aggregate supply price', there will be an incentive to entrepreneurs to increase their production and, if necessary, to raise costs by competing with one another, up to the point where they are finally equalized. As the 'proceeds', which entrepreneurs expect to receive from the production, eventually depend on the demand for the output, and as the 'supply price', which makes the production possible, directly reflects the supply conditions of the output, this very point denotes none other than the equilibrium of 'aggregate demand' for output and its 'aggregate supply' in the economy. (In fact, Keynes represented it as the intersection of the 'aggregate demand function' and the 'aggregate demand function' in his discussion.) Keynes called this equilibrium amount of 'aggregate demand' the 'effective demand' in the economy. Cf. *General Theory*, pp.23-6.

[4] Keynes himself made this point clear, as follows:

> The classical theory assumes, in other words, that the aggregate demand price (or proceeds) always accommodates itself to the aggregate supply. ... That is to say, effective demand, instead of having a unique equilibrium value, is an infinite range of values all equally admissible. (*General Theory*, p.26.)

By the way, in the above context, Keynes included in what he called the 'classical school' not only Ricardo and James Mill and their predecessors but also the followers of Ricardo, i.e., 'those who adopted and perfected the theory of the Ricardian economics, including (for example) J. S. Mill, Marshall, Edgeworth and Pigou'. Cf. *General Theory*, p.3

[5] As Keynes assumed both the method of production and the 'factor cost' per unit of employment to be given, the amount of employment and the level of output corresponds to each other in each individual firm and industry, and in the aggregate.

[6] Making use of the notion of 'propensity to consume', he formulated the amount of consumption as a function of the level of income in the economy. Cf. *General Theory*, chs. 8 and 9.

[7] Contriving the notion of 'marginal efficiency of capital', Keynes showed that the inducement of investment depends partly on the 'schedule of the marginal efficiency of capital' or the 'investment demand-schedule' and partly the rate of interest in the economy. Cf. *General Theory*, ch.11.

marginal efficiency of capital' or the 'investment demand-schedule') in a certain period of time might be assumed to be known from circumstances in the economy, what would determine the rate of interest? Keynes conceived of the determination the rate of interest as a purely monetary phenomenon: that is, it is determined by the demand for and the supply of money in the economy. In his explanation, in particular, it depends on the 'liquidity-preference schedule' of individual money holders and the quantity of money issued by the central authority.[8]

To sum up, given the 'liquidity-preference schedule' and the quantity of money in the economy, the rate of interest would be determined in its money market. Once the rate of interest is determined, the amount of investment would be determined correspondingly, given the 'schedule of the marginal efficiency of capital'. The thus determined amount of investment constitutes the 'effective demand' in the economy, together with that of consumption. Eventually, the level of income would be generated exactly in the same amount as the total 'effective demand'. For a certain 'propensity to consume', the level of income would adjust itself so as to equilibrate the aggregate demand and the aggregate supply in the commodity market. What is significant in this system of analysis is that there is no reason why the level of income, thereby determined, should be one of full employment. To go a step further, it suggests that any autonomous – i.e., independent of income – increment of 'effective demand', e.g. government expenditure, would bring forth the increase of income and the enhancement of employment in the economy, through the 'multiplier effect'.[9] This provides a basis for the active role of government in the market economy, as it may have control over the level of output and employment in the economy by means of its demand-management policy. Thus, Keynes's 'principle of effective demand' serves as a rationale of the 'mixed economy'.

There are two particular characteristics to note further in Keynes's theory of output and employment. One is the saving-investment relation, as a corollary of his 'principle of effective demand', and the other is the analytical setting of his conception of unemployment in the *General Theory*. In the course of analysis leading to the conclusion that an exchange economy is not always at the full employment equilibrium, it could be observed that the 'actual saving' is constantly equal to the 'predetermined' amount of investment in the economy, whatever decisions may be made to save. In other words, as long as income is generated in the same amount as the sum of consumption and investment, and as long as what is left in income after consumption is, by definition, to be saved, the amount of saving must, *ex post*, be equal to that of

[8] Cf. *General Theory*, ch.13.
[9] Cf. *General Theory*, ch.10.

investment. Indeed, it is in the process of equilibrium of saving and investment that the level of income is determined in the economy. For they are equalized in the economy as a whole, only through the adjustment of the level of income, since the one is assumed to be a function of the level of income and the other to be determined independently.[10]

As far as the analytical setting of the Keynes's conception of unemployment is concerned, the question is whether it is based on a static or a dynamic view of the productive capacity of an economy. While his 'principle of effective demand' is basically about the determination of the actual level of output *vis-à-vis* the potential level of output, the gap between them accounts for the existence of unemployment in the economy. Thus, his conception of unemployment must be subject to how he assumed the very potentiality of the economy, i.e., its productive capacity, in his analysis. Keynes conducted his analysis of output and employment on the basis of the Marshallian 'short period', in which all the 'factors of production', including technology and market conditions, in the economy are assumed to be given, while leaving the effects of changes in them out of consideration.[11] In consequence, he

[10] This is what makes Keynes's theory fundamentally different from the 'classical theory' as he called it. In the 'classical theory', saving and investment represent, respectively, the supply of and the demand for investible resources, and the rate of interest, as their price, is to be determined by the interaction of these supply and demand. Thus, together with a symmetrical notion that competitive wages ensure the equality between the supply of and the demand for labour, according to the 'classical theory', the equilibrium position of an economy is characterized as a set of market-clearing prices and that of associated quantities of individual commodities and 'factors of production'. Therefore, market forces would automatically lead the economy to the full employment of labour and other 'factors of production'; unless there exist certain 'structural' causes which prevent the market forces from operating properly, i.e., some 'market failures'. In this light, Keynes himself remarked, in the first chapter of his *General Theory*, as follows:

> ... the postulates of the classical theory are applicable to a special case only and not to the general case, the situation which it assumes being a limiting point of the possible positions of equilibrium. (p.3.)

That is to say, as Keynes was trying to show in the *General Theory* that the equilibrium position of a market economy is not always one of full employment, he eventually accomplished it by establishing that it is the level of income, rather than the rate of interest, which equilibrates saving and investment in the economy. For his own postulates of the 'classical theory', see *General Theory*, ch.2. And for his detailed discussions of saving-investment relation, see *General Theory*, chs. 6 and 7.

[11] Recently, there has been raised some issue on the analytical time horizon of Keynes's 'principle of effective demand': that is, whether it is concerned with the long-period 'normal' level of output or the short-period 'cyclical' one. The different analytical time horizons depend on whether or not we allow the price of commodities to yield a uniform rate of profit on the capital advanced in the production process through competition. In fact, as the concept of equilibrium in Keynes does not refer to a situation where all economic activities are carried out on their relevant demand and supply curves, but one which would not change of itself, unless it is disturbed, both analytical time horizons might be compatible with his analysis of output and employment in terms of 'effective demand'. Nevertheless, which was the whole system of his analysis actually designed to explain, one determined by the 'dominant and persistent' forces of the market economy or the other by its 'changeable and temporary' conditions? Keynes himself made it clear in his *General Theory*.

> We take as given the existing skill and quantity of available labour, the existing quality and quantity of available equipment, the existing technique, the degree of competition, the tastes and habits of the consumer, the disutility of different intensities of labour and of the activities

conceived of the existence of unemployment in the economy from a static point of view of its productive capacity. While he was not taking into account the effects of changes in either capital stock or labour force, due to *current* investment or consumption, on the productive capacity, in his analysis, he was rather concerned with both consumption and investment only as the monetary expenditure which constitutes 'effective demand' in the economy. Thus, in Keynes's analysis, the amount of unemployment corresponds to that part of

---

> of supervision and organisation, as well as the social structure including the forces, other than our variables set forth below, which determine the distribution of the national income. This does not mean that we assume these factors to be constant; but merely that, *in this place and context, we are not considering or taking into account the effects and consequences of changes in them.* (p.245; italics added.)

Thus, as Keynes's analysis was originally set up on the ground of Marshallian short period, in which the capacity of production in an economy was assumed to be given and the consequences of its changes were out of the scope, it must be confined to the determination of the 'cyclical', rather than 'normal', level of output in the economy. As a matter of fact, in his analysis, investment and consumption, which constitute the 'effective demand' and eventually determine the level of output in the economy, are assumed to have no effect on its capacity of production, nor *vice versa*; whereas, in a 'long-period' analysis of output and employment, if anything, the 'effective demand' and the productive capacity must be to affect each other.

Meanwhile, although he once admitted that 'Keynes developed his theory within what he saw as a short-period setting', Eatwell (1979) argued, to the contrary, that 'indeed, even on its own terms, Keynes's analysis does not warrant the appellation short-period', alleging that 'it is long-period implications of his analysis, as a theory of employment, which represent the significant contribution'. And, for example, he supposed that 'the fixed composition of the capital stock which defines Marshall's short period plays no role in Keynes's theory of employment – unemployment is, according to Keynes, not due to the shortage of a particular capital, but to a lack of effective demand'. (Cf. p.97.) However, as far as Keynes's analysis of investment, whose fluctuations mostly account for those of 'effective demand', relies on the notion of the 'marginal efficiency of capital', the very 'lack of effective demand' must be related to the 'shortage of a particular capital'. According to Keynes, the 'marginal efficiency' of any type of capital would diminish, as the investment on it increases. And, from this, he derived what he called the 'investment demand-schedule' or the 'schedule of the marginal efficiency of capital', as follows:

> If there is an increased investment in any given type of capital any period of time, the marginal efficiency of that type of capital will diminish as the investment in it increased, partly because the prospective yield will fall as the supply of that type of capital is increased, and partly because, as a rule, pressure on the facilities for producing that type of capital will cause its supply price to increase. ... Thus for each type of capital we can build up a schedule, showing by how much investment in it will have to increase within the period, in order that its marginal efficiency should fall to any given figure. We can then aggregate these schedules for all different types of capital, so as to provide a schedule relating the rate of aggregate investment to the corresponding marginal efficiency of capital in general which that rate of investment will establish. (*General Theory*, p.136.)

While, according to Keynes, the actual rate of investment in the economy would be pushed to the point on this schedule where the 'marginal efficiency of capital' in general is equal to the market rate of interest, the decreasing 'schedule of the marginal efficiency of capital' against aggregate investment, itself, was actually drawn on the presupposition that the overall composition of capital stock in the economy is fixed. Therefore, at least in that the 'schedule of the marginal efficiency of capital' simply reflects some short-period phenomena of investment behaviour, Keynes's 'principle of effective demand', in which investment is of greater importance than the other components of the 'effective demand', is essentially a short-period theory of output and employment; let alone the emphasis on 'uncertainty and expectations' in his analysis of investment, including the explanation of the rate of interest in terms of 'liquidity preference', which rather obviously characterizes the analytical time horizon of the whole system.

the *given* productive capacity in the economy, which is being idle at the actual level of output determined by the 'effective demand'.

The 'Political Effects of Luxury' and the 'Principle of Effective Demand'

Having discussed Keynes's theory of output and employment, we may now be able to compare it with Steuart's. Let us start with the notions of 'effective demand' and 'effectual demand', which underlie the whole system of their respective theories. As discussed previously, they are commonly concerned with the operation of the economy as a whole, rather than the value of an individual commodity. Essentially, they are based on the recognition of the reciprocity of demand and supply in the macroeconomic level. Nevertheless, in Steuart, the emphasis was on the interdependence between different economic sectors and among social classes; whereas, in Keynes, it was on the relation between income and spending in the aggregate. Therefore, Steuart's 'effectual demand' refers to the level of reciprocal demand for different commodities between sectors and classes through the medium of money; whereas Keynes's 'effective demand' the amount of aggregate demand actually realized by monetary spending in the economy.

From this dissimilarity between the notion of 'effectual demand' and that of 'effective demand', originate the differences in their respective theories of output and employment. As we may directly infer from these notions, first of all, the analytical focus of Steuart's theory was on the effect of the consumption of a certain commodity on the general level of output in the economy; whereas that of Keynes's theory was on the equilibrium of the aggregate demand, i.e., consumption and investment, and the aggregate supply, i.e., income, in the economy. Hence, the 'political effects of luxury' in the one and the 'principle of effective demand' in the other. According to the former, on the one hand, the level of output in an exchange economy is determined by the 'effectual demand' of various social classes for 'luxuries', materializing through the productivity of different economic sectors. On the other hand, according to the latter, the level of income, either spent or saved, in the economy is determined exactly in the same amount as the 'effective demand', composed of consumption and investment, as a result of the equilibrium of aggregate demand and aggregate supply. Therefore, while the productivity of economic sectors and the 'standard of taste' of social classes are the two main pillars in Steuart's 'political effects of luxury', the saving-investment relation, derived by way of equalizing income and 'effective demand' in the aggregate, is a primary corollary of Keynes's 'principle of effective demand'. Let us have a close look into these fundamentals of the respective theories of output and employment, from a comparative point of view.

According to Steuart, while all the sectors in the economy produce surplus or net produce and all the social classes consume both 'physical necessaries [necessities]' and 'luxuries', the productivity of economic sectors and the 'effectual demand' for 'luxuries' represent different faces of one coin. That is, unless the economic sectors are productive, there is no 'effectual demand' for 'luxuries'; and, unless there is any 'effectual demand', no economic sector produces anything. It is this juxtaposition of both analytical themes, i.e., productivity and luxury spending, on the same dimension in terms of his own notion of 'effectual demand' that distinguishes Steuart from the others before and after him, who dealt with one or the other separately.[12] On the other hand, as Keynes made use of the notion of 'propensity to consume (or to save)', the saving-investment relation implied in his 'principle of effective demand' eventually leads to its fundamental proposition that it is the level of income which equilibrates saving and investment in the economy as a whole. That is, if the 'propensity to consume (or to save)' is given as a certain ratio of what proportion of income is to be consumed (or saved), the level of income must adjust itself to equalize the amount of saving and that of investment in the economy, as long as the latter is determined independent of it. Thus, the greater (or the smaller) the propensity to consume (or to save), the higher the level of income, with a 'predetermined' amount of investment; and the greater the amount of investment, the higher the level of output, given the 'propensity to consume (or to save)'.[13] As far as it is ultimately concerned with the effect of spending, whether for consumption or for investment, on the level of income in the economy, Keynes's 'principle of effective demand' amounts to another version of the doctrine of the economic beneficence of 'spending-more', whose origin goes back to the economic writings of some mercantilist authors in the seventeenth and eighteenth centuries. Unlike those authors, Keynes carried out his analysis in aggregate monetary terms, as he did not categorize commodities into subsistence and luxury goods. Nevertheless, in common with them, Keynes did not explicitly take account of either the

---

[12] For instance, attaching great importance to the exclusive productivity of agriculture, F. Quesnay tried to show the crucial role of the expenditure of the rent revenue of the 'proprietors of land' in the determination of the level of output in the economy by means of his *Tableau Economique*, though the latter mechanism does not entirely depend on the former presumption. (Cf. the appendix to Ch.3 above); whereas B. Mandeville, in his *Fable of the Bees*, pointed to the beneficence of consumption of luxury goods, that is, the fallacy of composition regarding luxury spending. In fact, the emphasis on the productivity, on the one hand, dominated the economic doctrines of R. Cantillon and A. Smith, as well as those of the Physiocrats. On the other hand, the significance of the luxury spending was to be brought to light in the literature recurrently up until Keynes, in different guises, as represented by T. Malthus among others.

[13] In this context, the investment, as well as the consumption, is no more than a mere component of the 'effective demand' without any further effect on the productive capacity in the economy.

productivity of each individual economic sector in an economy or the productive capacity of the economy as a whole, in his analysis. This last point is what essentially differentiates Steuart's theory of output and employment from Keynes's and others'. In fact, apart from the inseparable relation between the productivity of economic sectors and the 'effectual demand' of social classes for 'luxuries', discussed above, there is one other thing which characterizes Steuart's theory: that is, its analytical setting, which allows of the effects of changes in the productive capacity of an economy, particularly the growth of its population.

Although both Steuart's and Keynes's theories of output and employment are concerned with the determination of the actual level of output *vis-à-vis* the potential level of output in an exchange economy, they are fundamentally different in their respective analytical settings. That is to say, while they commonly relate to the utilization of the productive capacity in the economy, the one approaches it in a dynamic context and the other in a static one. For Steuart, the analysis of output and employment cannot dispense with that of population, in that the level of output, the amount of employment and the size of population in an economy are all closely so related to each other that they must be determined concurrently; whereas, for Keynes, it is not the case, as he simply assumed the size of population to be given. In consequence, on the one hand, Steuart's analysis could encompass the effects of changes in the productive capacity of the economy, since labour is supposed to be the only input which could be augmented for further production, with land and other natural resources being 'physically' limited and various produced means of production being subject to the given state of technology. On the other hand, Keynes's analysis must confine itself to the determination of the relatively short-period cyclical level of output in the economy with the given capacity of production, as it assumes not only the amount of capital stock but also that of the labour force in the economy to be given. This difference between the analytical setting of Steuart's theory and that of Keynes's finally accounts for their disparate conceptions of unemployment.

Steuart conceived of unemployment as a result of the population outgrowing employment, due to the imbalance between economic sectors. According to him, the problem originates from the very fact that, in an exchange economy, production and consumption are 'alienated', i.e., these economic activities are conducted on separate accounts. In other words, the cause of unemployment in the economy lies in the disproportion between those who produce and those who consume. The former bears upon the amount of employment, whereas the latter upon the size of population. Particularly, the amount of employment depends on the production of both 'physical necessaries [necessities]' and 'luxuries', whereas the size of population on the consumption of 'physical necessaries [necessities]'.

Therefore, in Steuart's conception, unemployment might still exist in the economy, even if the equilibrium of production and consumption is always assured and there is thus no such thing as under-consumption. What matters is their composition. On this dynamic relation between the level of output, the amount of employment and the size of population in the exchange economy, he established that a lack of 'effectual demand' would cause some unbalanced capacity utilization between economic sectors and, thereupon, unemployment in the economy. On the other hand, Keynes understood the existence of unemployment in the economy from rather a static point of view of its productive capacity. That is, leaving out of consideration the consequences of changes in either capital stock or labour force, due to investment or consumption expenditure, he concentrated on the gap between the potential amount of employment, corresponding to the given productive capacity, and the actual amount of employment, generated by the 'effective demand' consisting of those monetary spendings, in the economy. Thus, according to Keynes, the existence of unemployment is due to the shortage of 'effective demand', which essentially denotes either under-consumption or under-investment in the economy, in the sense that part of the productive capacity of the economy is being idle in the actual level of output.

5. Economic Growth and Foreign Trade

In this chapter, we shall examine Steuart on economic growth and foreign trade. What we will discuss of his theory of growth is basically an extension of his theory of output in the last chapter. For, as already noted, his analysis of output, employment and population was carried out in a dynamic context of economic growth, in which labour was considered to be the only input which could be augmented to make further expansion of production possible, whereas both the necessary produced means of production and raw materials, including land, were deemed to be dependent on the technical conditions of production and the natural endowments of resources in the economy, respectively. Indeed, Steuart was chiefly concerned, in his *Inquiry*, with the growing process of an exchange economy, during which the potential productive capacity is not only to become more or less fully utilized but also to change itself as the population grows.[1] Apart from the problem of unemployment which we have already dealt with, there are some immanent limitations or constraints to the growth of output and population in the exchange economy. Steuart linked these limitations of economic growth to the gains from foreign trade. That is to say, the latter might help to remove or ease the former, depending on the state or stage of the economy. Thus, the first thing to do is to discuss briefly the relationship between economic growth and foreign trade, presumed in Steuart's *Inquiry*, on the basis of our previous analysis of his theory of output.

In the meantime, when he elaborated on economic growth in the *Inquiry*, Steuart constantly emphasized the general circumstances of the economy concerned, as is the case with the rest of his political economy.[2] In particular, the existence of foreign trade seemed to be the most significant parameter for the workings of the economy in his analysis. According to him, foreign trade itself is to be gradually introduced as the economy develops. Therefore, Steuart's theory of growth could not be properly treated without any reference to his unique account of the stages of change of an exchange economy in relation to foreign trade. We shall take up his three-stage theory of trade in the next section.

[1] As a matter of fact, the main theme of Book I of the *Inquiry* is the correlation between the level and the growth of output and those of population in an exchange economy.
[2] See the appendix to Ch.9 below, for a discussion of Steuart's method, which might be called empirico-historical relativism, in his political economy as a whole.

Steuart's analysis of economic growth and foreign trade seems to culminate in his discussions of the 'balance of wealth' and the 'balance of trade'. Here, we will meet with a fresh new concept of wealth in Steuart, which is different not only from the one in the mercantilists before him but also from the one in the 'classical' economists after him. Based on this unique concept of wealth, Steuart established his argument for the favourable balance of trade as a means of accumulating the wealth of a nation, which is his own version of growth theory corresponding to his theory of output. Closely examining these two notions, i.e., the 'balance of wealth' and the 'balance of trade', and their implications, we will get to the kernel of Steuart's coherent explanation of the inseparable relation of economic growth and foreign trade.

Finally, we shall make an attempt to formalize Steuart's analysis of economic growth and foreign trade, discussed thus far in this chapter, in association with his theory of output, examined in the previous chapter. We will set up a fairly simple model, which we abstract from his detailed and complicated arguments. In particular, we are leaving out considerations of the effects of both population growth and technical change on the level of output and thus on the wealth of a nation. With the help of this tentative model, nevertheless, we may firmly grasp how Steuart conceived of the relationship between economic growth and foreign trade in terms of his own concept of wealth. We will append to this chapter a comparative discussion of the concept of wealth in Steuart and in Smith.

1. THE LIMITS OF GROWTH AND THE BENEFITS OF TRADE

In Steuart's analysis, while both the level of output and the size of population in an exchange economy are to be determined simultaneously, they ultimately depend on the amounts of 'effectual demand' of different classes of people for various commodities produced in different sectors. The 'effectual demand', in turn, is affected by the productivity of the economic sectors and the luxury spending of the social classes. Thus, according to him, the increase of output and the augmentation of population, in a closed economy, are decided by two factors: how the productivity of economic sectors could be enhanced and how the 'taste of luxury' in people could be promoted. Given the state of technology in the economy, however, there are some limitations constraining these factors. In relation to the growth of population, Steuart summarized them into two circumstances: that is, 'moral' and 'physical incapacity (or impossibility)'. The one refers to the limitation directly resulting from the lack of 'effectual demand' for 'luxuries', whereas the other is due to the actual limits of natural resources in the economy.[3] In either case, the introduction of foreign trade proves to be a breakthrough, as far as it would bring about some extra demand for 'luxuries' from abroad and provide the economy with some additional subsistence in exchange.[4]

> As to the physical impossibility, the case can hardly exist, because means of procuring subsistence from other countries, when the soil refuses to give more, seem, if not inexhaustible, at least very extensive. A country therefore fully peopled, that is, in a physical impossibility of increasing their numbers, is a chimerical and useless supposition. The subject here under consideration is, the situation of a people, who find it their interest to seek for subsistence from abroad. This may happen, and commonly does, long before the country itself is fully improved: it decides nothing as to the intrinsic fertility of the soil, and proves no more, than that the industry of the free hands has made a quicker progress in multiplying mouths, than that of the farmers in providing subsistence. (*Works*, vol.1, pp.152-3.)

As a result of opening up foreign trade, the level of output would increase and the size of population would be augmented in the economy. It might be noted that, if a country could keep exporting 'luxuries', i.e., manufactures, in exchange for 'physical necessaries [necessities]', i.e., agricultural products, its level of output and its size of population would continue to increase in concert with each other, without any limit. That is, as far as the open economy is able to procure some sufficient 'effectual demand' for manufactures at home and abroad, it would constantly grow, avoiding any 'moral' or 'physical incapacity'.

Following what has been said so far, let us move on to discuss in detail what Steuart thought of the gains from foreign trade, in order to find out how it could be established between different countries. Basically, the reciprocal wants of the countries constitute the foundation of the trade. That is to say, one country wanting food could offer the 'superfluity of the industry of free hands', while the other abounding in grain and articles of subsistence might have a 'taste of elegance' and be eager for acquiring the 'manufactures and improvements' of its industrious neighbours. While one meets the other's wants, apparently, both sides of trade would benefit.

> If ... a spirit of industry has brought the country to a certain degree of population, this spirit will not be stopped by the want of food; it will be brought from foreign

[3] Cf. our discussion of Steuart's analysis of population in the previous chapter.

[4] In the case of 'moral incapacity', Steuart emphasized the role of government in creating 'reciprocal wants and dependences' among social classes and economic sectors within the economy so as to increase the 'effectual demand' and thus the level of output. Cf. *Works*, vol.1, pp.152-9. His argument for the active finance of government could be understood in the same context; however, we shall discuss it later in Ch.8 below, after examining his theory of money in Chs. 6 and 7 below, as it is *au fond* based on a monetary explanation of production, consumption and investment in an exchange economy. On the other hand, when a closed economy is caught in the 'physical incapacity', it reaches an actual upper limit in its extent of land, the fertility of soil, the improvement of technology, etc. Therefore, in this case, as it is virtually impossible for the agricultural sector to produce any more additional subsistence, foreign trade is the only way out. That is, only through the importation of subsistence from others, can the country further grow in its level of output and population.

> countries, and this new demand, by diminishing among them the quantity usually produced for their own subsistence, will prompt the industrious to improve their lands, in order to supply the new demand without any hurt to themselves. Thus trade has an evident tendency towards the improvement of the world in general, by rendering the inhabitants of one country industrious, in order to supply the wants of another, without any prejudice to themselves. (*Works*, vol.1, pp.157-8.)

As long as foreign trade provides trading countries with some additional 'effectual demand', whether for manufactures or for subsistence, and thereby raises their levels of output and population, it must be beneficial to both sides.

Steuart distinguished between two situations for any country to open foreign trade: 'passive' and 'active trade'.[5]

> ... wants are easily supplied, for the adequate value of the thing wanted. The next consequence is, the opening of foreign trade under its two denominations of passive and active. Strangers and people of distant countries finding the difficulty of having their wants supplied at home, and the ease of having them supplied from this country, immediately have recourse to it. This is passive trade. The active is when merchants, who have executed this plan at home with success, begin to transport the labour of their countrymen into other regions, which either produce, or are capable of producing such articles of consumption, proper to be manufactured, as are most demanded at home; and consequently will meet with the readiest sale, and fetch the largest profits. (*Works*, vol.1, p.247.)

The distinction between the two sorts of trade must be relative: namely, one represents the sort of trade by which a country may import those goods that are relatively difficult to produce at home, whereas the other the sort of trade by which a country may export those goods that are relatively easy to produce at home. In this context, the relativity refers to the competitiveness of the price of goods concerned between trading nations; however, it does not necessarily imply the 'comparative advantage', according to which a trading country must have some exportable goods whose price is 'comparatively' more competitive than the others' within the economy. Rather, it has to do with the 'absolute advantage'. As the price competition must be understood in absolute terms, it eventually marks both the first and the last resort of foreign trade.[6] Therefore, the competition among countries engaged in 'active trade' must be inevitable, whereas some may still be engaged in 'passive trade', by virtue of certain special circumstances, e.g., the abundance of natural resources. Steuart remarked,

> I apprehend that the whole system of modern politics is founded upon the basis of an active foreign trade. A nation which remains passive in her commerce, is at the mercy of those who are active, and must be greatly favoured, indeed, by natural advantages,

[5] According to Johnson (1937), the distinction between 'passive' and 'active trade' was originally made by M. Postlethwayt in his *Britain's Commercial Interest* (1757). Cf. Johnson (1937), pp.203-4 and pp.225-7. Meanwhile, for Steuart's own detailed discussions of the two sorts of trade, see chs. V, VI and IX, book 2, *Inquiry*; *Works*, vol.1, pp.247-62 and pp.276-88.

[6] As we will see later in the next section, according to Steuart, it is the competitiveness of export prices that eventually determines whether a country can open trade with others.

> or by a constant flux of gold and silver from her mines, to be able to support a correspondence, not entirely hurtful to the augmentation of her wealth. (*Works*, vol.1, p.276.)

Meanwhile, Steuart's characterization of 'passive' and 'active trade' must be understood in terms of his asymmetrical conception of different factors of production and different commodities. After supposing that the commodity, in general, is composed of two substances, i.e., 'matter' and 'labour', he argued that a trading country should be better off, if it exports more 'labour' than 'matter' and imports more 'matter' than 'labour'.[7]

> In all trade, two things are to be considered in the commodity sold. The first is the matter; the second is the labour employed to render this matter useful. The matter exported from a country, is what the country loses; the price of labour exported, is what it gains. If the value of the matter imported be greater than the value of what is exported, the country gains. If a greater value of labour be imported, than exported, the country loses. Why? Because in the first case, strangers must have paid, *in matter*, the surplus of labour exported; and in the second case, because the country must have paid to strangers, *in matter*, the surplus of labour imported. It is therefore a general maxim, to discourage the importation of work, and to encourage the exportation of it. (*Works*, vol.2, p.2; original italics.)

Relatively speaking, those raw materials and agricultural products, used directly or indirectly in the production process, contain more 'matter' and less 'labour'; whereas those manufactures, consumed immediately and having no further effect on production, contain more 'labour' and less 'matter'. Therefore, the more a trading country procures the former in exchange with the latter, the further it could carry on production. Thus, according to Steuart, 'the most profitable branches of exportation are those of *work*, the less profitable those of *pure natural produce*'.[8]

Now, from this postulate of the preferable pattern of trade based on the distinction between 'matter' and 'labour' in the commodity, it becomes clear how some trading countries fall into the category of 'passive traders', while others fall into that of 'active traders', and what they gain accordingly from their trade. While all trading countries wish to export more 'labour' (or less 'matter') and to import more 'matter' (or less 'labour'), only those which have abundant population could succeed in this since they are competing with each other. For, on the one hand, those countries which are abundant in natural resources, including land, but scarce in population could only export raw materials and agricultural products, i.e., 'matter'-intensive goods, so that they might import manufactures, i.e., 'labour'-intensive goods; on the other hand,

---

[7] On other occasions, instead, Steuart called the one the 'simple substance' or the 'production of nature', whereas the other the 'modification' or the 'work of man'. This composition of commodity corresponds to the division of its value into two parts: i.e., 'intrinsic value' and 'useful value'. We shall talk about this more, later, when we examine his discussion of the 'balance of wealth' and the 'balance of trade'.

[8] Cf. *Works*, vol.2, pp.1-10.

those which are scarce in natural resources but abundant in population might be able to export the manufactures so that they could import the raw materials and agricultural products. The former group of countries must be engaged in the 'passive trade', as long as they cannot help importing the 'labour'-intensive goods at the cost of exporting the 'matter'-intensive goods; whereas the latter group in the 'active trade', as far as they can afford to export the 'labour'-intensive goods in exchange for the 'matter'-intensive goods. Finally, while both would supply what they want through the foreign trade, whether 'passive' or 'active', the respective groups of trading countries benefit from it in different ways. On the one hand, the latter group engaging themselves in the 'active trade' could enhance their production and raise their level of output, by means of the raw materials and agricultural products, procured from abroad, together with the labour abounding at home. Particularly, the imported agricultural products would provide subsistence for some additional population, which, in its turn, could foster the further supply of labour and keep its wages down. On the other hand, the former group engaging themselves in the 'passive trade' could also enhance their production and raise their level of output, as they would further develop their natural resources and extend their cultivation of land so that they may export raw materials and agricultural products to acquire manufactures, in exchange, from abroad. In this case, however, it might be seen that they just drain their natural resources and exhaust their land, in order to consume 'luxuries'. Whenever they used up all these resources, they could no longer continue foreign trade, and, consequently, their level of output would decline.

We could summarize the above general discussion of the relation between the limits of economic growth and the benefits of foreign trade, as follows. First of all, the introduction of foreign trade could be a breakthrough for an exchange economy being faced with some limitations in the growth of output and population, as it would increase the 'effectual demand' for 'luxuries' and provide additional subsistence for the population. Second, as it depends on the nature of those limitations, the opening of trade for any country must be subject to its economic circumstances, particularly its initial conditions of production and consumption. In fact, there are two sorts of trade, 'passive' and 'active', in which a trading country may engage itself according to its economic circumstances. Last, the benefits from trade must also vary. The more 'labour'-intensive goods, such as manufactures, that a trading country exports and the more 'matter'-intensive goods, such as raw materials and agricultural products, that it imports, the more advantageous its foreign trade proves in terms of the long-run growth of the economy. On these, there follow two significant corollaries in Steuart's analysis of economic growth and foreign trade: i.e., his emphasis on the state of general circumstances of an exchange economy and his concept of wealth. While the one eventually leads to his three-stage theory of trade, the other leads to his analysis of two analogous notions of the 'balance of wealth' and the 'balance of trade'. We shall move on to examine them one after the other.

2. THE THREE STAGES OR CATEGORIES OF TRADE

Throughout his *Inquiry*, Steuart laid great emphasis on the general circumstances of the economy concerned.[9] He usually categorized them in terms of certain stages. When he talked about economic development and society in general, for instance, he suggested three stages in the evolution of society.[10] Again, in his analysis of economic growth in relation to foreign trade, Steuart was taking account of different stages in the process of change or development of modern exchange economy. He described them in terms of the following three categories of trade in general: 'infant', 'foreign' and 'inland trade'.[11] According to Steuart, these categories of trade may represent, in some cases, sequential stages through which an exchange economy passes or, in other cases, just intermittent phases between which it oscillates. As they are distinct from each other, the respective stages would correspondingly require some different strategies for the growth of the economy. Indeed, Steuart discussed the three stages of trade particularly in reference to certain policy recommendations for government.[12] Let us closely look into Steuart's discussions of each stage in turn with some special attention on the process of change from one stage to another.

2.1 'Infant Trade'

The stage of 'infant trade' represents the very beginning of development of an exchange economy.

> Infant trade, taken in a general acceptation, may be understood to be that species, which has for its object the supplying the necessities of the inhabitants of a country; because it is commonly antecedent to the supplying the wants of strangers. This species has been known in all ages, and in all countries, in a less or a greater degree, in proportion to the multiplication of the wants of mankind, and in proportion to the number of those who depend on their ingenuity for procuring subsistence. (*Works*, vol.1, pp.398-9.)

At this stage, the reciprocal wants among the people within the economy are the mainspring of all the economic activities. The more reciprocal wants, the

---

[9] Cf. the appendix to Ch.9 below, for Steuart's empirico-historical relativism in methodology.

[10] Cf. section 2, Ch.9 below.

[11] Instead of the term 'trade', he sometimes used 'commerce' in the *Inquiry*.

[12] It was strongly suggested, in his analysis, that government would play a significant role at each stage of trade. This reflects the fact that, in general, he was an advocate of the state interventionism and economic planning. Cf. Ch.10 below.

more production and consumption in the economy. Upon the progress of the 'taste of superfluity and luxury' among different social classes, backed up by the enhancement of the productivity in various industries, there would ensue the increment of 'effective demand' in the economy; and, thereby, its output, employment and population would increase. Therefore, as far as its domestic resources allow, the closed economy could constantly grow, provided that the 'effectual demand' was constantly augmented within the economy.

Under these circumstances, the role of government appears to be plain. It should be twofold: that is, to create the 'effectual demand' within the economy and at the same time to protect the domestic industries against foreign countries. According to Steuart,

> The ruling principle, therefore, which ought to direct a statesman in promoting and improving the infant trade of his people, is to encourage the manufacturing of every branch of natural productions, by extending the home-consumption of them; by excluding all competition with strangers; by permitting the rise of profits, so far as to promote dexterity and emulation in invention and improvement; by relieving the industrious of their work, as often as demand for it falls short; and, until it can be exported to advantage, it may be exported with loss, at the expence [expense] of the public. (*Works*, vol.1, p.402.)

That is, for a country at the stage of 'infant trade' to utilize fully its resources and increase its level of output, the government should encourage the domestic consumption of 'luxuries', i.e., manufactures, and discourage their importation from other countries until it is able to export them with profits. Sooner or later, the technological conditions of its economy would become advanced and the productivity of its industries would be enhanced so that it could manage the price of certain goods low enough to be competitive in the world market. The country would then open the door to foreign trade.

> In proportion as the prices of every species of industry are brought down to the standard of exportation, in such proportion will this species of trade its original character, and adopt the second. (*Works*, vol.1, p.402.)

Thus, the stage of 'infant trade' might be said to be a 'basis for establishing a foreign commerce', as the economy passes from the one stage to the other.

2.2 'Foreign Trade'

Once foreign trade is introduced to the exchange economy, many things, including the government's policy, must greatly change. Obviously, one of the most immediate and general effects of the transition from the stage of 'infant trade' to that of 'foreign trade' is the conspicuous increase of 'effectual demand' in the economy. Steuart remarked,

> The first and most sensible alteration will be an increase of demand for manufactures, because by supplying the wants of strangers, the number of consumers will now be considerably augmented. What again will follow upon this, must depend upon

> circumstances. If this revolution in the state of demand should prove to violent, the consequence of it will be to *raise* demand; if it should prove gradual, it will *increase* it. ... if the supply do not increase in proportion to the demand, a competition will ensue among the demanders; which is the common effect of such sudden revolutions. If, on the other hand, a gentle increase of demand should be accompanied with a proportional supply, the whole industrious society will grow in vigour, and in wholesome stature, without being sensible of any great advantage or inconvenience; the change of their circumstances will even be imperceptible. (*Works*, vol.1, p.279.)

As long as the economy opens itself to foreign trade gradually so as to keep the 'balance of work and demand' at all times, it can increase its level of output and augment its population by means of this additional source of 'effectual demand'. Thus, foreign trade would eventually be a great help to the economic growth. As we have seen in the last section, according to Steuart, the constant creation of 'effectual demand' and the stable multiplication of population are the two basic factors of the economic growth of a country, at whatever stage it is. Apparently, the opening of foreign trade benefits the country, if it can manage, in terms of both of these factors, directly or indirectly.[13]

To fully achieve such benefits from foreign trade, according to Steuart, it is necessary for the government to carry out some active economic policies. They seem to be mainly concerned with the general price level of the economy.

> ... the ruling principles of which [foreign trade] are to banish luxury; to encourage frugality; to fix the lowest standard of prices possible; and to watch, with the greatest attention, over the vibrations of the balance between work and demand. While this is preserved, no internal vice can affect the prosperity of it. (*Works*, vol.1, pp.402-3.)

That is, at the stage of 'foreign trade', while the government should make all possible efforts to lower the domestic price level, it must particularly discourage the consumption of 'luxuries' at home and at the same time keep the 'balance of work and demand' in all branches of industry in the economy, to that effect.

---

[13] Meanwhile, Steuart discussed the effects of sudden and violent introduction of foreign trade on both the economy as a whole and each class of the society. As a result of its sudden introduction, according to him, an abrupt increase of demand without the proportional augmentation of supply would bring forth the rise in the prices of both manufactures and agricultural products. Then, at its outset, some of the 'farmers' and the manufacturers may be better off, as their profits increase; whereas most of the 'proprietors of land' and those who live upon more or less determinate incomes in money would be worse off. In the end, however, this sort of foreign trade which is beneficial to only certain classes of people in the economy would not last, since the rise of prices would, sooner or later, infallibly worsen the competitiveness of its exports in the foreign markets. Thus, he concluded,

> Were revolutions as sudden as we are obliged to represent them, all would go to wreck; in proportion as they happen by quicker or slower degrees, the inconveniences are greater or smaller. (*Works*, vol.1, p.284.)

Cf. *Works*, vol.1, pp.279-84.

If a country cannot attract the other side of trade by any means, it would not continue to engage itself in foreign trade. Above all, if the country fails to keep the prices of exports low enough to defeat those of rival countries, *ceteris paribus*, the foreign trade will decline as a result of fierce competition between them. In this context, Steuart constantly emphasized that all the classes of people in the country engaged in foreign trade must be frugal and restrain themselves from domestic luxury to keep the cost of production down.

> The general society of mankind ... is here in a manner divided into two: the industrious providers are supposed to live in one country, the luxurious consumers in another. ... Luxury still tends as much as ever to the advancement of industry; the statesman's business only is, to remove the seat of it from his own country. When this can be accomplished without detriment to industry at home, he has an opportunity of joining all the advantages of ancient simplicity to the wealth and power which attend upon the luxury of modern states. He may preserve his people in sobriety, and moderation as to every expence [expense], as to every consumption, and make them enjoy, at the same time, riches and superiority over all their neighbours. (*Works*, vol.1, pp.347-8.)

The government should regulate the domestic consumption of 'luxuries', as otherwise it might eventually lead to the general inflation of the economy which would definitely hamper its foreign trade. At this stage, unlike the stage of 'infant trade', priority must be given to foreign markets rather than domestic markets and domestic demand must give way to foreign demand. Meanwhile, as it is the *excessive* demand for 'luxuries', relative to their supply, which raises their 'current price', the problem is associated with the 'balance of work and demand'.[14]

> ... when the balance gently vibrates, then work and demand, that is, trade and industry, like agriculture and population, prove mutually assisting to each other, in promoting their reciprocal augmentation. In order therefore to preserve a trading state from decline, the greatest care must be taken, to support a perfect balance between the hands employed in work and the demand for their labour. That is to say, according former definitions, to prevent demand from ever standing long at an immoderate height, by providing at all times a supply, sufficient to answer the greatest that ever can be made: or, in other words, still, in order to accustom my readers to certain expressions, to encourage the *great*, and to discourage the *high* demand. In this case, competition will never be found too strong on either side of the contract, and profits will be moderate, but sure, on both. ... For want of this just balance, no trading state has ever been of long duration, after arriving at a certain height of prosperity. (*Works*, vol.1, p.299; original italics.)

Thus, it is a matter of the greatest account for the economy at the stage of 'foreign trade' to secure the 'balance of work and demand' for all the

---

[14] For the relation between the 'current price' of individual commodities and their 'balance of work and demand' in Steuart's analysis, see sub-section 1.2, Ch.3 above.

industries, so that it may hold down its price level and compete with other countries in the foreign markets.[15]

Nevertheless, according to Steuart, the symptoms of 'growth and decay' always present themselves, despite all the possible efforts made by the 'statesman'.[16] That is to say, there are some immanent factors, in any exchange economy, which would necessarily destroy the 'perfect balance of work and demand'. Apart from what he called 'natural stops', e.g., the diminishing returns in agriculture which raise the price of subsistence and thereby that of all other goods as it is one of the factors which determine their 'intrinsic value', Steuart was particularly emphatic on the escalation of living standards in a trading country when he was explaining the transition of the stage of 'foreign trade' to the next.

> As long as a trading state is upon the rising hand, or even not upon the decline, and while the balance is kept right without the expedient of alternate diminutions, work will always be supplied from this quarter, cheaper than it possibly can be furnished from any other, where the same dexterity does not prevail. But when a nation begins to lose ground, then the columns which supported her grandeur, begin, by their weight, to precipitate her decline. The wealth of her citizens will support and augment the home demand, and encourage that blind fondness for high profits, which it is impossible to preserve. The moment these consolidate to a certain degree, they have the effect of banishing from the market the demand of strangers, who only can enrich her. It is in vain to look for their return after the nation has discovered her mistake, although she should be able to correct it; because, before this can happen, her rivals will have profited of the golden opportunity, and during the infatuation of the traders, will, even by their assistance, have got fairly over the painful struggle against their superior dexterity. (*Works*, vol.1, pp.313-4.)

As the profits of producers and merchants become 'consolidated', in consequence of the 'subversion' of the 'balance of work and demand' occasioned by the rising standard of living, the price level would be ever increasing in the trading country. As a result, the country would lose its ground in the competition against other countries in the world market, and in due course the stage of 'foreign trade' comes to its end.

> ... when the natural advantages of other nations constitute a rivalship, not otherwise to be overcome, the statesman must counterbalance these advantages by the weight and influence of public money; and when this expedient becomes also ineffectual, foreign trade is at an end; and out of its ashes arises the third species, which I call inland commerce. (*Works*, vol.1., p.403.)

Upon the extinction of foreign trade, the economy moves to the stage of 'inland trade'. After all, the relative advantage of foreign trade drifts from one country to another.

---

[15] For some macroeconomic implications of Steuart's discussion of the 'balance of work and demand', see section 2, Ch.3 above.

[16] He explained the symptoms of 'growth and decay' in the exchange economy in terms of the competition among trading nations. Cf. *Works*, vol.1, pp.309-14.

2.3 'Inland Commerce'

As an exchange economy switches over to the stage of 'inland commerce', it subjects itself to new principles which are totally different from those at the previous stage. According to Steuart,

> We must encourage oeconomy, frugality, and a simplicity of manners, discourage the consumption of every thing that can be exported, and excite a taste for superfluity in neighbouring nations. When such a system can no more be supported to its full extent, by the scale of foreign demand becoming positively lighter; then in order to set the balance even again, without taking anything out of the heavier scale, and to preserve and to give bread to those who have enriched the state; an additional home consumption, proportioned to the deficiency of foreign demand, must be encouraged. For were the same simplicity of manners still kept up, the infallible consequence would be a forced restitution of the balance, by the distress, misery, and at last extinction of the supernumerary workmen. I must therefore, upon such occasions, consider the introduction of luxury, or superfluous consumption, as a rational and moral consequence of the deficiency of foreign trade. (*Works*, vol.1, pp.348-9.)

As soon as foreign trade comes to an end without any possibility for restoration, the domestic demand for 'luxuries' should replace the previous foreign demand; otherwise, the industries would decline and the level of output in the whole economy would decrease consequently. It appears then that the situation at the stage of 'inland trade' would be similar to the one at that of 'infant trade'. That is, at these stages, it is necessary to encourage domestic consumption and to create 'effectual demand', in order to increase output, to enhance employment and to augment population in the economy. As both stages have the same character as a closed self-sustaining economy, the growth strategies for them also must be alike. Otherwise, the respective stages are quite different in their nature. The stage of 'infant trade' could be said to be a period of storing up economic potentials in preparation for foreign trade through which the economy would further grow; whereas that of 'inland trade' is one of keeping up the *status quo* after exhausting some relative advantages over other countries in foreign trade.

Meanwhile, according to Steuart, 'inland trade' is not definitely the final stage in the process of change or development of the modern exchange economy. If a country at this stage could manage to lower the price of commodities and make them vendible in the foreign markets, it could re-establish foreign trade from the decline or complete extinction. In fact, Steuart made some suggestions of how to let down the price of manufactures so as to render them exportable.[17] That is, apart from the direct control over

[17] In his *Inquiry*, ch.XVIII, book II, Steuart gave details of the causes of high prices of manufactures at home, relatively to those in foreign countries, and prescribed appropriate remedies for them. He enumerated those causes under four heads: 1) the consolidation of high profits with the real value of manufactures, 2) the rise in the prices of articles of the first necessity 3) the natural advantages of the other countries, and 4) the perfection of political economy in the other countries, such as their

'luxurious' consumption and the enhancement of productivity through developing technology, he particularly emphasized the application of government's public finance to that effect.[18] For instance, taxation might help to revive foreign trade.

> ... so soon as the wealth of a state becomes considerable enough to introduce luxury, and put an end to foreign trade; and when, from the excessive rise of prices, all hopes of restoring it are lost, then taxes become necessary, both for the support of government on the one hand, and, on the other, to serve as an expedient for recalling foreign trade in spite all the pernicious effects of luxury to extinguish it. (*Works*, vol.1, p.404.)

By imposing taxes on 'luxuries', the government could put a curb upon their domestic consumption. As far as the taxation keeps the demand low and prevents the 'consolidation' of profits, it would definitely serve to let the price level down and to restore the competitive power of previously exported goods. After all, at a certain stage of development of the modern economy, 'foreign trade' might alternate with 'inland commerce', depending on circumstances – domestic and foreign – including government policies.[19]

We have so far discussed Steuart's analysis of the three stages or categories of trade in relation to the process of development of an exchange economy. In so doing, we compounded the theoretical elements with the policy recommendations of his analysis. Indeed, as the whole of his political economy might be regarded as policy-oriented, it reflects the fact that he was in a sense an advocate of state interventionism and economic planning.[20] Our discussion in this section will provide some grounds for the further

---

superior technology, knowledge in trade, payment system, monetary circulation, abilities of statesman, and the application of public money. Then, he presented the methods of removing these causes in order, likewise. That is to say, as to the consolidation of profits, he proposed either to multiply the hands employed in those particular branches of industries where demand is high and make them frugal, or to check the domestic demand for the manufactures produced in those industries. Against the rising price of 'necessaries [necessities]', he recommended to increase their supply through importation, prohibition of other uses, and furtherance of technological change. To offset the other countries' natural advantages, Steuart put forth the use of public money, still emphasizing the frugality of various social classes in the economy. Finally, to compete with the others with superior technology, etc., he advised to find out the country's own merits and utilize them. Cf. *Works*, vol.1, pp.374-97.

[18] We shall discuss Steuart's argument for active finance, in general, later in Ch.8 below.

[19] In this light, Steuart established a principle of the demand-management policy of government in relation to foreign trade, as follows:

> ... when foreign demand begins to decline, domestic luxury must be made to increase, in order to soften the shock of the sudden revolution in favour of the industrious. For the same reason ... foreign trade must be opened upon every diminution of domestic luxury. (*Works*, vol.1, p.373.)

Thus, to sustain a certain stable amount of 'effectual demand' in the economy, the government should implement either 'inland commerce' or foreign trade. And, in this sense, they themselves might be seen as alternatives of the government economic policy.

[20] See Ch.10 below.

examination and formalization of Steuart's theory of economic growth and foreign trade later on.

3. THE 'BALANCE OF WEALTH' AND THE 'BALANCE OF TRADE'

After having examined Steuart's general discussions of the relation between economic growth and foreign trade in terms of the gains of trade and the stages of its development, we shall now get to the kernel of his theory of growth and trade. It starts with the analogy between the society of individuals and that of countries.

According to Steuart, as different countries are engaged in foreign trade, they form a 'new kind of society' among them, which is analogous to the one among individuals within each country. The analogy holds in two senses: i.e., the interdependence among the members of society and the concept of wealth for each member. On the one hand, Steuart classified the mutual dependence upon one country to another into two types: 'necessary' and 'contingent'.[21]

> It is necessary, when one of the nations cannot subsist without the assistance of the other, as is the case between the province of Holland, and those countries which supply it with grain; or contingent, when the wants of a particular nation cannot be supplied by their inhabitants, from a want of skill and dexterity, only. (*Works*, vol.1., p.362.)

To turn its foreign trade to full advantage, it is essential for a country to examine how far its dependence on other countries is 'necessary' and how far it is only 'contingent'.[22] Furthermore, as soon as the country opens its door to foreign trade, its matter of concern moves from on the one kind of society to the other. In other words, the mutual dependence among individuals within a country would be partly but significantly replaced with that among trading countries.

> While a people are occupied in the prosecution of foreign trade, the relations between the individuals of the state, will not be so intimate as when the producers and consumers live in the same society; such trade implies, and even necessarily creates a chain of foreign dependences; which proportionally diminish the mutual dependence which formerly subsisted among the citizens. (*Works*, vol.1, p.352.)

---

[21] For Steuart's discussion of the interdependence among various social classes and between different economic sectors within a country, see Ch.2 above. Meanwhile, the above classification of the mutual dependence among trading countries seems to correspond, by and large, to the division of foreign trade into two sorts, i.e., 'active' and 'passive trade', which we have already discussed in section 1 of this chapter. That is, the countries which 'necessarily' depend on other countries are likely to be engaged in the 'active trade'; whereas those which 'contingently' depend on others in 'passive trade'.

[22] Cf. *Works*, vol.1, pp.361-8.

This suggests that, after the introduction of foreign trade, things must greatly change in the economic mechanism of a country, including the government policy. In fact, as we have already seen in the last sections, the foreign trade furnishes an additional and, sometimes, alternative source of 'effectual demand' for the economy.

On the other hand, Steuart's concept of wealth also bears a good analogy between the level of the society of individuals within a country and that of international society. As this point represents the very key to our present discussion, it must be scrutinized in detail. First of all, he defined wealth as the 'circulating adequate equivalent'.

> By wealth I understand the circulating adequate equivalent. The desires of the rich, and the means of gratifying them, make them call for the services of the poor: the necessities of the poor, and their desire of becoming rich, make them chearfully [cheerfully] answer the summons; they submit to the hardest labour, and comply with the inclinations of the wealthy, for the sake of an equivalent in money. This permutation between the two classes, is what we call circulation; and the effects produced by it upon the political situation of the parties, at the precise time of the circulation, and the consequences, after it is completely effected, explain what is called the balance of wealth. (*Works*, vol.2, p.32.)

Thus, from the definition of 'wealth' as anything equivalent in circulation, Steuart further derived the notion of the 'balance of wealth' as the 'effects or consequences of the circulation'. It becomes now clear what he meant by that, as he put money, either metallic or paper money, on one side of the balance and what he called the 'prestations' or 'performances of any kind' on the other, as reciprocal equivalents for each other.[23] As the circulation goes on, the 'balance of wealth' turns in favour of the party who finally acquires money. For, while industry and 'effectual demand' makes wealth circulate, consumption turns the balance.

> Industry is the only method of making wealth circulate, so as to change its balance between the parties. (*Works*, vol.2, p.50.)

> The consumption ... is the only thing which makes the balance turn. While the consumable commodity remains entire in the hands of the purchaser, he still remains possessor of the value, and may, by inverting the operation, return to the possession of the same species of wealth he had before. (*Op.cit.*, vol.2, pp.37-8.)

---

[23] Steuart categorized the 'prestations' into four groups: that is, 'consumable' and 'inconsumable', as corporeal; and 'personal services' and 'rights in or to any thing whatever', as incorporeal. Then, he considered the effects of the circulation of money, as it has, for its object, the acquisition of those four kinds of 'prestations', in his *Inquiry*, book II, ch.XXVI 'Of the Vibration of the Balance of Wealth between the Subjects of a modern State'. In sum, according to Steuart, there is no vibration of the 'balance of wealth' in the cases of the acquisition of 'inconsumable' things, such as land and precious metals, and that of 'rights', such as servitudes, privileges or immunities, lending money at interest, etc.; whereas the 'balance' turns between parties either when 'consumable' commodities are consumed or when 'personal services' are performed. Cf. *Works*, vol.2, pp.31-51.

Thus, in Steuart's conception, wealth is no more than the 'means of purchasing whatever man can perform or produce'.

At the macroeconomic level, wealth as a stock could be augmented by the increase of output through the further creation of 'effectual demand';[24] at the same time, however, it has to be diminished by the consumption accompanying the very 'effectual demand', in a closed economy where the money, either 'real' or 'symbolical', serves as a means of hoarding value or storing wealth for individuals.[25] Thus, the wealth of a nation, as a whole, might not change at all in the closed economy during and after the circulation, though the 'balance of wealth' among individuals within the economy might 'vibrate'. In this regard, Steuart remarked,

> The essential characteristic of this vibration of the balance of wealth, is the change in the relative proportion of riches between individuals. (*Works*, vol.2, p.37.)

For instance, when Steuart advocated the use of 'symbolical money', he held that, although an increase in the circulation of money would create an

---

[24] As long as the output belongs to any of the four forms of 'prestations', categorized above, it becomes part of the wealth of a country. Steuart divided the value of commodity into two parts, i.e., its 'intrinsic value (or worth)' and 'useful value'. He attributed the former to 'simple substance', 'matter' or the 'production of nature'; whereas the latter to 'modification', 'labour' or the 'work of man'.

> The intrinsic value, therefore, is constantly something real in itself: the labour employed in the modification represents a portion of man's time, which having been usefully employed, has given a form to some substance which has rendered it useful, ornamental, or, in short, fit for man, mediately or immediately. ... The consumption of the intrinsic value of any commodity, takes place the moment the matter employed begins to diminish, and is completed so soon as it is consumed totally. The consumption of the useful value proceeds in like manner, in proportion as the use it is put to makes the value of it diminish, or disappear altogether. (*Works*, vol.2, p.36.)

While the compositional proportion between the two component parts of value varies in different commodities, the (total) value constitutes, in any case, what Steuart defined as wealth. Indeed, it might be said that the wealth itself is made up of the 'production of nature' and the 'work of man'. The one represents such natural resources as land and raw materials, whereas the other the labour employed in production. After all, the more 'effectual demand' created, the more output produced; the more natural resources utilized and the more labour employed, thereby, the more wealth augmented.

[25] Let us first note how Steuart defined 'real' and 'symbolical money'. According to him,

> By real money, is meant what we call coin, or a modification of the precious metals, which by general agreement among men, and under the authority of a state, carries along with it its own intrinsic value. By symbolical money, I understand what is commonly called credit, or an expedient for keeping accounts of debts and credit between parties, expressed in those denominations of money which are realized in the coin. Bank notes, credit in bank, bills, bonds, and merchants' books (where credit is given and taken) are some of the many species of credit included under the term symbolical money. (*Works*, vol.2, p.39.)

Thus, the 'real money', i.e., coins, has its own value as precious metals; whereas the 'symbolical money', i.e., paper money, itself has no value at all. Nonetheless, there is no difference between the two sorts of money in that both in common could make 'inconsumable prestations' circulate. Either they themselves are 'inconsumable prestations' or they are secured by them. As long as those 'inconsumable prestations' 'melted down' by them preserve the same value during the circulation, both 'real' and 'symbolical money' could serve to hoard value or store wealth. We shall discuss more about this, later when we deal with Steuart's theory of money and credit in the next chapter.

additional 'effectual demand' and enhance the level of output in the economy, it does not necessarily augment the wealth as a stock.

> Those nations, therefore, who circulate their metals only, confine industry to the proportion of the mass of them. Those who can circulate their lands, their houses, their manufactures, nay their personal service, even their hours, may produce an encouragement for industry far beyond what could be done by metals only. And this may be done, when the progress of industry demands a circulation beyond the power of the metals to perform. ... But does this species of circulation increase the riches of a state? Surely no more than it would increase the riches of France or England, to carry all the plate in the two kingdoms to be coined in the mint. The use of symbolical money is no more than to enable those who have effects, which by their nature cannot circulate (and which, by-the-bye, are the principle cause of inequality), to give, to the full extent of all their worth, an adequate circulating equivalent for the services they demand. (*Works*, vol.2, pp.41-2.)

In a closed economy, the use of 'symbolical money' would simply promote the 'vibration' of the 'balance of wealth' among individuals, without causing any change in its total amount. That is, as the 'real money' helps the 'vibration' of the 'balance of wealth' by just transforming precious metals into coins, both of which convey the same value; so does the 'symbolical money' help by 'melting down' those 'prestations' which cannot circulate for themselves. In either case, there would be no additional increase of wealth in the economy.

Before going further, let us sum up some implications of Steuart's discussion of the 'balance of wealth', examined so far. First, we could note that his notion of wealth is a *stock*, rather than *flow*, concept: it increases as the production goes on and decreases as consumption is made, both at the level of the economy as a whole and at that of each individual. For Steuart, the wealth of a nation or an individual is no more than unconsumed 'prestations'; in other words, it consists in potential consumption.[26] Second, as it literally implies, the 'balance of wealth' refers to the effects of the circulation of 'prestations', in one way, and money, in the other way around, on the wealth of individuals at the microeconomic level. The circulation gives rise to the 'vibration' of the 'balance of wealth' among individuals within the economy.[27] Finally,

---

[26] As for the concept of wealth, Smith's presented a good contrast to Steuart's. In Smith, wealth is a *flow* as it consists in potential production. We shall make a detailed comparison between them, in the context of economic growth and foreign trade, later in the appendix.

[27] Steuart considered the circulation of 'prestations' and money, which would make the 'balance of wealth' vibrate among individuals in the economy, to be a 'method of melting down the cause of inequality and rendering fortunes equal'.

> If therefore such variations in the balance of wealth depend on the difference of *genius* among men, what scheme can be laid down for preserving equality, better that of an unlimited industry equivalent to an universal circulation of all property, whereby dissipation may correct the effects of hoarding, and hoarding again correct those of dissipation? This is the most effectual remedy both against poverty and overgrown riches; because the rich and the poor are thereby perpetually made to change conditions. In these alterations in their respective situations, the parties who are changing by degrees, must surely in their progress towards a

therefore, Steuart's discussion of the 'balance of wealth' was rather concerned with the distribution of wealth, than its accumulation. It is particularly the case, as the creation of 'effectual demand' by means of or together with the increase of money supply would certainly raise the level of output in a closed economy, but the amount of wealth, as a stock, might still remain unchanged because of accompanying consumption; meanwhile, the 'balance of wealth' might 'vibrate' between individuals, however. All this is about a closed economy.

Now, if a country opens the door to foreign trade, the matter of the 'balance of wealth' is to be transformed into that of the 'balance of trade', as soon as it brings a new dimension to the circulation in the economy. In other words, as the foreign trade adds another sort of circulation, based on the mutual dependence among trading countries, to the domestic circulation among individuals within the economy, and as the one, sooner or later, dominates the other, the 'balance of wealth' would give its importance away to the 'balance of trade' in the economy, according to Steuart. Upon examining Steuart's discussion of this shift of concern for a trading country from the 'balance of wealth' to the 'balance of trade', we might reach a certain conclusion of Steuart's analysis of economic growth and foreign trade. We shall first look into the analogy between the 'balance of wealth' among individuals within a country and the 'balance of trade' among trading countries.

Above all, the two balances in common were defined in terms of wealth as a stock. In fact, the 'balance of trade' seemed to be regarded as the same thing as the 'balance of wealth' between trading countries, on the basis of the analogy between the society of individuals within a country and that of different trading countries.

> An industrious person who conduce his affairs with prudence, must either be in a way of growing richer by his industry, or of spending his income with oeconomy and discretion: so I must suppose a nation which is well governed, either to be growing richer by foreign trade, or at least in a state of not becoming poorer by it. (*Works*, vol.2, p.107.)

> ... both the one [a nation] and the other [a private person], by following a different conduct, may amass great sums of wealth, far above the proportion of it among their neighbour. (*Op.cit.*, vol.2, p.110; brackets added.)

Furthermore, as is the case with the 'balance of wealth' among private persons, the 'balance of trade' is to 'vibrate' among trading countries only as a result of consumption.

> total alteration, become, at one time or other, upon a level, that is to an equality; as the buckets in a well meet, before they can pass one another. (*Works*, vol.2, p.44.)

Thus, as the circulation goes on, the 'balance of wealth' turns against those who have money and who thereby consume, whereas it turns for those who want money and who therefore produce. In this sense, the circulation might be said to eventually help sustain the equality of wealth among people in the economy.

> It is not by the importation of foreign commodities, and by the exportation of gold and silver, that a nation becomes poor; it is by consuming these commodities when imported. The moment the consumption begins, the balance turns. (*Works*, vol.2, p.110.)

As long as the circulating equivalents used in trade, i.e., international money such as precious metals, preserve the same value before and after circulation, the 'balance of trade' between trading countries turns in favour of those who export consumable goods and acquire the equivalents and it turns against the others who import and consume the goods at the cost of the equivalents. Therefore, it might be said, that while the circulating equivalents serve as a means of storing wealth during the circulation, the countries with the favourable 'balance of trade' could accumulate their wealth through foreign trade, as they hold the equivalents instead of consuming the consumable goods at home.[28]

> While a favourable balance, therefore, is preserved upon foreign trade, a nation grows richer daily; and still prices remain regulated as before, by the complicated operations of demand and competition; and when one nation is growing richer, others must be growing poorer. (*Works*, vol.2, p.115.)

Thus, Steuart concluded that 'foreign trade, well conducted, has the necessary effect of drawing wealth from all other nations'.[29] Here arises a shift of concern for a trading country, as the 'balance of trade' occupies its interest in place of the 'balance of wealth'.

> It is as much as the duty of every statesman to watch over the conduct of those who hold the foreign correspondence of his people, as it is the duty of the master of a family to watch over those he sends to market. (*Works*, vol.2, p.107.)

It is the accumulation of wealth by means of foreign trade, rather than its distribution on the basis of domestic circulation, that becomes a matter of concern for the trading country. As far as the country keeps the 'balance of trade' in its favour, it could be augmenting the wealth as a stock.

Does this all merely amount to a traditional view of the so-called mercantilists on foreign trade and economic growth? To put it another way, does Steuart's view simply imply that the wealth of a nation consists in certain precious metals, as 'universal equivalents', and would increase as the nation

---

[28] In this regard, Steuart noted the significance of the existence of 'universal equivalent' for foreign trade.

> While trade was carried on by the exchange of consumable commodities, this operation also little interested the state: consumption then was equal on both sides; and no balance found upon either. But so soon as the precious metals became an object of commerce, and when, by being rendered an universal equivalent for every thing, they became also the measure of power between nations, then the acquisition, or at least the preservation of a proportional quantity of them, became to the more prudent, an object of the last importance. (*Works*, vol.1, p.433.)

We shall fully discuss Steuart's analysis of international money later in Ch.7 below.

[29] *Works*, vol.1, p.433.

brings them in by keeping its balance of trade favourable? Although Steuart, like the mercantilists before him, advocated the favourable balance of trade for the accumulation of wealth, their respective arguments were built on different grounds. Above all, Steuart's concept of wealth was more comprehensive than the mercantilists', though both of them commonly represented it as a stock, rather than a flow. The one allows its two alternative forms, i.e., either 'prestation' (which is equivalent to anything vendible) or money (both 'real' and 'symbolical'); whereas the other counts in only some precious metals, i.e., 'real' money. In other words, while the mercantilists identified wealth with precious metals, Steuart defined it as unconsumed 'prestations' or claims for them, that is, potential consumption.

On the basis of the concept of wealth thus defined, Steuart linked foreign trade to the accumulation of wealth by means of his own notion of the 'balance of trade'. He established it in terms of the above two alternative forms of wealth, on the analogy of the 'balance of wealth' between individuals within a country. The 'balance of trade' turns in favour of those countries who export 'consumable prestations' and, in return, acquire not only money, as international circulating equivalents, but also any 'prestations' whose value would be preserved throughout the circulation. The natural resources, e.g., raw materials, which could be used for further production, belong to the latter category of 'prestations'. Therefore, foreign trade would still prove to be advantageous to those countries who secure natural resources from it, even if the balance of trade, in the mercantilist sense, would turns against them.[30] As it were, according to Steuart, anything not to be consumed and anything to be used for further production would render the 'balance of trade' favourable, and contribute to the accumulation of wealth.

For the mercantilists who regarded 'universal equivalents' *themselves* as 'wealth', it might be said, that the more a country exports (and the less it imports), the more favourable the balance of trade; the greater the trade surplus, the more wealth it accumulates. For Steuart, on the other hand, wealth consists in either 'production of nature' or 'work of man', or some composite of both; therefore, as long as a trading country keeps these 'prestations' from being consumed at home and procures them from abroad, its 'balance of trade' would be 'favourable' and, thereby, its wealth would be augmented.

> ... whatever foreign commodity, of whatsoever kind it be, is found to be consumed within the nation he [statesman] governs, so far the balance of trade against her; and ...

[30] Cf. our previous discussion of Steuart's consideration of the composition of commodity in terms of 'matter' and 'labour' in section 1 above and the division of its value into 'intrinsic value' and 'useful value' earlier in this section. Meanwhile, in the above context, some intermediate goods, imported from abroad but employed in domestic production, must be the same sorts of 'prestations' as natural resources.

> so far as any commodity produced either by the soil, or labour of the inhabitants, is consumed by foreigners, so far the balance is for her. (*Works*, vol.2, pp.113-4; brackets added.)

> We must encourage oeconomy, frugality, and a simplicity of manners, discourage the consumption of every thing that can be exported, and excite a taste for superfluity in neighbouring nations. (*Op.cit.*, vol.1, p.348.)

In Steuart's analysis, the favourable balance of trade would help a country to accumulate wealth, so far as it results from the 'industry and frugality' of people.

Let us close this section by summarizing some distinctive features of Steuart's analysis of the relation of the balance of trade and the accumulation of wealth, particularly in contrast with that of those mercantilists before him. First of all, it is implicitly assumed in his analysis that there would be no correspondence between the balance of trade and the amount of precious metals in the economy, on account of the wide uses of 'symbolical money', i.e., paper money, between trading countries as between private individuals within an economy, on the one hand, and some other categories of the balance of payments than trade account, e.g., non-trade current account and capital account, on the other hand.[31] Second, in any case, money – either 'real' or 'symbolical'– is rather one of two alternative forms of wealth, than the wealth itself. The other form is 'prestation', i.e., anything vendible. Third, essentially, the wealth of a nation consists in its potential consumption, as is the case with individuals within the nation. Finally, therefore, a trading country could accumulate its stock of wealth, as long as it manages to acquire some additional potential consumption in the form of either money or 'prestation' through foreign trade. All these points seem to clearly manifest why Steuart laid so much emphasis on the favourable balance of trade, and how he supported his argument to that effect in his analysis of economic growth and foreign trade.[32]

---

[31] Cf. *Works*, vol.2, pp.123-35. According to Steuart, 'to judge of the balance of trade is one thing; to judge of the wealth of a nation as to specie is another'. Meanwhile, it appears that the 'balance of trade' in his own sense sometimes referred to a sort of 'overall balance of payments', including both current and capital accounts, in modern terminology. For instance,

> ... a balance may be extremely favourable without augmenting the mass of the precious metals; to wit, by providing subsistence for an additional number of inhabitants; by increasing the quantity of shipping, which is an article of wealth; by constituting all other nations debtors to it; by the importation of many durable commodities, which may be considered also as articles of wealth; as a well furnished house, a well stored cellar, an ample wardrobe, and a fine stable of horses, are articles which enhance the value of the inheritance of a landed man. (*Works*, vol.2, p.120.)

On occasions, in Steuart's *Inquiry*, it is this sort of balance of payments that was directly related to the accumulation of wealth of a trading country, irrespective of the amount of precious metals in the economy. We shall deal with more about his classification of the balance of payments later in Ch.7 below.

[32] Viner (1937; ch.1) provided an over-all view of the mercantilist arguments for a favourable balance of trade. He classified them into two large categories: i.e., those grounded on the 'desirability of more

4. ECONOMIC GROWTH THROUGH FOREIGN TRADE: A SIMPLE MODEL

In this concluding part of our present discussion of Steuart on economic growth and foreign trade, we shall first look into some theoretical implications of his analysis, examined so far, and, thereupon, make an attempt to formalize it into a macroeconomic model. This tentative model of growth would be purely instrumental in illustrating what we have already said in both the present and the previous chapter, abstaining from entering into details.[33]

In general, one of the important analytical differences between the theory of long-run growth and that of short-run output level might be whether or not in each case we allow the productive capacity of the economy, which could be increased to make further expansion of production possible, to be variable and

---

bullion' and those on the enhancement of 'employment'. (He called the latter the 'balance-of-labour doctrine'.) According to him, Steuart's argument belongs to the latter category, along with those of N. Barbon, J. Tucker, J. Harris and A. Young. (Cf. our previous discussion of Steuart's consideration of the composition of commodity in terms of 'matter' and 'labour' in section 1.) He observed,

> In the balance of labour doctrine the end was employment, and the favourable balance was the means, and even if its exponents did not themselves see clearly that income and consumption were in turn the rational ends of employment, and of economic activity in general, they at least made it easy to bring about a revolutionary change in the orientation of economic thought. (Viner (1937), p.55)

Apart from his view of the history of economic thought as a linear process of development, it seems that he did not pay due attention to each individual author. As far as Steuart was concerned, his economic doctrine was based on a different concept of exchange economy, in general, and a different concept of wealth, in particular, from Smith's. The point will become clear from our illustration of Steuart's analysis of economic growth and foreign trade in the next section, and from a comparison between the two contemporary authors' concepts of wealth in the appendix below. Meanwhile, according to Perrotta (1991), criticisms of mercantilism conventionally have been based on the following three accusations: (1) the absurdity of the exchange of unequal value or wealth between trading nations; (2) the confusion of wealth with money; and (3) the neglect of the growth of domestic production. Showing that none of them are well-grounded, he argued that 'the classical and postclassical paradigm of free trade and laissez faire is misleading for an understanding of the relationship established by the mercantilists between foreign trade and production growth' (p.302). In conjunction with our discussions so far, all those accusations seem to have little to do with Steuart's analysis of trade and growth. Thus, it might be said that he cannot be simply regarded as the 'last of the mercantilists' (Haney (1949), p.138), at least, in the conventional sense.

33 Akhtar (1978) also provided a formal outline of Steuart's growth model; he concentrated on the closed economy of the stage of 'infant trade'. According to him, 'it is in this context that Steuart's analysis of the growth problem is most clearly and systematically formulated'. He brought to light some particular characteristics of Steuart's theory of growth, e.g., the emphasis on the creation of the 'effectual demand' for agricultural surplus, the importance of the 'aspiration effect' in that process, and the crucial role of money and the public sector. In fact, all these represent what distinguishes Steuart's theory of growth from Smith's. As, in the latter, emphasis was rather on capital accumulation and technical change, the two theories form a good contrast in their analytical focus; the one on the demand side of the economy and the other on its supply side. Meanwhile, these contrasting focal points seem to be eventually linked to their respective concepts of wealth, quite different from each other, which in turn could be better understood in relation to their views of foreign trade. (Cf. the appendix below.) In the present model, we will highlight Steuart's analysis of the relation between economic growth and foreign trade, based on his own concept of wealth. Also cf. Akhtar (1979), for another macroeconomic model of Steuart's analysis of cyclical fluctuations in the 'developed economy', i.e., the closed economy of the stage of 'inland trade'.

determined endogenously. In Steuart's analysis of 'effectual demand', both the level of output and the size of population in an exchange economy are to be determined simultaneously, given the state of technology in the economy. As long as labour constitutes a major input in any production process, the potential productive capacity of the economy is to change as the population changes. Therefore, despite its apparent affinity with Keynes's 'effective demand', Steuart's notion of 'effectual demand' links the short-run cyclical determination of output to its long-run growth process, as the 'effectual demand' determines not only the degree of utilization or the level of employment but also the capacity of production or the size of population in the economy.[34]

Meanwhile, for an open economy, there are two sources of 'effectual demand': domestic and foreign. As we could note from Steuart's discussions of the relation of economic growth and foreign trade in general and those of the three stages or categories of trade in particular, these sources are sometimes alternative and sometimes complementary to each other for the growth of output level in the economy. In any case, the growth of output has recourse to that of 'effectual demand'. This seems to present a good contrast to some modern growth theories. In the latter theories, the analytical focus is rather on the capacity of production itself under the assumption that there always exists enough demand to soak up supply, i.e., at all times demand equals supply, in the economy. By contrast, in Steuart's analysis, the creation of 'effectual demand' is brought into focus on the supposition that, among those factors which decide the capacity of production in an exchange economy, the size of population is determined concurrently with the level of output by the amount of 'effectual demand', and the composition and scale of produced means of production and of natural resources are subject to the technical conditions of production and the initial endowments of the economy, respectively.[35] That is to say, while the one seems to be supply-side oriented, the other demand-side oriented. In parallel with this divergence of their focal points of analysis, the concept of wealth in the respective theories shows another contrast.

Steuart conceived wealth as potential consumption in the form of either money or 'prestation' – a stock amount at a certain point of time; whereas those modern growth theorists regard it as potential production in terms of 'annual produce' – a flow amount for a certain period of time.[36] As they are

---

[34] Cf. Ch.4 and its appendix, above.

[35] In the modern growth theories, while the growth of labour force or population is given exogenously at a certain rate, that of output is corresponding to that of produced means of production in aggregate terms. The so-called neoclassical growth models, including Harrod-Domar's, belong to these sorts of theories.

[36] It is believed that the flow concept of wealth originated from the Physiocrats. Nevertheless, it was A. Smith who actually established it as a fundamental of modern economics. Cf. the appendix below.

different in their concept of wealth, so they are different in their analysis of its accumulation. From the demand-side angle, to open up foreign trade and to keep the balance of trade favourable is the only way to procure some additional 'effectual demand' and to accumulate wealth as a stock; whereas, from the supply-side angle, to accumulate capital is to accumulate wealth as a flow, given the rate of growth of population and the amount of natural resources in the economy.

Based on his own concept of wealth as a stock, Steuart built up an argument for the favourable balance of trade. It laid a bridge between theory of economic growth and that of foreign trade. And yet, as we have already noted, Steuart's argument was different from that of the mercantilists before him. They were grounded on still different concepts of wealth and different definitions of the balance of trade. For the mercantilists, wealth was identified with money as 'universal equivalents', and the balance of trade was nothing but the amount of money acquired from or yielded to foreign countries. On the other hand, according to Steuart, not only money but also any unconsumed 'prestation' must constitute the wealth of a nation as that of an individual, and only consumption affects the 'balance of trade' among trading nations as it does the 'balance of wealth' among individuals.

Now, let us try to present a simple model on the basis of our discussions so far of Steuart's analysis of output, trade and growth, concentrating particularly on the relation between the accumulation of wealth and the balance of trade.[37]

Above all, we may represent Steuart's analysis of the level of output for an open economy in terms of 'effectual demand', as follows:[38]

$$Y = C_d + X \tag{1}$$

where Y: level of output

C_d: amount of consumption of domestically produced goods

X: amount of exportation.

That is to say, the level of output is determined by the amount of 'effectual demand', both domestic and foreign, for its own products. In the open economy, the consumption is to be supplied with either its own or foreign products. In other words, the whole consumption in the economy consists of domestic products and imports.[39] Thus,

[37] In this model, we will take no account of money, price level, and exchange rate, except money as one of alternative forms of wealth. After fully discussing Steuart's theory of money, we will set up another macroeconomic model of the simultaneous determination of output, price level and exchange rate, in Ch. 7 below. However, the two models are of different nature in their analytical time horizons: that is, while the present model relates to the long-run growth of the economy in terms of the accumulation of its stock of wealth, the one in section 2, Ch.7 below, has to do with the short-run cyclical movements of its level of output and balance of trade.

[38] All the variables in the present model are expressed in aggregate (value) terms.

[39] In this context, the 'consumption' comprises both the consumption of consumer goods and the use of producer goods.

$$C = C_d + M \tag{2}$$

where C: total amount of consumption
M: amount of importation.

By definition, the balance of trade is the difference between the amount of exportation and that of importation. Thus,

$$T = X - M \tag{3}$$

where T: balance of trade.

Therefore, from the above three equations (1 - 3),

$$T = X - M = (Y - C_d) - (C - C_d) = Y - C.$$

That is to say, the balance of trade eventually amounts to the difference between what the economy produces and what it consumes during a certain period of time.[40]

Meanwhile, according Steuart, the wealth of a nation, as a stock at a certain point in time, consists in two forms, i.e., 'prestation' and money. Thus, at the end of a certain period,[41]

$$W = P_1 + P_2 + G$$

where W: amount of wealth
P_1: amount of 'consumable prestations'
P_2: amount of 'inconsumable prestations'
G: amount of money.

Therefore, a change in the wealth of a nation must be equal to the sum of changes in its respective component parts. That is,

$$\Delta W = \Delta P_1 + \Delta P_2 + \Delta G. \tag{4}$$

Among those component parts of wealth, the amount of 'consumable prestations' in the economy would increase as either production at home or importation from abroad goes on, and decrease as either consumption at home or exportation to abroad keeps on. Thus,

$$\Delta P_1 = (Y + M) - (C + X). \tag{5}$$

Second, the amount of 'inconsumable prestations', i.e., any other assets than money – such as land and precious metals, also changes in the economy, as they are sometimes 'melted down' or 'liquidated' into money. Thus,

---

[40] We shall fully examine the implication of the absorption approach to the balance of payments in Steuart's macroeconomics, later when we deal with his theory of international money, particularly his analysis of the relationship between the balance of payments and the domestic economy. Cf. section 3, Ch.7 below.

[41] The amount of wealth and that of each component part of it, i.e., W, P_1, P_2 and G, are stock quantities; whereas the other variables, i.e., Y, C_d, C, X, M, T and L, are flow quantities.

$$\Delta P_2 = -L \tag{6}$$

where L: amount of 'liquidation'.

Finally, in the open economy, the amount of money, either 'real' or 'symbolical', would increase either domestically through the 'liquidation' of 'inconsumable prestations' or internationally through the favourable balance of trade. Thus,

$$\Delta G = L + T. \tag{7}$$

Therefore, from all the above equations (1 - 7),

$$\begin{aligned} \Delta W &= \Delta P_1 + \Delta P_2 + \Delta G \\ &= \{(Y + M) - (C + X)\} + \{-L\} + \{L + T\} \\ &= Y - C \\ &= T. \end{aligned}$$

That is to say, the wealth as a stock would be augmented, only if production exceeds consumption in the economy; and what remains in the production after the consumption is the same as the balance of trade.[42]

With the help of this simple but illustrative macroeconomic model, we may grasp the gist of Steuart's analysis of economic growth and foreign trade, i.e., its demand-side-oriented, stock-concept-based and trade-surplus-favoured character. And yet, his argument seems to be so much more sophisticated and systematic than that of anyone before, or even after, him that we could not merely relegate him to the status of an 'obscure and contradictory' mercantilist.[43]

---

[42] By implication, if there is no foreign trade in the economy, as is the case in the stages of 'infant trade' and that of 'inland trade', there would be no addition or reduction in the stock of wealth. For, in the above equations, $Y = C = C_d$ and $T = 0$; therefore, $\Delta W = 0$. In Steuart's own words,

> Here there is no question of either an increase or diminution of her wealth, but merely of making it circulate in the best manner to keep every body employed. (*Works*, vol.2, p.16.)

Thus, in his analysis of economic growth and foreign trade, no trade, no growth.

[43] Cf. Roll (1942), pp.125-7.

APPENDIX: Steuart and Smith

Throughout the evolution of economic doctrines, there have been many contemporary controversies, as well as sequential challenges of new theories to old ones, without distinction of any branch of the discipline. The controversies and the challenges, themselves, represent the process of evolution as such. While the debate between Ricardo and his contemporaries on various subjects was a good example for the former in the last century, Keynes's refutation of the 'classical school' is one for the latter in this century. What was then the relation between Steuart (1713-80) and Smith (1723-90), each of whom made his own *Inquiry*, published by the same publisher, with a nine-year interval? Despite the fact that apparently there seems to be no *formal and explicit* relation between them, either controversial or challenging,[1] it is quite well known that the theoretical approaches adopted and the ideological views expressed in their respective *Inquiries* present a distinct contrast.[2] Let alone the question why or how, one of the two Scottish

[1] This is particularly true in that Smith did not even mention Steuart, name or work, in his work. According to Sen (1957; pp.2-3), nevertheless, Smith deliberately did not do so in order to refuse to Steuart's work any public recognition whatsoever. As he referred to Smith's letter to W. Pulteney in 1772, some relevant part reads,

> ... I have the same opinion of Sir James Stewarts Book [*Inquiry*] that you have. Without once mentioning it, I flatter myself, that every false principle in it, will meet with a clear and distinct confutation in mine [*Wealth of Nations*]. ... (Smith (1977), p.164; brackets added.)

This passage was already quoted by Ingram (1888; p.87) and Stettner (1945; p.453). Also see Marx (1859), pp.167-8.

[2] Hutchison (1988) observed,

> The two fundamentally contrasting *Inquiries*, Steuart's of 1767 into the principles of political economy, and Smith's of 1776 into the wealth of nations, epitomized the two opposing macro-economic viewpoints and doctrines, 'classical' and 'anti-classical' (or mercantilist-Keynesian) of the ensuing two centuries. (p.368.)

While revealing that Smith had borrowed many technical points from Steuart, Sen (1957) warned that 'the main injustice that has been done to Steuart as well as to Smith was to imagine that they represented different stages in the same line of development'. He suggested that any comparison between them should be made in terms of their different broad perspectives and not on the basis of some technical details without reference to the general context.

> The *Political Oeconomy* is as much of a piece as the *Wealth of Nations*. These works must be compared as a whole or not at all. ... The real comparison between Steuart and Smith is, then, a comparison between their fundamentally different approach to economic problems. ... as a purely technical performance in the attempt to develop the economics of control the Political Oeconomy will stand comparison with the Wealth of Nations as a purely technical performance in the endeavour to develop the economics of laissez-faire. The balance of merits and demerits considered simply as an intellectual effort is almost the same. (Sen (1957), pp.185-6.)

contemporaries so overshadowed the other that no due attention has been attracted to him in the history of economic discipline,[3] in the present discussion, we shall concentrate on what essentially renders them so different from each other – especially, *inter alia*, the concept of wealth in their respective major works.

As indicated in its full title, the central theme of Smith's *Inquiry into the Nature and Causes of the Wealth of Nations* seemed to relate to the very concept of wealth, with regard to which it was quite different from another *Inquiry* that had already existed as the 'first comprehensive treatise in English', i.e., Steuart's *Inquiry into the Principles of Political Oeconomy*.[4] Since we have already been exposed to Steuart's concept of wealth in the preceding chapter, let us sketch out some general features of Smith's. Smith's *Wealth of Nations* starts with the definition of wealth.

> The *annual* labour of every nation is the fund which originally supplies it with *all the necessaries and conveniences of life* which it *annually* consumes, and which consist always either in the immediate produce of that labour, or in what is purchased with that produce from other nations. According therefore, as this produce, or what is purchased with it, bears a greater or smaller proportion to the number of those who are to consume it, the nation will be better or worse supplied with all the necessaries and conveniences for which it has occasion. (*Wealth of Nations*, vol.1, p.1; italics added.)

Thus, according to him, the wealth of a nation is what its economy 'annually' produces, whether 'necessaries [necessities]' or 'conveniences' and whether

---

Meanwhile, Anderson and Tollison (1984) even argued that Steuart was virtually the 'complete antithesis of Smith' in the sense that 'Smith correctly perceived Steuart to be his chief intellectual opponent' and 'the latter significantly influenced the course of development of *Wealth* – a work which might have taken on a less critical tone and complexion in Steuart's absence'. However, it seems that they went too far, when they stated that 'if Smith had a strawman, it was most definitely the totalitarian mercantilism of Steuart'. We shall discuss Steuart's view of the market economy and the role of the state in our Conclusion (Ch.10) below, after going through a rigorous analysis of his *Inquiry*.

[3] Cf. Johnson (1937), pp.209-10; Schumpeter (1954), p.176 n.; Sen (1957), pp.1-5 and pp.186-9; Vickers (1959, pp.240-3; 1970); Skinner (1966), pp.lxxxiii-lxxxiv; Akhtar (1978), pp.72-4; Anderson and Tollison (1984); Eltis (1987); and Hutchison (1988), pp.349-51.

[4] In the 'Anecdotes of the Author' subjoined to the *Works, Political, Metaphysical and Chronological, of Sir James Steuart*, in 6 vols., 1805, the editor, his son known as General Sir James Steuart, compared the two *Inquiries* in the following way:

> It is, indeed, singular, that two such writers, as Sir James Steuart, and Dr. Adam Smith, should have risen, in the same nation, during the same age, and written on the same subject, under different forms. ... The great object of Sir James Steuart was to form into *a regular science*, the complicated interests of *domestic policy*. To explain, wherein consists the revenue of the people; and secondly, the revenue of the state was the fundamental purpose of Dr. Smith. (*Works*, vol.6, pp.388-9; original italics.)

This passage points to the fact that, granted the originality of each, Steuart's *Inquiry*, as an 'Essay on the Science of Domestic Policy in Free Nations' (its subtitle), presented a general scope of the subject; whereas Smith's, afterwards, showed quite new modes of thinking in some specific terms, e.g., the concept of wealth as a flow of revenue or income, on that ground.

consumed within or without the economy.[5] The concept of wealth, implied in this definition, could be characterized in terms of a *flow* quantity in association with the *production* in the economy. This is a striking contrast to the concept of wealth in Steuart. For the latter, it is a *stock* quantity in association with the *consumption* in the economy. From these different starting points, their divergent systems of political economy originated.

As for Steuart who saw wealth as the stock amount of potential consumption, the only way for a nation to accumulate it is to have a favourable balance of foreign trade.[6] In his analysis, while the level of output in the economy is to be determined by the 'effectual demand' – both domestic and foreign, everything produced should be consumed either within or without the economy in one way another; therefore, to accumulate wealth as potential consumption, it is necessary to produce more but to consume less by exporting more and importing less.[7] On the other hand, for Smith who perceived wealth in terms of the flow amount of potential production, the productivity of labour and the accumulation of capital are the two crucial factors in the growth of wealth, which further hinge on the progress of the division of labour and the increment of savings out of the 'annual produce', respectively.[8]

> The greatest improvement in the productive powers of labour, and the greater part of skill, dexterity, and judgment with which it is any where directed, or applied, seem to have been the effects of the division of labour. (*Wealth of Nations*, vol.1, p.7.)

> Capitals are increased by parsimony, and diminished by prodigality and misconduct. Whatever a person saves from his revenue he adds to his capital, and either employs it himself in maintaining an additional number of productive hands, or enables some other person to do so, by lending it to him for an interest, that is, for a share of profits.

---

[5] From the opening passage, quoted above, onward, Smith regarded the 'real wealth' (or 'real revenue') of a country as a synonym of the 'annual produce of its land and labour'. For example, see *Wealth of Nations*, vol.1, pp.4, 264, 267, 359, 368 and 473; vol.2, p.197.

[6] See section 3 in the preceding chapter.

[7] See section 4 in the preceding chapter.

[8] Indeed, this is the main theme of the first two books of Smith's *Wealth of Nations*. Elsewhere, he neatly summarized it, as follows:

> The annual produce of the land and labour of any society can be augmented only two ways; either, first, by some improvement in the productive powers of the useful labour actually maintained within it; or, secondly, by some increase in the quantity of that labour. The improvement in the productive powers of useful labour depend, first upon the improvement in the ability of the workman; and, secondly, that of machinery with which he works. ... The increase in the quantity of useful labour actually employed within any society, must depend altogether upon the increase of the capital which employs it; and the increase of that capital again must be exactly equal to the amount of the savings from the revenue, either of the particular persons who manage and direct the employment of that capital, or of some other persons who lend it to them. (*Wealth of Nations*, vol.2, pp.197-8.)

Thus, the more savings, the more capital; then, given the state of technology, the more employment of labour, the more production. For some discussions of Smith's theory of growth, in general, and of his treatment of capital in relation to it, in particular, see Hollander (1973), chs. 6 and 7, and Bowley (1979), respectively. The latter shed light upon the role of capital as the major influence on growth in Smith's analysis. Also see Eltis (1984), ch.3, for an account of Smith's theory of growth in quite modern terms.

> As the capital of an individual can be increased only by what he saves from his annual revenue or annual gains, so the capital of a society, which is the same with that of all the individuals who compose it, can be increased in the same manner. (*Op.cit.*, vol.1., pp.358-9.)

While the productivity of labour upon the division of labour should be subject to the technical conditions of the economy, its relation to the accumulation of capital through saving-investment, or *vice versa*, seems to be the key to Smith's theory of growth.

Smith took the case of a weaver as an example to show that the accumulation of capital is a precondition for the division of labour.[9]

> A weaver cannot apply himself entirely to his peculiar business, unless there is beforehand stored up somewhere, either in his own possession or in that of some other person, a stock sufficient to maintain him, and to supply him with the materials and tools of his work, till he has not only completed but sold his web. This accumulation must, evidently, be previous to his applying his industry for so long a time to such a peculiar business. (*Wealth of Nations*, vol.1, p.291.)

To go a step further, Smith observed that the accumulation of capital might be not only a necessary but also a sufficient condition for the division of labour.

> As the accumulation of stock, in the nature of things, be previous to the division of labour, so labour can be more and more subdivided in proportion only as stock is previously more and more accumulated. The quantity of materials which the same number of people can work up, increases in a great proportion as labour comes to be more and more subdivided; and as the operation of each workman are gradually reduced to a great degree of simplicity, a variety of new machines come to be invented for facilitating and abridging those operations. As the division of labour advances, therefore, in order to give constant employment to an equal number of workmen, an equal stock of provisions, and a greater stock of materials and tools than what would have been necessary in a ruder state of things, must be accumulated beforehand. (*Wealth of Nations*, vol.2, pp.291-2.)

Therefore, in Smith's analysis, the accumulation of capital might be said to be the main cause of the wealth of nations, as 'it naturally leads to the improvement in the productive powers of labour', given the growth of population and the state of technology in the economy.

Eventually, on account of their different concepts of wealth, the contrast between the theories of growth in the two contemporary *Inquiries* becomes plain: one is demand-side oriented, whereas the other supply-side oriented. In Steuart's where wealth is regarded as the stock amount of potential consumption existing in the economy at a certain point of time, to open up foreign trade and to keep the balance of trade favourable is the only way to accumulate it. On the other hand, in Smith's where wealth is conceived as the flow amount of potential production attainable in the economy for a certain

[9] It is well known that the concept of capital as advances in the production process, as described above, had already appeared in the writings of the Physiocrats before Smith. Cf. our appendix to Ch.3 above.

period of time, the accumulation of capital is the most important in the growth of wealth.

6. National Money and Interest

When Steuart was writing his *Inquiry*, he treated every branch of political economy separately chapter by chapter, and gradually introduced more complicated combinations into the initial and fundamental circumstances as he went on from one to another. This is particularly the case with his discussions of money and credit which immediately follow those of trade and industry in the *Inquiry*. That is, after having discussed both the 'balance of wealth' between individuals within a nation and the 'balance of trade' between trading nations, he needed to explain the nature and functions of money and to deal with some related subjects, as, according to him, it is the circulation of money, nationally and internationally, which gives rise to the 'vibration' of those 'balances'. In the two following chapters, we shall examine Steuart's theory of money and credit; one in a closed-economy setting and the other in an open-economy. In so doing, we will particularly try to grasp it in the broad context of his macroeconomic analysis.

To start with, in this chapter, we shall articulate all the functions of money, assumed in Steuart's economics as a whole. They will serve as a basic tool-kit for our further analysis. Then, we shall move on to his discussion of coin, i.e., metallic money, as a proxy for the ideal money having all those functions. Exposing some intrinsic and extrinsic imperfections of coin as such, Steuart demonstrated their consequences and suggested some remedies for them. We shall also deal with his discussions of the value of the money-unit in terms of coin and the relative prices between coin, bullion and other commodities. Meanwhile, Steuart regarded paper money as a supplement of coin; nonetheless, he strongly argued for a wide use of it in every practical sense. By paper money, actually, he meant any and every sort of credit in its conventional sense. Thus, in connection with paper money as credit, we will meet his analysis of the interest of money. We shall particularly focus on his discussions of the nature of interest and the determination of its rate. Basically, while he saw the interest of money as an opportunity cost of its loan, he considered the rate of interest to be determined by the demand and supply conditions in the loans market as the price of money. After disclosing its relation to the rate of profit in his analysis, we shall illustrate the determination of the rate of interest by means of a fixed-price model. We will also examine his discussion of the legal rate of interest. At the end of the chapter, we shall synthesize all that has been said thus far into a self-contained macroeconomic model. As this model is designed not only to bind together all he discussed of national money and credit but also to link it to the rest of his macroeconomic analysis, it may take the place of a conclusion to this chapter.

1. THE FUNCTIONS OF MONEY

Throughout his *Inquiry*, Steuart assumed, implicitly or explicitly, four functions of money, which indeed comprehend all those attributed to it in modern monetary theory: that is, a measure of value, a medium of exchange, a means of payment and a store of value.[1] The present discussion of the functions of money seems to be particularly important as well as necessary, in that they were closely related to his treatment of coin and paper money and directly underlying his analysis of credit and interest. Let us examine them in turn.

1.1 Money as a Measure of Value

At the very outset of his full-dress analysis of money and credit in Books III and IV of the *Inquiry*, Steuart defined money as follows:

> Money, which I call of account, is no more than an arbitrary scale of equal parts, invented for measuring the respective value of things vendible. (*Works*, vol.2, p.270; original italics.)

That is to say, according to him, money is by definition to serve as a measure of value, no matter how the value of things might be determined.[2] Therefore, the denomination of money, taken for the unit of account, is supposedly just a scale for measuring the value of commodity. It is precisely analogous to any other sort of scale for measurement in general.[3]

---

[1] Cf., e.g., Davidson (1978). Also cf. Monroe (1923), p.21, p.48, pp.83-4 and pp.161-2, for a historical account of the functions of money presumed in the monetary theories before Adam Smith.

[2] As we noted in our previous discussion of his theory of value, Steuart mainly referred to the value of commodities as being determined by the 'demand and competition' in the markets. (See. Ch.3 above.) He himself neatly summarized this point in conjunction with the function of money as a measure of value as follows:

> The value of things depends upon many circumstances, which however may be reduced to four principal heads: First, The abundance of the things to be valued. Secondly, The demand which mankind make for them. Thirdly, The competition between demanders; and Fourthly, The extent of faculties of the demanders. The function therefore of money is to publish and make known the value of things, as it is regulated by the combination of all these circumstances. (*Works*, vol.2, pp.271-2.)

Thus, according to Steuart, while the value of commodities is nothing else than its price determined by the supply and demand in the markets, it needs to be expressed in terms of a common unit. This commensurable unit of value is money of account.

[3] Steuart remarked,

Now, once we understand that money is just a 'scale of equal parts' for measuring value, we might naturally lead on to the following question: 'what ought to be the standard value of one part'? To answer this question, let us turn to Steuart's explanation of the process of measuring value.

> ... so soon as one part becomes determined, by the nature of scale, all the rest must follow in proportion. The first step being perfectly arbitrary, people may adjust one or more of those parts to a precise quantity of the precious metals; and so soon as this is done, and that money becomes realized, as it were, in gold and silver, then it acquires a new definition; it then becomes the *price, as well as the measure of value*. (*Works*, vol.2, p.275.)

Thus, above all, it might be noted that, though anything vendible could readily be adjusted to the scale of value, it does not necessarily mean that it should thereby become the scale itself. This is because anything vendible has its 'price' for which an adequate equivalent is required and paid in return; and because, as long as it is determined in the market, the 'price', as the exchange ratio between them, varies and fluctuates according to circumstances. It therefore becomes clear that the ideal scale cannot be fixed to anything material whose value also changes as other things do. Steuart remarked,

> Money of account, therefore, cannot be fixed to any material substance, the value of which may vary with respect to other things. The operations of trade, and the effects of an universal circulation of value, over the commercial world, can alone adjust the fluctuating value of all kinds of merchandise, to this invariable standard. (*Works*, vol.2, p.277.)

Therefore, in Steuart's analysis, money as a measure of value merely represents a synonym of the 'money of account', which is no more than an 'imaginary' common scale or unit.[4]

> Money of account, which I shall here call *money*, performs the same office with regard to the value of things, that degrees, minutes, seconds, &c. do with regard to angles, or as scales do to geographical maps, or to plans of any kind. (*Works*, vol.2, p.271.)

Thus, money (of account) is just an 'imaginary scale' for measuring the value of commodity.

[4] Steuart described what would be the 'invariable standard' as follows:

> That money, therefore, which constantly preserves an equal value, which poises itself, as it were, in a just equilibrium between the fluctuating proportion of the value of things, is the only permanent and equal scale, by which value can be measured. (*Works*, vol.2, p.276.)

Is not this analogous to what Ricardo was seeking for in his labour theory of value? (Cf. Ricardo (1951-73), vol.1, pp.43-7.) As for Ricardo who tried to find an 'invariable measure of value' as ideal medium to 'sieve' only that change of the (supply) price of commodity occasioned by the change in the quantity of labour 'embodied' from that occasioned by the change in the rate of profit, it must be a special commodity which is produced in the average proportion of labour and capital of all industries in the economy; otherwise, it must be Sraffa's 'standard commodity' which is also purely theoretical. Cf. Sraffa (1960). As far as Steuart, who conceived the value of commodity as no more than its market price, was concerned, any common scale or unit might serve as a 'invariable standard', as long as 'all is merchandize with respect to this standard and, consequently, it stands unrivalled in the exercise of its function of a common measure' (*Works*, vol.2, p.277). In fact, Steuart gave two examples of this 'invariable standard': one was the 'florin banco' issued by the Bank of Amsterdam in those days, the other a certain scale adopted by the inhabitants in the African coast of Angola

Under the general circumstances of the economy where things were normally valued, anyhow, in terms of such 'artificial' or 'material money' as gold and silver coin, Steuart's discussion of money as a measure of value involved rather a practical problem, i.e., how good (or bad) the *real* money could be as a proxy for the *ideal* money. In other words, as far as Steuart was concerned, the matter in hand was how proximately the metallic coin could perform the office of money as a measure of value.[5]

1.2 Money as a Medium of Exchange

As we saw in our previous discussion of his basic macroeconomic model,[6] this is another function of money actually assumed in Steuart's *Inquiry*. The function of a medium of exchange is closely related to that of a measure of value, in that the process of exchange presupposes that of measuring value, as soon as it goes beyond the person-to-person level. Initially, some precious metals, such as gold and silver, were employed for the use of a medium of exchange, since they have certain physical properties which render them suitable for that, e.g., homogeneity, divisibility and durability.[7] As the operations of 'trade and industry' become more complicated and diversified, and, above all, as the process of exchange is carried out impersonally, things are to be valued before exchanged. Then, any medium of exchange must be an 'adequate equivalent for every thing alienable', and, at the same time, it must be, more or less, a proper measure of value. That is, the precious metals could adequately play their role as a medium of exchange, only if they themselves could properly serve as a measure of value; and *vice versa*, for the metals could be employed as a measure of value only in so far as they could be exchanged with things whose value is to be measured. Now, again, the question is, practically, how well the coin, made of precious metals, might

(*Works*, vol.2, pp.276-7). Cf. our previous discussion of his theory of value in Ch.3 above; particularly, sub-section 1.4.

5 As we shall fully discuss Steuart's analysis of coin as a proxy for ideal money in the next section, suffice to say that he put great emphasis on having a proper measure of value for the enhancement of trade and 'alienation' in the economy.

> The value of commodities therefore, depending upon circumstances relative to themselves and to the fancies of men, their value ought to be considered as changing with respect to one another only: consequently, any thing which troubles or perplexes the ascertaining these changes of proportion by the means of a general, determinate and invariable scale, must be hurtful to trade, and a clog upon alienation. This trouble and perplexity is the infallible consequence of every vice in the policy of money and coin. (*Works*, vol.2, p.273.)

In fact, apart from the whole of Book III ('Of Money and Coin') in his *Inquiry*, two of Steuart's other major economic writings were mainly concerned with the imperfections or inconveniences of coin, their prejudicial consequences on the economy and some remedies against them: i.e., *A Dissertation upon the Doctrine and Principles of Money Applied to the German Coin* (1761) and *The Principles of Money Applied to the Present State of the Coin in Bengal* (1772).

6 Cf. section 2, Ch.2 above.

7 Cf. *Works*, vol.2, pp.278-9.

perform the office of money as a medium of exchange as well as a measure of value.[8]

In an analytical sense, money as a medium of exchange is no less significant than money as a measure of value in Steuart's economics, as he postulated a certain relation between the amount of money circulating and the level of output in the economy. Leaving aside his monetary analysis of the level of output for our later detailed discussions,[9] let us briefly note how emphatic Steuart was on the importance of maintaining an 'adequate' proportion between the level of output and the amount of money as a circulating equivalent, i.e., money as a medium of exchange.

> ... a statesman who intends to increase industry and domestic consumption, should set out by providing a circulating fund of one kind or other, which ought always to be ready, and constantly at the command of those who have any sort of real equivalent to give for the consumption they incline to make: for as specie may oftentimes be scarce, a contrivance must be fallen upon immediately to supply the want of it. (*Works*, vol.2, pp. 59-60)

As we might notice from this, for the use of money as a medium of exchange, there is no difference between metallic coin and paper money secured on those 'solid properties' which could not circulate for themselves, such as land. According to Steuart, the latter simply supplies the want of the former in the economy where more 'circulating equivalents' are needed than the former can provide.[10] To find out how paper money could supplement coin in the process of exchange, we must discuss another function of money assumed in Steuart's analysis.

1.3 Money as a Means of Payment

It is this function of money which ultimately allows us to understand the nature of paper money and its relation to coin. Steuart illustrated the function of money as a means of payment as follows:

---

[8] Cf. the next section.

[9] In a closed-economy setting, we will discuss Steuart's monetary explanation of the level of output both in a fixed-price model at the end of section 3 and in a flexible-price model in section 4 of this chapter. After dealing with some subjects relating to international money, we will discuss it in an open-economy setting in the next chapter.

[10] In consequence of the introduction of paper money, as another source of 'circulating equivalents', into the economy, its level of output would certainly be enhanced.

> Those nations, therefore, who circulate their metals only, confine industry to the mass of them. Those who can circulate their lands, their houses, their manufactures, nay their personal service, even their hours, may produce an encouragement for industry far beyond what could be done by metals only. And this may be done, when the progress of industry demands a circulation beyond the power of the metals to perform. (*Works*, vol.2, p.41.)

As mentioned earlier, we shall fully discuss Steuart's analysis of the relation of money and output, later in this chapter and in the next chapter. And we shall discuss some other effects of the use of paper money later in connection with other functions of money.

> Let us suppose (A) to be a proprietor of a bit of land, and (B) an industrious workman; in order that (B) may purchase the land of (A), it must be supposed that (A) is very extravagant, and that he inclines to consume a much greater proportion of work than what is equivalent to all the surplus produce of his land. Now, in order to supply (A) to the value of the land itself, (B) must distribute his work to many different persons, and take in exchange, not such things as he has use for himself, but such as may be found useful to (A). But so soon as (A) has to pay (B) the whole surplus of his land, what fund of credit will he find in order to engage (B) to furnish more? He cannot pay him in land, this fund is not susceptible of circulation; and every expedient that could be fallen upon to keep accounts clear between them, is neither more or less than the introduction of *money*, either *real* or *symbolical*. ... we may suppose that (A) having no more circulating equivalent to give (B) for his work, and being desirous to consume of it to the value of his land, shall agree to issue notes of hand, every one of which shall carry in a right to an acre of land, to a fruit tree, to ten yards of the course of river, &c. and that every parcel of property, shall be esteemed at a certain proportion of work. This agreement made, he goes on with his consumption, and pays regularly, and adequately, the value of what he receives. (*Works*, vol.2, pp.39-40.)

Thus, for paying what one owes to another, conventionally, two kinds of money could be used: 'real money', i.e., coin made of precious metals, and 'symbolical money', i.e., paper money secured on 'solid properties'.[11]

According to Steuart, the essential difference between payment in 'real money' and that in 'symbolical money' lies in whether one or the other leaves any further action or performance behind it.

> He who pays in coin, puts the person to whom he pays in the real possession of what he owed; and this done, there is no more place for credit. He who pays in paper puts his creditor in possession only of another person's obligation to make that value good to him: here credit is necessary even after the payment is made. (*Works*, vol.2, p.269.)

That is, while the use of 'symbolical money' is based on certain credit, that of 'real money' is not.[12] This is because the latter has its own 'intrinsic value', whereas the former has not and, thus, must rely on one or another sort of 'intrinsic value' in terms of credit. Meanwhile, the value of 'symbolical money' is still affixed to that of 'real money' in the sense that the former is usually expressed in those denominations or units which could be 'realized' in the latter; otherwise, 'it is impossible to fix any determinate standard-worth for the denominations contained in it'.[13] Then, after all, 'symbolical money' is

---

[11] Steuart defined 'real' and 'symbolical money' in the following way:

> By real money, is meant what we call coin, or a modification of the precious metals, which by general agreement among men, and under the authority of a state, carries along with it its own intrinsic value. By symbolical money, I understand what is commonly called credit, or an expedient for keeping accounts of debt and credit between parties, expressed in those denominations of money which are realized in coin. (*Works*, vol.2, p.39.)

In particular, he included under the term 'symbolical money' not only bank notes but also credit in bank, bills, bonds, and merchants' books. Cf. *Works*, vol.2, p.39 ff.

[12] For Steuart's illuminating explanation of credit in general and paper money in particular, see *Works*, vol.2, pp.268-9.

[13] *Works*, vol.2, p.269.

nothing but a 'species of credit', which represents an obligation to pay a certain 'intrinsic value'. And, as a symbol by which credit is reckoned or an expedient for keeping accounts of debt and credit between parties, it performs the office of a means of payment, as well as 'real money'.[14]

1.4 Money as a Store of Value

Finally, this is another function of money assumed in Steuart's political economy as a whole. Apparently, the 'real money' or coin certainly has the function of storing value, as it has its own 'intrinsic value' as a commodity, either as metal or as product which entails some expense for its manufacture on top of that. What about the 'symbolical' or paper money? It seems that, although paper money itself scarcely has any value, it could also serve as a store of value, as long as it is secured on certain 'solid properties', such as land or any precious metal. In fact, according to Steuart, paper money just represents those 'melted-down' 'solid properties' which cannot circulate for themselves, but which preserve the same value during its circulation on their behalf.[15]

> Nothing is so easy as to invent a money which may make land circulate as well as houses, and every other thing which is of a nature to preserve the same value during the time of circulation. Whatever has a value, may change hands for an equivalent, and whenever this value is determined, and cannot vary, it may be made to circulate, as well as a pound of gold or silver made into coin. ... The use of symbolical money is no more than to enable those who have effects, which by their nature cannot circulate (and which, by-the-bye, are the principal cause of inequality), to give, to the full extent of all their worth, an adequate circulating equivalent for the services they demand. (*Works*, vol.2, pp.40-2.)

Thus, paper money holds exactly the same amounts of value as the 'melted-down' properties. Therefore, it could be said that not only the 'real money' or coin transformed from precious metals but also the 'symbolical' or paper money secured on 'solid properties' performs the office of money as a store of value.[16]

---

[14] Thus, in conjunction with the function of money as a means of payment, one of the effects of the use of paper money is the existence of the interest of money. We shall further discuss credit and the interest of money in section 3 of this chapter.

[15] Also see *Works*, vol.2, pp.39-42.

[16] In consequence, the circulation of paper money also vibrates the 'balance of wealth' among individuals within the economy, as that of coin does. Cf. *Works*, vol.2, p.40. This is another effect of the use of paper money, owing to its function as a store of value. It is in addition to the enhancement of output level in the economy, due to its function as a medium of exchange, and the existence of interest, because of its function as a means of payment.

2. COIN AS A PROXY FOR IDEAL MONEY

Despite his rigorous description of the nature of ideal money, Steuart admitted, as a matter of fact, that some sorts or other of 'artificial or material money' had been used in reality.[17]

> From the infancy of the world, at least as far back as our accounts of the transactions of mankind reach, we find they had adopted the precious metals, that is silver and gold, as the common measure of value, and as the adequate equivalent for everything alienable. (*Works*, vol.2, p.278.)

Now, the question is how well this 'artificial or material money' could perform in place of ideal money. Is there any inherent imperfection in the former, which prevents it from performing the office of the latter? Basically, according to Steuart, the problem arises from the difference between its 'price considered as a measure' and its 'price considered as an equivalent for value', whenever money is made of any material substance.[18] As we already mentioned in the previous section, coin made of precious metals has two faces: as money and as a commodity. From this immanent nature of 'material money', result its several 'moral and physical' imperfections. Let us briefly recapitulate them from Steuart's *Inquiry*, and closely examine his discussions of both their consequences and the remedies which he suggested for them. All this is a prerequisite for a complete account of Steuart's theory of money, as it underlies our further analysis.

2.1 The Imperfections of Coin

Two of the most decisive imperfections of coin as a proxy for ideal money are directly related to the fact that the material, of which it is made, itself is a commodity whose value fluctuates, depending on circumstances. First of all, it prevents coin from properly carrying out the function of money as a measure of money.

> ... the substance of which the coin is made, a commodity, which rises and sinks in its value with respect to other commodities, according to the wants, competition, and caprices of mankind. (*Works*, vol.2, p.288.)

Thus, how could anything be measured in terms of a scale which also varies on occasions?

Second, the situation could become even worse, if there are more than one sort of coin, e.g., if both gold and silver coins are used, in the economy.

---

[17] Steuart's description of ideal money was primarily concerned with the function of money as a measure of value, as he thought that this was the principal cause of imperfections of any 'artificial or material money'. (Cf. *Works*, vol.2, pp.270-8.) We shall see soon why it is the case.

[18] *Works*, vol.2, p.274.

> ... the rivalship between the metals, and the perfect equality which is found between all their physical qualities, so far as regards purity, and divisibility, render them so equally well adapted to serve as the common measure of value, that they are universally admitted to pass current as money. What is the consequence of this? ... There is no determinate invariable proportion between their value. ... when they are both taken for measuring the value of other things, the things to be measured, ... without changing their relative proportion between themselves, change however with respect to the denominations of both their measures. (*Works*, vol.2, pp.282-3.)

That is to say, unless the relative value of the different precious metals of which coins are made is kept perpetually invariable, things to be measured may constantly vary in their value, as the relative value changes.

Besides the above two major imperfections, Steuart enumerated those other inconveniences which would accompany the use of coin.[19] They relate to the wearing of coin during its circulation, the difficulty of its exact manufacture, the expense for coinage, and the arbitrary change of its nominal value by the government or authority. Let us move on to Steuart's discussions of what would follow these imperfections and inconveniences of coin.

2.2 The Consequences of the Imperfections of Coin

According to Steuart, the immediate result of those imperfections and inconveniences which any 'material money' is liable to, is the inevitable discrepancy between its actual and nominal value.[20] Corresponding to each

---

[19] See *Works*, vol.2, pp.289-90. In connection with these imperfections and inconveniences of coin, Steuart remarked on some relative advantage and disadvantage of the 'real' (or 'material') and the 'symbolical' money.

> The advantage, therefore, found in putting an intrinsic value into that substance which performs the function of money of account, is compensated by the instability of that intrinsic value; and the advantage obtained by the stability of paper, or symbolical money, is compensated by the defect it commonly has of not being at all times susceptible of realization into solid property, or intrinsic value. (*Works*, vol.2, p.288.)

Thus, the 'real money' is secure but unstable in its value; whereas the 'symbolical money' is insecure but stable in its value. This point reflects that, in Steuart's conception, the former is of the nature of a commodity, while the latter is of a sort of credit.

[20] In fact, as long as the nominal value of coin keeps on a par with its actual value, whatsoever, as a commodity, nothing could be wrong with it as a proxy for ideal money. It would perform all the functions of money perfectly. Upon the variations of the relative value with respect to other commodities, its actual value necessarily deviates from its nominal value. Now, the problem is how to grasp the actual value of coin, in that there is no other scale for value than coin itself. Then, what would happen, if we measure the value of one sort of coin, say, made of gold, by another, say, made of silver? Steuart observed,

> Let us suppose an ox to be worth three thousand pounds weight of wheat, the one and the other to be worth an ounce of gold, and the ounce of gold to be worth exactly fifteen ounces of silver. If the case should happen, that the proportional value between gold and silver should come to be as 14 is to 1, would not the ox, and consequently the wheat, be estimated at less in silver, and more in gold, than formerly? I ask farther, if it would be in the power of any state to prevent this variation in the measure of the value of oxen and wheat, without putting into the unit of their money less silver and more gold than formerly? (*Works*, vol.2, pp.283-4.)

imperfection of coin, as discussed above, let us first discuss briefly how its actual value deviates from its nominal value, and then examine some further effects of this.

First of all, as the price of the precious metals, of which coin is made, fluctuates subject to the demand and supply in their markets, the actual value of the coin also changes accordingly and deviates from its nominal value.[21] Second, when there are more than one sort of precious metals used for coin in the economy, changes in their relative prices give rise to the disparity of the money-unit between different sorts of coins.

> ... let us suppose the proportion to change; that the silver, for example, should rise in its value with regard to gold; will not follow, from that moment, that the unit realized in the silver, will become of more value than the unit realized in the gold coin? (*Works*, vol.2, pp.298-9.)

The 'realization' of different value for the money-unit among different sorts of coins simply reflects that the actual value of either of them deviates from its nominal value. Third and finally, the wearing of coin during circulation, the inaccuracy of its manufacture, and the imposition of coinage, all represent some causes for the discrepancy between its actual and nominal value; whereas the arbitrary manipulation of coin by the authority, as such, leads to the deviation of the nominal value of coin from its actual value by way of either raising or debasing it.[22]

Now, according to Steuart, this discrepancy between the actual and the nominal value of coin, as an immediate result of its intrinsic or extrinsic imperfections, could be categorized in two circumstances: as it were, general and partial.[23] As we look further into what would follow these two circumstances, we shall discuss some eventual and prejudicial consequences of those imperfections of coin.

In the case of a general rise or fall of the actual value of coin relative to its nominal value, there ensues an increase or decrease of the value of the money-unit attached to the coin, as it becomes equivalent to a greater or lesser

---

Thus, as the relative value of different coins with respect to each other changes, the value of other commodities varies, depending on which coin is employed to measure it. With every variation in the actual value of gold coin, the same denomination acquires a different value in silver coin from what it used to do, and *vice versa*. But still it would not be known whose value has changed among them.

[21] We shall closely examine the relation between the value of coin, bullion and other commodities, at the end of this section.

[22] Cf. *Works*, vol.2, pp. 302-7.

[23] The general discrepancy is the case where all the coins in the economy, together, rise or fall in their actual value, relatively to their nominal value: e.g., the general change in the price of bullion, the equal loss of weight after a long time of circulation, the imposition of coinage, and the general raising or debasing of coin by the authority. On the other hand, the partial discrepancy is the case where only part of coins in the economy change in their actual value, relatively to their nominal value: e.g., the change in the relative value of different precious metals, of which the coins are made, the unequal wearing among coins during the circulation, and the manufacture of coins of uneven weight. Cf. *Works*, vol.2, pp. 302-7.

quantity of every other commodity than before. Steuart laid down a firm principle on this point,

> That the value of the money-unit of account is not to be sought for in the statutes and regulations of the mint, but in the actual intrinsic value of that currency in which all obligations are acquitted, and all accounts are kept. (*Works*, vol.2, pp.303-4.)

That is, the money-unit in the economy would naturally change in its value according to the actual value of coin, as the latter in itself is a commodity.[24]

In the case of a partial rise and fall of the actual value of coin relative to its nominal value, on the other hand, those coins which are relatively worth more than the others would be immediately picked up from the circulation and melted down or exported, as they could be sold as bullion at above the value they bear as coin.[25] Moreover, all debtors would choose the other coins, which are worth relatively less, to pay their debts, as they have the option of paying in what they think fit, so far as by law all coins should currently pass as equivalent.[26] Then, eventually, none but those coins which have relatively less actual value would remain in circulation. Bad money drives out good![27] Thereupon, the value of the money-unit would gradually fall, since everything then must be sold and bought for more coins than before.

Meanwhile, every variation in the value of the money-unit would have the effect of benefiting the class of creditors at the expense of that of debtors, or *vice versa*.[28]

---

[24] We shall deal closely with the determination of the value of the money-unit in the economy where some 'material money' is used, later in this section.

[25] Steuart took as an example the case of the British coin in his day. According to him, the proportion between the gold and silver in the coin was found to be as 1 to 15.2, whereas the relative market price between them as bullion in the year of 1759 might be 1 to 14.5; and a great deal of the coins in circulation were worn out and became lighter. As a result, silver coins and relatively heavier coins were melted down into bullion by money-jobbers. Otherwise, they were carried out of the country either to pay the balance of trade or to be sold for foreign bullion. Here, we could note that all this business of money-jobbers was directly related to the dual character of coin, i.e., as money and as a commodity. Steuart himself remarked,

> ... although there be many who look no farther than at the stamp on the coin, there are others whose whole business is to examine its intrinsic worth as a commodity, and to profit of every irregularity in the weight and proportion of the metals. (*Works*, vol.2, p.320.)

Cf. *op.cit.*, vol.2, pp.313-28.

[26] Steuart pointed out that, as another result of the disorder in the British coin, described in the above note, the pound sterling in silver was really no more the standard, since nobody would pay it at the rate of gold to silver as 1 to 15.2, as nobody would be compelled to it. See *Works*, vol.2, pp.313-28.

[27] The result is what is conventionally known as Gresham's law. Marshall (1923) described its substance as follows:

> As when the level surface of the sea falls it is the highest rocks that first stand out, so when there is a gradual fall of the level surface of the currency value of all coins which have the same rating, it is the specie of these that will be the first to be taken to the melting-pot. The best will go first, and then the next best; it is the worst that will remain. (p.60.)

For a further explanation of Gresham's law, including its historical background, see Marshall (1923), pp.60-2. Also cf. *New Palgrave* (1987).

[28] Cf. *Works*, vol.2, pp.307-312.

> ... every *diminution* of the metals contained in the money-unit, must imply a loss to all creditors; and ... in proportion to this loss, those who are debtors must gain. ... On the contrary, whatever *augmentation* is made of the money-unit, such augmentation must be hurtful to debtors, and proportionally advantageous to creditors. (*Works*, vol.2, p.311.)

To conclude, from what has been said so far, we have noted that the imperfections of coin as a proxy for ideal money occasion the deviation of its actual value from its nominal value, which in turn manifests itself in terms of the change of the value of the money-unit in the economy. In particular, the general discrepancy between the two would cause the value of the money-unit either to increase or decrease, depending on which is greater; whereas the partial discrepancy between them would result in the decrease only of the value of the money-unit, as the coins with relatively less value would expel those with relatively more. Then, we are now facing another question: that is, after all this, how is the current value of the money-unit determined in the economy where any sort of 'material money' is used? Is it merely a relative scale for measuring value, which has no determinate value at all? We shall look into this question after we have examined what Steuart suggested for lessening those imperfections and inconveniences of coin, discussed so far.

2.3 The Remedies for the Imperfections of Coin

As we noted earlier, in Steuart's analysis, the first and the most crucial imperfection of coin. i.e., its inappropriateness as a measure of value, directly relates to its dual character as money and as a commodity. No sooner do the metals, of which coin is made, vary in their value according to the supply and demand conditions of the markets, than its actual value also changes, and thus it inevitably fails to serve as a measure of value. As is actually the case with any 'material money', there would be no direct remedy against this imperfection of coin. To obviate or reduce its immediate and longer-term impacts on the economy, instead, the question is how to keep the nominal value of coin on a par with its actual value. In fact, this is what the remedies for this as well as other imperfections and inconveniences of coin are all about in Steuart's analysis. In the meantime, his discussions of the remedies concentrate particularly on the imperfections of coin relating to the variation in the relative price of metals to one another.

Steuart considered the following five alternative expedients for dealing with the problem associated with the change of the relative price of metals.[29]

> First, By considering one only as the standard, and leaving the other to seek its own value, like any other commodity. Secondly, By considering one only as the standard,

[29] Cf. *Works*, vol.2, pp.291-5. Also cf. Marshall's symetallism as a particular suggestion for the problem of a bimetallic currency (Marshall (1923), pp.64-7).

> and fixing the value of the other from time to time by authority, according to the market price of the metals shall vary. Thirdly, By fixing the standard of the unit according to the mean proportion of the metals, attaching it to neither. ... Fourthly, To have two units, and two standards, one of gold, and one of silver, to allow every body to stipulate in either. Fifthly, or last of all, to oblige all debtors to pay, when required, one half in gold and one half in the silver standard. (*Works*, vol.2, pp.291-3.)

The first expedient is a simple monometallic system, in which the standard is affixed to only one of the precious metals in the economy. As it is attached to a certain amount of the metal chosen, the standard appears to be invariable. However, as soon as the relative price of the metal, with respect to other metals and commodities, changes, it would turn out to be either debased or raised. As discussed earlier, this consequence basically results from the dual character of coin as money and as a commodity. In any case, it would not be so harmful as the bimetallism in which the standard is affixed to two different metals at the same time. That is, although the value of the money-unit changes, there would be no melting down or exporting coins, except for some extrinsic imperfections of coin, e.g., wearing, inaccurate manufacture, and government's intervention.[30]

The second one is a slightly modified monometallic system, in which only one metal serves as the standard and the rest of metals are linked to it for their value by the regulation of government. As far as it fixes the relative value of metals in a determinate proportion, this expedient helps keep stable the value of the money-unit. To that extent, it might correct the shortcoming of the simple monometallism. However, as far as the regulation is subject to both time lags and the mutual agreement of both parties of contract, the fixed proportion of the relative value of metals would be liable to deviate from their relative market price. Then, it would face the same inconvenience as a pure single-standard system; i.e., either overvaluation or undervaluation of the money-unit.[31] Why could not the government itself adjust the denomination of the money-unit?

We come to the third expedient: fixing the standard to the mean proportion of different metals. If, upon the variation of their relative value, the money-unit is set in the mean proportion of metals, its value would be less variable than if it is fixed to a certain amount of one or another metal (or both), by

---

[30] Besides, in a monometallic system, sometimes creditors and sometimes debtors would gain, depending on whether the value of the money-unit increases or decreases; whereas, in a bimetallic system, the creditors can never gain, since it always decreases. Cf. *Works*, vol.2, pp.298-302.

[31] Particularly, as both creditors and debtors must agree to adjust their contracts in accordance with the government regulation of the proportion of the relative value of metals, it is not likely to happen, in reality, upon every variation in it without any gain or loss to either of them. This is because, while the standard sticks to a certain amount of the same metal once and for all, both creditors and debtors must revise the sum of money which they lent and borrowed, as the value of the money-unit changes.

virtue of the very nature of mean value.[32] That is, whenever the relative value of metals changes, the mean-proportion standard would be debased or raised to a relatively lesser degree than any other monometallic or bimetallic standard.[33] For this system of mean-proportion standard to work, however, it is crucial to calculate the mean value and to regulate accordingly the denomination of the money-unit at the very moment the relative price of metals changes in the market.[34]

The fourth expedient seems to be a sort of double-standard system, in which two different standards are competing each other. The system could only work if there were no mint par. The exchange rate between different coins is to be determined by the relative price of metals in the market. Although the value of the money-unit in each standard might change as to the market price of the metal on which it is based, there would be no melting down or exporting of coins, except for some extrinsic imperfections of coin, since each standard is using a different unit.[35]

---

32 Steuart illustrated how to calculate the mean proportion of metals, as follows:

> Suppose, then the value of gold to be to the value of silver, as 1 to 14. Then 100 grains of gold will be worth 1400 grains of silver. Suppose, that next year, the proportion shall change, and that it shall come to be as 1 to 15; then 100 grains of gold will be worth 1500 grains of silver. Here then, are two different values in silver for the same quantity of gold. ... Take one half of the sum, or 1450. This I call the mean proportion of the silver. On the other hand, as to gold ... 96 5/6 grs. [is] the mean proportion of the gold. Supposing, therefore, the unit to have been determined at 100 grs.. of gold, and at 1400 grains of silver, as soon as the proportion comes to 15 it must be changed to 96 5/6 grs. of gold, and 1450 grs. of silver. (*Works*, vol.2, pp.292-3.)

To preserve the money-unit exactly in the mean proportion of different metals, it is necessary, upon every variation in their relative value, either to make a new coinage or to alter the denomination of the existing specie.

33 In this context, Steuart advocated using the mean-proportion standard in measuring the value of the 'merchandize which has not varied in its relative value to any thing but to gold and silver' (*Works*, vol.2, p.299). Meanwhile, under this system, paying and being paid in the mean proportion of different metals, neither debtors nor creditors would wholly gain or lose upon any variation in their relative value. By contrast, in the case of monometallism or bimetallism, either of them might gain or lose the whole difference between the actual and the nominal value of coin, whenever the former deviates from the latter. Cf. *Works*, vol.2, p.302.

34 Although he appreciated this system even as the 'introduction of a pure ideal money of account' (*Works*, vol.2, p.300), Steuart explicitly make the crucial point, as follows:

> I have one observation only to make in this place, to wit, that the regulation of fixing the unit by the mean proportion, ought to take place at the instant the standard unit is affixed with exactness both to gold and silver. If it be introduced long after the market proportion between the metals has deviated from the proportion established in the coin, and if the new regulation is made to have a retrospect, with regard to the acquitting of permanent contracts entered into, while the value of the money unit had attached itself to the lower currency, in consequence of the principle above laid down, the restoring the money-unit to that standard where it ought to have remained (to wit, to the mean proportion) is an injury to all debtors who have contracted since the time the proportion of the metals began to vary. (*Works*, vol.2, pp.300-1.)

For detailed explanations of the adoption of the mean proportion of metals as an ideal unit and its usefulness as well as impracticability, see *Works*, vol.2, pp.297-307. As Steuart took the case of the British coin, cf. *Works*, vol.2, pp.329-38 and 414-23.

35 Steuart did not discuss this and the next expedient in detail in his *Inquiry*.

As to the last expedient, Steuart himself regarded it as 'blending the value of the two metals together, so as to make them virtually but one'.[36] That is, if the different metals should always go together in the same proportion in any transaction or contract, there would no problem owing to the variation of their relative price to each other in the market.

Now, let us close our discussion of Steuart's suggestion for the remedies against the imperfections of coin by briefly mentioning the rest of them, mainly those against some extrinsic ones.[37] First of all, as to the wearing of coin during its circulation, Steuart recommended that it be struck in a large solid piece, having as little surface as possible, and to circulate it by weight, rather than by its nominal value, to prevent cutting-off. Second, as to the inexact manufacture of coin, he simply called for the government's strict attention. Third, as to the expense of coinage, Steuart offered no particular solution but noted its implication for foreign trade.[38] Finally, as to the adulteration or change of standard by the government, Steuart warned that it would only hurt the public credit of the government.

2.4 The Value of the Money-unit

We could notice, by now, that all the imperfections and defects of coin, discussed so far, would affect the value of the money-unit in the economy through the discrepancy, either general or partial, between its actual and nominal value. How then does the money-unit actually have its current value? Could it be materialized into a certain determinate amount of anything tangible at all?[39] Here we shall examine Steuart's discussion of how it is determined.

Basically, according to Steuart, the value of the money-unit in the economy, where any sort of 'material money' is used as circulating

---

[36] *Works*, vol.2, p.295.

[37] Cf. *Works*, vol.2, pp.295-6.

[38] We shall discuss more about the expense of coinage in connection with Steuart's analysis of the relative prices of coin, bullion and other commodities at the end of this section of the present chapter, and in connection with the rate of exchange and the balance of payments in the next chapter.

[39] To illustrate this question, let us take the case of the pound sterling in Steuart's time as follows:

> ... there must be found in England two legal pounds sterling, of different values; the one worth 113 grains of gold, the other worth 1718.7 grains of silver. I call them different; because these two portions of the precious metals are of different values all over Europe. (*Works*, vol.2, p.329.)

Nevertheless, it will be proved, as the present discussion goes on, that despite all those imperfections of coin, including the variations in the relative value of different metals, which might render it so ambiguous, there must still be a certain determinate value of the pound sterling in terms of both coins, gold and silver. In any case, conceptually, the current value of the money-unit is different from the actual value of coin itself, though a certain specie is sometimes supposed to represent the money-unit of a country. The one relates to money in general, and the other to every individual coin in particular.

equivalents, is determined in the operations of trade, domestic and foreign, in the following way.[40]

> The operations of trade bring value to an equation, notwithstanding the greatest irregularities possible, and so in fact a pound sterling has acquired a determinate value over all the world by means of foreign exchange. ... Exchange considers the pound sterling as a value determined according to the combination of the values of all the different currencies, in proportion as payments are made in the one or the other; and as debtors generally take care to pay in the worst species they can, it consequently follows, that the value of pound sterling should fall to that of the lowest currency. Were there a sufficient quantity of worn gold and silver to acquit all bills of exchange, the pound sterling would come down to the value of them; but if the new gold be also necessary for this purpose, the value of it must be proportionally greater. All these combinations are liquidated and compensated with another, by the operations of trade and exchange; and the pound sterling, which is so different in itself, becomes thereby, in the eyes of commerce, a determinate unit, subject however to variations, from which it never can be exempted. (*Works*, vol.2, pp.330-1.)

That is, above all, while the coins with the least actual value come to circulate first and gradually others with relatively greater actual value would join later on as the operations of trade and exchange go on, the current value of the money-unit, e.g., that of pound sterling, is to do with the actual value of the coins thus circulating in the economy at a certain point of time. Thus, for instance, the general wearing of coins during circulation definitely diminishes the value of the money-unit in the economy.[41] To be more particular, on Steuart's account, the value of the money-unit is determined, through the operations of trade and exchange, in terms of the average of the actual value of all the coins circulating in the economy. He himself drew a principle concerning the value of the money-unit,

> That in the countries where the money-unit is entirely affixed to the coin, the actual value of it is not according to the legal standard of that coin, but according to the mean proportion of the actual worth of those currencies in which debts are paid. (*Works*, vol.2, p.332.)

Therefore, it might be additionally noted that the quantity of paper money issued in the economy is nothing to do with the value of its money-unit in terms of the material of which coin is made.[42]

---

[40] Steuart's analysis of the current value of the money-unit of one country relative to that of another, i.e., the rate of exchange, will be dealt with in the next chapter.

[41] Even Steuart stated that 'the wearing of one shilling had the effect of contributing towards the diminution of the value of the pound sterling every where' (*Works*, vol.2, p.331).

[42] In this light, Steuart dismissed the proposition that the great quantity of paper money in England tended to diminish the value of the pound sterling in his day.

> The payments, therefore, made in paper money, never can contribute to the regulation of the standard of the pound sterling; it is the specie received in the liquidation of that paper money which alone can contribute to mark the value of the British unit; because it is affixed to nothing else. (*Works*, vol.2, p.332.)

That is, as long as the paper money is affixed to the coin, the value of the money-unit in the economy solely depends on the actual value of the latter. In any case, here Steuart was talking about the value

Now, in practice, how could we perceive the average of the actual value of coins circulation in the economy, as the value of its money-unit? The question does not seem to be too difficult.

> When people buy bullion with current money at a determinate price, this operation, in conjunction with the course of exchange, ought naturally to mark the actual value of the pound sterling with great exactness. (*Works*, vol.2, p.333.)

That is, as coin itself is made of precious metals, the market price of bullion would reflect its actual value; and unless it has more than one value at a time, the former price would represent the reciprocal of the value of the money-unit.[43] Therefore, the market price of bullion might be said to be a 'very tolerable measure' of the current value of the money-unit in the economy where coin made of precious metals circulates as a proxy for ideal money.

---

of the money-unit as the grains of gold and silver which it could command. Meanwhile, in his analysis of the relation between the price level and the quantity of money, both coin and paper, which we shall discuss later in this chapter, he conceived the value of the money-unit as its relative price with respect to commodities other than gold and silver.

43 Let us cite an example from Steuart's *Inquiry*, to show how the market price of bullion marks the pound sterling.

> If therefore the price of standard bullion in the English market, when no demand is found for the exportation of the metals, that is to say, when upon change paper is found for paper, and when merchants, versed in these matters, judge exchange (that is remittances) to be at par, if then, I say, silver bullion cannot be bought at a lower price than 65 pence the ounce, it is evident that this bullion might be bought with 65 pence in shillings, of which 65 might be coined out of the pound troy English standard silver; since 65 pence per ounce implies 65 shillings for the 12 ounces or pound troy. (*Works*, vol.2, p.333.)

To put it another way, if the market price of silver were to stand uniformly at 65 pence per ounce or 65 shillings per pound troy (1 shilling = 12 pence; 1 pound troy = 12 ounce), then the shillings with which it is bought would be coined exactly with 1/65 a pound troy; otherwise, nobody would sell it for or buy it with the bullion. (Here it is assumed that there is no expence [expense] for coinage.) And consequently the pound sterling would be just worth 20 shillings of 65 to the troy. If, in another time, the standard silver bullion should sell for 62 pence per ounce or 62 shillings per pound troy, then 62 shillings would be coined out of a pound troy and the pound sterling would become worth 20 shillings of 62 to the pound troy. From this, therefore, we could notice that the value of the pound sterling would increase or decrease accordingly as the market price of bullion falls or rises, that is, they move reversely to each other. Moreover, once bullion stands at a certain common market price, e.g., so many pence per once, then the value of the pound sterling could be grasped in terms of its weight.

> The pound troy contains 5760 grains. This, according to the standard, is coined into 62 shillings; consequently, every shilling ought to weigh 92.9 grains. Of such shillings it is impossible that ever standard bullion should sell at above 62 pence per ounce, supposing the exportation of them to be free. If therefore such bullion sell for 65 pence, the shillings with which it is bought must weigh no more than 88.64 grains standard silver; that is, they must have lost 4.29 grains, and are reduced to 1/65 of a pound troy. (*Works*, vol.2, p.334.)

That is, the market price of bullion indicates the relative price of money as the bullion serves as a sort *numéraire*; and, at the same time, it indicates the changes in the weight of coin as the bullion could be converted into the coin and *vice versa*.

2.5 The Relative Prices of Coin, Bullion and Commodities

According to Steuart, the prime necessity for money of account lies in reducing all sorts of weights and measures to an 'equation of value', i.e., its role as an 'universal scale of proportional value'. And yet coin as its metallic proxy could not play such a role properly, because of some intrinsic and extrinsic imperfections. In the metallic system, meanwhile, the money-unit would be valued in terms of the average of the actual value of all the pieces of coin, composing its currency. And if there is no imposition of coinage, this value of the money-unit would be the exact reciprocal of the market price of bullion. In what follows, we shall further discuss Steuart's analysis of the relation between coin, bullion and other commodities, particularly their relative prices with respect to each other.

Let us start with Steuart's remark on the price of coin.

> Since gold and silver, then, are commodities like any other thing, the invariable scale of value must measure them as well as every other commodity, and money of account must be considered in no other light, than as a scale for expressing the proportional value of grains of metals, yards of stuffs, pounds of wares, bushels of grain, or gallons of liquors. In this view, when we mention a hundred pounds, it is just as proper to consider this value relatively to the measure of any merchandize, as to the metallic measure of the coin. (*Works*, vol.3, p.3.)

That is to say, coin, as a commodity, has its own price like any other. It depends on the grains or weight of precious metals which each individual coin contains. If no expense is needed for the manufacture of coin, the grains of metals in coin would be worth as much as those in bullion. Therefore, the price of coin would be the same as that of bullion. If it costs anything to manufacture coin, the grains of metals in coin would rise in value, relative to other commodities including bullion, in proportion to the cost of coinage. Then, the price of coin should be that of bullion plus the cost of coinage.[44]

Meanwhile, the price of bullion may vary according to the demand and supply conditions of the market, in general, and the balance of payments, in

---

[44] According to Steuart,

> ... if by the laws and customs of a country, coin be absolutely necessary for buying and selling, this coin must be had; and if there be but one person who can make it, the price he thinks fit to demand for it can be the only measure of the value of fabrication. The grains of the metals, therefore, in the coin, must rise in their proportional value to yard of cloth, and gallons of liquor, in proportion to the cost of coinage, as the pounds of wool and silk must rise in their value in proportion to their manufacture. ... since the value of coin must rise in proportion to every commodity, it must also rise with respect to the metal it is made of, just as wool manufactured rise with respect to wool which is not manufactured. (*Works*, vol.3, p.5.)

See also *Works*, vol.3, pp. 3-4. In addition to the changes in the relative prices of coin, bullion and other commodities, we may here take note of the exclusive privilege of the state in the manufacture of coin. As a result, the state could impose coinage at its own discretion, while people might still believe, upon its authority, that it is the stamp on the coin, rather than the grains of metals in it, which constitutes its value. Cf. *Works*, vol.3, pp.4-5.

particular.[45] What would happen to the relation between the price of coin and that of bullion, if the latter rises as a result of an adverse balance of payments?

> Let us suppose, that for a certain time the country (F) has absolute occasion for the cloth of the country (E). The merchants of (F) who carry on his trade, must send bullion to (E) to pay for this cloth. But the merchants of the country (F) who deal in bullion, perceiving the usefulness of it for this trade, will then raise the price of the 100 of it above the 92 grains in coin (the common market price of bullion before this trade was known), and according to the demand made for the foreign cloth, the bullion will rise in the country (F), until 100 grains of it become exactly worth 100 grains in coin. The bullion can never rise higher; because at this period, the coin itself will be exported for bullion; and the country of (E) will accept of 100 grains in their coin as willingly as in any other form. Nor it ever fall lower than 92 grains; because the mint in the country (F) is always ready to give that price for all the bullion which is brought to coined. (*Works*, vol.3, p.6.)

That is, while the price of bullion rises as its demand increases for the adverse balance of payments, it would make the price of coin fall *relatively* from the sum of both the price of the grains of precious metals, contained in it, and the cost of coinage, as the highest, to the former only, as the lowest. In fact, it fluctuates within that range, depending on the balance of payments in the economy.[46]

As soon as coin has lost the additional price of the cost of coinage by a 'circumstance purely relative to itself as a metal', it exerts an influence on the price of commodities other than bullion. According to Steuart, the variations in the price of any commodity would be constantly determined by the 'proportion of the grains of the metal it costs to acquire the coin which is its price'.

> The consequence, therefore, of this revolution ought to be, that as the merchandize, *bullion*, has got up 8 *per cent.* with regard to the *coin*, and as the price of all merchandize ought to be in proportion to the grains of bullion to which that price amounts, the revolution having annihilated the 8 *per cent.* advance upon the coin, ought to have the same effect with respect to price as if coinage were given gratis. (*Works*, vol.3, p.7.)

---

[45] It is assumed, in Steuart's analysis, that the balance of payments between countries are to be cleared in bullion.

> By the balance of trade, I here constantly understand a certain quantity of bullion sent by one country to another, to pay what they have not be able to compensate by an exchange of their commodities, remittance, &c. (*Works*, vol.3, p.28.)

(In the present context, the 'balance of trade' actually refers to a sort of 'overall balance of payments'.) Thus, the demand for bullion would increase as a result of an adverse balance of payments, as it should then be sent abroad.

[46] Thus, even if we do not assume the non-existence of the cost of coinage as we did in the previous discussion, the value of the money-unit in the economy might be measured as the reciprocal of the market price of bullion whenever there is such great demand for it as to equalize the price of bullion and that of coin. In any case, the value of the money-unit is the reciprocal of the price of coin in terms of the grains of precious metals.

Thus, if the price of bullion rises, then the price of any other commodity ought to rise in the same proportion. On the other hand, if the price of bullion drops as its demand diminishes, for instance, for a favourable or less unfavourable balance of payments, then the price of coin would rise back whereas the price of other commodities would fall relatively.[47]

To sum up, according to Steuart, when the cost of coinage is imposed by the state, the price of bullion would fluctuate within certain limits, depending on its demand and supply, as 'the value of coin, as a metal, prevents bullion from rising higher than its full denomination as money and the mint price of bullion preserves it from falling lower than what the mint is willing to give for it'.[48] While the demand and supply of bullion is mostly influenced by the balance of payments in the economy, its price would regulate that of every other commodity through its relation to coin: that is, upon the unfavourable balance of payments, the price of other commodities would rise up in proportion as the relative price of bullion with respect to coin goes up ; whereas, upon the favourable balance of payments, they would fall in proportion as the relative price of bullion goes down.[49]

---

[47] Cf. *Works*, vol.3, p.7. However, Steuart himself admitted an exceptional case, which 'tends greatly to destroy the due proportion of value between coin and merchandize', in association with the 'consolidation of profits'. That is, in general, 'it is far easier to make a price rise than to make it fall'; in particular, the imposition of the cost of coinage by the state may, on many occasions, have the effect of attaching the price of commodities to the denominations of coin, rather than the grains of bullion. Thus, after the balance of trade is quite 'overturned', rather than 'fluctuating', against the country for a long time, the price of commodities would not fall back later when the balance becomes favourable to it.

> When wars, e.g., occasion a wrong balance to continue for many years against a nation, this keeps coin at par with bullion for a long time. Is it not very natural, that during this time manufactures should estimate their work according to the coin, and not as formerly, according to the bullion? The consequence of this is, that when peace returns, and when coin begins to rise above the price of bullion, the manufactures to stick to the denominations of coin, instead of descending in value (as they ought to do by theory) along with the bullion. (*Works*, vol.3, p.12.)

Steuart added that this might happen particularly to the commodities for home-consumption and those peculiar to the country; otherwise, the force of competition among trading countries would pull down their price. Cf. *Works*, vol.3, pp.10-4.

[48] *Works*, vol.3, p.9.

[49] This is quite a striking contrast with Hume's price-specie-flow mechanism. According to this, if a country has a deficit in the balance of payments, its general price level would fall as a result of the outflow of specie; whereas if it has a surplus, the general price level would rise as a result of the inflow of specie. From Steuart's point of view, Hume's argument seemed to be based on two false premises: the identification of national money with international money, on the one hand, and the quantity theory of money, on the other. For the latter, we shall discuss Steuart's alternative theory of money , price and output later in this chapter, after examining his analysis of the interest of money. As far as the former is concerned, Steuart distinguished coin as national money from bullion as international money for the existence of the cost of coinage imposed by each state. Whenever one goes up, the other goes down in relative value to each other. And the general price level moves in the opposite way around to the value of national money. We shall further discuss Steuart's analysis of the relation of the balance of payments and price level, particularly in conjunction with both the rate of exchange and the level of output, in the next chapter.

3. THE INTEREST OF MONEY

From our previous discussion of the functions of money assumed in Steuart's economics, we notice that basically he considered the circulation of paper or 'symbolical' money to supplement that of coin or 'real money' in the economy when the latter falls short of what is required. As we have already seen, in fact, paper money could perform all the functions of money which coin does; except that of a measure of value, for its value is still affixed to that of coin, so that it could not be a measure of value of its own. According to Steuart, what essentially makes a difference between these two kinds of money is that the one relies on credit, whereas the other does not. Indeed, paper money is nothing but a symbol by which credit is reckoned , or itself a 'species of credit'.[50] In association with the notion of paper money as an expedient for keeping accounts of debt and credit between parties, we will eventually come across Steuart's analysis of interest, which is the very gist of his theory of money. After briefly looking at the relation of credit and interest in his analysis, we shall inquire, in specific terms, into his discussions of the nature of interest and the determination of its rate. Especially, we will direct our attention to the relationship between the interest of money and the 'profit of trade and industry', and try to formalize the simultaneous determination of the rate of interest and output level in a fixed-price model. And finally we shall discuss some implications of all this for a particular question: that is, the legal stipulation of the rate of interest.

3.1 Credit and the Interest of Money

Steuart defined credit in general, as follows:

> Credit is the reasonable expectation entertained by him who fulfils his side of any contract, that the other contracting party will reciprocally make good his engagement. (*Works*, vol.3, p.141.)

That is, in a most broad sense, credit is a 'well established confidence' between the creditor who gave it and the debtor who receives it in what relates to the performance of their engagements. While the 'confidence' is the soul and essence of credit, it must have for its object a 'willingness' and a 'capacity' in the debtor to fulfil his obligation, both of which in their turn depend upon the 'person' himself than upon his 'faculties'.[51] On the basis of this general concept of credit, we may infer that owing or borrowing a certain sum of value or money involves a certain form of credit which relates to some particular 'engagement', i.e., obligation of paying it back in a distant period of

---

[50] In this context, what is meant by paper money comprehends all sorts of bills and notes, including convertible bank notes. Cf. sub-section 1.3 in this chapter.
[51] Cf. *Works*, vol.3, pp.137-46.

time. Now then, the question in hand is whether, at the time of fulfilling the obligation, the debtor should pay the creditor only that exact sum of money, borrowed and lent, or pay some interest as well on top of it. Why? Before addressing ourselves to the task of closely examining Steuart's view on this question, let us consider his historical account of it.

Above all, Steuart ascribed the payment of interest, as the basis of money loan, to the general development of trade and industry in a modern economy.

> The lending of money without interest, was very common before the introduction of trade and industry. Money then was considered as a barren stock, incapable of producing fruit; and whenever the quantity of it, in any country, exceeded the uses of circulation, the remainder was locked up in treasures: in which case, the exacting of interest for it appeared unreasonable. Things are now changed: no money is ever locked up; and borrowed, the regular payment of interest for it, is as essential to the obtaining of credit, as the confidence of being repaid the capital. (*Works*, vol.3, pp.146-7.)

That is, before trade and industry were established in the economy, there was not much need for money in circulation and consequently a great amount of coin was actually 'locked up'. As coin far exceeded all its use, so paper money based on credit was superfluous. Therefore, it was not so common in those days for creditors to ask some interest for lending money. Upon the development of trade and industry, however, there has been more and more need for money in circulation. As a result, whenever the amount of coin existing in the economy could not meet its demand, one or another sort of paper money had to be introduced. Therefore, after a certain stage in the development of trade and industry, there is always found such excess demand for coin that those who lend it might just as well claim some interest on their loan to those who borrow it. Thus, it cannot be borrowed without any premium or price being given for the loan. According to Steuart, this premium or price for loan is the interest of money.

Furthermore, as money may not be lent without interest, it now becomes an essential requisite for credit, which underpins the whole system of trade and industry in the modern economy.[52]

> While people borrowed in order only to procure a circulating equivalent for providing their necessaries, until they could have time to dispose of their effects; and while there was seldom any certain profit to be made by the use of the money borrowed, as now, by turning it into trade, it was very natural to consider the lender in an unfavourable light; because it was supposed that his money, had it not been lent, must have remained locked up in his coffers. But at present, when we see so many people employed in providing stores of necessaries for others, which, without money, cannot be done; were the loan upon interest forbidden, it would have the effect of locking up the very instrument (money) which is necessary for supplying the wants of society.

[52] From the passage quoted, we may notice that, according to Steuart, there are two kinds of money demand, i.e., for consumption and for production. We shall fully examine this later on.

> The loan, therefore, upon interest, as society now stands composed, is established, not in favourable of lenders, but of the whole community. (*Works*, vol.3, p.153.)

Thus, without interest, credit would no longer exist and, therefore, trade and industry would become suffocated for the lack of circulating equivalents. Consequently, there would be neither profit for those who carry out trade and industry nor benefit for the whole society.[53] Let us now further explore the nature of interest in Steuart's analysis.

3.2 The Interest of Money as an Opportunity Cost

In any transaction, one or another means of payment is necessary for balancing accounts between contracting parties. As we have already seen, both kinds of money, coin and paper money, could be used as such a means of payment. According to Steuart, however, they have different effects when performing that function of money. That is, the payment made by means of coin does not leave any further action; whereas the one made by paper money does. For the former has its own 'intrinsic value', whereas the latter is merely a 'species of credit'. In the meantime, no sooner have these two kinds of money entered into circulation, than they become circulating equivalents, i.e., money as a medium of exchange. Thus, both of them could serve as a means of payment and as a medium of exchange.[54]

In proportion to trade and industry actually operating in an economy, there should be a certain amount of circulating equivalents. That is, as the level of output goes up or down, the quantity of money as a medium of exchange should increase or decrease, accordingly. Is there anything which guarantees the quantity of money already existing in the economy to supply no more and no less than that of the money required for trade and industry? To quote Steuart,

---

[53] As alluded to in the above passage, Steuart related the interest of money to the 'profit of trade and industry'. We shall further discuss this point later. Meanwhile, for more about Steuart's historical account of the relation between credit and interest, see *Works*, vol.3, pp.151-4.

[54] In fact, as Steuart pointed out, paper money supplements coin as a medium of exchange at the very moment it is issued.

> The utility of this kind of credit, or paper-money, is principally at the instant of its entering into circulation; because it is then only that it supplies the want of real specie; and by this invention the desire to consume creates, as it were, the circulating equivalent, without which the alienation of the produce of industry would not have taken place; consequently, the industry itself would have suffered a check. But in the after-circulation of this paper-money from hand to hand, this utility comes to cease; because the subsequent consumer, who has another man's paper to give in exchange, is already provided with a circulating equivalent, and therefore, were it not for the wearing of the specie, or difficulty of procuring of it, it is quite indifferent both to the state, as well as to circulation, whether this paper continue to pass current, or whether it be taken up, and realized by the debtor, and gold and silver be made to circulate in its place. (*Works*, vol.2, p.60.)

Thus, once it is issued, paper money is not different from coin, as a medium of exchange. Cf. section 1 in this chapter.

> ... the current money of a country is always in proportion to the trade, industry, consumption, and alienation, which regularly take place in it; and when it happens that the money already in the country is not sufficient for carrying on these purposes, a part of the solid property, equal to the deficiency, may be melted down (we have called it) and made to circulate in paper: that as soon again as this paper augments beyond this proportion, a part of what was before in circulation, must return upon the debtor in the paper, and be realized anew. (*Works*, vol.3, p.147.)

That is to say, if the quantity of money existing is less than the one required, then either the coins previously 'locked up' would come out to circulate (or some bullion would be brought to the mint to be coined) or additional paper money would be issued, being secured on 'solid properties', through its function as a means of payment. On the other hand, if the former is more than the latter, then the excessive quantity of money, over and above what is necessary for the circulation, must be 'stagnating' or 'regorging', as it is 'superfluous' for a means of payment, and, sooner or later, will be 'realized'. By the 'realization' of money, Steuart meant 'tuning it into some shape whereby it may produce an income' or the 'purchase of some kind of income with it'. The 'realization' could be possible for both kinds of money, because they commonly serve as a store of value: in the case of coin, it may be converted into bullion, whereas, in the case of paper money, the process of 'realization' would involve the payment of interest by the debtors to the creditors presented in the paper, unless it is paid up in coin.[55] Thus, while the paper money represents a 'specie of credit', the interest paid by the debtors to the creditors would amount to a sort of opportunity cost of what the former owe the latter.

> Money, while it is employed in circulation, can carry no interest; the moment it is lies idle to one, were it but for a day, it may be worth interest to another, who willingly pays for the use of it, when he has occasion either to buy what he wants, or to pay what he owes. (*Works*, vol.4, p.321.)

To put it another way, according to Steuart, while the quantity of money as a means of payment and that of money as a medium of exchange should come to be equal by way of issuing paper money or its 'realization' in the economy, the latter process would entail the payment of interest by the issuers of paper money to its receivers for the opportunity cost of the money loan.

Then, from the conception of the interest of money as an opportunity cost, it naturally follows that its rate presents itself as the price of money, borrowed and lent. Thus, in Steuart's analysis, the actual rate of interest is to be determined by the demand and supply in the credit market, a market for borrowing and lending money.

> ... at all times, there is in every state a certain number of persons who have occasion to borrow money, and a certain number of persons who desire to lend: there is also a

[55] Cf. *Works*, vol.3, pp.147-9 and vol.4, pp.320-1.

> certain sum of money demanded by the borrowers, and a certain sum of money to be lent. The borrowers desire to fix the interest as low they can; the lenders seek, from a like principle of self-interest, to carry the rate of it as high as they can. From this combination of interests arises a double competition, which fluctuates between the two parties. If more be demanded to be borrowed, than there is found to be lent, the competition will take place among the borrowers. Such among them as have the most pressing occasion for money, will offer the highest interest, and will be preferred. If, on the other hand, the money to be lent exceed the demand of the borrowers, the competition will be upon the other side. Such of the lenders, as have the most pressing occasion to draw an interest for their money, will offer it at the lowest interest, and this offer will be accepted. (*Works*, vol.3, pp.154-5.)

Just like the price of other commodities, the rate of interest is fixed by the operation of 'double competition', with the borrowers and the lenders of money being on either side. That is, if more money is demanded for borrowing than offered for lending, the competition among the borrowers brings up the rate of interest; whereas, if more money is offered than demanded, the competition among the lenders brings down the rate of interest.[56]

3.3 The Interest of Money and the 'Profit of Trade and Industry'

Now, if the interest of money is an opportunity cost of its loan, where does the opportunity cost come from? Apparently, it depends on all possible uses of money, so the actual rate of interest is to be determined by the demand for and the supply of money loans. According to Steuart, however, it depends on the 'profit of trade and industry' in the last resort.[57] This point will become clear if we examine his discussion of the relation between the rate of interest, determined in the credit or money-loan market, and that of profit, regulated by the 'trade and industry' in the commodity market.

---

[56] Steuart pointed out a similarity and a difference between the price of money and that of any other commodity. According to him, on the one hand, as the one should be regulated by the 'principle of demand and competition' so as to be 'just and adequate', 'the only thing which can fix a standard for it is frequent and familiar alienation', as is the case with the other. On the other hand, 'the price of money, i.e., the rate of interest, is susceptible of a far greater stability and uniformity than the price of any other thing', since money is of general use, rather than of particular use, and of the same quality, rather than of different quality. See *Works*, vol.3, pp.155-6.

[57] Steuart's notion of 'profit of (or upon) trade and industry' is different from that of 'profit upon capital' appearing in the later literature. It is actually equivalent to another notion of his used in a different context, i.e., the 'profit upon alienation'. Cf. sub-section 3.1, Ch.3 above. Meanwhile, here and there in his *Inquiry*, we could find the concept of capital as either monetary or physical means of production. For instance, cf. *Works*, vol.1, pp.224-5 and pp.396-7, and vol.2, p.111. And sometimes he also assumed a sort of profit upon capital advanced in the production process. For instance, cf. *Works*, vol.2, p.76. Despite the fact that Steuart seems to be well aware of the role of capital in the production process and to have actually in his mind a clear notion of profit upon capital, however, it is the analytical focus of his economics which differentiates it from that of those others who categorized the 'profit upon capital' as a distinct income of its own, and who placed much emphasis on the accumulation of capital for the long-run growth of the economy. Cf. our discussions of his analysis of value and distribution in Ch.3 above, and that of growth and trade in Ch.5 above; particularly, the appendices to the respective chapters.

Above all, he proposed a hypothetical principle concerning the relation between the two rates.

> Were the interests of trade and industry so exactly established, as to produce the same profit on every branch of them, the money borrowed for carrying them on, would naturally be taken at the same rate [on every branch of them]. (*Works*, vol.3, p.158; brackets added.)

That is, hypothetically, the interest rate should be in proportion to a uniform rate of 'profit upon trade and industry' among all their different branches in the economy. He went on to discuss some obstacles to this proportional relation between them. On the one hand, for instance, the actual rates of profit might be different among different branches of trade and industry in the economy, so there might be different rates of interest in proportion to them.

> ... some branches afford more, some less profit. In proportion, therefore, to the advantages to be reaped from borrowed money, the borrowers may offer more or less for the use of it. (*Works*, vol.3, p.158.)

On the other hand, while there are two sorts of people who demand to borrow money, those who borrow 'to dissipate' might be relatively less sensitive to the rate of interest, than those who borrow 'to profit'.[58]

> Besides the class of men who borrow *in order to profit* by the loan, there is another class, who borrow *in order to dissipate*. The first class never can offer an interest which exceeds the proportion of their gains: the second class, finding nothing but want of credit to limit their expense, become a prey of usurers. (*Works*, vol.3, p.158; original italics.)

Thus, the demand for money loans 'to profit' would equilibrate the proportional relation between the rate of interest and that of profit, whereas the demand for money loans 'to dissipate' would disturb it.

Nevertheless, Steuart held that there are still some analytical or practical grounds which may allow us to suppose a certain proportional relation between the rate of interest and that of profit. Let us examine them in turn, corresponding to those obstacles discussed above. First, for the divergence of profit rates among different branches of trade and industry, Steuart clearly noted the 'average' concept.

> The profit on trade would strike an average among the industrious classes; and this average would fall and rise, in proportion to the flourishing or decay of commerce. (*Works*, vol.3, p.158.)

---

[58] In other words, according to Steuart, people demand to borrow money for two purposes, i.e., either to produce or to consume. From this, it may be postulated that in a macroeconomic sense there are two sorts of demand for money: one for production and the other for consumption. And, as explicitly described in the passage quoted, they are different in nature: that is, the one is sensitive to the rate of interest and the other insensitive. We shall return to this point, later when we try to set up a formal model of Steuart's theory of money in the next section.

Thus, while different rates of profit among different branches of trade and industry would converge into an average of them, the rate of interest would be proportional to it. Second, as to that sort of demand for money loans which is insensitive to the rate of interest, Steuart suggested what might be called a wealth effect, or even a demonstration effect, which would keep the rate of interest from being too high or too low as a result of that.

> ... the rise of interest has so much the effect of depreciating the value of every species of solid property, that spendthrifts are quickly stripped of it, by the growing accumulation of that canker worm, interest; their ruin terrifies many from falling into the hands of the other class, who spend less than their income; these new possessors introduce, by their example, a more frugal set of manners. (*Works*, vol.3, p.159.)

Thus, as the interest rate goes up or down, the wealth of those who borrow money 'to dissipate' would diminish or increase in its relative value with respect to money. Therefore in so far as their demand for money loans would be, more or less, stabilized, it could not disturb too much the centripetal force toward the proportional relation between the rate of interest and that of profit.[59]

To sum up, according to Steuart, while the rate of interest on money loans would be, on average, in proportion to that of 'profit upon trade and industry', the proportional relation might be disturbed mainly by two factors. One is the lack of competition in the commodity market: that is, the commodity market is not always so competitive that it could bring about a uniform rate of profit among different branches of trade and industry in the economy. The other is the existence of some demand for loans which is insensitive to the rate of interest in the credit market: that is, money is borrowed not only for production but also for consumption. Nevertheless, as long as there is any equilibration in the proportional relation between the rate of interest and that of profit, the interest of money could be said to rest on the 'profit upon trade and industry'. In this sense, the latter is the only source of opportunity cost of the former.

---

[59] In addition, Steuart took into account the effect of a direct control of credit by the state, as it would help to keep the rate of interest stable.

> The spendthrifts must have credit; that is, they must have it in their power to repay interest what they have borrowed: any impediment to credit, will have the effect either of diminishing the demand for money and consequently of lowering the rate of interest, or of introducing unlawful usury. If we suppose the rate of interest well determined, and usury prevented by a regular execution of good laws, it is very certain, that a statesman by hurting the credit of extravagant people, will keep the rate of interest within due bounds. (*Works*, vol.3, p.161.)

We will discuss Steuart's treatment of usury in conjunction with the legal rate of interest, later in the last section of this chapter.

3.4 The Rate of Interest, Production and Consumption: A Fixed-price Model of their Simultaneous Determination

From the discussions so far in this section, we may realize that, according to Steuart, the rate of interest is determined by the demand for and the supply of money loans in the credit market, as their price. There are two sorts of demand for money loans, according to their uses: namely, one for production and the other for consumption. It is the demand for money loans for the use of production which eventually accounts for some proportional relation between the rate of interest and that of profit. While production and consumption constitute the supply and the demand side of the commodity market, respectively, the determination of the rate of profit has to do with that of the 'current price' of commodities in that market.[60] Therefore, the money and the commodity market are so inseparably interrelated that they should be equilibrated at the same time. In this last part our discussion of Steuart's analysis of the interest of money, we shall present a formal model of the simultaneous determination of the rate of interest and the level of output in the economy.[61]

Before we go any further, we need to clarify what is meant by the 'commodity' and 'money' markets in this context. As we suppose 'production' to comprehend all sorts of 'trade and industry', including not only the production of corporeal commodities but also the performance of incorporeal services and other mercantile business, we may simply call all these things 'commodities'. They are bought and sold in the 'commodity' market. On the other hand, we generalize Steuart's discussion of the two uses of demand for money loans, i.e., for production and for consumption, to assume that there are correspondingly two sorts of demand for money, *not only loans but also balances*: that is, the demand for money to produce and the demand for money to consume. While these two uses of money form the demand side of what is called the 'money' market, the actual circulation of money in the economy represents its supply side.

We shall examine both commodity and money markets to find out their equilibrium conditions in relation to the rate of interest and the level of output in the economy. Let us start with the commodity market. There are two components of the 'effectual demand' for commodities in the economy: the consumption of consumer goods and the use of producer goods in the production process. According to Steuart, the one depends on the 'propensity

---

60 Cf. Ch.3 above.

61 For the sake of the simplicity of the analysis, we shall adopt a fixed-price model. Therefore, all the variables of quantity appearing here in this sub-section are supposed to be expressed in value terms, on the assumption that price level is given. When we attempt to synthesize, in the next section, all that has been said so far about Steuart's theories of value, distribution, output and money, we shall allow it to be flexible, introducing some other variables and relations.

of the rich to consume'; whereas the other depends on the 'disposition of the poor to be industrious'.[62] Here in this model, we simply assume the proportion between them to be given as a certain ratio in the economy as whole. Thus,[63]

$$D_f = C + U \tag{1}$$

$$C = p_c\, D_f \ \ (\text{or } U = d_p\, D_f) \tag{2}$$

where D_f: amount of 'effectual demand'
C: amount of the consumption of consumer goods
U: amount of the use of producer goods
p_c: 'propensity to consume' (given)
(or d_p: 'disposition to produce' (given): $p_c + d_p = 1$).

Meanwhile, the level of output is determined by the 'effectual demand' in the economy.[64] Thus,

$$Y = D_f \tag{3}$$

where Y: level of output.

Next, let us turn to the money market. There are two sorts of demand for money: i.e., to consume and to produce. The demand for money to consume is insensitive to the rate of interest, but must be a positive relation with the amount of consumption. It could be assumed that the one is proportional to the other.[65] Thus,

$$L_c = k\, C \tag{4}$$

---

[62] Cf. *Works*, vol.2, p.53.

[63] We may note that the distinction between the consumer goods and the producer goods might enable us to introduce the saving-investment relation into our model. That is, if we regard the use of producer goods as investment and further separate savings from the flow of national income, then we would eventually embrace the saving-investment relation in the present model. For instance, if we assume that some part of income is to be spent for consumption and the rest is being saved, then we have an additional equation, as follows:

$$Y = C + S$$

where S: amount of savings.

From this and equations (1) and (3), we could derive the equilibrium condition of savings and investment, i.e., S = U. (Then, Steuart's notions of the 'propensity to consume' and the 'disposition to produce' out of the total 'effectual demand' could be seen as equivalent to those of the 'propensity to consume' and 'propensity to save' out of national income in Keynes's analysis.) Apart from this, as we have already noticed, there are some other parallels in their respective monetary analyses: e.g., two sorts of demand for money, one sensitive and the other insensitive to the rate of interest, and two components of 'effectual demand' or 'effective demand', consumption and investment. As far as the saving-investment relation is concerned, however, Steuart did not explicitly describe it either in his analysis of output or that of money; though it seems not too difficult to see an anticipation of Keynes's monetary analysis of output through a rational reconstruction of Steuart's.

[64] Cf. the previous discussion of Steuart's theory of output in Ch.4 above.

[65] Steuart described the proportional relation between them as the 'proportion of circulating money with respect to the desires of consumers to consume'. Cf. *Works*, vol.2, p.53.

where L_c: demand for money to consume
k: constant.

While those who demand money to produce seek the gains from the difference between the 'profit of trade and industry' and the interest of money, they need the money, either self owned or borrowed, mainly for the working capital in the production process. As we assume the wages of labour to be paid at the end of production process, the money goes only to what is paid for producer goods. Therefore, we may postulate that the greater difference between the rate of 'profit' and that of interest, the more use of producer goods, and the greater demand for money. Thus,

$$U = U(\bar{r} - I), \quad U' > 0 \tag{5}$$

$$L_y = L_y(U), \quad L_y' > 0 \tag{6}$$

where E: amount of the employment of goods for production
$\bar{r}$: rate of profit (given)[66]
i: rate of interest
L_y: demand for money to produce.

In sum, the total demand for money in the economy consists of the consumers' and producers' demand. Thus,[67]

$$M_d = L_c + L_y \tag{7}$$

where M_d: total demand for money.

Meanwhile, the total supply of money in the economy has two sources: i.e., from coin made of precious metals or from paper money secured on 'solid properties'. The one is confined to the whole amount of the precious metals in the economy; whereas the other is to the whole value of the 'solid properties'. When the one alone falls short of the 'circulating equivalents' required for all transactions in the economy, the other supplements its shortage by way of 'melting down' the 'solid properties', subject to the state of credit of the economy. Thus,

$$M_s = \overline{M}_1 + M_2(\alpha) \tag{8}$$

where M_s: total supply of money
$\overline{M}_1$: quantity of coin (given)[68]

---

[66] As we mentioned before, Steuart's notion of profit is based on the 'trade and industry' in a broad sense, rather than on the capital advanced. As he called it the 'profit upon alienation' on other occasions, therefore, its rate is to be dependent on the contingent circumstances of the commodity market. Here, we assume the rate of profit to be given exogenously, along with the price of commodities.

[67] While the demand for money to consume is for the consumers' transactions, the demand for money to produce is for the producers' working capital. Thus, both sorts of demand for money, either balances or loans, could be added to give us the total demand for money in the economy.

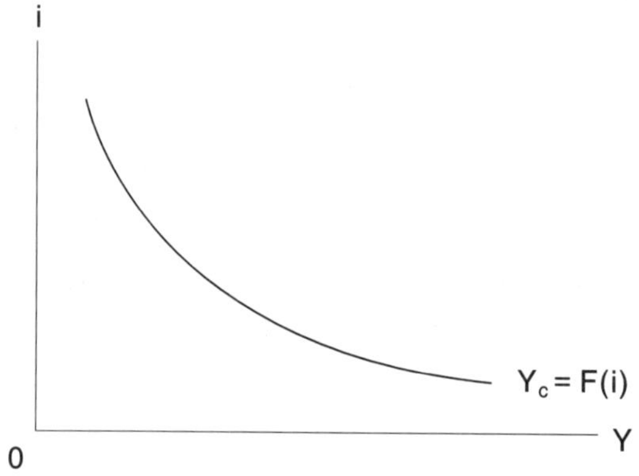

Figure 6.1 Commodity market

M_2: quantity of paper money
α: parameter of the state of credit

And, the total demand for money should be equal to the total supply of money in the economy. Thus,

$$M_d = M_s. \tag{9}$$

From equations (1) - (9), we could obtain all the equilibrium values of 9 unknowns, including both the equilibrium rate of interest and the equilibrium level of output in the economy.

To visualize the equilibrium situation in the co-ordinates of the rate of interest and the level of output, let us specify the equilibrium conditions of both commodity and money markets. That is, from the commodity market equilibrium condition, we have

$$Y = D_f \qquad \text{(from 3)}$$
$$= C + U \qquad \text{(from 1)}$$
$$= p_c D_f + U(\bar{r} - i); \qquad \text{(from 2 and 5)}$$

therefore,

$$Y_c = F(i),\ F' < 0. \tag{10}$$

We may depict the relation between the level of output and the rate of interest in the commodity market, in Figure 6.1.

[68] As our model is based on a closed economy and no conversion between coin and bullion is taken into account, the quantity of coin in the economy could be assumed to be given as a fixed quantity.

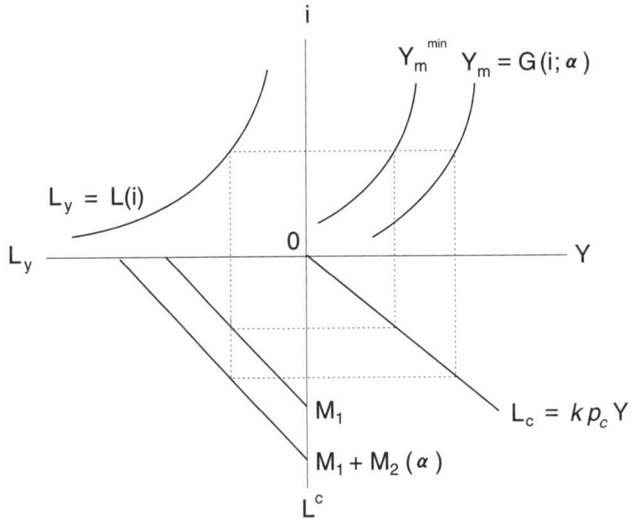

Figure 6.2 Money market

On the other hand, from the money market equilibrium condition, we have

$$M_s = M_d \qquad \text{(from 9)}$$

$$\overline{M}_1 + M_2(\alpha) = L_c + L_y \qquad \text{(from 7 and 8)}$$

$$= k\,C + L_y(U) \qquad \text{(from 4 and 6)}$$

$$= k\,p_c\,Y + L_y(U(\bar{r} - i)); \qquad \text{(from 2, 3 and 5)}$$

therefore,

$$Y_m = G(i;\,\alpha),\ \ G' > 0. \qquad (11)$$

We may also depict the above relation between the level of output and the rate of interest in the money market, in Figure 6.2.[69]

At last, we can obtain the equilibrium values for the level of output and the rate of interest from equations (10) and (11), and find the equilibrium point in the co-ordinates of the two variables by putting Figure 6.1 and Figure 6.2 together (see Figure 6.3). From this simple fixed-price model of Steuart's

---

[69] From equations (5) and (6), we could get the relation between the demand for money to produce and the rate of interest, shown in the north-west quadrant of the above diagram: that is, $L_y = L(i)$, $L' < 0$. The one is negatively related to the other, for those who demand money for production purposes must be fully sensible to the rate of interest in comparison with that of profit, which we assume to be given exogenously. Meanwhile, curve Y_m in the north-east quadrant must be subject to the state of credit in the economy (α).

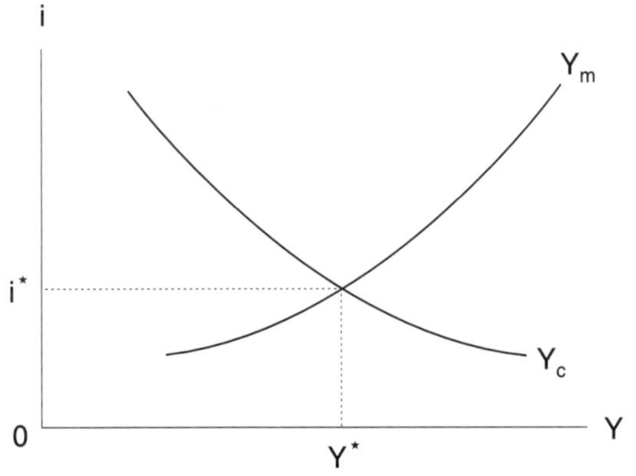

Figure 6.3 The simultaneous equilibrium of commodity and money markets

analysis of money, it becomes obvious that, while the rate of interest, as the price of money, adjusts itself in the money market, it takes part in determining the level of output in the commodity market; after all, both markets should be equilibrated at the same time.[70]

Is this system stable enough? In other words, is the equilibrium situation self-restoring in the above model, whenever it is disturbed for some reason? For instance, Steuart himself suggested how it might work when the rate of interest is set too high.

> ... when trade and industry flourish, and when a monied [moneyed] interest is formed, in consequence of the melting down of solid property, and still more in consequence of a State's contracting great debts; were the money-lenders to attempt to raise the rate of interest to the standard of spendthrift, the demands of trade, &c. would soon be cut off: the stagnation would then swell so fast in their hands, that it would in a manner choke them, and in a little time interest would fall to nothing. Whereas by contenting themselves with the standard of trade, the largest supplies (provided for the borrowers) easily find a vent, without raising the rate of interest so high as to be hurtful to any interest within the state. (*Works*, vol.3, p.160.)

That is to say, if the rate of interest is too high, then not many entrepreneurs would demand money for their production. It occasions a fall in the rate of interest in the money market. As a result, the more use of producer goods, the greater the 'effectual demand', and the higher the level of output in the

[70] We shall further elaborate on this point in a flexible-price model later on. In any case, the result is pretty similar to the IS-LM analysis, originally introduced by Hicks (1937). That is, the curve denoting relation between the level of output and the rate of interest in the commodity market (Y^c) bears some analogy with IS curve, while the one in the money market (Y^m) does so with LM curve. In the present model of Steuart's monetary analysis, however, there is no explicit saving-investment relation, and we need neither the 'schedule of the marginal efficiency of capital' in the commodity market nor 'liquidity-preference schedule' in the money market. Cf. note 63 above.

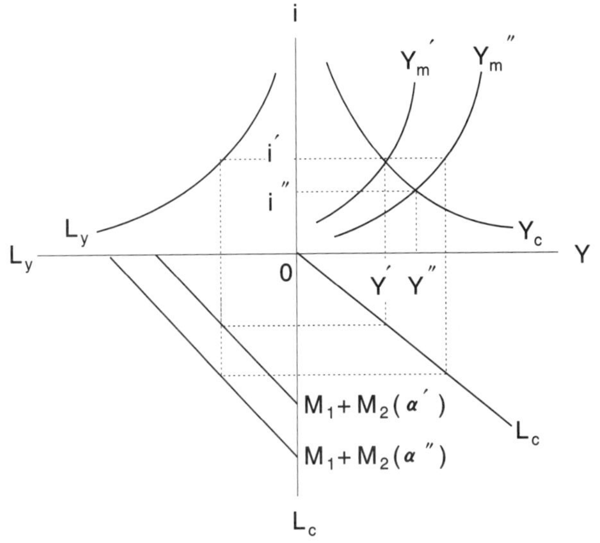

Figure 6.4 The effects of the increase of paper Money

commodity market. As the level of output gradually increases, the falling of the rate of interest would slow down in the money market. After all, sooner or later, the equilibrium would be restored at a lower rate of interest.

Finally, we shall close the present discussion with the application of the above model to Steuart's argument for the wide use of paper money based on a good state of credit in the economy.[71] The argument could be summarized as follows (cf. Figure 6.4). If credit is better established ($\alpha' < \alpha''$) in the economy, the circulation of paper money could increase ($M_2(\alpha') < M_2(\alpha'')$). As the total supply of money consequently expands (as shown in the south-west quadrant of the above diagram), the level of output at each rate of interest could increase ($Y_m' \rightarrow Y_m''$) in the money market. Then, after a process of

[71] While Steuart was advocating paper money as a 'good expedient to accelerate circulation and to give birth to industry', he accused a poor state of credit in the economy of impeding the use of paper money and, thereby, the progress of its 'trade and industry'.

> The greatest of all obstacles to industry in its infancy, is the general want of credit on both sides. The consumers having no circulating value, the difficulty of liquidating what they owe by the alienation of their lands, prevents their getting credit; and the many examples of industrious people giving way, on account of bad payments, discourages others from assisting them in the beginning of their undertaking. (*Works*, vol.2, p.59.)

For what Steuart said about the effect of the circulation of paper money on the level of output in the economy, see *Works*, vol.2, pp.40-1, pp.53-66 and *passim*. Also cf. our previous discussion of paper money in this chapter.

adjustment, the economy would settle down in a new equilibrium situation (E′ → E″). In the end, as a result of the increase in the circulation of paper money, the rate of interest would fall (i′ < i″), whereas the level of output would increase (Y′ < Y″).

3.5 The Legal Rate of Interest

Up to this point, we have seen how the rate of interest, as the price of money, is determined by its demand and supply: particularly, through a fixed-price model, we have observed how both money and commodity markets could reach equilibrium in the process of the determination of interest rate. Nevertheless, there still might be those who demand money most urgently and borrow it at a higher interest rate than usual. This accounts for the existence of usury, which has been rather common even in modern days. Meanwhile, keeping the interest rate low has been regarded as most essential to 'trade and industry', in general, and foreign trade, in particular; for it would help induce more production in the economy and bear some comparative advantage for its exports in the international market.[72] Exactly in these two senses, i.e., against usury and for 'trade and industry', Steuart discussed, in his *Inquiry*, various methods of bringing down the rate of interest in the economy, especially, the stipulation of a certain rate by law.[73] In what follows, we shall examine his discussions of the legal rate of interest, and, in particular, some of its

---

[72] Steuart remarked,

> ... low rate of interest is the soul of trade; the most active principle for promoting industry, and the improvement of land; and a requisite, without which it is hardly possible that foreign commerce can be no longer supported. (*Works*, vol.3, p.173.)

To fully inquire into his argument for the low rate of interest, we may have to be rather more realistic than discussing it in a fixed-price model. That is to say, as far as the price level of an economy goes, we need to discuss it in a flexible-price model, in which the price level, as well as the rate of interest, functions as an intermediary variable in both money and commodity markets. Furthermore, as far as the balance of trade goes, we must consider the rate of exchange as well. As we move on, we shall gradually take these variables into account and extend our present model later on in the next section and in the next chapter.

[73] For some methods of lowering the rate of interest in the economy, other than the legal rate of interest, see *Works*, vol.3, pp.161-81. Meanwhile, on the state's regulations of interest rate in general Steuart observed,

> ... hitherto all regulations made concerning interest, have been calculated either for bringing it down, or for preventing its rise. The distress which may come upon a state, by its falling too law, is a phaenomenon which has not yet manifested itself in any modern state, by any symptom I can at present recollect. (*Works*, vol.3, p.163.)

He denied the existence of what is called the 'liquidity trap', i.e., a sort of disequilibrium caused by too low a rate of interest in the economy. As far as Steuart was concerned, the rate of interest could not be too low to result in a low level of output in the economy. Rather, according to him, it is usually occasioned by the lack of 'effectual demand' upon the imbalance between industries. (Cf. Ch.4, above.) Here comes the logic behind his advocacy for the government's active public finance. (Cf. Ch.8, particularly section 3, below.)

consequences, utilizing the analytical device which we developed in the last sub-section.

Let us start with Steuart's explanation of the relation between the rate of interest, as the price of money, and the price of stocks, e.g., treasury bonds, which yield a certain percentage of their face value to their holders.

> The current value of money, I think, is best to be determined by the price of stocks. If a 4 *per cent.* sells at par, money may be said to be then at 4 *per cent.* If the same stock fall to 89, then the value of money rises to near 4 1/2: if the same stock rise to 114, then the value of money falls to about 3 1/2; and so in proportion. According, therefore, as stock is found to rise, the price of money falls, and *vice versa.* (*Works*, vol.3, p.168.)

Thus, there is an inverse relation between the current rate of interest and the market price of stocks.[74] Now, if the government stipulates the rate of interest at a lower level than the current market rate, then the creditors who lend money would withdraw their loans in order to buy stocks which yield relatively more returns. Consequently, as the demand for stocks is increasing, their price is rising. The price of stocks would continue to rise right up to the point where their internal rate of return becomes equal to the legal rate of interest, so that the inverse relation between the current rate of interest and the price of stocks could be restored. Meanwhile, as a result of the withdrawal of money loans, the total supply of money diminishes proportionally in the economy.[75] On this diminution of money supply, there would definitely follow an abrupt decrease in the amount of 'effective demand' in the economy for the want of 'circulating equivalents', as long as the current rate of interest is stipulated by law, rather than determined in the money market. Then, the decrease in the level of output would be inevitable. Steuart illustrated with an example all these chain reactions to the legal rate of interest, as follows:

> Suppose, then, the price of money to be at 4 per cent. and that government should pass a law, forbidding any man to lend at above 3 per cent., what would be the consequence? ... Would not the consequence be, that the creditors of private people

---

[74] If we suppose the market price of stock to be equal to the total present value of its annual return,

$$P_s = \overline{R}/(1 + i) + \overline{R}/(1 + i)^2 + \overline{R}/(1 + i)^3 + \ldots\ldots = \overline{R}/i$$

where P_s: market price of stock
$\overline{R}$: annual return of stock (given).

Therefore, $i = \overline{R}/P_s$. That is, the price of money, i.e., the rate of interest, is inversely proportional to the price of stock.

[75] Apart from the purchase of stocks, Steuart, assuming extensive operations of trade and credit between countries, also noted the outflow of money abroad to seek for a higher rate of interest, in consequence of bringing down the domestic rate of interest by law below the international level. Steuart even supposed that 'the monied [moneyed] interest (from a certainty of disappointing the intention of government in making the law) might form a concert among themselves to lock their money, even though it should remain dead in their hands'. Cf. *Works*, vol.3, pp.170-2. Thus, it might be said that all these circumstances together would bring about the shortage of currency in the economy where the legal rate of interest is lower than the market rate.

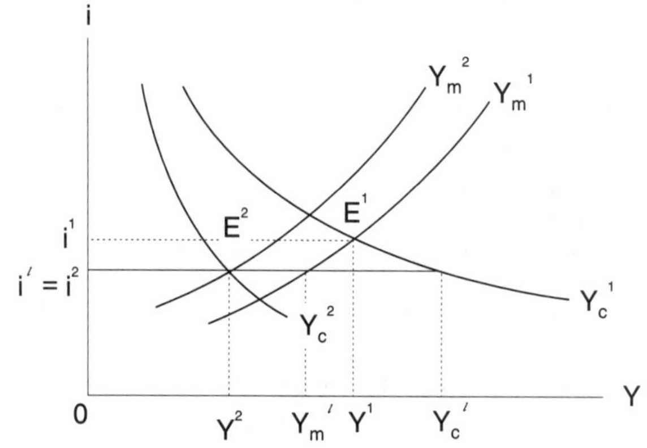

Figure 6.5 The consequences of the legal rate of interest

> would demand their money, in order to get 4 per cent. in buying stock, and would not this additional demand for stocks make them rise? ... The purses of all monied people, would, for some time at least, be fast shut against their demand. What a shock again, would this be to all inland trade, what distress upon all creditors for accounts furnished and upon those who supply daily wants! (*Works*, vol.3, pp.169-70.)

In other words, the government's stipulation of a legal interest rate lower than the 'conventional' or market rate would immediately bring about a big discrepancy between the level of output and the amount of 'effectual demand' in the economy. This disequilibrium situation would ultimately result in a lower level of output in the economy than before.

We can clearly see this result in Figure 6.5. That is to say, when the rate of interest is forced down to the legal level (i^l), there would first exist a gap between the levels of output, *compatible with the legal rate of interest*, in both commodity and money markets ($Y_c^l - Y_m^l$). It ultimately reflects the discrepancy between production and consumption, as too much money goes to producers and too little money to consumers. The ensuing leakage in the supply of money, mainly due to the difference between the legal rate of interest and the internal rate of return in stocks, would make the situation even worse, as it further squeezes the level of output in the money market ($Y_m^1 \rightarrow Y_m^2$). In the meantime, as the rate of 'profit upon trade and industry' falls, the level of output in the commodity market would rapidly contract ($Y_c^1 \rightarrow Y_c^2$).[76] After all, a new equilibrium would be established at a far lower level of output, in compliance with the legal rate of interest, than before ($E^1 \rightarrow E^2$).

[76] As we assume the price of commodities to be fixed in this model, we simply suppose that, as a result of the disequilibrium between production and consumption, the rate of 'profit upon trade and industry' would fall down until a equilibrium is restored in the economy.

On this ground, Steuart maintained that 'many inconveniences might manifest themselves, were government to force down the value of money beyond the ordinary operations of demand and competition'.[77]

4. MONEY, PRICE AND THE LEVEL OF OUTPUT (I): THE CONSUMPTION-PRODUCTION THEORY OF MONEY

In this concluding section of our examination of Steuart's analysis of national money and interest, we shall present a self-contained macroeconomic model, synthesizing what we have discussed so far in this chapter and the rest of his macroeconomic analysis. Basically, while an attempt is made to build up a flexible-price model of Steuart's theory of money, extended from the previous fixed-price model, it relates to his analysis of the relationship between the rate of interest, price level and the level of output in the economy as a whole.

To begin with, let us briefly discuss Steuart's critical review of his predecessors on money, price and output. He summarized Montesquieu and Hume's doctrine 'concerning the influence of riches upon the increase of prices', in the following three propositions.[78]

> First, The prices (say they [Montesquieu and Hume]) of commodities are always proportioned to the plenty of money in the country. So that the augmentation of wealth, even fictitious, such as paper, affects the state of prices, in proportion to its quantity. Secondly, The coin and current money in a country is the representation of

[77] *Works*, vol.3, p.171. Steuart raised the issue of the legal rate of interest initially to dismiss Sir Josiah Child's view on it. Cf. *Works*, vol.3, pp.163-7.

[78] It seems that Steuart referred to Montesquieu's *Spirit of the Laws* (1748) and Hume's *Political Discourses* (1752). As that sort of quantity theory of money which he criticized could be traced back to Locke's *Considerations* (1691) and *Further Considerations* (1695), Steuart himself noted,

> Who was the first author of this doctrine, I cannot say. I find it in Mr. Locke, and in the Spectator for the 19th of October 1711; but they have been beautifully illustrated by Monsr. de Montesquieu; and Mr. Hume has extended the theory, and diversified it prettily in his political discourses. (*Works*, vol.2, p.84.)

Meanwhile, among others, Skinner (1967) gave an interesting account of Steuart's critique of the quantity theory, concentrating on both its purpose and content. According to him, however, it still leaves us with a question: 'how do we integrate the concept of hoarding and the rate of interest with the quantity theory? (p.289.)' As we shortly find out, the present examination of Steuart's analysis of money, price and output will give a certain answer to this question. In fact, our model to be set up later will be firmly based on Steuart's very integration of the concept of hoarding and the rate of interest with the quantity theory of money. For Steuart's monetary analysis in general, Sen's work (1947) is quite illuminating. Pointing out that those few who have written about Steuart have 'merely tried to evaluate him in the light of Smithian doctrines and have almost completely failed to appreciate the true significance of his economic, especially monetary, ideas, which were on an absolutely different plane', he remarked,

> The most surprising thing, however, is that even Lord Keynes, whose monetary ideas have some resemblance to Steuart's, should fail to mention him, although he rakes up from oblivion a fairly large number of earlier writers who professed views similar to his' (p.19)

Also cf. Vickers (1959; ch.12) and Akhtar (1979). For some general background of the 18th century pre-Smithian quantity theory of money, see Monroe (1923), part V, ch.XXX.

> all the labour and commodities of it. So that in proportion as there is more or less of this representation (money), there goes a greater or less quantity of the thing represented (commodities, &c.) to the same quantity of it. From this follows, that Thirdly, Increase commodities, they become cheaper; increase money, they rise in their value. (*Works*, vol.2, p.84.)

Thus, in the last analysis, what is meant by these propositions is that there is always an exact proportion either between the quantity of money and price level or between the quantity of money and the level of output in the economy.[79] Steuart criticized, rather incisively, the above doctrine of the proportional relation among money, price and output, and put forward his own argument, as follows:[80]

> What then will become of the additional quantity of coin, or paper money? I answer, that in both cases it will enter into circulation, in proportion to the *rise* or *augmentation* of demand; with this difference, that in the first case, it will have the effect of raising prices; because the supply is not supposed to augment in proportion: in the second, prices stand as they were; because the supply is supposed to augment in proportion. ... But if upon the increase of riches it be found that the state of demand remains without any variation, then *the additional coin* will probably be locked up, or converted into plate. ... As for the paper-money, so soon as it served the first purpose

---

[79] The above three propositions could be represented in the following equation:

$$M = 1/v\ P\ y$$

where M: quantity of money
v: velocity of circulation of money (given)
P: price level
y: level of output.

That is to say, if the level of output is determined elsewhere or assumed to be constant, price level is always in proportion to the quantity of money existing in the economy (proposition 1). If price level is determined elsewhere or assumed to be constant, the level of output is always in proportion to the amount of money existing in the economy (proposition 2). And if the quantity of money is given exogenously, there is always an inverse relation between price level and the level of output (proposition 3).

[80] Steuart remarked,

> ... nothing is so easy in an hypothesis, as to establish proportions between things, which in themselves are beyond all the powers of computation. (*Works*, vol.2, p.104.)

For the details of Steuart's criticism of the quantity theory of money, described above, see *Works*, vol.2, pp.78-104. It is interesting to note (and, in fact, quite well known,) that Cantillon also made a similar comment on Locke's quantity theory.

> ... he [Locke] has clearly seen that the abundance of money makes every thing dear, but he has not considered how it does so. The great difficulty of this question consists in knowing in what way and in what proportion the increase of money raises prices. (*Essai,* in Higgs (1931), p.161.)

Skinner (1967), quoting the above passage, pointed out that 'Cantillon thus set out *how* changes in the supply of money affect price levels and in so doing endeavoured to elucidate the causal sequences involved'. Moreover, according to him, 'precisely the same is true of Hume's essay *Of Money*, taken as a whole, as of Steuart's *Principles*'. Cf. Skinner (1967), p.227. On the other hand, Blaug (1985), also quoting the same passage, observed that Cantillon's stress was rather on the fact 'that an increase in M will not only raise the level of prices but will also alter the structure of prices, depending upon the initial recipients of the new cash and their relative demand for goods'. He called the differential effect of a cash injection, as governed by its nature, 'Cantillon Effect'. Cf. Blaug (1985), pp.20-3.

> of supplying the demand of him who borrowed it, (because he had at that time no coin,) it will return upon the debtor in it, and become realized; because of the little use found for it in carrying on circulation. Let the specie of a country, therefore, be augmented or diminished, in ever so great a proportion, commodities will still rise and fall according to the principles of demand and competition ... (*Works*, vol.2, p.86; original italics and parentheses.)

That is to say, according to Steuart, the price level would change, if and only if there is any change in the demand and supply conditions of the commodity market; therefore, the fluctuation of the price level is far from being exactly proportional to the quantity of money existing in the economy, except by mere chance.[81] On the other hand, *mutatis mutandis*, the level of output would vary, if and only if there is any movement in the equilibrium of production and consumption in the economy; therefore, the variation in the output level is far from being exactly proportional to the quantity of money existing in the economy, except by mere chance.

Is there no causal relation at all, in Steuart's analysis, between the quantity of money, price level and the level of output in the economy? As can be seen from the passage quoted above, indeed, some part of additional supply of money might increase consumption and thus the demand for commodity; whereas the rest might just stagnate and consequently bring down the rate of interest. As a result of the fall in the rate of interest, more production would go on and thus the supply of commodity would increase. After all, it seems that, as the additional supply of money might raise both the demand for and the supply of commodities at the same time, the level of output would definitely rise but the price level would still depend on which side preponderates in the commodity market. In other words, according to Steuart, the supply of money would affect both the price level and the level of output simultaneously by way of changing the rate of interest; though there is no exact proportion between them. Let us now explore in detail how Steuart saw the relationship between money, price and output, and establish a formal model of it.[82]

---

[81] Again, in Steuart's own words,

> ... the riches [money] of a country have no determinate influence upon prices; although, I allow, they may accidentally affect them: what I mean is, that they may influence them; but they cannot regulate them. (*Works*, vol.2, p.93; brackets added.)

Thus, according to him, the quantity of money existing in the economy is neither the only nor a definite factor which affects the price level. As Steuart provided some instances concerning those other factors which might influence the demand and supply conditions of commodities, see *Works*, vol.2, pp.87-93.

[82] As far as Steuart was concerned, the supply of money consists of the quantity of money actually circulating, rather than merely existing, in the economy. The difference between the two quantities of money, according to him, is mainly due to the existence of paper money, hoarded coin and foreign trade. Meanwhile, Steuart sometimes ascribed the disproportion between money, price and output to this difference between money in circulation and that in existence. (Cf. *Works*, vol.2, pp.93-104.)

We shall first examine both money and commodity markets in turn to derive certain basic relations between variables, and then summarize them into a few equations to visualize the equilibrium situation of the economy as a whole.[83] To begin with, let us look at the money market. As money is an essential requisite for not only consumption but also production, it is demanded for both economic activities. Thus,[84]

$$M_d/P = l_c + l_y \qquad (1)$$

$$l_c = k_1 \, c \qquad (2)$$

$$l_y = k_2 \, u \qquad (3)$$

where M_d: total demand for money
P: price level
l_c: demand for money to consume
k_1: constant
c: amount of the consumption of consumer goods
l_y: demand for money to produce
k_2: constant
u: amount of the use of producer goods.

On the other hand, money existing in an economy either circulates or is hoarded. In other words, the quantity of money actually circulating in the economy equals that of money existing less that of money being hoarded, while the hoarding of money might depend on the rate of interest.[85] Thus,

---

Nevertheless, the point in the present analysis is how the supply of money, i.e., the quantity of money in circulation, could affect the price level and the level of output in the economy.

[83] For our present model, we will reproduce some parts of the previous fixed-price model, while introducing new variables and relations and making some necessary modifications to expand it. This time, particularly, we should specify most variables in real terms, as we allow the price level to be flexible. We shall denote them in small letters, in contrast with those in value terms in capital letters.

[84] As we did in the previous fixed-price model, we assume here that the wages of labour are paid at the end of production process; therefore, the money employed as working capital in the production process is to be spent on producer goods. And we further assume, for the simplicity of modelling, that the demand for money to produce is in proportion to the amount of the use of producer goods in the economy, i.e., $l_y = k_2$ u, in parallel with the demand for money to consume, which is in proportion to the amount of consumption of consumer goods, i.e., $l_c = k_1$ c. As a matter of fact, Steuart himself sometimes considered the 'proportion of circulating money with respect to the desires of consumers to consume' (k_1) and the 'proportion of circulating money with respect to those of the industrious to produce' (k_2) to be constant. Cf. *Works*, vol.2, p.53. Meanwhile, these assumptions, together with those regarding the supply of money which we will soon make below, allow us to see how Steuart succeeded in 'integrating the concept of hoarding and the rate of interest with the quantity theory of money'. Cf. note 78 above.

[85] According to Steuart, if the quantity of money existing is greater than that of money circulating in the economy, it would become either 'locked up' or 'realized'. Meanwhile, if the latter is greater than the former, either some of those coins previously 'locked up' must come back into circulation or some additional paper money must be issued. Indeed, as we could notice from his analysis of the interest of money in the previous section, while the continuous process of issuing and 'realizing' paper money accounts for the payment of interests for money loans, the individual potential creditors' decisions of either hoarding or lending money depend on the rate of interest. Thus, the amount of money hoards

$$M_s = \overline{M}_e - M_h \tag{4}$$

$$M_h/P = h(i), \;\; h' < 0 \tag{5}$$

where M_s: supply of money
$\overline{M}_e$: quantity of money existing (given)
M_h: quantity of money being hoarded
i: rate of interest.

And the demand and supply should be equal in the money market. Thus,

$$M_s = M_d. \tag{6}$$

Next, let us turn to the commodity market. In Steuart's monetary analysis, basically, production is supposed to be carried out with a view to earning net profit, i.e., gross profit less either actual or potential interest for the money employed in the production process. Therefore, the greater the difference between the rate of profit and the rate of interest, the more money is demanded for production; and, consequently, the more goods are used in the production process, the more production is carried out; while the rate of profit dependent on price level.[86] Thus,

$$y = y(u), \;\; y' > 0 \tag{7}$$

$$u = u(r - i), \;\; u' > 0 \tag{8}$$

$$r = r(P), \;\; r' > 0 \tag{9}$$

where y: amount of production
r: rate of profit.

On the other hand, the 'effectual demand' for the commodities produced consists of two components, i.e., the consumption of consumer goods and the use of producer goods in the production process, with a certain proportion between them being given.[87] Thus,

$$d_f = c + u \tag{10}$$

$$c = p_c\, d_f \;\; (\text{or } u = d_p\, d_f) \tag{11}$$

where d_f: amount of 'effectual demand'
p_c: 'propensity to consume' (given)
(or d_p: 'disposition to produce' (given); $p_c + d_p = 1$).

in the economy depends on the rate of interest in the money market. Meanwhile, we assume the quantity of money existing in the economy to be given out of the model.

[86] According to Steuart, both the wages of labour and the 'profit upon trade and industry' are determined, *ex post*, after the price of commodities is determined. Cf. the previous discussion of his theory of value and distribution in Ch.3.

[87] Cf. the fixed-price model in the previous section.

Finally, according to Steuart's analysis, the level of output in the economy is determined by the amount of 'effectual demand'. Thus,

$$y = d_f. \quad (12)$$

All these equations (1 - 12) represent the basic relations of our model.[88]

Now, we shall manipulate further the above basic equations to look closely at the equilibrium situation of the economy. Above all, from the demand side of the economy, we could get the following result.

$$M_s = M_d \quad \text{(from 6)}$$
$$\overline{M}_e - P\,h(i) = P\,(l_c + l_y) \quad \text{(from 1, 4 and 5)}$$
$$= P\,(k_1\,c + k_2\,u) \quad \text{(from 2 and 3)}$$
$$= P\,k\,d_f;\ \ k = k_1\,p_c + k_2\,d_p.^{89} \quad \text{(from 10 and 11)}$$

Therefore,

$$d_f(P, i) = 1/k\,(\overline{M}_e/P - h(i)),\ \ \partial d_f/\partial P < 0,\ \partial d_f/\partial i > 0 \quad (13)$$

where k: weighted money-balance constant.

From the supply side of the economy, on the other hand, we may obtain a production function, as follows:

$$y = y(u) = y(u(r(P) - i)). \quad \text{(from 7, 8 and 9)}$$

Therefore,

$$y(P, i) = y(u(r(P) - i)),\ \ \partial y/\partial P > 0,\ \partial y/\partial i < 0. \quad (14)$$

Then, as we add the equilibrium condition of the commodity market (equation 12) to these two summarizing equations (13 and 14), we could find out the equilibrium level of output (y), price level (P) and interest rate (i) in the economy.

On the basis of the three equations (12, 13 and 14), we may visualize how they are simultaneously determined. That is, first of all, we could note that the amount of 'effectual demand' (d_f) is negatively related to price level (P) in the commodity market but positively related to the rate of interest (i) in the money market; whereas the amount of production (y) is positively related to price level (P) in the commodity market but negatively related to the rate of interest in the money market. By combining them in each market, we could see the simultaneous determination of the level of output ($y = d_f$), price level (P) and

---

[88] Since the above system of equation has 12 unknowns and equations, respectively, it could be solvable.

[89] As we assume p_c and d_p to be given outside of model, k is also a constant; for

$$k = k_1\,c/(c + u) + k_2\,u/(c + u) = k_1\,p_c + k_2\,d_p.$$

We may call it weighted money-balance constant.

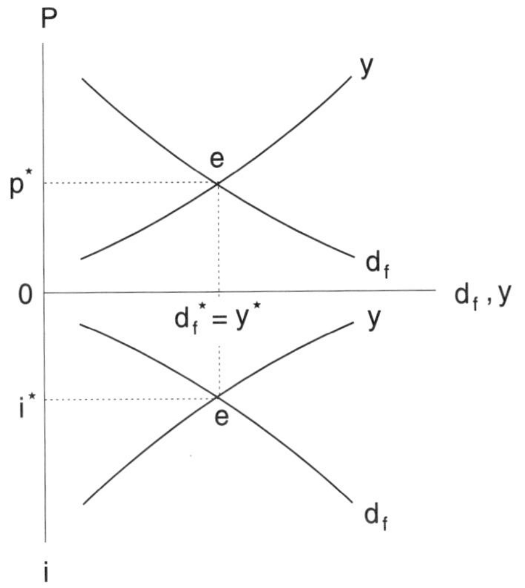

Figure 6.6 The simultaneous determination of price, output and the rate of interest

the rate of interest (i) in Figure 6.6. From this, then, it is evident that, in Steuart's analysis, the commodity and the money market are so closely interrelated that the level of output, price level and the rate of interest should be determined simultaneously through their respective equilibrium conditions.

Finally, let us examine what would happen to the above equilibrium situation, if there is any exogenous change in the supply of money, e.g., an increase in the quantity of money existing in the economy as a result of some favourable balance of trade.[90] We may illustrate this with Figure 6.7. If the supply of money increases exogenously for some reason, in the first place, it would directly affect either the amount of consumption in the commodity market or the rate of interest in the money market – to be exact, both at the same time. That is to say, on the one hand, as supply exceeds demand in the

[90] As a matter of fact, to fully discuss the relation between money, price and output in an open economy, the analysis of foreign exchange, in general, and the rate of exchange and the balance of payments, in particular, must be premised. Hence, as we deal with Steuart's analysis of international money in the next chapter, we shall again take up the same subject but in a different setting. Meanwhile, in the present context, the discussion of the effects of an exogenous change in the supply of money on price level, the level of output and the rate of interest is intended to serve a double purpose. That is, on the one hand, it would help us to clearly understand how Steuart's analysis of money differs from his predecessors' who held on to the quantity theory, discussed earlier in this section; on the other hand, it might at the same time give us a chance to observe how the equilibrium situation could be restored in the economy, whenever it is disturbed by any impact exogenous to our model of his analysis. We will rely on a diagrammatic presentation rather than differential calculus.

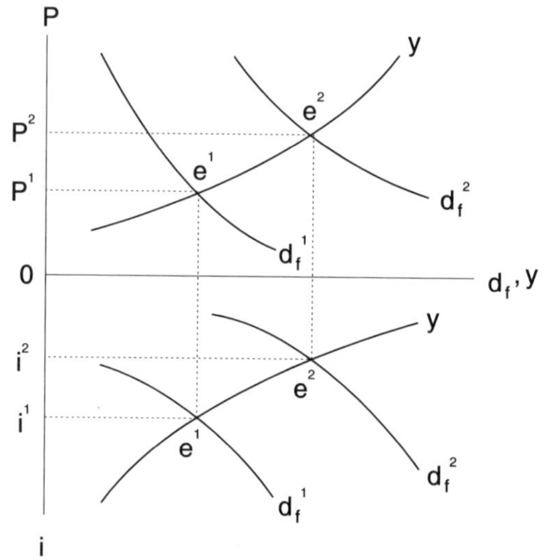

Figure 6.7 The effects of the increase of money supply on price, output and the rate of interest

money market, the rate of interest would fall; on the other hand, as more money is available than before, the amount of consumption would increase, which denotes the increase of 'effectual demand' in the economy ($d_f^1 \rightarrow d_f^2$). As a result, sooner or later, the price of commodities would rise. Therefore, while the rate of interest falls in the money market, the price level rises in the commodity market ($i^1 \rightarrow i^2$; $P^1 \rightarrow P^2$).[91] This would induce more production in the economy.[92] As soon as the production equals the consumption, both the rate of interest and the price level would stop to settle down to another equilibrium situation ($e^1 \rightarrow e^2$). In the new equilibrium, the level of output and the price level would be higher than before, whereas the rate of interest would be lower than before. After all, the initial exogenous increase of money supply has been absorbed partly into the circulation for consumption and partly into that for production in the economy.

To conclude, we may summarize that, according to Steuart, there is no proportional relation either between the supply of money and price level or

[91] In fact, we may note that, as the price level rises, the supply of money in real terms would slightly diminish. And, as a result, the increase of 'effectual demand' would be a bit hampered; whereas the falling-down of interest rate would occur more slowly.

[92] While the augmentation of production would certainly entail some additional increment of 'effectual demand', the latter in its turn would give rise to some extra demand for money to produce.

between the supply of money and the level of output in the economy, in that the supply of money would certainly affect both price level and the level of output *at the same time* through its influence on the rate of interest.[93] In his analysis of money, indeed, those three variables, i.e., price level, the level of output and the rate of interest, are to be determined simultaneously via the equilibrium conditions of both commodity and money markets in the economy.

[93] Naturally, according to Steuart, there is no exact inverse relation between price level and the level of output with a given quantity of money supply, either. All in all, he rejected the quantity theory of money which presumed certain proportional, either directly or inversely, relations between money, price and output, as our discussion so far has proved. He gave a clear and lucid illustration of what he was arguing against the quantity theory of money, as follows:

> Suppose the specie of Europe to continue increasing in quantity every year, until it amounts to ten times the present quantity, will price rise in proportion? I answer, that such an augmentation might happen, without the smallest alteration upon prices, or that it might occasion a very great one, according to circumstances. Were industry to increase to ten times what it is at present, that is to say, were produce of it to increase to ten times its present value, according to the actual standard of prices, the value of every manufacture and produce might remain without alteration. This supposition is possible: because no man can tell to what extent demand may carry industry. If, on the other hand, the scale of demand could be supposed to preponderate, so as to draw all the wealth into circulation, without having the effect of augmenting the supply (which I take to be impossible), then prices would rise to ten times the present standard, at least in many articles. (*Works*, vol.2, p.104.)

Thus, for Steuart, in so far as there could not be found any cause-and-effect or any definite relation among money, price and output, they must depend on some other factors than each other. As the system of analysis is under-determined, so to speak, there should be introduced some more equations and variables into it so as to get rid of any unnecessary degree of freedom. One of these additional variables – in fact, the most important of them all – is the rate of interest, which is to be determined endogenously in the system.

7. International Money

Following the last chapter, we shall continue to examine Steuart's theory of money and credit. In this chapter, however, it will be dealt with in a different context, i.e., in an open-economy setting. As far as the subject of money and credit is concerned, what essentially makes things different in an open rather than a closed economy is the presence of trade and capital movements between countries, which entail the operation of what Steuart called 'money of the world'. If there is any balance due by one trading country to another, it must be paid with some sort of international money. Thus, we shall start with a general discussion of the operation of foreign exchange, accompanying international trade and capital movements, as presented in Steuart's *Inquiry*. Then, in the next section, we move on to some particulars of Steuart's analysis of international money: that is, the determination of exchange rates between the currencies of different countries, its relation to the balance of payments, and the effects of the balance of payments on domestic circulation in the economy. Finally, we shall complete our discussion of Steuart's theory of money and credit, as a whole, by extending our previous model of his macroeconomic analysis of national money to an open-economy context in order to comprehend those new variables and relations introduced in his analysis of international money. We will deal separately with Steuart's analysis of banking in the appendix, in so far as it is descriptive rather than theoretical.

1. FOREIGN EXCHANGE

As we have seen in the last chapter, according to Steuart, money performs four functions in a closed economy: that is, a measure of value, a medium of exchange, a means of payment and a store of value. Both coin made of precious metals and paper money secured on 'solid properties' could by and large be used for all these functions of money. In the presence of extensive transactions and credit between different countries, it is necessary for money to carry out another function: that is, to make good the international balance of payments. Apparently, the payments between countries seem to bear some analogy with those between individuals within a country. As different currencies are used in different countries, however, the way the payments are made must be more complex between countries than between individuals within the same country. And, moreover, the foreign circulation of money would inevitably affect its domestic circulation in the economy. To get down to his analysis of international money, let us briefly discuss Steuart's observations on how the balance of payments between countries could be categorized into different sorts and how it would eventually become cleared.

According to Steuart, there are two sorts of balance of payments between countries: i.e., the 'balance of trade' and the 'general balance of payments'.

> The first [the balance of trade] marks the total loss of the nations when her imports exceed the value of her exports; the second [the general balance of payments] comprehends three other articles, viz. 1. the expense of the natives in foreign countries; 2. the payment of all debts, principal and interest, due to foreigners; 3. the lending of money to other nations. (*Works*, vol.3, p.216.)

Thus, while the 'balance of trade' for a country refers to the (value) amount of exports less that of imports in its current account, the 'general balance of payments' relates to the rest of the current account plus the whole capital account. And these two balances put together make what Steuart called the 'grand balance'.[1] How, then, would this balance be made good in the end?

Assuming various operations of banking, both domestic and foreign,[2] Steuart noted that there would be only two alternatives in clearing the balance of payments due by one country to another: either paying it in hard currency or having it on loan.

> ... either the grand balance must be paid out of the national stock of coin, or it must be furnished by foreigners upon a loan from them; the interest of which must be paid out of that part of the solid property the nation which has been melted down into paper. (*Works*, vol.3, p.219.)

That is, both coin made of precious metals and international loan secured on 'solid properties' eventually constitute the means of foreign exchange. This raises a basic question on the subject of international money: on what basis are bills exchanged and is the balance paid between different countries where different money-units are used? In other words, how is the rate of exchange, as the ratio between the money-units of respective countries, determined, so that all the reciprocal transactions between them can be worked out and

---

[1] *Works*, pp.216-7.

[2] For instance, Steuart supposed,

> ... it is alleged that nothing but coin can be employed in paying this grand balance. To this I answer, that in such a case the credit of a bank may step in, without which a nation which runs short of coin, and which comes to owe a grand balance must quickly be undone. We have said that while exchangers transact the balance, the whole load of providing coin lies upon banks. Now the whole solid property melted down, in their paper, is in their hands; because I consider the securities given them for their paper, to be the same as the property itself. Upon this property, there is a yearly interest paid to the bank: this interest, then must be engaged to foreigners by the bank, in lieu of what is owing to them by the nation; and when once a fund is borrowed upon abroad, the rest is easy to the bank. (*Works*, vol.3, p.218.)

Cf. the appendix below.

accordingly their balance of payments be made good? To answer this question, then, becomes the first task of our specific discussions of Steuart's analysis of international money in the next section.

2. THE RATE OF EXCHANGE AND THE BALANCE OF PAYMENTS

In this section, we shall closely examine some significant aspects of Steuart's analysis of international money, particularly those related to the rate of exchange and the balance of payments. Let us start with his explanation of the determination of the rate of exchange between the currencies of different countries.

2.1 The Rate of Exchange, the Price of Bullion and the Balance of Payments

As far as both countries adopt the same metallic standard, it appears not too difficult to fix the rate of exchange between their currencies. That is, as the value of the money-units in the respective countries would depend on the amounts of the precious metal contained in their coins, the exchange rate, as the ratio between the value of their money-units, could be represented simply in terms of the relative proportion of those amounts. However, the problem is that, in each country, the relative value of coin with respect to other commodities including bullion does not solely depend on the amount of precious metal in it. In other words, apart from the problem of some imperfections of coin which render the amount of metal contained in one coin different from that in another even within the same country,[3] the value of the money-units in each country must change, as the relative value of coin changes with regard to other commodities including bullion, according to circumstances, particularly when the government of each country imposes the price of coinage in different proportions.[4] Therefore, it may not be in proportion to the amount of precious metal in the coin. Given then that the money-unit in each country has no determinate value, how could the rate of exchange be calculated at all? Steuart suggested an answer to this, as follows:

> This being the case, the way to calculate the real par of exchange between nations, who have in common no determinate and invariable money, exclusive of coin, is to consider fine gold and silver as the next standard. This is a merchandize which never varies in its quality. Fine gold is always the same in every mass; and weight for weight, there is no difference in its value or quality any where. This standard being

[3] For example, coins might be manufactured without precision and be wearing irregularly during circulation. Cf. sub-section 2.1 in the last chapter.
[4] Cf. sub-section 2.5 in the last chapter.

> once adopted, the calculation of the real par becomes an easy operation to those who know the course of the bullion market in the two places exchanging. (*Works*, vol.3, p.426.)

That is, if there is any sort of commodity which is exactly the same and common among different countries, such as bullion in Steuart's conception, the rate of exchange between their currencies could be found out by comparing the domestic prices of that commodity in terms of the respective money-units. In other words, according to Steuart, the rate of exchange between different currencies is determined by the relative amount of bullion which the money-unit of each currency can command in each country's market, rather than the relative amount of precious metal contained in the coin representing the money-unit of each currency. For example,

> The general rule ... is to settle the real par of different coins, not according to the bullion they contain, but according to the *bullion* they are worth in their own market at the time. If 1000 pounds weight of guineas can purchase at London 1000 pounds weight of standard bullion; and that 1000 pounds of the same weight of louis can buy at Paris 1080 pounds weight of the same standard bullion; then the 1000 pounds weight of guineas is at the real par with 925 926/1080 [that is, 1000 x 1000/1080] pounds weight of the louis, and not worth 1000, as is commonly supposed. (*Works*, vol.3, pp.30-1; brackets added.)

Under the metallic standard, therefore, the price of bullion in a country ultimately reflects the exchange rate of its own currency against others: that is, if the former price goes up, the latter rate falls down, and *vice versa*.

Furthermore, according to Steuart, it might be supposed that bullion would be the only medium of exchange in every international transaction; for, without the mediation of banking, there might be the actual transportation of bullion from one country to another.

> When one nation pays to another the price of what they buy, the interposition of bullion is unavoidable; and the whole operation consists in comparing the value of bullion in the one and in the other nation. Suppose France owe to England 1000 pounds sterling; what regulates exchange here, is the quantity of bullion in Paris and in London. The French merchant inquires first, what is the quantity of bullion in London, which at the time is equal to the sum he wants to pay? and next, what this quantity of bullion will cost him to procure in the Paris market? Upon this the par of exchange ought to be regulated. Whatever is given more than this quantity is the price of transportation, when the balance of trade is against France. (*Works*, vol.3, pp.16-7.)

In consequence, while the price of bullion basically depends on its demand and supply conditions of the market, it would particularly be affected by the balance of payments in the economy. That is, whenever the balance turns unfavourable, the price of bullion, as its relative price with respect to coin, would go up. It would rise until it becomes at par with coin, i.e., no price of coinage is paid. On the other hand, whenever the balance of payments is in

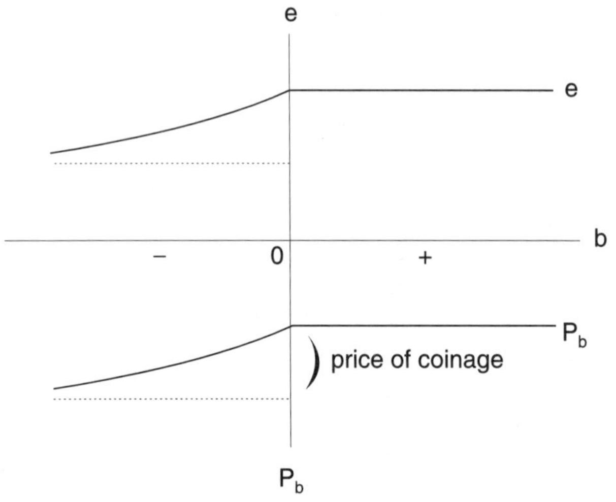

Figure 7.1 The balance of payments, the price of bullion and the rate of exchange

the country's favour, the price of bullion would fall to the mint price, so that the full price of coinage would be paid.[5]

Therefore, we may summarize our discussions of Steuart's analysis of exchange rate, so far, as follows: if a country has an adverse balance of payments, its exchange rate would be devalued, as far as the price of bullion would rise; whereas, if it goes into the black, the exchange rate would be revalued, since the bullion price would get back to the mint rate.[6] We could

---

[5] Actually we have already explained this relation between the relative price of bullion with respect to coin and the balance of payments in the economy, in sub-section 2.5 in the last chapter.

[6] In addition, we might note that, in Steuart's analysis, as the rate of exchange between different currencies eventually represents none other than the relative price of coin with respect to other commodities including bullion in one country in comparison with that in another, it would also depend on some factors other than the balance of payments, such as the price of coinage and the degree of weight loss during circulation, which may exert influences on the value of coin directly. He did not fail to mention this point.

> At present our exchange becomes favourable from the weight of our currency, and the balance against France upon her trade; which, in Paris, raises the price of bullion with which we pay our French debts. On the other hand, our exchange becomes unfavourable from the lightness of our currency, from the coinage we pay to France, and balance against us; which last carries off all our new guineas; and in the Paris market, sinks the value of that bullion in which we pay our French debts. (*Works*, vol.3, pp.431-2.)

Also see *Works*, vol.3, pp.433-4. Lastly, we may note that Steuart called the rate of exchange the 'par of exchange', and regarded some extra expenses for paying the actual balance, over and above the 'par', as the 'price of exchange', which include the 'price of transportation', insurance and the exchanger's profit. Cf. *loc.cit.* In this context, we could observe that the present analysis parallels Marshall's (1923) discussion of 'gold point', when he talked about the 'limits of variation of the

depict the relation between the balance of payments, the price of bullion and the rate of exchange in Figure 7.1. In Figure 7.1, the lower part describes the relation between the balance of payments and the price of bullion (P_b): that is, when the country has a deficit ($b < 0$), the price of bullion is positively related to the balance of payments; whereas, when it has a surplus ($b > 0$), the price of bullion remains at its mint price. Correspondingly, the upper part describes the relation between the balance of payments and the rate of exchange (e): that is, while the price of bullion in the country reflects the exchange rate of its currency against others, the latter would depreciate with a deficit balance; whereas, with a surplus, it would appreciate.

2.2 The Balance of Payments and the Domestic Circulation of Money

Now, let us move on to further exploring the effects of the balance of payments on the domestic economy. Steuart described the initial situation of the domestic circulation of money in the economy without any international balance of payments, as follows:

> Now the state of trade, of manufacture, of modes of living, and of the customary expense of the inhabitants, when taken together, regulate and determine what we may call the mass of ready-money demands, that is, of alienation. To operate this multiplicity of payments, a certain proportion of money is necessary. This proportion again may increase or diminish according to circumstances; although the quantity of alienation should continue the same. (*Works*, vol.3, p. 226.)

Thus, the domestic circulation of money depends on what is called 'ready-money demands' or 'alienation', either production or consumption, in the economy, which requires a certain quantity of money in circulation, with its velocity given.[7]

Then, what would happen to the domestic circulation, if the economy has the foreign sector, i.e., international trade and capital movements? According to Steuart,

> (A) is the total mass of money (coin and paper) necessary at home: (A) is composed of (B) the coin, and of (C) the paper-money, and (D) stands for that mass of coin, or metal, or bills, which goes and comes according as the grand balance is favourable or unfavourable with other nations. ... When a favourable balance of trade brings the price of exchange below par, and brings coin into the country, the consequence is, either to animate trade and industry, to augment the mass of payments, to swell (A),

exchanges between countries whose currencies are based on gold'. Cf. Marshall (1923), pp.144-7. Note that his 'gold point' referred to the 'price of exchange' rather than the 'par of exchange'. According to him,

> If the premium on the bill is just equal to the cost of carriage of gold, so that it is indifferent to a merchant whether he buys a bill or sends the gold, it is said that "gold point" has been reached. (Marshall (1923), p.227)

Also see *ibid.*, pp.225-8.

[7] Cf. our discussion of Steuart's analysis of national money in the last chapter; section 4, in particular.

> and still to preserve (C) in circulation; or else make (A) regorge, so as to sink the interest of money below the bank lending price: in this case people will carry back the regorging part of (C) to the bank, and withdraw their securities; which is consolidating, as we have called it, the property which had been formerly melted down, for want of this circulating equivalent (money). ... Those who owe this balance (D), and who are supposed to have value for it, in the currency of the country, must in order to pay it, either exhaust a part of (B), by sending it away, or they must carry a part of (C) to the bank, to be paid for in coin. If they pick up a part of (B) in the country, then the coin in the circulation, being diminished below its proportion, the possessors of (C) will come upon the bank for a supply, in order to make up (B) to its former standard. Banks complain without reason. If they carry part of (C) to be changed at the bank, for the payment of (D), they thereby diminish the quantity of (C); consequently there will be a demand upon the bank for more notes, to support domestic circulation; because those notes which have been paid in coin by the bank are returned to the bank, and have diminished the mass of (C); which therefore must be replaced by a new melting down of solid property. (*Works*, vol.3, pp.227-8 and p.230.)

From this, first of all, we could note that if the country has a favourable balance of payments, it would bring some additional quantity of coin to the economy from abroad. And, as a result, either the domestic circulation would increase or some part of paper money already existing in the economy would stagnate and eventually become 'realized'. On the contrary, if the country owes some balance to the others, some quantity of coin would flow out abroad. And, consequently, either the domestic circulation would decrease or more paper money would be issued to supply the deficiency of circulating equivalents.

Meanwhile, as Steuart himself explicitly noted in the passage quoted above, the balance of payments would also affect the rate of interest in the economy. In other words, while the balance of payments brings about the increase or decrease in the quantity of coin in the economy, it would result in a fall or rise in the rate of interest, along with the 'realization' or new issuing of paper money. In fact, as the inflow or outflow of coin, due to the balance of payments, would give rise to the increase or decrease in the total supply of money in the economy, though the quantity of paper money might be partly changed, so it would ultimately affect not only the level of output and price level but also the rate of interest in the economy. That is to say, on the one hand, a favourable balance of payments would expand the domestic circulation of money with a lower rate of interest, so that it could result in higher levels of output and price. On the other hand, an unfavourable balance of payments would squeeze it with a higher rate of interest, so that it could result in lower levels of output and price.[8]

[8] In section 4 of the last chapter, we have already seen what would happen to the level of output, price level and the rate of interest if there is some exogenous increase of money supply in the economy.

In sum, from our discussions in this section, we may conclude that, according to Steuart, the balance of payments affects an open economy in two ways: while it exerts an influence on the price of bullion and sets the rate of exchange of the currency against others, at the same time it also has an effect on the domestic circulation of money by way of changing the supply of money in the economy.

3. MONEY, PRICE AND OUTPUT (II): AN ABSORPTION APPROACH TO THE BALANCE OF PAYMENTS

When we examined Steuart's analysis of the rate of exchange and the balance of payments in the last section, we particularly focused on the relation between those and the effects of the balance of payments on the domestic circulation of money in the open economy. We dealt with the two things separately. That is, assuming *ceteris paribus*, we merely discussed one after the other. However, while the balance of payments affects both the rate of exchange and the domestic circulation of money at the same time, the latter themselves are also inter-related. Moreover, as far as the latter might in their turn influence the former the other way around, they all, including the balance of payments, must be treated as endogenous variables. We need then a system to determine them all simultaneously: that is, a general, rather than partial, equilibrium analysis. In this final section of our discussion of Steuart's analysis of international money, therefore, we shall present a general equilibrium model of his theory of money, price and output in an open-economy setting, as an extension of the previous one in a closed-economy setting.[9]

First of all, let us look at Steuart's discussion of the relation between the foreign and domestic sectors in the economy, as it constitutes the gist of our present analysis. According to him,

> If domestic consumption be equal to the sum of both [the produce of industry and the quantity of importation], the country must annually lose the value imported. ... If domestic consumption do not exceed the produce of industry, this will prove that exportation is at least equal to importation. ... If the domestic consumption should really fall short of the produce of industry, it marks a flourishing foreign trade. (*Works*, vol.2, pp.73-74; brackets added.)

That is, for a trading country, if the domestic consumption is greater than the domestic production, the importation exceeds the exportation; if the domestic consumption equals the domestic production, the importation equals the exportation; and, if the domestic consumption equals the domestic production,

[9] Cf. section 4 in the last chapter.

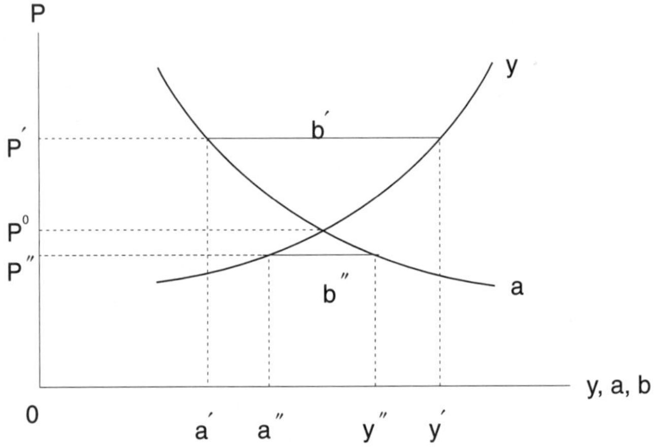

Figure 7.2 Production, absorption and the balance of trade

the exportation exceeds the importation. We may summarize this in an equation as follows:[10]

$$y + m = a + x \qquad (15)$$

where y: amount of domestic production
m: amount of importation
a: amount of domestic consumption, i.e., absorption
x: amount of exportation.

Therefore, if we define

$$b = x - m, \qquad (16)$$

then

$$b = y - a \qquad (17)$$

where b: balance of trade or payments.

Thus, the balance of trade represents no more or no less than that part of the domestic production which exceeds or falls short of the domestic consumption. In other words, the balance of trade in a country exactly amounts to the excess of the economy's production over its absorption.[11]

---

[10] As we extend the macroeconomic model of a closed economy, established in section 4, ch.5 above, we will number the additional equations due to the introduction of foreign sector continuously from the previous equations (1 - 14).

[11] Perlman (1990) quoted the same passage, as we did above, from Skinner's edition (1966) and remarked that 'a clearer statement of what in the 1950s became known as the absorption approach to the balance of trade is hard to find in the literature' (p.126). While his account of Steuart's analysis of the balance of payments encompasses both current and capital accounts, it does not seem to build upon the full context of Steuart's macroeconomics. In the present discussion, on the contrary, we shall emphasize the macroeconomic implications of Steuart's absorption analysis, while simplifying

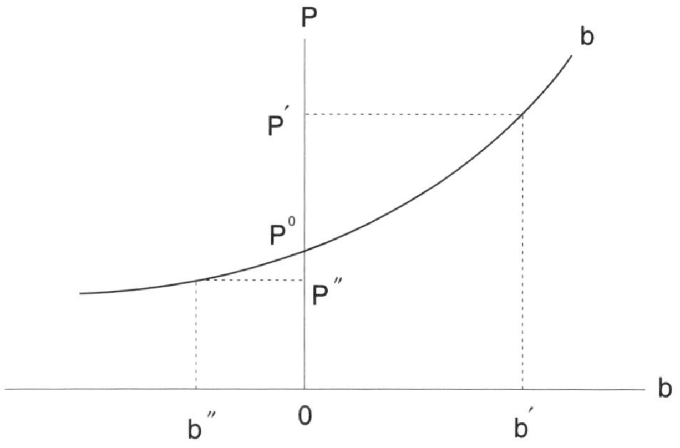

Figure 7.3 Price level and the balance of trade

On the basis of our previous analysis of Steuart's monetary explanation of output and price, we may describe the relationship between the domestic production, absorption and the balance of trade, as shown in Figure 7.2.[12] That is to say, depending on price level, the balance of trade is determined in terms of the difference between the amount of production and that of absorption in the economy: whenever one exceeds the other, there would exist either trade surplus or deficit ($y' > a'$, $b' > 0$; $y'' < a''$, $b'' < 0$). We could transform Figure 7.2 into another on the co-ordinates of price level and the balance of trade, as shown in Figure 7.3. It shows what amount of the balance of trade could be compatible with each price level in the economy. How then is the price level to be determined in the open economy?[13]

As far as the price of commodities goes, in Steuart's analysis, the country concerned is basically too 'small', relative to the rest of the world, to set it according to the country's own domestic supply and demand conditions; so to

---

the balance of payments as due to trade only. Meanwhile, a prototype of the absorption approach to the balance of payments could be found in Alexander (1952). Also cf. Johnson (1958), Ch.6 'Towards a General Theory of the Balance of Payments'.

[12] Figure 7.2 is basically borrowed from our previous discussion of Steuart's analysis of the simultaneous determination of price, output and the rate of interest. (Cf. section 4, Ch.6 above.) But, while curve y in the diagram still depicts the amount of domestic production, curve a represents the amount of domestic absorption, rather than the amount of 'effectual demand', in an open economy. In the open economy, the whole 'effectual demand' is made up of not only domestic absorption but also exportation. In any case, the absorption denotes both the consumption of consumer goods and the use of producer goods in the present model.

[13] In fact, we substituted equation (17) for equation (12), i.e., the equilibrium condition of the commodity market in our previous model of a closed economy. As it has an additional unknown (b), we need, at least, another equation to complete our system, unless some more unknowns and equations are introduced. (Note that a (absorption) replace d_f ('effectual demand') in the previous system.) Cf. section 3 in the last chapter.

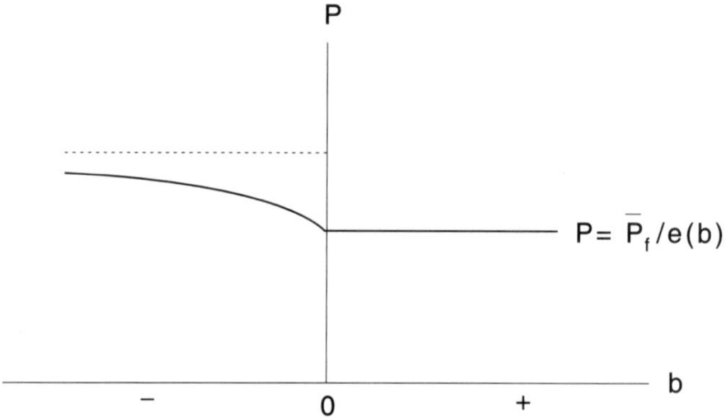

Figure 7.4 Domestic price level and the balance of payments

speak, it is a mere price-taker in the international trade.[14] Once the price of commodities is determined in the world market, it would be translated in terms of the country's own money-unit by the help of the foreign exchange rate: that is,[15]

$$P = \overline{P}_f/e \qquad (18)$$

where $\overline{P}_f$: price level in the world market (given)
e: rate of exchange.

Meanwhile, as we have discussed in the last section, the rate of exchange is regulated by the price of bullion in the economy, which in turn has to do with its state of the balance of payments.[16] Thus,

$$e = e(b). \qquad (19)$$

[14] As we have previously seen in his analyses of value, output, trade and growth, the awareness of and the emphasis on the competition among trading countries, especially regarding the price of commodities, was ever present in Steuart. For instance, he stated,

> ... as to manufactures for exportation, which are not peculiar, but which are produced by different countries, the prices of these are violently pulled down by the force of foreign competition; and the workmen are obliged to diminish them. (*Works*, vol.3, p.12.)

Of course, Steuart admitted that there might be some commodities whose price would not be subject to the international competition, such as those for home-consumption and those peculiar to the country concerned. (Cf. *Works*, vol.3, pp.10-4.) But, for the sake of the simplicity of modelling, we shall ignore these exceptional cases.

[15] Basically, in this context, the country's exchange rate is nothing more than the relative value of its currency with respect to the foreign one, which could be expressed as the inverse of relative domestic price level with respect to foreign price level: i.e.,

$$e = \overline{P}_f/P.$$

[16] Cf. sub-section 2.1 above.

Therefore, if we substitute equation (19) into equation (18),

$$P = \overline{P}_f/e(b). \tag{20}$$

That is to say, the domestic price level would ultimately depend on the state of the balance of payments in the economy. We could visualize this relation between the domestic price level and the balance of payments, with reference to the previous diagram of the balance of payments, the price of bullion and the rate of exchange, as in Figure 7.4.[17] It shows us the domestic price level, translated from the given foreign level by means of the exchange rate based on the price of bullion, at each amount of the balance of payments which an open economy may have at a given point of time.

Finally, from the intersection of the two conditions which any open economy must be subject to, i.e., the equalization of supply and demand in the domestic market (equation 17) and the price competition in the world market (equation 20), we could obtain the equilibrium domestic price level and the equilibrium balance of trade in the open economy.[18] We can see some of the results of this *interim* equilibrium situation of the open economy by interposing Figures 7.3 and 7.4 describing equations (17) and (20) to overlap each other, as shown in Figure 7.5.[19] That is to say, domestic price level and the balance of trade would be determined simultaneously, once foreign price level is given: if the foreign price level is high enough ($\overline{P}_f'$), the balance of trade would turn favourable ($b' > 0$), though the domestic price level would rise (P'); if the foreign price level is low enough ($\overline{P}_f''$), the balance of trade

---

[17] We could obtain Figure 7.4 by simply multiplying a given foreign price level by the inverse of the rate of exchange depending on the balance of payments, while omitting the relation between the balance of payments and the price of bullion in the lower half of Figure 7.3.

[18] We have then 13 unknowns and equations (1 - 11, 17 and 20), respectively, in our model of an open economy. While we replaced equation (12) in the previous model of a closed economy with equation (17), we added another one (20) as we have an additional unknown (b) introduced. (If we have another unknown (e), then we need another equation (19).) Cf. section 3 in the last chapter. Meanwhile, if the economy concerned is supposed to be 'large' enough to be the price-setter, rather than a price-taker, in the world market, the foreign price level (P_f) must be determined endogenously and, therefore, we need at least one more equation to complete the simultaneous equation system. For instance, if we specify exportation (x) and importation (m), as functions of P, P_f and e, and adopt equations (15), (16), (18) and (19), rather than equations (17) and (20), then we have 17 unknowns, including x, m, b, P_f and e, and the same number of equations, i.e., equations (1) - (11), (15), (16), (18), (19) and two equations for x and m.

[19] In our previous discussion of the balance of payments and the domestic circulation of money (subsection 2.2 above), we analysed the impact of the balance of payments on the domestic economy, on the assumption that the balance would be cleared between countries, in one way or another. As a result, we observed that it would affect the equilibrium situation of the level of output, price level and the rate of interest, by way of increasing or decreasing the supply of money in the economy. In contrast, in the present discussion, we examine a sort of *interim* equilibrium situation, where the balance of payments, either surplus or deficit, is supposed to still exist in the economy. In other words, apart from its character of general equilibrium analysis, the above model is based on the supposition that the balance of payments – to be precise, the balance of trade – would remain uncleared without exerting its full influence on the domestic economy. In reality, has any moment of time ever existed without any balance between trading nations? Or, has any balance ever existed without being paid between them?

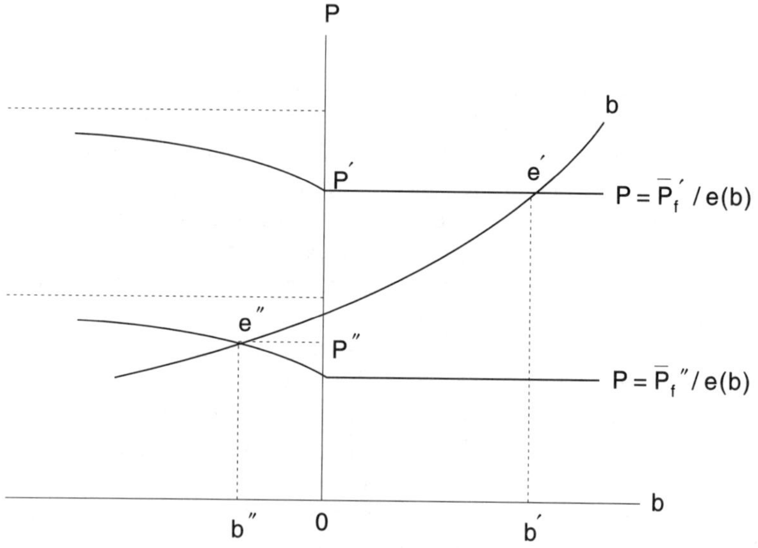

Figure 7.5 The determination of domestic price level and the balance of trade

would turn unfavourable (b″ < 0), though the domestic price level would fall (P″).

To conclude, as we explored Steuart's theory of international money in this chapter, we particularly tried to grasp it in the broad context of his whole macroeconomics. To this effect, we expanded the macroeconomic model of his theory of national money, developed in the previous chapter, to comprehend those new variables and relations attributable to international transactions and payments. As a result, we could complete his monetary analysis of output and price in an open-economy setting and better understand its contents and characteristics.

APPENDIX: Steuart on Banking

In his *Inquiry*, Steuart dealt in detail with the functions and operations of banking in an exchange economy. As its contents show, no doubt, his analysis of banking would stand on its own.[1] Nevertheless, it could be seen as an integral part of his theory of money, in the sense that the one relates to the other's institutional background and its policy implications. In other words, considering the whole scheme of his political economy enunciated in his *Inquiry*, we might regard Steuart's analysis of banking as subsidiary to his theory of money. The point becomes clear, if we look closely at the way how he actually treated the subject. As he examined the workings of various banks based on different sorts of credit, he carried out his analysis, from start to finish, in terms of their effects on the monetary mechanism of an exchange economy, in general, and the circulation of money in the economy, in particular.[2] Therefore, while Steuart's analysis of banking would deserve its own place in his economics, it could be better understood in the context of his theory of money. On the other hand, it is also true that one could not complete any discussion of his theory of money, national and international, without considering his analysis of banking, so far as the latter laid the foundations of the former. In this appendix, we shall present some aspects of Steuart's analysis of banking, which have some particular bearing on his theory of money, discussed in the previous two chapters, as either its premises or corollaries.

Let us start with Steuart's discussion of the functions of banking in general, in the exchange economy. According to him,

> Upon the right establishment of banks, depends the prosperity of trade, and the equable course of circulation. By them solid property may be melted down. By

[1] Part II of book IV in the *Inquiry* was entitled 'Of Banks'.

[2] In this light, Steuart remarked,

> The great operations of domestic circulation may be better discovered by an examination into the principles upon which we find banking established, than any other method I can contrive. It has been by inquiring into the nature of those banks which are the most remarkable in Europe, that I have gathered the little knowledge I have of the theory of domestic circulation. (*Works*, vol.3, pp.195-6.)

In fact, Steuart's discussion of banking provides an analytical basis not only for the national circulation of money but also for its foreign or international circulation and even for the public credit of government. He treated the latter two, respectively, in Part III ('Of Exchange') and Part IV ('Of Public Credit') of book IV in his *Inquiry*, just after the analysis of banking. In our previous chapters, we have already discussed both national and international circulation of money; whereas we will discuss the public credit of government in the next chapter on his theory of public finance.

> means of banks, money may be constantly kept at a due proportion to alienation. If alienation increase, more property may be melted down. If it diminish , the quantity of money stagnating, will be absorbed by the bank, and part of the property formerly melted down in the securities granted to them, will be, as it were, consolidated anew. Banks must pay, as agents for the country, the balance of their trade with foreign nations. Banks keep the mints at work; and it is by their means principally, that private, mercantile, and public credits are supported. (*Works*, vol.3, pp.199-200.)

That is to say, by means of operating various kinds of credit, banks facilitate the circulation of money in the economy, as they, nationally, supply money in accordance with the demand for it and, internationally, balance accounts with other trading countries. For Steuart, banking is the 'great engine for the circulation of money' in the exchange economy.[3] How it works depends on what sort of policy a particular bank adopts and what kind of credit it rests on. Thus, to see how banks facilitate the circulation of money in the exchange economy, we need beforehand to explore Steuart's categorization of various banks.

Steuart first classified banks or their business, according to their policy, into two sorts: i.e., 'banks of circulation' and 'banks of deposit and transfer'. The former refer to 'those banks which issue notes payable in coin to bearer'; whereas the latter 'those which only transfer the credit written down in their books from one person to another'.[4]

> These two species of banks differ essentially in two particulars. First, That those of circulation serve the purpose of melting down unwieldy property into money; and of preserving the quantity of it at the proportion of the uses found for it. Those of deposit, are calculated to preserve a sum of coin, or a quantity of precious moveables, as a fund for carrying on the circulation of payments, with a proportional value of credit or paper money secured upon them. Secondly, In the banks of circulation, the fund upon which the credit is built, is not *corporeally* in the custody of the bank; in the other it is. (*Works*, vol.3, pp.390-1; original italics.)

Thus, what makes them different from each other is that the 'banks of circulation' issue paper money on the basis of certain credit, whatever it is secured upon; whereas 'those of deposit and transfer' simply transfer credit while preserving the fund or security. As a result, while both sorts of banks would facilitate the circulation of money and enhance its supply in the economy, the 'banks of circulation' could perform far better than 'those of deposit and transfer'.[5]

---

[3] *Works*, vol.3, p.189.
[4] *Works*, vol.3, p.196.
[5] According to Steuart,

> Both indeed may be called banks of circulation, because by their means circulation is facilitated; but, ... circulation undoubtedly reaps far greater advantages from banks which issue notes transferable every where, than from banks which only transfer their credit on the very spot where the books are kept. (*Works*, vol.3, p.196.)

Steuart further divided the 'banks of circulation' or their business into three, in terms of the nature of credit on which they rest: i.e., those upon 'private credit', upon 'mercantile credit', and upon 'public credit'. According to him, the three different kinds of credit could be defined, respectively, as follows:

> [Private credit] is established upon a security, real or personal, of value sufficient to make good the obligation of repayment both of capital and interest. ... [Mercantile credit] is established upon the confidence the lender has, that the borrower, from his integrity and knowledge in trade, may be able to replace the capital advanced, and the interest due during the advance, in terms of agreement. ... [Public credit] is established upon the confidence reposed in a state, or body politic, who borrow money upon condition that the capital shall not be demandable; but that a certain proportional part of the sum shall be annually paid, either in lieu of interest, or in extinction of part of the capital; for the security of which, a permanent annual fund is appropriated, with a liberty, however, to the state to free itself at pleasure, upon repaying the whole; when nothing to the contrary is stipulated. (*Works*, vol.3, p.190.)

Thus, basically, the nature of different kinds of credit depends on the object of confidence or security for the credit concerned, rather than on who is the debtor or creditor.[6] 'Private credit', secured on a determinate value sufficient to acquit both capital and interest, is deemed the most solid among them. 'Mercantile credit', wholly subject to the opinion and speculation of debtor's integrity and ability, is the most precarious. The solidity of 'public credit', built on the pledge of the perpetual payment of a certain annual income, depends on circumstances.[7] On the basis of one or another of these three kinds of credit, any 'bank of circulation' must be established and conducted.[8] As Steuart went through with his analysis of banking according to the above categorization of banks, let us take up each of the different kinds of banks, in turn, for his detailed explanations of how it works.

The 'banks of deposit and transfer' were supposed to have some uses other than for promoting the domestic circulation of money in the economy, which we shall discuss later on.

[6] For Steuart's general discussion of credit, confidence or security, and the interest of money, see sub-sections 3.1 and 3.2 in Ch.6 above.

[7] Apart from the object of confidence or security for credit and the degree of its solidity, according to Steuart, there are some other characteristic differences between the three sorts of credit: that is, the difficulty of establishment, the ease of transfer and the stability of confidence. Cf. *Works*, vol.3, pp.191-3.

[8] Steuart himself conceded that, in practice, there might be some banks based on a certain combination of the three kinds of credit.

> ... although I represent each of the three kinds of banks as having a cause of confidence peculiar to itself, to wit, either private, mercantile, or public credit; yet we shall find a mixture of all the three species of credit entering into the combination of every one of them. (*Works*, vol.3, p.199.)

For analytical purposes, however, he assumed that each of them typifies the whole business of a particular bank.

The 'Banks of Circulation upon Private Credit'

These banks are those which issue notes or paper money on the basis of private mortgage. Since the security is most palpable and solid, the banks could still work in the countries where trade and industry are yet in their infancy. As 'circulating equivalents' are usually wanting for the lack of credit in those countries, the 'banks of circulation upon private credit' would help develop all the more trade and industry in the economy, as they 'melt down' 'solid property' and convert it into paper money for the use of circulation.[9]

Basically, these banks are set up privately for the gain of the profits from the interest of loans, out of which are deducted the loss of interest of money reserved, the cost of their management, and other expenses including those for international transactions.

> In proportion, therefore, as the interest upon the money advanced by the bank in consequence of the securities, exceeds the loss of interest on the coin in the bank, the expence [expense] of management, and providing funds abroad to pay balances, in the same proportion is their profit; which they may either divide, accumulate, or employ, as they think fit. (*Works*, vol.3, p.202.)

What then would regulate the limit of their loans upon a certain amount of 'solid property' in the economy? To answer this question, Steuart suggested what would determine the proportion between reserves and loans of the 'banks of circulation upon private credit'.

> In proportion to the notes issued in consequence of these credits, they provide a sum of coin, such as they judge to be sufficient to answer such notes as shall return upon them for payment. Nothing but experience can enable them to determine the proportion between the coin to be kept in their coffers, and the paper in circulation. (*Works*, vol.3, p.201.)

Thus, as the reserve ratio varies according to circumstances, the extent of loans does not necessarily depend on the amount of reserves kept in the banks. Neither does it depend on the mount of 'original capital' of the banks. Rather, it would only be subject to the general state of credit in the economy.[10]

> ... the solidity of a bank which lends upon private security, does not so much depend upon the extent of their original capital, as upon the good regulations they observe in granting credit. In this the public is nearly interested; because the bank securities are really taken for the public, who are creditors upon them in virtue of the notes which circulate through their hands. (*Works*, vol.3, p.205.)

This point seems to be particularly relevant to Steuart's analysis of money in two senses. On the one hand, it underlay his argument for the use of paper

---

[9] CF. *Works*, vol.3, p.197. Steuart took the banks in Scotland in his day as an example.

[10] This accords with what we have assumed in our fixed-price model of simultaneous determination of the rate of interest, production and consumption (sub-section 3.4, Ch. 6 above). That is, in that model, we assumed that the supply of money is subject to the state of credit in the economy (parameter α).

money. That is to say, as long as the economy's state of credit is stable enough, there is no actual limit to the circulation of paper money, apart from the amount of 'solid property' available for the 'private credit' in the economy; therefore, the first thing for the economy, suffering from the shortage of 'circulating equivalents', to do is establish a good state of credit so as to use paper money.[11] On the other hand, it also has to do with his postulate of the supply of money. Given the state of credit in the economy, the loans of the 'banks of circulation upon private credit' would be influenced by the rate of interest: the higher the rate of interest goes up, the more profitable the loans become for the banks. Thus, the supply of money would ultimately depend on the rate of interest.[12]

The 'banks of circulation upon private credit' also deal with some international transactions. Unless the balance between trading countries is cleared in hard currency, e.g., coins, the banks would have a part in settling their accounts. For instance,

> ... as nations who have coin, pay their *grand balance* out of their coin, to the diminution of this species of their property, so nations who have melted their solid property into symbolical money, must pay their *grand balance* out of the symbolical money; that is to say, out of the solid property of which it is the symbol. But this solid property cannot be sent abroad. ... in such case the credit of a bank may step in, without which a nation which runs short of coin, and which comes to owe a *grand balance* must quickly be undone. ... Upon this solid property, there is a yearly interest to the bank: this interest, then, must be engaged to foreigners by the bank, in lieu of what is owing to them by the nation; when once a fund is borrowed upon it abroad, the rest is easy to the bank. (*Works*, vol.3, pp.217-8.)

Thus, upon the security of 'solid property', loans could still be made for international transactions from the domestic banks, which simply transmit the 'private credit' to foreign banks. In this case, although some additional 'solid property' is 'melted down', it would not augment the mass of 'circulating equivalents' in the economy.[13]

---

[11] Steuart remarked,

> ... it appears that there is no impossibility for a people to throw the whole intrinsic value of their country into circulation. (*Works*, vol.2, p.41.)

For his discussions of the state of credit, the circulation of paper money and its effects on both the level of output in the economy and the 'balance of wealth' among individuals, see *Works*, vol.2, pp.40-2 and pp.53-66. In fact, we have already analysed them in the context of his theory of national money and interest in Ch.6 above. Cf., particularly, sub-sections 1.3, 1.4, and 3.4 in that chapter.

[12] In our previous model of Steuart's consumption-production theory of money (section 4, Ch.6 above), we presented the supply of money as being positively related to the rate of interest.

[13] For a detailed examination of Steuart's analysis of how the balance of payments affects the domestic circulation of money, see sub-section 2.2 in Ch.7 above.

The 'Banks of Circulation upon Mercantile Credit'

As already mentioned, the 'mercantile credit' is in its nature the most precarious of all and, therefore, it could only exist on a good and stable state of credit in the economy. On the hand, after a certain stage of development of trade and industry, the supply of paper money, based on 'private credit', would fall far short of its demand in the economy. Thus, as soon as credit becomes well established in the course of the development of trade and industry, the 'banks of circulation upon mercantile credit' would be introduced into the economy. They do not lend upon any mortgage or any determinate fund provided for the repayment of either capital or interest, but upon the integrity and capacity of the debtors. Among others, the principal branches of their business are concerned with discounting bills of exchange and making loans to the government upon the faith of taxes for a short period of time.[14]

While the business of the 'banks of circulation upon mercantile credit' is chiefly concerned with commerce and exchequer, these banks are more useful for promoting the circulation of money than augmenting its quantity in the economy. In other words, in contrast to those 'banks upon private credit' which multiply the currency by 'melting down' the 'solid property' which cannot circulate by itself, the 'banks upon mercantile credit' rather facilitate its circulation by discounting bills of exchange for merchants and by taking up exchequer bills for the government. For instance,

> The intention of this operation of discounting bills, is plainly to employ the cash of the bank in a way to draw an interest for it; but as merchants allow their money to lie dead for as short a time as they possibly can, the bank must have quick returns for what they advance upon discount, in order to be constantly ready to answer all demands. This is no loss to the bank, a prodigious advantage to trade. (*Works*, vol.3, pp.297-8.)

> The bank of England is to exchequer, what a private person's banker is to him. It receives the cash of the exchequer, and answers its demand. ... The large sums the bank is constantly receiving of public money, and the great assistance it obtains from thence in carrying on the other branches of its trade, enable it at present to make advances of money to government at 3 *per cent.* (*Op.cit.*, vol.3, pp.302-4.)

Nevertheless, as these banks still issue paper money to the merchants and the government in the interim before the one's bills of exchange and the other's revenue become due, they must be classified as the 'banks of circulation', rather than those of 'deposit and transfer'. In fact, like the 'banks of circulation upon private credit', they also issue paper money far more than the stock which they keep as reserves.[15]

---

[14] Cf. *Works*, vol.3, pp.198-9 and pp.295-315. Steuart represented the Bank of England in his day as a good example of this kind of bank, and described in detail its primary business under the following headings: 1. the circulation of the trade of London; 2. the exchequer business of Great Britain; 3. the paying of the interest of all the funds transferable at the bank; and 4. the trade in gold and silver.

[15] Cf. *Works*, vol.3, pp.206-7.

The 'Banks of Circulation upon Public Credit'

Relative to the others, these banks appeared most recently. They were originally designed to finance governmental spending. They issue paper money on the security of a fund appropriated for the perpetual payment of the interest. Thus, as long as the fund remains intact so that the interest could be paid regularly, the banks would continue their business and, thereby, promote the circulation of money in the economy.[16]

Without entering into details of Steuart's discussion of the 'banks of circulation upon public credit', let us gain a general idea on how, according to him, they work. He illustrated it in terms of an actual establishment of a bank of this sort, i.e., the Royal Bank of France, in his day.[17] He observed,

> The Regent [The Duke of Orleans] perceived, that in consequence of the credit of Law's bank, people grew fond of paper-money. The consequence of this, he saw, was to bring a great quantity of coin into the bank. The debts of France were very great, being, as has been said, above 2000 millions. The coin, at this time, in France, was reckoned at about 1200 millions, at 60 livres the marc, or 40 millions sterling. The Regent thought, that if he could draw either the whole, or even the greatest part of this 1200 millions of coin into his bank, and replace the use of it to the kingdom, by as much paper, secured on his word, that he should then be able to pay off, with it, near one half of all the debts of France; and by thus throwing back the coin into circulation, in paying off the debts, that it would return of itself into the bank, in the course of payments made to the state; that credit would be thereby supported, as the bank would be enabled to pay in coin the notes as they happened to return, in the course of domestic circulation. (*Works*, vol.3, pp.326-7; brackets added.)

As described here, the Regent's original plan for paying off the previously accumulated public debts seemed to be plausible enough to carry out. Indeed, the government could have issued sufficient paper money upon public credit

[16] Apart from banking, we shall look into Steuart's analysis of public credit and debts in Ch.8. It constitutes his theory of public finance, together with his analysis of taxation. As we approach it particularly in macroeconomic terms, we will discuss, for instance, the effects of public credit and debts on the circulation of money in the economy, as a whole, and thereby on price level and the level of output, in that chapter.

[17] In fact, Steuart explained the workings of the 'banks of circulation upon public credit' with particular reference to the 'Royal Bank of France', erected during the regency of the Duke of Orleans in the early 18th century. The bank was primarily planned to assist the government in paying off its public debts after the death of Louis XIV – the project was known as 'Mississippi scheme'. Steuart took great pains to give full details of the scheme in 13 chapters, including some chronological anecdotes, in his *Inquiry* (chs.XXIII-XXXV, Part II, Book III; *Works*, vol.3, pp.315-90). It starts with his account of John Law's establishment of a bank upon 'private credit' – the 'General Bank of Law and Company' – in 1716, which was eventually vested in the monarch and named 'Royal Bank' in 1719. After the transfer, the bank changed to a different kind: i.e., one upon 'public credit'. However, on Steuart's account, since the credit was secured on rather a 'precarious' fund than a 'permanent' one, it was to be overthrown in due course. As the bank led to total bankruptcy in 1721, the project ended up in failure. Steuart described it as a 'golden dream for a short space of 506 days'. Cf. Thiers (1859). For a short account of Law's monetary theory and 'Mississippi scheme', see *The New Palgrave* (1987). His major work on money and banking is *Money and Trade Considered: With a Proposal for Supplying the Nation with Money* (1705). In conjunction with the theories of creeping inflation in the 18th century, Blaug (1985) called him 'perhaps the best exponent of the doctrine that "money stimulates trade"' (p.19).

and paid all the debts, if the credit had been at all sustainable. However, unless it was certain that the bank was keeping a proper reserve fund for payments on demand, nobody would take paper money. And unless a permanent annual fund was appropriated for the payment of the interest from the government side, how could the bank procure the reserve fund? After all, the paper money issued for paying off the debts was secured on nothing except the government's own word. Thus, as soon as the public credit lost its ground, there occurred runs on the bank. The scheme proved a failure. According to Steuart, while one of the most important principles of credit is that 'a *permanent* and *well secured* fund of interest is always equal in value to a corresponding capital', the fund in the above scheme was 'at first real and did exist; but it was rendered *precarious*, by a blundering administration: then credit failed, and in that convulsion, the fund of interest was fraudulently diminished by an act of power'.[18]

The 'Banks of Deposit and Transfer'

So far, we have examined the three kinds of what Steuart called the 'banks of circulation' in turn. Now, let us move on to his discussion of some banks of a totally different nature: i.e., the 'banks of deposit and transfer'. An essential difference between them is that one issues paper money on the basis of certain credit, whereas the other does not issue any paper money but, instead, transfers credit itself while preserving its fund.[19] Thus, the principal business of the 'banks of deposit and transfer' is to preserve well the fund deposited, on which credit is given for its value.[20] Of what use then is this business?

Steuart gave an account of the utility of the 'banks of deposit and transfer' with an actual example of the Bank of Amsterdam in his day.[21] According to him,

> The original intention of the States of Holland, in establishing the bank of Amsterdam, was to collect a large capital in coin within that city, which might there perpetually

[18] *Works*, vol.3, pp.371-2.

[19] The paper money issued by the one is easily transferable everywhere, whereas the transfer of credit carried out by the other is only confined within the banks, themselves, where the fund is preserved. Therefore, as mentioned earlier, as far as the promotion of circulation goes, one is far better than the other.

[20] Thus, as soon as a bank lends or disposes of any part of the fund deposited, it becomes of mixed nature – both 'bank of deposit and transfer' and 'that of circulation'.

> Were it [i.e., coin locked up in the vaults] at any time to be diminished below the value of the credits written in their books, the nature of the bank would be changed. Were the coin to be lent on good security, such a bank would then immediately become a bank of circulation upon mortgage; since it would be the same as if the credit had been at first granted upon this security. Were the coin disposed of for no value, the bank would be from that moment bankrupt in fact, although the secret might be kept for a long time. (*Works*, vol.4, pp.352-3.)

Cf. *op.cit.*, vol.3, p.391.

[21] Cf. *Works*, vol.3, pp.391-415.

> remain, buried in a safe repository. ... Now the credit in the books of the bank, which is every day transferable at the bank, answers every purpose, either for payment or loan: and the proprietor has neither the trouble of receiving the species, nor any risk from robbery, or false coin. (*Works*, vol.3, pp.392-3.)

Thus, instead of issuing paper money, the bank was to grant credit upon the security of coin preserved in the repository. While the safe preservation of the coin deposited was the very ground of the credit, the bank was of great use for commerce, mainly, in the following two ways.

> The first advantage the city reaped from this institution, was, to secure the residence of trade in that city. Capitals transferable only at the bank, laid the proprietors under a necessary of fixing their dwelling where funds were, where only they could be turned to account. ... Another was, to prevent the inconveniences to which a small state was exposed, by the introduction of bad coin, from all the neighbouring countries in Europe, with whom they trade. (*Works*, vol.3, pp.394-5.)

That is to say, on the one hand, since all the bills of exchange should be paid in coin to the bank, from which their holders would obtain transferable credit for their value, trade must have been carried on only in the place where the fund was preserved. On the other hand, the establishment of the bank could also help prevent the circulation of bad coins in the economy by rejecting them when the payments were made. Therefore, the bank could well support trade and commerce in the economy by simply transferring credit while preserving coin in good condition and without recourse to issuing any paper money.

8. Public Finance

In this chapter, we shall examine Steuart's theory of the oldest branch of economics, i.e., the one dealing with public revenue, spending and borrowing, presented in his *Inquiry*. Among the economic writers of the mid-seventeenth century to the end of the third quarter of the eighteenth century, or around then,[1] Steuart seems to have been exceptional in the sense that his discussions of public finance formed a striking contrast to those of others. In particular, his views on public credit and debts appear to have been directly opposed to those held by the majority of his contemporaries and even the 'classical economists' later on.

We shall start with his analysis of taxation as a means of securing revenues for a government's spending, and move on to that of public borrowing as another source of revenue for the government. Then, the overall view of his analyses of government's revenue, spending and borrowing, discussed thus far, will be followed. As an attempt is made to formalize Steuart's system of fiscal policy in that final section, it would become apparent that his theory of public finance was firmly based on his macroeconomic analysis of money,

[1] The majority of historians call this period the age of absolutism in Europe. After several wars and conflicts between different sides within and outside most European countries for the preceding 120 years or so – conventionally described as the wars of religion, the countries were being transformed into so-called nation-states on the basis of the 'absolute' power of those monarchs who entered into an alliance with the third estate. Along with this characteristic feature of the political scene in those years, the then newly emergent bourgeoisie were gradually taking the place of, or at least taking their place with, the feudal lords, as the ruling class of society, in the social aspect of these nation-states. Economically, this time also saw many changes and developments. As a result of both internal and external expansion of markets, which became apparent as early as the mid-fifteenth century, the domestic and international circulation of commodities and money in those countries was to increase enormously. The wealth of nations, defined in whatever way, was yearly growing in its trend, in spite of sometime violent fluctuations or interruptions. The moneyed interest, such as merchants and manufacturers, were emerging as rivals of the landed interest and, as time went on, the conflict between them became obvious, particularly in some government policy issues, e.g., those of public debts and taxation. In fact, the increase of public debts throughout this period, which was still prolonged in the next century or so, was one of the burning issues in the economic as well as the social sphere of those days. That is, often accelerated by government expenditure for executing foreign wars between the then expanding nation-states, the ever increasing public debts affected the existing class strata of society, as the moneyed people, as stockholders, became a dominant class of the society. And the impact of public debts on the economy was considered by most of the contemporary economic authors to be devastating and destructive for they might dissipate resources and disrupt a smooth circulation of goods and money in the economy as a private debt might do to the debtor. As far as the taxation was concerned, there were, over this period, relentless debates on the objects of taxation and the incidence of various taxes, together with those on the actual methods of collecting them, since all these questions were closely related to the interests of social classes and economic sectors in the country. For the economic history of this period, see Heaton (1936), chs.XIII-XVI; for its general history, see Zaller (1984) and Woloch (1982).

price and output. Rather, it could be seen as a logical corollary of the latter analysis in the light of his general position on the active role of government in adjusting and guiding the economy.[2]

1. TAXATION

As far as Steuart was concerned, two main issues were involved in the theme of taxation. One is its effects upon the workings of an economy, e.g., upon the price of commodities, the rate of interest, the level of output and the balance of trade in the economy. Throughout his *Inquiry*, Steuart considered taxation to be a potent tool of the economic policy of government and discussed its effects on certain facets of the economy. The other issue concerns the nature of particular taxes, especially their impact on the different interests of individuals or classes in the society. While concentrating chiefly on the latter issue in the last book of the *Inquiry*, entitled 'Of Taxes and of the Proper Application of their Amount', Steuart investigated the different consequences of the imposition of different sorts of taxes. In this case, the taxation might be regarded as an important part of government's social policy. After all, according to Steuart, taxation is not merely a source of public revenue but it constitutes an efficacious instrument of both the economic and the social policy of government, together with public spending.

Needless to say, it is difficult to separate the macroeconomic aspect of taxation from the microeconomic, as they are mutually dependent and interact. In Steuart's analysis, nevertheless, they were disentangled in such a methodical way that a comparison could be made between different kinds of taxes. That is, for each kind of tax, both macroeconomic and microeconomic aspects were fully taken into account and coherently integrated into a system representing one of the options available for a government as policy devices.

Here in this section, we shall derive what Steuart called the 'fundamental principle of taxation' from his definition of tax in general. Then, we shall look at his classification of various taxes, bringing into focus their different natures, particularly in relation to their shifting and incidence. Next, we shall further examine his discussions of the consequences of the two alternative taxes, i.e., 'proportional' and 'cumulative', at a micro-level. At the end of the section, we will examine Steuart's account of their effects on the economy, as a whole, at a macro-level.

---

[2] We have already dealt with Steuart's macroeconomic analysis of money, price and output in the previous two chapters – Chs. 6 and 7 above. Meanwhile, for a detailed discussion of his interventionist view of the role of the state in his political economy as a whole, see Ch.10 below.

1.1 The 'Fundamental Principle of Taxation'

Although there are certain characteristic differences between all kinds of burdens, under the name of tax, which can possibly be imposed by the state in all ages of the world, there must be some features common to them, upon which its definition may be founded. According to Steuart,

> I understand therefore by tax, in its most general acceptation, *a certain contribution of fruits, service, or money, imposed upon the individuals of a state, by the act or consent of the legislature, in order to defray the expences [expenses] of government.* (*Works*, vol.4, p.173; original italics.)

He represented it as a 'fundamental principle of taxation' that the 'fruits' not the 'funds' are to be impaired by the tax; that is, it should fall upon revenue or income rather than capital or principal.[3]

> ... however different they [taxes] may prove in their effects and consequences, they all agree in this, that they ought to impair the fruits and not the fund; the expences [expenses] of the person taxed, not the savings; the services, not the persons of those who do them. .... This is a fundamental principle in taxation; and therefore public contributions, which necessarily imply a diminution of any capital, cannot properly be ranged under the head of taxes. (*Works*, vol.4, p.175.)

On the basis of this fundamental principle, as we shall see as we move on, Steuart offered a positive as well as a normative analysis of taxation.

1.2 The Classification of Taxes

First of all, Steuart classified modern taxes into three kinds, according to their natures and respective objects of taxation: that is, 'proportional' taxes upon 'alienation', 'cumulative or arbitrary' upon 'possessions', and 'personal' taxes exacted in 'service'.[4] A 'proportional' tax is paid by those who buy a commodity to consume, as it is 'consolidated' with the price of the commodity. A 'cumulative or arbitrary' tax is to affect the possessors of a certain sort of property which bears an income. It is 'cumulative', in the sense that it is levied on the past, not present, gains which exist in the form of

---

[3] In response to the criticism, in the *Monthly Review*, Aug. 1767, that 'every man whose goods are embarked in the political vessel, risks the whole; and in equity, as in all other cases of insurances, ought to pay, in the language of commercial policies, *as interest may appear*: which will be in proportion to the whole risk, and not in proportion to the profits, or fruits', Steuart explained why 'taxes should impair the fruits only, and not the fund', as follows:

> My reason for excluding in my definition of a tax, all contributions from funds ... is that they cannot, by their nature, be annual and perpetual, as taxes, which affects growing fruits only, may easily be. Were such contributions out of property, to be annually levied, over and above the full extent of the value of the fruits or income; the contributors would be reduced to beggary; and the taxable fund itself would in time, become the property of the state. (*Works*, vol.4, pp.177-8, n.)

Cf. *Works*, vol.4, pp.176-8, n.

[4] For some examples of these different kinds of taxes, taken by Steuart, see *Works*, vol.4, pp.173-6.

'property'; whereas it is 'arbitrary', in that it is laid upon the 'income' of the property, rather than upon any determinate piece of labour or article of consumption. A 'personal' tax is imposed on the person himself, not on his consumption or income, in terms of his personal service, not money or any equivalent.

Meanwhile, according to Steuart, the 'fund for taxation' or tax base in every kind of tax may be classed under one of the following headings: i.e., the produce or fruits of the earth, the produce of the industry of man, or his personal service. As to both the produce of the earth and that of the industry of man, the net produce alone is liable to taxation, and every contribution should bear a just proportion of this. In other words, that part only of the produce which remains after deducting an equivalent for all necessary expenses in making the production possible is to be taxed with regard to the land and the workman, respectively. Then, both of them might be subject to either the 'proportional' or the 'cumulative' tax, depending on whether or not they 'pass through alienation' – in other words, whether or not they are traded in the market. As to the 'incorporeal' work itself, on the other hand, it is to be affected by the 'proportional' tax upon its consumption; otherwise, in the case of no alienation, it may be laid under either the 'cumulative' or the 'personal' tax, according to how to pay, i.e., in money or in work itself. Now, let us move on to a detailed discussion of Steuart's analysis of the nature of the 'proportional' and the 'cumulative' tax, particularly their shifting and incidence.

'Proportional' taxes

With regard to 'proportional' taxes, which are equivalent, more or less, to what we call indirect taxes in modern terminology, Steuart first noted a problem arising from the fact that the composition of input is different from that of output in the economy of commodity production. That is, if we assume, rather unrealistically, the input and the output of production to be homogeneous, it would be no problem for a state to impose 'proportional' taxes on the commodities brought to the markets to sell, as those commodities might be regarded as just the 'fruits' or net produce, rather than any part of the 'funds' or what Steuart called 'physical necessary [necessity]'.[5]

---

[5] Steuart also considered the existence of the advance for production, 'either out of the producer's own stock or that of others'. In this case, according to him, the amount of output equivalent to that advance as 'physical necessaries [necessities]' should not be liable to taxation; otherwise, the tax upon it should be 'drawn back' to the producer.

> ... though in fact a farmer possesses all his crop after harvest, yet part of it, *as to him*, is virtually consumed either out of his own stock, or that of others, who have furnished him food and necessaries all the time it was coming forward. ... as the farmer is supposed to have paid the tax upon what he has borrowed and consumed, he must *draw it back* from those who, in

> Nothing would be so easy as a general rule for imposing proportional taxes, did the labourers of the ground actually consume a part of the fruits of the earth, and the other industrious classes a part of their own work, in lieu of the whole of this physical-necessary. In this case, nothing but what remained of fruits and work, not already consumed by the immediate producers, would come to market for the use of those who do not work; but who have an equivalent to give for it, out of the produce of past industry. Were this, I say, the case, ... then at the time of alienation a tax proportional to the value of the alienation might, with the greatest propriety, be imposed. ... Nothing would come to be refunded to the labourer or workman, at the sale of his surplus. This surplus would be equal to the whole produce of the earth, and the whole industry of the country, deducting the physical-necessary of all the industrious. ... it is supposed to be consumed in the very production of the surplus, as the aqueous part of sea water is consumed before you can have salt. (*Works*, vol.4, pp.180-1.)

Thus, the state could take a certain proportion of the 'surplus' only, produced in the economy, upon its alienation, if it alone, and not the whole of its gross produce, were brought to the market.[6]

Nevertheless, the above simple representation of the operation of 'proportional' taxes seems to be far from matter of fact in the modern economy of commodity production, where the composition of input is quite different from that of output and where not only the net produce but the whole output is usually intended to be sold in the market. In fact, Steuart's analysis of 'proportional' taxes was mainly concerned with this more realistic situation; though he examined the simple case to provide a general idea of the problem. Thus, he came to the point immediately after the above hypothetical illustration.

> What perplexes our notions in the theory of proportional taxation, is, that the industrious man, instead of bringing his surplus only, to market, is obliged to bring the whole of his work. (*Works*, vol.4, pp.183-4.)

> their turn, are to consume his crop: and if he draws it back, he cannot be said to pay it, although the state profits of it as much as if he did. (*Works*, vol.4, pp.181-2; original italics.)

[6] Actually, Steuart meant by this that the 'proportional' taxes would fall upon the buyers, rather than the sellers, of the 'surplus', as they were supposed to affect only the 'idle', who do not work but already have money to afford it, but never the 'industrious'. Meanwhile, we may note here that money, not only as a medium of exchange but also as a store of value, is supposed to exist and be used in the economy.

> Now what is here called surplus, relatively to the industrious, is the necessary fund of consumption for all the rich and idle; consequently, were the state to diminish any part of the *quantity*, the idle and the rich would be deprived of a sufficiency. ... without *money* there could be no tax imposed: for were the state to take their proportion of the real surplus, and dispose of it out of the country, a part of the inhabitants would be starved. But by an equivalent's being found, quite different from the surplus itself, of no use for subsistence, the whole produce of industry is left for the use of those who have it; the state takes what part of the equivalent they please from the idle; and nobody starves, except such as have neither money, nor industry, nor the talent of exciting the compassion of the charitable. (*Works*, vol.4, pp.182-3; original italics.)

For a discussion of the functions of money assumed in Steuart's analysis, see section 1, Ch.6 above.

There are two things which Steuart took into account in dealing with the problem of heterogeneity between the input and the output of production, in relation to the imposition of 'proportional' taxes. One is the price of output brought to the market; the other is the distinction between 'necessaries [necessities]', including subsistence and intermediate goods, and 'luxuries'.[7] If the price of output exceeds the value of the producer's 'physical necessary [necessity]', then some 'profits' accrue to him. Therefore, these 'profits' may either be taxed or not, as the state shall think fit. Depending further on whether the tax falls upon the producer or seller, or upon the consumer or buyer, it might be either of a 'cumulative' or of a 'proportional' nature.

> If this [the profit] be taxed in the hands of the industrious man, before it suffer an alienation, the tax will be of a cumulative nature. If it be left free to him, and taxed to the person who buys it, it will be of the proportional kind. ... In the first case, it will check the growing wealth of the industrious man; in the second, it will accelerate the dissipation of the buyer. (*Works*, vol.4, p.184.)

Thus, according to Steuart, when a tax of the 'proportional' kind is laid upon the consumer or buyer of a commodity, what he should pay for the commodity, as a result, consists of three components: namely, the prime cost, i.e., every expense necessarily incurred in producing it or the value of 'physical necessary [necessity]', of the producer or seller, his profit, and the tax. Meanwhile, the producer or seller has got the prime cost of the commodity refunded and also acquires his profit from selling it.

In the economy where commodities are generally produced by means of commodities, there are two kinds: intermediate and final goods. Among the final goods, according to Steuart, some are consumed by the 'industrious' as 'necessaries [necessities]', e.g., their subsistence; whereas others by both the 'idle' and the 'industrious' as 'luxuries'. On the other hand, the intermediate goods are, by definition, employed in the production process as 'necessaries [necessities]'. In his analysis of 'proportional' taxes, this distinction between 'necessaries [necessities]' and 'luxuries' among commodities serves to identify their shifting and incidence. That is to say, according to Steuart, 'proportional' taxes upon 'necessaries [necessities]' will shift to 'luxuries', and their incidence is upon the 'idle' and the 'industrious' who consume 'luxuries'. Steuart illustrated all this by an example.

> A tanner sells his leather to a shoemaker; the shoemaker in paying the tanner for his leather, pays the tanner's subsistence and profit, and the tax upon leather. The man who buys the shoes for his own consumption, refunds all this to the shoemaker,

[7] According to Steuart, those goods which are needed for production, e.g., the subsistence goods for labourers and the intermediate goods in the production process, are 'necessaries [necessities]'; and those which are not are 'luxuries'. Therefore, it was supposed in his use of the terms that the 'industrious' who work might consume both 'necessaries [necessities]' and 'luxuries', whereas the 'idle' who do not work would never consume any 'necessaries [necessities]'. Cf. Ch.2, particularly section 1, above.

> together with his subsistence, profit, and the tax upon shoes; consequently, the price of shoes are raised, only by refunding the taxes paid by the industrious. (*Works*, vol.4, p.187.)

Thus, we may note from this that while the price of a commodity (say, shoes) is composed of both the value of 'physical necessaries [necessities]' or the necessary expense and the profit of its producer (the shoemaker), the buyer (of the shoes) should pay a 'proportional' tax on top of it. Meanwhile, the necessary expense (of the shoemaker) is in its turn composed of the previous producer's (the tanner's) necessary expense and profit, and another 'proportional' tax upon the intermediate goods (the leather from the tanner), and so on. In the end, as those 'proportional' taxes levied on previous intermediate goods shift on to the final goods, the buyer or consumer of the latter goods should pay not only the immediate 'proportional' tax upon them, but also those upon the former goods through their price. Moreover, the incidence of even those 'proportional' taxes on the subsistence goods for the producers of both final goods and intermediate goods is also on the buyers or consumers of the very final goods. In other words, the buyers or consumers of the final goods ('luxuries'), not of the subsistence goods nor of any intermediate goods ('necessaries [necessities]'), pay all the 'proportional' taxes – i.e., those levied on these final goods as well as those previously levied on any intermediate goods and the subsistence goods for the producers of both final goods and intermediate goods. Consequently, the 'proportional' taxes are proved to affect only 'those who dissipate', whereas those who Steuart called 'physical necessarians' can draw them back by raising the price of commodity.[8]

---

[8] Unless it is always possible to draw a clear-cut line between 'luxuries' and 'necessaries [necessities]', how could the two classes of people be distinguishable from each other? In fact, the distinction between the two classes is ambiguous, as is that between the two supposedly different commodities. Cf. section 1, Ch.2 above. Nevertheless, we may say that, according to Steuart, if some of what he called 'physical-necessarians' might *exceptionally* consume certain 'luxuries', the competition among them would prevent them from continuing to do so. Therefore, as 'the extravagance and idleness of particular workmen does not check industry, nor raise prices', only that part of expense which is necessary for production could be 'drawn back' from the sale of commodities. With regard to the above example of a shoemaker, Steuart made this point clear.

> ... if the shoemaker's subsistence shall happen to include either their tavern expences [expenses], or his consumption on idle days, he will not draw these back; because other shoemakers who do not frequent the tavern, and who do not idle, will undersell him; he must therefore take his extraordinary expence [expense] out of his profits; and if his profit be not sufficient, he must run in debt to the tavern-keeper. (*Works*, vol.4, p.187.)

On the other hand, according to Steuart, those he called on other occasions the 'industrious' might consume 'luxuries', as they are usually supposed to acquire some profits upon their industry. Then, in this particular respect, they could be regarded as being quite the same as the 'idle'. That is, both the 'industrious' and the 'idle' are in effect exactly alike, so far as they commonly 'dissipate'.

> ... with respect to the consumption of superfluities by the manufacturing classes, they also must be considered as being of the class of the rich and idle, as much as the first Duke of England. (*Works*, vol.4, pp.189-90.)

After all this, we may conclude that the price of 'luxuries' paid by buyers is composed of (i) the whole value of the 'necessaries [necessities]' of the producers, i.e., their subsistence and intermediate goods, (ii) their profits, and (iii) the 'proportional' taxes, both upon the 'necessaries [necessities]' and upon the 'luxuries'. That is to say, the whole reimbursement of all payments and repayments at the previous stages of production comes upon the buyers or consumers of 'luxuries'. In particular, all 'proportional' taxes are eventually paid by those who consume 'luxuries'. Steuart came to this point, when he said:

> How absurd, therefore, is it either to say, that all taxes fall ultimately upon land; or as others, for no better reason, pretend, that they fall upon trade. I say, that this class of taxes [the proportional taxes] ... never can fall either upon, or affect any person but the idle; that is to say, the not industrious consumer. If there be found a possibility for any consumer to draw back the tax he has paid, I say he is of the class of the industrious, in one way or other: and farther I say, that such a tax raises the price of the commodity. But by drawing back, I understand, that the repayment is an inseparable consequence of his having paid the tax. (*Works*, vol.4, p.189.)

'Cumulative' taxes

Next, we shall turn to Steuart's discussion of the nature and consequences of 'cumulative' taxes, which appear to be analogous to what we call direct taxes these days. As mentioned before, according to him, 'cumulative or arbitrary' taxes are those which are imposed upon properties, i.e., 'the past industry, gains or advantages of fortune', which bear certain incomes. Thus,

> The nature of all these taxes, is, to affect the possessions, income, and profits of every individual, without putting it in their power to draw them back in any way whatever; consequently, such taxes tend very little towards enhancing the price of commodities. (*Works*, vol.4, p.191.)

First of all, unlike 'proportional' taxes, the imposition of 'cumulative' taxes might become arbitrary at the discretion of the state, as it is upon the *latent or*

If the 'industrious' class might *generally* consume certain 'luxuries' and 'consolidate' their profits upon industry into the price of commodity, then they would draw back not only the 'necessary expence [expense]' for production but also the 'extraordinary expence [expense]' for their 'dissipation'. In this case, Steuart called for the state intervention so as to introduce competition among them and to bring down the price level of the economy.

> When therefore the extravagance of the manufacturing classes becomes general, and when the rate of the market can afford them great wages, relatively to the price of necessaries, such profits consolidate into the price of the manufacture ... The statesman then must endeavour to create a competition among them, by introducing fresh and untainted hands into such branches. This will be a sure check upon the dissipation of the industrious, and ... will prevent all frauds, all pretences for the rise of the price of labour on account of taxes. (*Works*, vol.4, p.190.)

Then, however, there still remains some ambiguity in the distinction between 'necessaries [necessities]' and 'luxuries', i.e., that between subsistence wages and 'consolidated' profits, in particular.

potential consumption, rather than upon the *realized or actual* consumption. To lessen this inconvenience of 'cumulative' taxes, Steuart suggested:[9]

> First, ... the more such taxes [cumulative taxes] are proportional to the subject taxed; Secondly, the more evidently this proportion appears; and Thirdly, the more frequently and regularly such taxes are levied; the more they will resemble proportional taxes, and the less burden will be found in paying them. (*Works*, vol.4, p.192.)

Second, on many occasions, the 'cumulative' taxes might be found to be a burden to the 'physical-necessarians', i.e., those who only consume their 'physical-necessaries [necessities]', so long as they cannot be 'drawn back'. In fact, they would be no less burdensome to the 'industrious' in general, who otherwise could accumulate their wealth faster from the profits upon their trade and industry. As this wealth might be employed for the further advancement of trade and industry, according to Steuart, every deduction from their profits through 'cumulative' taxes is a diminution of such a useful fund. Third, however, the 'cumulative' taxes might prove to be suitable for thwarting the 'superfluity' of those 'rich and idle' who earn certain incomes from their properties, such as land, without any industry. Thus, on the whole, we may observe that 'cumulative' taxes are less preferable than 'proportional' ones, in so far as they are apt to be arbitrary; whereas the former are more effective than the latter in preventing a certain class of society from overgrowing in terms of its wealth. Steuart remarked,

> When cumulative taxes are laid upon any of the industrious classes, they tend to check growing wealth ... But as to the class of land proprietors, that is to say, the more wealthy inhabitants, who live upon a revenue already made, the impropriety of cumulative taxes is much less. They are however burdensome, and disagreeable in all cases, and ought to be dispensed with, when the necessary supplies can be made out by proportional taxes, without raising the prices of labour too high for the prosperity of foreign trade. (*Works*, vol.4, p.196.)

Now, on the basis of some general discussions, so far, of the two different taxes, let us further proceed to make a close comparison between them so as to better understand them.

1.3 The Comparison between 'Proportional' and 'Cumulative' Taxes

As the payment of taxes in general is made in money, the *quantities* of commodities in the private sector still remain the same, whether before or after their imposition by the government. An apparent change after the imposition is the increase of the mass of circulation, as the taxes should be paid either out of the money circulating in the purchase of commodities, in the case of 'proportional' taxes, or out of the income arising from certain properties, in

[9] As Steuart illuminated this by some examples, see *Works*, vol.4, pp.192-5.

the case of 'cumulative' taxes. Therefore, it is necessary for the state to augment the supply of money, in proportion to the increase of circulation resulting from the imposition of taxes, in order not to cause a general depression of the economy owing to the lack of 'circulating equivalents'.[10] Meanwhile, as we noted earlier, the *price* of commodities might change after the imposition of taxes, depending on their nature. Leaving Steuart's macroeconomic analysis of taxation in his *Inquiry* for the next section, let us examine now his comparative account of the consequences of the imposition of the two different kinds of taxes at a micro-level, particularly their effects on the price of commodities.

The effects of 'proportional' taxes on the price of commodities

The 'proportional' and 'cumulative' taxes are different in their respective objects of taxation. That is, the former are levied on commodities upon their 'alienation', whereas the latter on incomes of properties. Hence, it seems that, while the 'cumulative' taxes are nothing to do with the price of commodities, the 'proportional' ones raise it in proportion to their amounts. Moreover, as far as the 'proportional' taxes are concerned, those laid on the intermediate goods of production and those on the subsistence goods for labourers are subsequently to shift on to the price of final goods and those of non-subsistence goods, respectively, after they are 'consolidated' with the price of commodities. Therefore, as the incidence of all the 'proportional' taxes is upon those who consume non-subsistence final goods which Steuart called 'luxuries', the price of these commodities must rise, in the end, by the whole amount of the taxes laid on the intermediate and subsistence goods employed for their production, as well as those on themselves. And, of course, those intermediate and subsistence goods whose production process requires further intermediate and subsistence goods, also rise in their price by the amount of taxes paid by previous producers and labourers as well as the present ones. Therefore, Steuart said:

> ... when the commodity is not consumed by the purchaser, then upon a subsequent alienation he is refunded all he paid. I consider him therefore, in this case, not as *paying*, but as *advancing* the amount of the [proportional] tax for another; and while any part of the commodity remains unconsumed, there still remains the equivalence for a proportional part of the tax in the hands of him who advanced it. ... In all kinds of this imposition we find the tax regularly reimbursed from hand to hand; it adheres so closely to the commodity, that it becomes as essentially a part of the value, as carriage, packing, and the like incident charges, enter into the prices of goods. (*Works*, vol.4, pp.197-8; original italics.)

---

[10] See Ch.6 above, for Steuart's analysis of the relation between money, price and the level of output, particularly section 4, in which the velocity of circulation of money in the economy was assumed to be given.

Thus, according to Steuart, the 'proportional' taxes can never affect those 'industrious physical-necessarians' who do not consume any 'luxuries', and can never be avoided by those 'rich and idle' who do, as far as the price of commodities goes up after their imposition in such ways as we described above.

Then, having said that those 'proportional' taxes on subsistence goods raise the price of other commodities, is it true in Steuart's analysis that the price of the subsistence goods actually regulate the wages of labourers?[11] To be more specific, is it the case that the 'proportional' taxes on subsistence goods directly raise the wages of labourers?

> Were proportional taxes to raise the price of subsistence, and by that circumstance to discourage manufactures, we should see the generality of workmen living with sobriety, depriving themselves of superfluity, confining themselves to the plain but sufficient physical-necessary, working with all the assiduity a man can support, and still not be able to supply the market at the ordinary rates. (*Works*, vol.4, pp.200-1.)

Therefore, according to Steuart, since 'it is the rate of the market for labour and manufactures, and not the price of subsistence, which determines the standard of wages', those 'proportional' taxes on subsistence goods do not always cause the wages of labourers to increase, unless they are at the subsistence level.[12] Thus, Steuart strongly denied an alleged proposition against 'proportional' taxes, that 'they have the effect of raising the price of labour, and the produce of industry, and thereby prove hurtful to the prosperity of foreign trade'.

> ... it is generally thought, because taxes are higher in England than in some other countries, that foreign trade should therefore be hurt by them. But the sloth and idleness of man, and the want of ambition in the lower classes to improve their circumstances, tends more, I suspect, to lessen the productions of industry, and thus to raise their price, than any tax upon subsistence which has been hitherto imposed in this kingdom. (*Works*, vol.4, p.201.)

That is to say, as long as labourers can afford, on the average, some 'luxuries', the rise in the price of subsistence goods, occasioned by the imposition of

---

[11] The answer is no. According to Steuart, the wages of labourers are not regulated by the price of subsistence goods, but the price of commodities which they are employed to produce.

> Could a weaver, for example, live upon the air, he would still sell his day's work according to the value of the manufacture produced by it, when brought to market. As long as he can prevent the effects of the competition of his neighbours, he will carry the price of his work as high as is consistent with the profits of the merchant, who buys it from him in order to bring it to market; and this he will continue to do, until the rate of the market be brought down. (*Works*, vol.4, p.200.)

This view is after all in accord with his proposition that the wages are determined by the demand and supply of labour. Cf. sub-section 3.2, Ch.3 above.

[12] If the rate of wages were to be at a certain level of subsistence for the labourers – whatever the level is – then rises in the price of subsistence goods, either resulting from taxes or natural scarcities, must lead to an upturn of the rate and thus to a general advance in the price of other commodities. This is the case which we described previously.

'proportional' taxes on them, is hardly accompanied with any increase of their wages and thus of the price of other commodities.[13] Thus, from this analysis of the relation between the 'proportional' taxes and the price of commodities in Steuart's *Inquiry*, we may draw a conclusion as follows: while 'proportional' taxes in general raise the price of commodities being taxed immediately in proportion to the respective amounts of the taxes, those on intermediate goods shift on to final goods but those on the subsistence goods may or may not shift on to 'luxuries', depending on the level of wages in the economy. Unless the level of wages is one of subsistence, the 'proportional' taxes on subsistence goods usually do not shift. The reason for this, according to Steuart, is that although the price of subsistence goods *influences* that of other commodities, it does not *regulate* the wages of labourers. That is, as 'we do not see wages fluctuate with the price of living', we *cannot* conclude that 'a rise in the price of subsistence, occasioned by taxes, should raise wages more than when the price is raised by a natural scarcity'. Meanwhile, the wages of labourers are determined, instead, by the demand and supply in the labour market, and the demand for labour in its turn by the demand for commodities.[14]

What about the effect of those 'proportional' taxes imposed on both intermediate and non-subsistence final goods, upon the price level of the economy, where the rate of wages is above the subsistence level so that those on subsistence goods may not affect the rate of wages and thus the price of other commodities, as discussed just now? On their part, as we have seen

---

13 In this light, Steuart concluded,

> ... if foreign trade suffer by the high prices of commodities in our markets, the vice does not proceed from our taxes, but from our domestic luxury, which swells demand at home. Were we less luxurious, and more frugal in our management in general, all classes of the industrious, from the retailer down to the lowest manufacturer, would be satisfied with more moderate profits. (*Works*, vol.4, p.203.)

Therefore, according to him, if a country is in such a situation that its goods are not exported, because of their high prices, while the rate of wages is high enough for the labourers to be 'luxurious', then the government should promote competition among them by 'multiplying hands' so that their wages could only afford the 'physical-necessary [-necessity]' and at the same time the supply of goods could be augmented for both its domestic and foreign markets. Also cf. *Works*, vol.4, pp.206-7. Meanwhile, Steuart supported the use of export bounty to compensate the rise of prices occasioned by taxes, rather than the abolition of the taxes. Cf. *Works*, vol.4, pp.202-4.

14 In Steuart's own words,

> I must observe, that when manufacturers can thus capitulate with their employers, and can insist upon an augmentation of their wages, the demand of the market must be greater than the supply from their work. This is the circumstance which raises the price of labour. Let the demand of the market fall, the prices of labour will fall, in spite of all the reasons which ought to naturally to make them rise. ... Let the demand of the market rise, manufacturers may raise their wages in proportion to the rise of the market. (*Works*, vol.4, pp.204-5.)

Therefore, the price of subsistence goods *influences only on some special occasions* the rate of wages and thus the price of other commodities. See our previous discussion of his theory of wages in sub-section 3.2, Ch.3 above.

previously, there would be the impact of increasing the general price level of the economy, since the price of intermediate goods would increase only by the amounts of the taxes on them; whereas the price of non-subsistence final goods would increase by not only the amounts of the taxes on *them* but also those on the intermediate goods as they shift on to them. In fact, those 'proportional' taxes on subsistence goods also might partly contribute to raising the price level, in that their price would increase by the amounts of the taxes on them, although these amounts are not supposed to shift on to the non-subsistence final goods under the assumption that the rate of wages is above the subsistence level. Whether or not the rate of wages is above the subsistence level, does this general rise of price level imply any diminution or retrenchment in the total amount of consumption in the economy? According to Steuart,

> In answer to this, I must observe, that all the amount of proportional taxes is refunded to the industrious consumer, so far as they are raised on articles *necessary* for his subsistence; and when he is either idle, or consumes a superfluity, he is classed along with the idle and rich. Now if the rate of market price be high, relatively to the income of certain individuals, it can only be because the supply of the things they want to consume is not above the proportion of the demand of those who are richer. If, therefore, the rate of the market afford such profits to manufacturers as to render them idle and luxurious, how can the augmentation of these profits, by the abolition of taxes, and consequently diminution of the price of subsistence, ever diminish the competition of the rich, unless the supply be augmented? (*Works*, vol.4, p.209.)

Thus, as far as the domestic consumption is concerned, there would be no change in its *real* amount as a result of either the imposition or abolition of 'proportional' taxes upon it, because the movement of the price level has nothing to do with any alteration in the balance of supply and demand in the economy, while it has already represented the market conditions in *nominal* terms. Moreover, any change in the amount of profits, after the imposition or abolition of the taxes, might prevent the price level from further moving, since it helps the demand to stay stable by virtue of the fact that the profits would decrease or increase accordingly as the price of subsistence goods rises or falls.[15]

---

[15] Nevertheless, it is quite possible that the higher price level after the imposition of 'proportional' taxes might dampen foreign demand. In this case, Steuart suggested the application of the government bounty to bring down the price of exports.

> ... as far as taxes, which are imposed either to supply the exigencies of the state, or to cut off consolidated profits, enjoyed by manufacturers in consequence of our own extravagance, have contributed either to raise them, or to support them when raised, above the foreign standard, a full equivalent, in the way of bounty, must be given for them, in order to bring the exportation price of goods below the level of foreign competition. (*Works*, vol.4, pp.209-10.)

Cf. note 13 above.

The effects of 'cumulative' taxes on the price of commodities

So much for Steuart's discussions of the effects of 'proportional' taxes upon the price of commodities. Let us now move on to examine whether, according to him, there is any possibility of some 'cumulative' taxes affecting the price of commodities, though they are supposed not to. Basically, as we have seen earlier, the objects of imposition for the 'cumulative' tax are the income from various sorts of properties, rather than the consumption of certain commodities. Since, therefore, 'alienation' is not necessary in imposing the 'cumulative' tax, it neither directly relates to the price of commodities, nor can it be 'drawn back'. Consequently, on the one hand, it shifts nowhere and its incidence is on the very possessors of those properties whose incomes are subject to the taxation. On the other hand, although it may indirectly affect the price of some commodities through its effect on the incomes of their consumers and thus on their demand for them, it does not directly affect the price of particular commodities as the 'proportional' tax does. Furthermore, as it is paid in money, rather than in kind, there would be no change, apart from that income effect, in the market conditions of any particular commodity, upon which its price might bear.[16]

The transformation of taxes

Nonetheless, despite these apparent differences in their respective objects of taxation, incidences, and effects on the price of commodities, the two kinds of taxes were actually seen, in Steuart's analysis, to be 'transformable' into each other, in practice. As far as 'cumulative' taxes are concerned, in some cases, they could virtually be 'drawn back' and exert direct influences upon the price of commodity. For example,

> ... were a cumulative tax so levied as to prevent the proprietor [the consumer] from spending what the state intends to make him pay out of his income, he who pays it

---

[16] Even if a 'cumulative' tax were to be paid in kind, Steuart asserted, it would not make so much difference, particularly so far as the tax-payers are concerned.

> When a man pays his land-tax out of his rent, what remains to him will not buy of any thing than if he had paid nothing. Nay, were the state to indulge him and take his tax in corn, the corn which remains to him would not bear an advanced price, unless the state should export the quantity he had given; and then indeed, by diminishing the supply, it might raise the price of grain in general; but every one having grain to sell would profit of the rise upon the price, as well as the landlord, whose share does not commonly amount to one third of the crop. (*Works*, vol.4, p.221.)

Thus, unless any part of the commodity paid to the state as a 'cumulative' tax goes out of the country, its supply and demand conditions of the domestic market would remain the same after the imposition of the tax. Even then, i.e., in the case of the rise in its price due to the exportation, the tax-payers still could not be said to 'draw back' any part of what they have paid as the tax, since non-payers would also sell the commodity at an equally higher price.

Meanwhile, as we are at the moment concentrating on a microeconomic analysis of the effects of taxes on the price of particular commodities, we shall leave the income effect of taxes for a later discussion.

> would thereby acquire one great alleviation of his burden. ... When a brewer pays the excise, the tax, as to him, is of the cumulative nature. It is so in a certain degree, no doubt, as may be seen without farther explanation; but it still so far retains its own nature as to be easily drawn back from the consumer. (*Works*, vol.4, p.221; brackets added.)

Thus, those 'cumulative' taxes imposed on some incomes from the production of commodities might be 'drawn back' by the tax-payers later on when they are sold for the price which comprehends the taxes. Then, the nature of those taxes is exactly the same as that of 'proportional' taxes, as they shift on to the consumers who, according to the principle of the latter taxes, should pay for their 'dissipation'.[17] And whether to consume or not to consume these commodities at the price comprehending the taxes is entirely up to those who want to consume them. On the contrary, according to Steuart, if the liberty of choice between consuming and not consuming certain commodities does not lie with the consumers, those 'proportional' taxes levied on them must be of a 'cumulative' nature, in spite of their appearances.

> If the liberty not to consume be taken away, as in the *gabelle* [salt-tax] in some provinces in France, then the imposition changes its nature and becomes a cumulative tax, as may be easily perceived. (*Works*, vol.4, p.225; brackets added.)

Therefore, on account of this liability of the two different kinds of taxes to transform into one another, Steuart emphasized the importance of the proper methods for both imposing and collecting each kind of tax, given the initial purposes of taxation and the nature of each kind.[18]

The advantages of 'proportional' taxes over 'cumulative' taxes

Finally, before closing this section, we shall summarize what Steuart saw as the advantages of 'proportional' taxes over 'cumulative' ones. As we have already seen, according to him, the amount of 'proportional' taxes is ultimately taken from the 'superfluity' of the 'rich and idle consumers', while they are *advanced* by one set of the 'industrious producers' and refunded by another until at last they fall upon those who cannot 'draw them back' from anybody and thus must *pay* them. Therefore, the whole burden of the 'proportional' taxes is supposed to be confined to the inconveniences of

---

[17] In this context, Steuart added, in the above example,

> He [the brewer] thinks no more of frauds; he no more grudges what he pays; and becomes in a manner collector of that imperceptible duty *advanced* by him, and *paid* by all his customers. (*Works*, vol.4, p.226; original italics but brackets added.)

[18] For Steuart's discussion of the expense of collecting 'proportional' taxes and the oppression of many restrictions designed for preventing frauds in the collection, see *Works*, vol.4, pp.210-9. Also see *op.cit.*, vol.4, pp.277-300, for Steuart's observations upon the land-taxes of England and France at his time, and his suggestions for the proper method of imposing a land-tax. Cf. his comparative analysis of the methods of collecting taxes, particularly between the 'farming' and the 'management of commissioners appointed by the state' in *op.cit.*, vol.4, pp.300-6.

advancing their amount by the 'industrious' and to the payment of them by the rich and idle, which diminishes their income *in proportion to the amount of their consumption.* On the other hand, the amount of 'cumulative' taxes is taken directly from the income of any possessor of certain properties, regardless of the rich and idle or the industrious, and they cannot usually be drawn back. Therefore, the burden of the 'cumulative' taxes is supposed to be laid on none but those who literally pay them and the payment diminishes their income *without any reference to the amount of the consumption* they have made. From these contrasts in the object of taxation, incidence and relation with consumption, between the two kinds of taxes, Steuart concluded,

> ... no objection can lie against proportional taxes, so far as they affect the industrious; because they draw them completely back: and that great objections lie against cumulative taxes, when they affect the industrious, because they cannot draw them back at all; and consequently, they may affect the physical-necessary of the contributor, in case no profit should remain to him upon his labour. On the other hand, I think little objection can be made to cumulative taxes, when they are imposed upon possessions, which produce a visible annual revenue, clear to the proprietor. (*Works*, vol.4, pp.221-2.)

Thus, in that the 'proportional' taxes never affect the industrious whereas the 'cumulative' ones may do, the former are preferable to the latter.[19] Besides this advantage in favour of 'proportional' taxes, according to Steuart, there is still another, i.e., the less tax-resistance.

> In the cumulative taxes, the person who pays does not always perceive the reason of his paying. He imagines that he is taxed merely because it is known that he is able to pay a certain sum. In the proportional, the deceit is of another nature. When a person buys a consumable commodity, which has paid an excise, he does not perceive that the price he pays for it comprehends a tax upon his past gains, in favour of the public; he concludes the whole to be necessary, in order to procure what he has an inclination to consume. (*Works*, vol.4, p.222.)

Although the 'proportional' taxes may be perceived by those who *advance* them, they may not easily felt by those who really *pay* them. For the ones who eventually draw them back, there is no reason for resisting the taxes; for the others as consumers, there is only the option of consuming or not. On the other hand, the 'cumulative' taxes might meet with some resistance, particularly when they are levied in such ways as to affect the 'physical-necessaries [necessities]' of the industrious who are left no possibility to draw them back or to raise the price of their work because of competition. Unlike 'proportional' ones, 'cumulative' taxes may create unequal competition

---

[19] In another place, Steuart put it as follows:

> ... if this tax [the proportional tax] be improperly laid on, the defect will manifest itself by checking consumption only; whereas in the other [the cumulative tax], it will be known by the distress also of the individuals. (*Works*, vol.4, pp.224-5.)

between people of the same profession or work, as the latter cannot all be levied on them so equally as on the former, because of a variety of circumstances.[20]

1.4 The Macroeconomic Analysis of Taxation

After having thus far examined Steuart's discussion of the nature of different kinds of taxes, particularly their respective objects of imposition, incidences and effects on the price of commodities at a micro-level, we shall now move on to his account of the impact of these taxes on the economy as a whole, so that we may have a complete picture of the analysis of taxation in his *Inquiry*.

Taxation and public spending

Let us start with Steuart's characteristic view of taxation in connection with public spending.

> Raising money by taxes must always be burdensome, less or more, to those who pay it; and the advantages resulting from taxes can proceed only from the right application of the money when it is raised. ... If the money raised be more beneficially employed by the state, than it would have been by those who have contributed it, then I say the public has gained, in consequence of the burden laid upon individuals; consequently, the statesman has done his duty, both in imposing the taxes, and in rightly expending them. (*Works*, vol.4, p.227.)

Thus, Steuart considered taxation in general as an act of 'saving' out of the private sector 'in order to procure a public fund to be expended for the public benefit' in a macroeconomic sense. The justification of 'restraining the liberty of individuals in order to promote the common good' depends ultimately on how properly the fund raised is then spent. The criterion of proper taxation *and* public spending lies in whether, out of the alternatives, the public gain is greater or less than the private loss. Now, the question is how the one could be weighed against the other.

---

[20] Apart from the above two merits and demerits of 'proportional' and 'cumulative' taxes, Steuart pointed out another inconvenience which might occur in paying some 'cumulative' taxes.

> Those who come under such taxes [cumulative taxes], do not always consider that their past industry, gains, or advantages of fortune, are here intended to suffer a diminution, in favour of the state; for which out-going they have, perhaps, made no provision. When people of the lower classes, instead of being subjected to proportional taxes, are laid under such impositions, there results a great inconvenience. They are allowed to receive the whole profit of their industry, ... the state however reserving to itself a claim for a part of it: this, instead of being paid gradually, as in a proportional tax, is collected at the end of the year, when they have made no provision for it, and consequently, they are put to distress. (*Works*, vol.4, pp.191-2.)

That is, as the 'cumulative' taxes are not paid at the time of consumption or in any way bit by bit, the tax-payers may not be so provident as to make any allowance for what they are to pay at a certain point of taxation. Hence, distress and tax-resistance. To remove this inconvenience, therefore, Steuart proposed either the frequent and regular imposition of the taxes, or the 'retention' or withholding of them at the source of income, instead of allowing it to be received and afterwards obliging it to be refunded. Cf. *Works*, vol.4, pp.192-5 and p.222.

> ... the imposition of taxes is a method of bringing money into circulation; ... those of the proportional kind have the effect of drawing from the rich an additional price upon every thing they buy, which goes for the use of the state, and which otherwise would not have entered into circulation at that time. ... taxes promote industry; not in consequence of their being raised upon individuals, but in consequence of their being expended by the state; that is, by increasing demand and circulation. (*Works*, vol.4, p.271.)

That is to say, taxation would encourage trade and industry in the economy, not by taking the money from individuals but by throwing it into the hands of the state which spends it. As far as taxation and subsequent public spending draw money into circulation, which otherwise would not have entered into it, they would certainly help to raise the level of output in the economy. Even when the money raised through the taxation might have been spent in the private sector, the public spending, compared to the private spending, would be more certain, extensive and constant.

> It is no objection to this representation of the matter, that the persons from whom the money is taken, would have spent it as well as the state. The answer is, that it might be so, or not: whereas when the state gets it, it will be spent undoubtedly. Besides, had it been spent by individuals, it would have been laid out for the supply of private wants, which are not near so extensive as those of the public: and farther, when money is so taken from rich individuals, it obliges them to find out a way of procuring more, out of their solid property; and when this facility is not procured for them by their statesman, we see how taxes become both oppressive and ill paid. On the contrary, when it is provided, either by the returns of foreign trade, which greatly augment the coin of a country; or by banks, which melt down property into paper circulation; we see taxes augmenting constantly, without creating any impediment to consumption, or discouragement to industry. (*Works*, vol.4, pp.272-3.)

Thus, according to Steuart, provided that there is a sufficient supply of money in the economy, the taxation, being accompanied with the subsequent spending by the state, would add another, more stable, source of 'effectual demand' to the economy, and thus it could prove to be an effective policy instrument of the government for promoting trade and industry and thereby increasing the level of output in the economy.[21]

On the other hand, taxation in general, and the 'proportional' kind in particular, has some influence upon the price level of the economy, as we have seen in the previous section. That is, as far as those individuals who pay taxes are concerned, since the taxes are in one way or another taken from certain

---

[21] In this context, Steuart said:

> If these [principles of money, circulation and taxation] be just, we shall discover by them, how it happens that in countries where taxes are high, where living is dear, and where every circumstance seems to render the means of subsistence difficult to obtain, people live in the great plenty, are best and most easily subsisted, and that industry there makes the greatest progress. (*Works*, vol.4, p.270.)

Thus, according to him, the higher the taxation, the more prosperous the economy, in some cases. Steuart took some historical facts as examples. Cf. *Works*, vol.4, pp.273-7.

amounts of their income which they have already acquired, they could not buy things either as much as they used to or for the same price as before the imposition of the taxes. Whichever is the case, it implies a certain impact of the taxation upon the price level in the economy.

> After the imposition of taxes, the individuals of a state, who have already a determinate income, begin to pay greatly more than they used to do for every thing they consume. A great part of this additional price goes to the public, and is thereby laid out for national purposes. (*Works*, vol.4, p.229.)

In what follows, we shall take a close look at Steuart's analysis of how different taxes affect some major macroeconomic variables, particularly the general price level and the level of output or activity, in the economy.[22]

'Proportional' taxes and the circulation of money

First of all, we shall examine Steuart's discussion of the impact of those 'proportional' taxes laid on 'alienation', e.g., consumption, upon the circulation of money in the economy. Basically, according to him, the circulation of money is to be proportional to the 'alienation'; whereas its amount is determined by the quantity of money circulating and its velocity of circulation in the economy.

> As to this [the state of circulation], we have frequently observed, how it must be in proportion to alienation. This proportion is not determined by the value or denominations of the money circulating; but by this value with the frequency of transitions from hand to hand. (*Works*, vol.4, p.233.)

Given its velocity, the circulation of money would increase after the imposition of the 'proportional' taxes. Therefore, the supply of money should be augmented accordingly in the economy; otherwise, the amount of 'alienation' ought to be diminished, and thus the taxes themselves might become unproductive. Steuart remarked,

> ... when methods can be fallen upon to increase money according to the uses found for it, taxes will continue to produce, consumption will not diminish, and circulation will keep pace with them. (*Works*, vol.4, p.239.)

How then could the supply of money in the economy be augmented? According to Steuart, the price of all commodities is determined by 'demand and competition' in their markets. Thus, in proportion to the competition of those who come to the markets with their money to buy the commodities, a larger or smaller amount of money is brought into circulation. Meanwhile, as we have seen in the previous discussions of 'proportional' taxes, these taxes are imposed by the state, in a way, as if it interposed at the time of alienation

---

[22] For the reason given above, Steuart's macroeconomic analysis of taxation always goes together with that of public spending in his *Inquiry*. Therefore, in the rest of this section, we will examine the impact of taxation on the economy, as a whole, in connection with public spending.

and exacted a certain value in money from the buyers of commodities. Therefore, as the amounts of the 'proportional' taxes are added to what the buyers used to pay for the commodities before their imposition, either these buyers should give up buying them or they should bring more money with them to the markets. Hence, there would be an additional amount of money brought into circulation, if the latter is the case. According to Steuart,

> ... in proportion to the [proportional] tax, an additional sum of money is drawn into circulation, which would otherwise have remained in the pocket of the purchaser; consequently, on imposing proportional taxes, they cannot, at first, exceed that proportion of money which is found in the pockets of the consumers, over and above what they used to pay for what they consumed. (*Works*, vol.4, p.238.)

Thus, in so far as there is a certain amount of money which has been 'locked up' before the imposition of 'proportional' taxes, some additional amount could augment the supply of money in the economy after the imposition.[23]

What will happen, if the consumers just give up buying any more of those commodities on which some 'proportional' taxes are imposed, as they think their price after the imposition is too high, even though they have some extra money 'locked up'? What is more, if there exists no money, whatsoever, because it has been locked up in the economy, causing the amount of consumption in its private sector definitely to diminish with the imposition of 'proportional' taxes, may the state, then, still impose them? And, on what ground? To the first question, Steuart answered as follows:

> Could we suppose, that before the imposition of taxes, every person in a state had laid it down as a rule, to spend the whole of his income, but none of his treasure, in the consumption of what is brought to market, it is plain, that in a luxurious nation, taxes might be carried so high as to draw the last farthing of the treasure into circulation, even though it were supposed to exceed the value which demand had fixed for all that was formerly brought to market. But without a luxurious turn this would not be the case. There are countries abounding with coin, which it is impossible to come at by proportional taxes. The reason is plain: the value which demand fixes upon the total of the articles of consumption exposed to sale in the country, bears but a trifling proportion to the coin which remains locked up. This was the case in ancient Greece. In this case, proportional taxes never can exhaust the treasure; because were they to be made high upon articles of the first necessity, all the poor would starve; if upon articles of superfluity, demand would stop. (*Works*, vol.4, pp.239-40.)

Thus, if the 'proportional' taxes are imposed at too high a level, then the amount of consumption in the private sector would decrease, even if there exists some hoarded money in the economy. If they are too high upon 'necessaries [necessities]', the 'labourers' might starve as their wages would not increase accordingly. If they are too high upon 'luxuries', the level of

---

[23] Steuart provided some historical evidence for this proposition, that 'taxes must come out of that money which exceeds what was necessary for carrying on alienation before they were imposed'. Cf. *Works*, vol.4, pp.238-9.

output in the economy would diminish as its 'effectual demand' would decrease.[24]

Next, how could the imposition of 'proportional' taxes still benefit the economy, despite the fact that it would dampen the consumption of the private sector, if no money has been hoarded at the time of the imposition? To answer this question, we now have to find out how the fund raised by the imposition of taxes would be spent subsequently by the state. That is, we need to trace the course in which the money taken from the private sector by the imposition is later brought back into circulation. Steuart explained it rather neatly, as follows:

> I shall call the value, fixed by demand, for all that comes to market (Y). The sum levied in consequence of the alienation of it, or in other words, the sum of proportional taxes (X). And the whole money of the country (Z). ... as soon as the money of the country is brought into circulation, then (Z) will be exactly equal to the sum of (Y) and (X). ... Let us proceed to examine the progress of (Y) and (X) as they continue in circulation. (Y) is no sooner come into the hands of the industrious seller, but he has occasion to go to market: that moment I consider him as one of the rich; and the money which, at the time he sold, he had acquired the denomination of (Y), now resumes that of (Z). When he comes to buy a commodity with what was formerly his (Y), there is immediately a part of it converted into a new (X), and the remainder keeps the denomination of (Y) in the hands of him from whom he buys. ... Let us next follow the progress of (X). Upon the first alienation of any part of what comes to market for the consumption of the proprietors of (Z), a proportional part of (Z) is transformed into (X), and is carried into the public coffers. ... Taxes are not raised, in our days to remain in treasures, but to answer the exigencies of the state. The moment, therefore, that the money arising from them comes out of the public coffers, it loses the character of (X) and resumes that of (Z), by being brought to market in order to buy a commodity. This new (Z), as we may call it, no sooner returns into circulation, it becomes again converted into (Y) and (X), with this difference, however, that what came from the exchequer, so far as it is converted into (X), returns directly into it again. (*Works*, vol.4, pp.240-3.)

From this, we may notice two things: i.e., the extent of 'proportional' taxes and the nature of the public spending as a result. For the former, we may observe that the sum of the taxes (X) would soon far exceed the whole amount of money in the economy (Z), as they are levied on all the transactions carried out by both its private and public sectors.[25] For the latter, on the other hand, it is evident that the subsequent public spending following the taxation would be, at least, of the same nature as the private consumption, which might partly

---

[24] How high is too high? According to Steuart, it ultimately depends on the 'spirit of the people'.

> Proportional taxes, therefore, can be raised in proportion only to the desire of spending money; and as this desire depends upon the spirit of the people, so much the extent of taxes. (*Works*, vol.4, p.240.)

In this discussion, we leave aside the effects of public spending which is supposed to accompany any taxation.

[25] According to Steuart, the 'proportional' taxes might be carried to their utmost extent, when they are imposed on the whole gross product of the economy. Cf. *Works*, vol.4, pp.243-6.

be hampered by that very taxation. If, however, the public spending could be more stable and less precarious than the private as we mentioned before, the imposition of 'proportional' taxes and the subsequent spending of the fund raised thereupon by the state might turn out to be a preferable alternative, so far as the maintenance of the 'effectual demand' of the economy and the enhancement of its level of output are concerned. At the same time, moreover, this powerful policy instrument of government could be better employed, when it is applied to discouraging the 'superfluity of the rich and idle' and encouraging the 'industry and ingenuity of the industrious', so as to further enhance the level of output and employment in the economy.[26]

> The whole of such expences [expenses of the state] is thrown into circulation, as much as if the rich proprietors had laid it out themselves upon articles entirely adapted the their own taste. Is it not evident, that in this way of appropriating the income of a country, it must produce a more extensive encouragement to industry of all kinds, than if the proprietors only had spent it? ... Does not the experience of former ages show how apt private opulence is to sink into treasures, when a taste for industry does not animate the lower classes to create new objects of desire in the wealthy? Wherein is a state benefited by the luxurious gratifications of the rich, unless it be by the employment they procure for those who provide the objects of luxury? Those very gratifications are, in one sense, taxes upon the rich in favour of the industrious: they increase expence [expense], and throw money into circulation. (*Works*, vol.4, pp.229-30.)

We have now examined how, according to Steuart, the 'proportional' taxes would affect the circulation of money in the economy and consequently its price and output level, under various circumstances. What then about the 'cumulative' taxes?

---

[26] In this context, Steuart further suggested two things for the proper application of the taxation and public spending: one for the imposition of the 'proportional' taxes to render the taxation itself more productive, and the other for the use of the public fund to make the foreign trade favourable.

> Subsistence and necessaries might be taxed low in proportion to the abilities of those of the lower classes; articles of luxury might be taxed in a higher proportion, in order to draw the more into the exchequer. (*Works*, vol.4, p.244.)

> When a due proportion of the amount of taxes is properly laid out in premiums, for the encouragement of the industrious, the prices of labour upon articles of exportation, may be brought so low, that all nations who do not follow the like policy, must languish and decay. (*op.cit.*, vol.4, p.231.)

Since, according to Steuart, the wages of labourers usually do not depend on the price of subsistence, too high a 'proportional' tax upon it might force some of them, who could not 'draw it back', into a condition of starvation, and the tax itself might therefore become unproductive. In the meantime, if the wages are so low as to be just at a subsistence level, all the 'proportional' tax upon the subsistence must be drawn back by the labourers. Besides, all those 'proportional' taxes upon intermediate goods are always drawn back from the final goods. Therefore, if it might happen that some 'proportional' taxes accordingly raise the price of exports, the government should furnish the export industries with some export bounties or subsidies to make them competitive in the international market. Cf. our previous discussions on these in the last section above.

'Cumulative' taxes and the circulation of money

At a macroeconomic level, the 'cumulative' taxes seem to affect the circulation of money in an economy in a way quite similar to the 'proportional' ones. That is, the former are also supposed to take out a certain amount of money from the private sector in one way as the latter do in another, and thus may tighten the circulation in that sector as the latter may do. And subsequently the former would also bring the fund raised through them into circulation, by means of the public spending of the government, as the latter would do. As we have discussed in the previous section, one of the main differences between them is that the one comes out directly from the income of the private sector whereas the other emerges indirectly through its spending. Therefore, while the 'proportional' taxes would raise the price of commodities both *immediately* by being superadded to it and *in the longer term* by their income effect, the 'cumulative' ones might raise it later via their income effect *only*. On the other hand, as far as the amount of consumption in the private sector is concerned, it might diminish in both cases, as they both commonly reduce the money circulating which is in fact the whole income of the sector, until the public spending subsequently follows the imposition of the taxes; unless there is some extra amount of money, apart from the income, which has been 'locked up' before the imposition. Indeed, we already examined this aspect of taxation and public spending in general, when we dealt with the impact of 'proportional' taxes on the economy as a whole.

Therefore, it appears that the only difference which still exists between the two taxes at the macroeconomic level is the way in which they affect the price level of the economy: i.e., one raises it both *immediately* and *in the longer term*, and the other *only in the longer term* through income effect. Yet, there is another difference, which is almost symmetrical to the first one: that is, for the 'proportional' tax which necessitates certain 'alienation', it is impossible to impose it on that part of the income which is going to be 'locked up' or that part of the 'stock' which is already locked up and has never come out for consumption; whereas, for the 'cumulative' one which does not necessitate any alienation, it is possible. In other words, only the 'cumulative' tax, never the 'proportional' tax, can be imposed by the government on those savings of individuals which would not appear in 'alienation' any more.[27]

---

[27] We have already noted, in the previous section, that Steuart generally preferred the imposition of 'proportional' taxes to that of 'cumulative' ones. At this particular juncture, he was opposed rather strongly to the latter.

> When proportional taxes are carried to their full extent, I then presume every one will be obliged to pay as much as possible; ... and therefore, were cumulative, or personal taxes, to be superadded on those who already pay all they can, they would, by affecting them unequally, deprive many of their physical-necessary, or small profits; and consequently destroy the proper balance of their competition. ... taxes can be increased in proportion only to the spirit of dissipation in the people. To force money, therefore, out of the hands of those who do not

> Were [proportional] taxes thus carried out to their utmost extent, still every person in the state must be left at liberty to save, or to spend the whole, or any part of his stock, or income; which is not the case when cumulative taxes are imposed. (*Works*, vol.4, pp.244-5.)

Therefore, the savings locked up in the private sector belong to the domain of the 'cumulative' tax. Apart from these dual aspects of the two kind of taxes, in a macroeconomic dimension, there is not much difference between them. After discussing Steuart's analysis of public credit and debts in the next section, we shall make an attempt to build up a formal model of his theory of public finance as whole, which will comprehend what we have discussed so far in this section.

2. PUBLIC CREDIT AND DEBTS

In this section, we shall examine Steuart's analysis of public credit or borrowing as another important means of securing revenues for a government's spending, apart from taxation. As is the case with his analysis of taxation, it could be fully anatomized and grasped in the context of his macroeconomics as a whole. In fact, if we approach Steuart on public credit and debts in the same vein as in the last section dealing with his discussions of taxation, we may finally portray the whole scope of his theory of public finance, remaining faithful to his own logic. We could represent it in terms of the first single principle of public finance in his political economy – i.e., the active role of the state in adjusting and guiding the economy by means of its fiscal policy.[28]

Specifically, in the present section, we shall first examine his discussions of the nature of public credit, especially in comparison with that of other sorts of credit, and its social and economic consequences. Then, after further exploring his discussions of the various methods of contracting and paying off public debts, and the public bankruptcy of the state as a result of excessive debts, either domestic or foreign, we shall finally close this section by disentangling some macroeconomic implications of his analysis of public credit and debts.[29]

> incline to spend it, is forcing the spirit of the people; if it be not tyranny, it is at least great severity. (*Works*, vol.4, p.246.)

[28] Cf. our macroeconomic model of Steuart's theory of public finance in the next section. For a general discussion of his view on the role of the state in an exchange economy, see Ch.10 below.

[29] Stettner (1945) gave a due account of some distinctive features of Steuart's analysis of public debts, particularly in comparison with that of two of his contemporaries, i.e., Hume and Smith. Based on some factual evidences, he showed that 'only in Steuart's discussion did the development and role of British credit during the eighteenth century receive adequate recognition and understanding' (Stettner (1945), p.454). According to him, 'Steuart sees it as the function of the state to draw stagnant funds out of hoards, via taxation or public borrowing, and channel them into useful and productive government expenditures, thus ensuring that the income flow will complete its circuit'

2.1 The Nature of Public Credit

Steuart defined 'public credit', as against both 'private' and 'mercantile credit', in the following way:[30]

> This [Public credit] is established upon the confidence reposed in a state, or body politic, who borrow money upon condition that the capital shall not be demandable; but that a certain proportional part of the sum shall be annually paid, either in lieu of interest, or in extinction of part of the capital; for the security of which, a permanent annual fund is appropriated, with a liberty, however, to the state to free itself at pleasure, upon repaying the whole; when nothing to the contrary is stipulated. The solidity of this species of credit depends upon circumstances. (*Works*, vol.3, p.190.)

In this definition, the most characteristic feature of public credit, which makes it different from the other sorts, lies in its 'nature of security' or 'object of confidence', rather than in the conditions of the debtor or borrower. That is to say, whereas the other sorts of credit depend on either the existence of a security, real or personal, whose value is sufficient to acquit both capital and interest, or the confidence to the lender that the borrower may be able to replace the capital advanced and the interest due during the advance, the public credit rests only on the visible security of a fund appropriated for its annual payment, either perpetual or determinate, apart from the stability of 'public faith'.[31] Thus, we may note, on the one hand, that Steuart's classification of credit is based on its object of security, no matter who is the debtor or borrower, and that the solidity of the security is essential to each kind of credit. As far as the public credit is concerned, on the other hand, it could be well sustained, as long as the annuity continues regularly to be paid and the fund appropriated for this remains entire.

2.2 The Consequences of Public Borrowing

First of all, as we have already discussed, the essence of public credit depends on the payment of annuities, i.e., the annual payment of the interest for the money borrowed and, sometimes, of part of the capital. In a sense, we may say, the annuities of public credit are bought by those who lend to the state, for the price of the capital. On the other hand, the state ultimately pays the annuities out of its revenues from taxation. In Steuart's analysis of taxation, as discussed in the previous section, the tax revenue of a state is supposed to

(*ibid.*, pp.475-6). We will mainly point to this characteristic of Steuart's view on public finance in this section. It will be made even clearer, as we set up a monetary general equilibrium model of his analysis of public finance in the next section.

30 For Steuart's discussions of credit, in general, and 'public credit', in comparison with 'private' and 'mercantile credit', in particular, see *Works*, vol.3, pp.137-46 and pp.189-93, respectively. And also cf. sub-section 3.1, Ch.6 and the appendix to Chs. 6 and 7 above.

31 In addition to the different nature of 'security' or 'object of confidence' for each of the three kinds of credit, Steuart mentioned some other characteristics of them, i.e., differences in the difficulty of establishing, the ease of transfer and the stability of confidence. Cf. *Works*, vol.3, pp.191-3.

have two main sources, i.e., the imposition of 'proportional' taxes on commodities and that of 'cumulative' taxes on incomes. In either case, the tax revenue in effect comes from the national income, indirectly or directly. Therefore, while the public credit creates a new branch of 'solid personal property', i.e., stock, which bears certain incomes or annuities; it seems, above all, to result in the transfer of incomes from the tax-payers to the stock-holders.

> The capital of the public debts is the price which has been paid for the annuities due to the creditors, and is now no more money to them than land is money to the landlords. It may turned into money, no doubt; but so may land. ... While it is fixed, that is, given for any permanent value, it ceases to be money; when it is called in, it becomes money again. Let stock, therefore, suffer ever so many alienations from hand to hand, it still continues stock: it never can become land, it never can become money, until it be paid off by the government. Stock, therefore, I here consider as one great branch of solid personal property; as far as the security of government is solid and good; and such as, may be melted down into money by banks, as well as any other thing. ... this fund is formed out of the income of whole nation; consequently by *fund*, here, I do not understand the capital, which exists no more, but the interest which is drawn for it: it is this interest, I say, which is paid from the land, the money, the trade, the industry, &c. which forms one great branch of the monied [moneyed] interest of England. ... The more the national debts increase, by the monied [moneyed] interest realizing into this branch of solid property the funds, the more taxes must augment. (*Works*, vol.4, pp.123-4.)

Thus, according to Steuart, one of the significant results of public borrowing by the state is the transfer of wealth between social classes in the economy.

> When a statesman, therefore, establishes a system of public credit, the first object which should fix his attention is to calculate how far the constitution of the state, and its internal circumstances, render it expedient to throw the revenue of it into the hands of a moneyed interest. ... In political bodies every separate interest will consult its own; and in the contest between those who will be made to pay, and those who are to receive the taxes, under the denomination of creditors, the security of public credit will become precarious. (*Works*, vol.4, pp.3-4.)

Therefore, as the government borrows money from a certain group of people in the economy and appropriates a part of every branch of revenue for the payment of it, the consequence will be, in the first place, to transfer income to the creditors. And, as a result, unless all the interests in the economy are duly considered and a sort of sinking fund for paying off the debts is properly raised, the solidity of public credit itself may become endangered. In the case of foreign debts, the public borrowing may occasion the transfer of wealth from one country to another.

Along with its social effects mentioned above, public borrowing has obviously some influence on the workings of the economy, including its own fate. As we shall fully investigate, later on, how public borrowing was supposed to affect the economy as a whole in Steuart's analysis, let us just note briefly its apparent economic consequences. First of all, as the state should pay annuities for the money borrowed, it might augment the incomes of individuals who lend money to the state, if the money would otherwise be hoarded in their coffers.

> ... the effect of public borrowing, or national debt, is to augment the permanent income of the country, out of stagnating money, and balances of trade. (*Works*, vol.4, p.130.)

Therefore, second, public borrowing might have the effect of providing an employment for the hoarded money in the economy.

> If stagnation in one part be found to interrupt circulation in another, public borrowing, for domestic purposes, has the good effect of giving vent to the stagnation, and throwing the money into a new channel of circulation. (*Works*, vol.4, p.130.)

Third, since it is ultimately taxes which are mortgaged for public debts, the taxes must be multiplied in the end to pay the annuities of the debts, and all these circumstances would result in the increase of circulation of money in the economy.

> [When] recourse is had to credit, money is borrowed, debts are contracted, [and] taxes are augmented; all this increases circulation, which demands a supply of currency. (*Works*, vol.4, p.120; brackets added.)

Meanwhile, the ever increasing public indebtedness might bring forth some other consequences. One of those might be a public bankruptcy.

> If natural causes be left to work their own effects, without a systematical plan of borrowing, the consequence will be a bankruptcy, and a total failure of public credit, at least for some time. (*Works*, vol.4, p.4.)

Thus, unless the public debts, as a result of public credit, are paid off in one way or another, their gradual increase might unavoidably cause the general bankruptcy of the state and a collapse of the public credit itself. Another consequence of escalating public debts might be an abrupt and unilateral repudiation of them by the state.

> If a state should find the mass of their own debts to amount to so great a sum as to be insupportable, they might have recourse to a total, or partial abolition of them by an act of power. (*Works*, vol.4, p.4.)

Although this case appears to be different from the above one in that it takes place by a deliberate act of the government, it could be also regarded as a public bankruptcy, either partial or general. In fact, both cases appear to represent certain limitations of public credit. Thus, let us next turn to Steuart's discussions of how public debts could be paid off and what would happen otherwise.

2.3 The Repayment of Public Debts and Bankruptcy

Obviously, as the public borrowing and spending of a state expands more and more, its public debts should continually increase, if it does not pay back the principal. After all, according to Steuart, unless the annual payments for its borrowing exceed the interest and thus gradually pay off the principal as well, the state running public credit to an increasing extent would come to one of these three results: i.e., either the natural extinction of its public debts, a public bankruptcy, or the repayment of the debts under certain special schemes.

> We may therefore conclude, that one of three events must happen, viz. either First, Debts will swell to such a pitch as at last to pay themselves: or, Secondly, The nation will be involved in a bankruptcy: or, Thirdly, They will be fairly paid off, or at least circumscribed within reasonable bounds. (*Works*, vol.4, p.136.)

Actually, the first of these results seems to be an extreme and rather unrealistic case which is supposed to be what would follow when public credit and taxes are carried to their utmost extent as we discussed in the previous sub-section. That is to say, if the state continues to borrow money from the private sector until all the sources of taxation, for the payment of annuities for its debts, are exhausted, then it might not need to trouble to impose taxes and pay the annuities with them; since the fact is then that the state first takes all the incomes of the private sector and later returns them as the annuities, which then becomes a situation without any public debts and taxes.[32]

> ... the state then [when public debts and taxes are carried to the greatest height possible] be in possession of all that can be raised on the land, on the consumption, industry and trade of the country; in short, of all that can be called income, which it will administer for the public creditors. When this come to be the case, debts become extinguished of course; because they come to be consolidated with the property: a case which commonly happens when a creditor takes possession of an estate for the payment of debts equal to its value. (*Works*, vol.4, p.134.)

Meanwhile, Steuart admitted that in practice most of public debts would sooner or later disappear, in one way or another, before they reach their highest level.

> If we judge of them from what past experience has taught us, we may conclude, that, in one way or another, all debts contracted will in time disappear, either by being paid,

---

[32] In fact, Steuart conceded this result of increasing public debts as being merely contingent and hypothetical, though he still strongly argued against another result, a public bankruptcy.

> The whole of this hypothesis is, I readily agree, destitute of all probability; because of the infinite variety of circumstances which may frustrate such a scheme. I introduced it merely to show where the constant mortgaging of a public revenue *may* end; and to disprove the vulgar notion, that by contracting debts beyond a certain sum, *a trading nation which has a great balance in its favour*, must be involved in an unavoidable bankruptcy. To say that a *nation* must become bankrupt to itself, is a proposition which I think implies a contradiction. (*Works*, vol.4, p.135; original italics.)

Cf. *op.cit.*, vol.4, pp.134-6.

> or being abolished: because it is not expected that posterity will groan under such a load any longer than it is convenient; and because in fact we see no very old public debts as yet outstanding, where interest has been regularly paid out of a fund which has remained in the possession of a state. (*Works*, vol.4, p.117.)

Thus, as a matter of fact, the public debts are more likely either to be paid off or to involve the country in a public bankruptcy, whether unavoidable or deliberate, than to increase to an unlimited extent. Now then, let us move on to Steuart's discussions of the various methods of paying off public debts and the public bankruptcy of a state.

Methods of repayment

Steuart noted that when a state contracts public debts, the foundation of its public credit is the existence of a sure and sufficient fund for performing the engagements contracted. Consequently, as the fund never can be formed but from taxes, the more public debts are contracted, the more must the taxes be imposed. In contracting the debts, on the other hand, the first article to be agreed upon is the rate of interest. As, in Steuart's analysis, the rate of interest is determined by the supply and demand of money in the money market, the government intending to borrow must use all possible means to increase the quantity of money in circulation. Regarding these two aspects of contracting public debts, Steuart made his point as follows:

> The method, therefore, of borrowing money to the best advantage, is previously to establish a fund of credit, arising from annual taxes; to provide the people who are to pay them, with credit or money in proportion to their property or industry; and to prevent the latter from ever failing for want of the medium, money, for carrying it on. (*Works*, vol.4, p.151.)

Thus, according to him, the only way for the state to borrow money from the private sector without any excessive burden of the debts later on, is to previously provide a fund for making good what is agreed upon with the creditors, by means of imposing the taxes for that purpose and, at the same time, increasing the supply of money in the economy. Otherwise, the state should at least work out a certain way to pay off the public debts already contracted, in order to avoid a bankruptcy and thus to preserve its public faith.

Steuart then proceeded to consider some advantages and disadvantages of the several methods of discharging public debts. First, a state may pay off the long term debts all at once, by refunding to the creditors the whole capital and all arrears of the interest. In that case, according to Steuart, it would occasion a sudden and violent impact on the economy, e.g., a sharp fall in the rate of interest.

> Could a treasure be brought from India (let me suppose) sufficient at once to discharge the debts of Great Britain, circulation would become so glutted with money, that interest would fall to nothing. This would be a temporary loss to all the former

> creditors, until they had time to lend to the other states of Europe. (*Works*, vol.4, p.161.)

Therefore, as the velocity of circulation of money falls, the activity level of the economy would decline heavily.

Second, when public debts are paid off partially every year from a sinking fund set apart for discharging the capital and interest, there would be no adverse effect on the economy, as long as the repayment is executed gradually. It should not result in any stagnation of money in the private sector. Only the price of stock might change accordingly.

> If, upon the establishment of such a plan, the stock be found to rise, it will be a proof that either the interest formerly paid was below the common rate, or that the credit of the state was looked upon as precarious: if it should sink, contrary conclusions may safely be drawn. (*Works*, vol.4, p.161.)

That is, the price of stock would rise or fall accordingly as the rate of interest in the money market is less than or greater than the own rate of return of the stock.

Third, public debts may be paid off every year, by incorporating the sinking fund into the money appropriated yearly and placing all that is paid beyond the interest as payment in part of the capital.

> Had England at the time government first established a sinking fund, arising out of the savings which were made upon reducing the rate of interest, from time to time, continued to pay to the creditors the same annual sums as formerly; and thereby applied what was paid beyond the interest, to the payment of the capital, there could not have been any misapplication of the sinking fund; and the debts by this time would have been greatly diminished. (*Works*, vol.4, p.162.)

Thus, as long as there is no misapplication of the sinking fund, this method would effectively diminish the debts.

Fourth, the reduction of the rate of interest upon the money borrowed may be said, in a sense, to pay off some part of the debts.

> The fourth method of reducing debts is that adopted by Great Britain, viz. by reducing the interest paid upon them. From this we discover the reason why taxes, even in time of war, are seldom augmented in this kingdom much above the proportion of the interest of the money borrowed. (*Works*, vol.4, p.162.)

By increasing the supply of money in the economy, the state may reduce the rate of interest upon its borrowing, as some of the money in the private sector might stagnate.

From these discussions of the various ways of paying off public debts,[33] we may confirm the conclusion of our last sub-section of Steuart's macroeconomic analysis of public credit and debts: i.e., the functional role of

---

[33] In addition to those four mentioned briefly above, Steuart spelled out some other methods for the repayment of public debts, including that of converting them into annuities for lives or paying them off below their original value by means of lotteries. Cf. *Works*, vol.4, pp.159-69.

public borrowing. To be precise, according to him, while the public borrowing and subsequent spending by the state affect the circulation of money and commodities in the economy under certain monetary conditions, the repayment of the debts might produce adverse results to the economy. It depends on the methods of repayment as well as the circumstances of the money market. If the money market is tight enough, the repayment of public debts by the state would release some extra money for the private sector and drop the rate of interest, so the economy might become activated further. Otherwise, i.e., if there is some money already stagnating in the private sector, a sudden and large-scale repayment could further the stagnation of money, so it would only aggravate the situation and the economy would never get out of depression.

Public bankruptcy

Now, in the last part of our analysis of Steuart on public credit and debts, we shall turn to his discussions of public bankruptcy as one of the results which a state running public credit to an increasing extent might face. First of all, we may note that, although Steuart was directly opposed to a public bankruptcy itself, his argument actually allowed of some exceptions.

> I shall advance no argument to prove that the scheme of a public bankruptcy is either lawful, honourable, or expedient, if voluntarily gone into by a state; because I think it is diametrically opposite to every principle of good government. It is a maxim uncontroverted, that a contract ought to be binding between the parties contracting, and that it ought to be fulfilled in every article. If the public good be alleged as an overruling principle, to which every other must give way, I readily admit the justness of the exception. There is another of equal force, the impossibility of performance. (*Works*, vol.4, p.136.)

Thus, according to Steuart, the state may become bankrupt in two ways: either by its deliberate act for the 'public good' or as a consequence of unavoidable circumstances due to the 'impossibility of its performance'. For the latter, it might suffice to take the following example.

> Were the trade and industry of England to decay, the amount of all the permanent taxes might so far diminish, as to prove insufficient to pay the interest of the national debt, and defray the expence [expense] of civil government. (*Works*, vol.4, p.137.)

On the other hand, as regards the former way of bankruptcy, i.e., a bankruptcy by a deliberate act of power with a view to expediency, the state intending to execute it should devise a plan to prevent all the harmful consequences of bankruptcy in general. In what follows, let us first examine Steuart's discussion of the harmful consequences of bankruptcy in general, and then move on to his explanation of what reasons a state may still have for breaking faith with its creditors, despite all those consequences. Finally, we shall come to his evaluation of what would be gained, after all, by doing so.

In either case of bankruptcy mentioned above, according to Steuart, some natural and immediate consequences of the bankruptcy would probably follow one after another. They are:

> First, Every creditor of the state would become poorer in proportion to the diminution of his income. Secondly, Consumption and the demand for work would diminish in proportion to the part of that income withheld, which the creditors annually expend for these purposes. Thirdly, Trade would *directly* suffer, in proportion to that part of said revenue yearly thrown into it by the public creditors at present; and it would *consequently* suffer, in proportion to the hurt resulting to private credit, from the consequences of the bankruptcy. (*Works*, vol.4, pp.137-8; original italics.)

Thus, not only would the creditors of public debts directly lose their capital, but also the whole trade and industry of the country might directly and indirectly suffer from the bankruptcy, as it would affect the 'effectual demand' of the economy.

Despite these harmful consequences of bankruptcy in general, according to Steuart, a state may decide to declare it by law with a view to achieving other policy objects.

> I imagine, they would begin by ordering the amount of all that is paid to the creditors, to be set apart as a fund for the execution of the plan. They would purchase all over England, every article of produce and manufacture which might remain upon hand for want of a market: they would feed all those who would be forced to be idle for want of employment: ... they would furnish credit to all the merchants subsisting, in proportion to what they had lost by the extinction of the funds: they would establish offices everywhere, to supply the wants of those who would be totally ruined, until by degrees they could re-establish confidence, the parent of trade, the mother of industry. ... none would suffer but the unhappy creditors. (*Works*, vol.4, p.139.)

Thus, instead of paying off public debts, a state may want to spend the money on public expenditure to create demand, to enhance employment and to supply credit, for the economy as a whole, if it could make sure that the result would compensate the loss incurred to the creditors in any way.[34] Suppose the scheme could be fairly carried out – in whatever way – as initially intended, what would happen in the end?

> If by the supposition all taxes be kept alive, for at least a certain time, in order to prevent a total confusion, certainly no body could gain during this period; even the state itself would lose, because every branch of consumption would infallibly diminish. But that time elapsed, and taxes reduced to the lowest, who would be the gainers? ... a sudden abolition of taxes, in consequences of a bankruptcy, would be advantageous to no body, but to creditors upon mortgage, and to the idle: not to landlords; because their incomes would diminish more than in the proportion of the

[34] However, Steuart was rather doubtful of the outcome of 'executing such a complicated plan for human wisdom'.

> As far as human prudence is insufficient for going through so great a detail all at once; so far would the effects of a general bankruptcy add hurtful consequences to those which in every case are unavoidable. (*Works*, vol.4, p.140.)

> present land-tax ... : not to manufacturing classes; because at present they pay no taxes, but in proportion to their idleness or extravagance ... : the monied [moneyed] interest, not secured on land would I suppose be extinguished; trade and credit at an end. ... In such a situation, the interest of money would rise beyond all bounds; and a debt which might have been considered as a trifle before, might then carry off an estate. The idle also who live peaceably upon a very moderate income, would find a great advantage from the fall of price for want of consumption, and from the distress of the industrious. (*Works*, vol.4, pp.140-1.)

Thus, according to Steuart, a public bankruptcy by a deliberate act of government, no matter by what means it is accomplished, would inevitably lead to the diminution of 'effectual demand' and the rise of interest rate(s) in the economy. As it reduces the income and the consumption of the private sector, the amount of taxes would diminish, and thus, even if government spending accompanies the public bankruptcy, the whole amount of effectual demand in the economy would not reach the previous level. On the other hand, as the breakdown of public credit might influence the state of private credit, it would raise the rate of interest as the object of confidence for the latter. Therefore, the total failure of credit and the contraction of circulation would bring about the decline of the level of output and employment in the economy.

What about foreign debts? As we noted before, Steuart suggested that, in a situation where the public borrowing might overheat the economy as it would raise the rate of interest, if all the money in the economy is already engaged in its private sector, the state ought to borrow money from abroad in order to avoid a recession at home for want of money, even at the expense of sending the interest out of the country. While the interest sent abroad, together with the balance of trade, constitutes the 'general balance of payments' of a country, the state would eventually pay both interest and capital of its foreign debts with the balance of trade of the private sector, either through taxation or public credit at home. What would happen to a country with increasing foreign debts, if it still has an unfavourable balance of trade?

> Suppose, I say, that by continuing to carry on long and expensive wars, the sum of interest paid to strangers should exceed all that the nation gain by her trade. In this case, there must be a general balance of payments against her every year, which very soon would manifest itself by the most fatal consequences. ... In such a situation, I fairly acknowledge, that I cannot discover any expedient to avoid a bankruptcy. (*Works*, vol.4, pp.143-4.)

Thus, a state might also become bankrupt due to foreign debts, if its balance of trade could not afford even the interest of the debts, let alone the capital.[35]

---

[35] According to Steuart, a bankruptcy due to foreign debts is more likely to happen than one due to domestic public debts.

The consequences of a bankruptcy due to foreign debts, according to Steuart, seem to be no less harmful to the economy than one due to domestic public debts.

> The greatest of all the inconveniences proceeding from a bankruptcy, is the ruin of industry, and the stop put to circulation. Can it then be supposed, that a country might execute so glaring a scheme of treachery to all her neighbours, and still continue her correspondence with them in the open way of trade? Certainly not. Were all foreign trade to be stop at once, what a revolution would it occasion! The circulation of foreign trade, in the city of London only, exceeds perhaps the amount of all the taxes. A stop put to this would occasion such a stagnation, as would ruin the nation as much as if the bankruptcy were to become universal. (*Works*, vol.4, p.147.)

In fact, as the insolvency of foreign debts might put an end to all foreign trade and credit of the country, the bankruptcy would result in the curtailment of foreign demand and the diminution of circulation, and thus lead to the decline of output and employment in the economy. The more its economy depends on foreign trade and credit, the more harm the bankruptcy does to the country. Therefore, although Steuart was in favour of public borrowing, in general, and foreign debts, in particular, he was warning rather strongly against some harmful results of a bankruptcy which might be attendant upon them. Although, as we discussed earlier, he logically inferred that the domestic public debts in an increasing trend might not necessarily cause a bankruptcy, he showed that a country with an unfavourable balance of trade would most likely go into it due to foreign debts, which does as much harm to the economy. On this account, answering the question of how to determine the exact extent of public credit in an economy, Steuart pointed out some guides to the government policy for public debts, domestic and foreign, as follows:

> ... it is not necessary that public credit should ever fail, from any augmentation of debts whatever, due to natives; and that it must fail, so soon as the nation becomes totally unable either to export commodities equal to all their imports and foreign debts, or to pay off a proportional part of their capital, sufficient to turn the balance to the right side. From this proposition two corollaries may be drawn. First, That the most important object in paying off debts, is get quit of those due to strangers. Secondly, That whatever circumstance has a tendency towards diminishing the burden of foreign debts, should be encouraged. (*Works*, vol.4, p.146.)

Thus, according to Steuart, the repayment of foreign debts must take priority over that of domestic debts in a government's public finance.

To what extent then could a state establish public credit in a modern economy? In Steuart's own words, is there any 'impossibility of performance' in that? In fact, this question relates to the gist of Steuart's analysis of public

---

The idea of a nation's becoming bankrupt to itself, I have always looked upon as contradiction; but that it may become bankrupt to the rest of the world, is quite consistent with reason and common sense. (*Works*, vol.4, p.144.)

credit and debts. In answering the question, it is necessary to closely examine the effects of public borrowing on the workings of the economy. Hence, we shall next present the macroeconomic aspect of Steuart's theory of public credit and debts.

2.4 The Macroeconomic Analysis of Public Credit and Debts

We may note from the previous discussion of Steuart's analysis of taxation that, although the public finance of government – taxation and public spending in particular – is basically a monetary phenomenon, it is so interrelated with other economic activities that it may affect both price and output level in the economy as a whole. In Steuart's macroeconomic analysis, money is not neutral. Any monetary phenomenon exerts influence on the real activity level of the economy. According to him, money is a linking ring of the circular chain of all the economic activities in a country.[36] In his analysis of public credit and debts, Steuart made this point clear as follows:

> Now, as we have seen how industry creates wealth; how wealth and confidence create credit; how credit creates debts and taxes; how these again occasion an augmentation of money, by melting down of property; and how this property becomes transferred to a new set of men, once the monied [moneyed] interest, who afterwards acquire the lands, and consolidate this quantity of money which is become superfluous to circulation; does not this chain of consequences represent a kind of circle, returning into itself? And is it not plain, that without the intervention of this engine, namely the money created in proportion to the demand for it, the chain would be cut off, before it could reach the link from which it first set out? (*Works*, vol.4, pp.120-1.)

That is to say, money is the means of forming all the economic activities, both private and public, in the country into a circular chain. Therefore, the analysis of money must be the key to our discussion of Steuart's theory of public credit and debts.

As mentioned previously, according to Steuart, public credit is established basically through the 'realization' of money into stock. Obviously, when the government borrows money from the private sector, the creditors must be those who are able to lend it as a result of their income exceeding their spending. And, as the government pays annuities for its debts with tax revenue, the public credit as such would not affect the economy as a whole. In other words, the public credit itself seems to have no further effect on the economy, as it only transfers income from one group to another in the country. As is the case with taxation, according to Steuart, public credit exerts its full influence on the economy by way of the subsequent public spending of the money borrowed.

[36] For a detailed discussion of Steuart's analysis of national money, see. Ch.6 above.

> If the loan be made at home, the money is no sooner paid in, than it is spent; and as we may suppose that it would not have been lent, had either the lenders found it necessary for their current expence [expense], or had they found a more profitable way of realizing it than by lending it to government, we consider it as having been in a state of stagnation; but being lent to government, it is thrown into a new channel of circulation. (*Works*, vol.4, p.126.)

Thus, if there is a certain amount of money stagnating in the economy, the public borrowing, accompanied with public spending, might help bring it into circulation, and thereby promote trade and industry. It may, therefore, be used as a government policy instrument to boost the economy and increase its level of output.

In the above discussion, we assumed that public borrowing is supplied with money stagnating in the private sector, which the possessors are willing to 'realize' into stock: that is, if they cannot do better with that money, they lend it to the state; otherwise, they do not. However, on some occasions, the public borrowing might overheat the economy as it would raise the rate of interest, if all the money in the economy is already engaged in its private sector.

> While the uses of domestic circulation absorb all the money in the country, that is to say, when there are private persons ready to borrow all the money to be lent, at this time government cannot borrow at home; and if they did, by offering a high interest for it, the borrowing would do harm to circulation; because it would raise interest at home, or disappoint those who would gladly borrow it, for little more than the interest offered by the government. (*Works*, vol.4, p.128.)

In this situation, according to Steuart, the government ought to borrow money from abroad in order to avoid a recession at home for want of circulating equivalents, i.e., money, even at the expense of sending the interest out of the country.

> ... if the high interest at home proceed from want of money, that is to say, from circulation not being full enough, it is their interest to borrow [abroad], were it for nothing else than to supply circulation; because unless this be full, all industry must languish. (*Works*, vol.4, p.129.)

From the discussion so far, we may note that, according to Steuart, public borrowing, accompanied with spending later on, could play a positive role in enhancing the level of output in the economy. How far then may the public credit be extended? The answer appears to be obvious:

> ... abstracting from circumstances which may disturb the gradual progress of this operation, before it can arrive at the *ne plus ultra*, debts may be increased to the full proportion of all that can be raised for the payment of the interest. (*Works*, vol.4, p.132.)

That is, as far as the state can raise taxes to pay the annuities for the debts, the public credit might continue to expand. Now, the question is how far the taxes may be imposed for the payment? As we have seen in the previous section of Steuart's analysis of taxation, *theoretically* there would be no limit to the extent of 'proportional' taxes; whereas 'cumulative' taxes could be carried to the full value of all sorts of properties in a country. Therefore, at least from the theoretical point of view, there would be no definite bound, beyond which public credit must come to a stop. In other words, according to Steuart, while a government could borrow money from the private sector and spend it with a view to boosting the economy, the extent of its borrowing might not necessarily reach any limit, except in the case when the existing money in the economy becomes insufficient for the whole circulation of both private and public sectors so that it may make the rate of interest soar too high.[37] According to Steuart, then, the only theoretically feasible qualification which circumscribes the extent of a state's public credit seems to be concerned with its functional role in regard to the workings of the economy, in general, and the money market, in particular. As long as there is a certain amount of money stagnating in the private sector, or at least unless the initial rate of interest in the economy is too high for the state to borrow without incurring further discouragement to the 'effectual demand' of the private sector, the public borrowing and subsequent spending by the state would have the good effect of facilitating the circulation of money and commodities and thus giving an impetus to the economy.

3. REVENUE, SPENDING AND BORROWING: A MACROECONOMIC MODEL OF ACTIVE FINANCE

Thus far, in the previous sections, we have discussed Steuart's analysis of two alternative sources of revenue for government spending, i.e., taxation and public borrowing, and particularly their effects on the workings of the economy as a whole. As a result, we may note that, according to him, both taxation and public borrowing, being accompanied with public spending, can be used as an effective policy tool for a government to adjust and guide the economy, and especially to regulate its price and output level. In the present section, we shall further pursue this aspect of Steuart's analysis of public finance, i.e., its functional role in the workings of the economy.[38]

[37] The above rather hypothetical argument, that public debts may increase infinitely as long as public borrowing and spending throw idle money in the private sector into a new channel of circulation to help the economy to get out of stagnation, reflects Steuart's criticism of the proposition, widespread in his day, of the inevitability of public bankruptcy. Cf. the previous section.

[38] Sen (1957) already drew attention to Steuart's argument for the 'functional' role of public finance, and he remarked that 'it would not be any great exaggeration to say that A. P. Lerner's chapter on functional finance seems almost a paraphrase of Steuart' (p.122). Cf. his quotation from Lerner (1944), p.xx, and also Lerner (1943), from which the term 'functional finance' originated. Lerner (1944) himself described it as follows:

> The central idea is that government fiscal policy, its spending and taxing, its borrowing and repayment of loans, its issue of new money and its withdrawal of money, shall be taken with

Specifically, while we have an overall view of Steuart's discussions of government revenue, spending and borrowing, we shall present a formalized version of his theory of public finance in what follows.

Above all, as previously discussed, the public finance of government, *au fond*, is a monetary phenomenon. Therefore, it is necessary for us to briefly review Steuart's monetary explanation of the circular process of production and consumption in an economy with no public finance, before we get down to his analysis of public finance. To begin with, then, let us set out the initial situation of the economy without the public sector, on the basis of his analysis of money.[39]

According to the previous macroeconomic model of Steuart's monetary analysis, the initial equilibrium situation of an economy, before any tax is imposed and before any public spending or borrowing is made, could be represented in the following twelve equations. That is,

(The demand for money)

$$M_d/P = l_c + l_y \qquad (1)$$

$$l_c = k_1 c \qquad (2)$$

$$l_y = k_2 u \qquad (3)$$

where M_d: total demand for money
P: price level
l_c: demand for money to consume
k_1: constant
c: amount of the consumption of consumer goods
l_y: demand for money to produce
k_2: constant
u: amount of the use of producer goods;

(The supply of money)

$$M_s = \overline{M}_e - M_h \qquad (4)$$

$$M_h/P = h(i), \ h' < 0 \qquad (5)$$

where M_s: supply of money

an eye only to the *results* of these actions on the economy and not to any established traditional doctrine about what is sound or unsound. (p.298; quoted by Francis M. Bator, 'functional finance', *The New Palgrave* (1987).)

Meanwhile, as our discussion in this section would soon prove, although Steuart's macroeconomic analysis of public finance, particularly its implications for government policy, apparently anticipated what might be called a Keynesian fiscal policy, derived from the 'principle of effective demand', it was based on his *own* monetary explanation of the economic activities of private and public sectors, which is fundamentally different from Keynes's in many respects. Cf. Chs. 4 and 6 above.)

[39] For detailed discussions of Steuart's monetary model of price and output, see section 4, Ch.6 above.

$\overline{M}_e$: quantity of money existing (given)
M_h: quantity of money being hoarded
i: rate of interest;

(The equilibrium condition of money market)

$$M_s = M_d; \tag{6}$$

(The supply of commodities)

$$y = y(u),\ \ y' > 0 \tag{7}$$

$$u = u(r - i),\ \ u' > 0 \tag{8}$$

$$r = r(P),\ \ r' > 0 \tag{9}$$

where y: amount of production
r: rate of profit;

(The demand for commodities)

$$d_f = c + u \tag{10}$$

$$c = p_c\, d_f\ \ (\text{or } u = d_p\, d_f) \tag{11}$$

where d_f: amount of 'effectual demand'
p_c: 'propensity to consume' (given)
(or d_p: 'disposition to produce' (given); $p_c + d_p = 1$);

(The equilibrium condition of commodity market)

$$y = d_f. \tag{12}$$

These are the basic equations of our model. Apart from the one for the equilibrium condition of commodity market (equation 12), the rest can be reduced to the following two equations. That is,

(The demand side of economy)

$$d_f(P, i) = 1/k\,(\overline{M}_e/P - h(i)),\ \ \partial d_f/\partial P < 0,\ \partial d_f/\partial i > 0 \tag{13}$$

where k: weighted money-balance constant;

(The supply side of economy)

$$y(P, i) = y(u(r(P) - i)),\ \ \partial y/\partial P > 0,\ \partial y/\partial i < 0. \tag{14}$$

From the above three equations (12, 13 and 14), we can obtain the equilibrium level of output (y), price level (P) and interest rate (i) in the economy. We may visualize their simultaneous determination in Figure 8.1. Now, it becomes clear that, in Steuart's analysis, commodity and money markets are so closely interrelated that the level of output, price level and the rate of interest should be determined simultaneously.

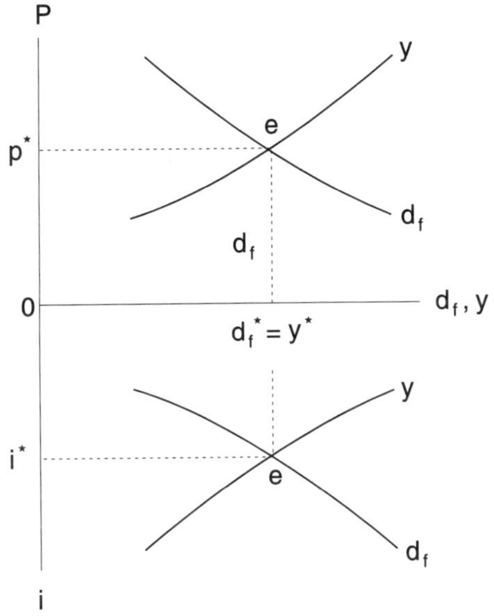

Figure 8.1 The simultaneous determination of price, output and the rate of interest in the economy without public finance

Having set out the initial situation of the economy without any taxation, public spending or borrowing, we are ready to examine his analysis of the active finance of government. Let us now introduce new variables and relations, due to the existence of the public finance, to the previous basic equation system. As we assume that the government would spend without regard to its tax revenue, part of its expenditure might be defrayed by the public borrowing. That is, while the revenue of public finance relies on both taxation and public credit, its amount should be equal to that of the expenditure. Thus,

$$g = t + b \qquad (15)$$

where g: amount of public spending
t: total amount of tax revenue
b: amount of public borrowing.

Meanwhile, it is also assumed that both 'proportional' tax on commodity and 'cumulative' tax on income are imposed at the same time.[40] Thus,

[40] For the sake of the simplicity of the model, we assume here the 'cumulative' tax to be imposed as a lump-sum on income; although it makes no substantial difference to the present analysis if it is assumed to be otherwise. Cf. the previous section of Steuart's analysis of taxation in this chapter.

$$t = t_p + t_c \tag{16}$$

$$t_p = r_{tp}\, d_f \tag{17}$$

where t_1: amount of 'proportional' tax
t_2: amount of lump-sum 'cumulative' tax
r_{tp}: rate of 'proportional' tax.

Then, we need to modify some of the previous basic equations (1 - 12) so as to accommodate these new variables and equations. On the one hand, we have another use for which money is demanded, apart from to produce or to consume: that is, to pay the 'cumulative' tax.[41] Thus,

$$M_d/P = l_y + l_c + l_t \tag{1}'$$

$$l_t = k_3\, t_c \tag{18}$$

where l_t: demand for money to pay tax
k_3: constant.

On the other hand, the public spending of government also constitutes part of the 'effectual demand' in the economy, as well as the consumption of consumer goods and the use of producer goods, with a certain proportion between them being given. Thus,

$$d_f = c + u + g \tag{10}'$$

$$c = p_c\,(d_f - g) \quad (\text{or } u = d_p\,(d_f - g)). \tag{11}'$$

Now, let us recapitulate the whole system of equations relevant to the present model, as follows:

(The demand for money)

$$M_d/P = l_y + l_c + l_t \tag{1}'$$

$$l_c = k_1\, c \tag{2}$$

$$l_y = k_2\, u \tag{3}$$

$$l_t = k_3\, t_c; \tag{18}$$

(The supply of money)

$$M_s = \overline{M}_e - M_h \tag{4}$$

$$M_h/P = h(i),\ h' < 0; \tag{5}$$

(The equilibrium condition of money market)

Meanwhile, for detailed explanations of what is related to Steuart's analysis of taxation, public credit and debts, see the previous relevant sections as we formalize them here in this section.

[41] As the 'proportional' tax is superimposed on the price of commodities and is assumed to be collected by the government immediately on its purchase or sale, it is not necessary for either consumers or producers to demand money in order to pay the tax.

$$M_s = M_d; \tag{6}$$

(The supply of commodities)

$$y = y(u),\ y' > 0 \tag{7}$$

$$u = u(r - i),\ u' > 0 \tag{8}$$

$$r = r(P),\ r' > 0; \tag{9}$$

(The demand for commodities)

$$d_f = c + u + g \tag*{(10)$'$}$$

$$c = p_c\,(d_f - g)\ \ (\text{or } u = d_p\,(d_f - g)); \tag*{(11)$'$}$$

(The equilibrium condition of commodity market)

$$y = d_f; \tag{12}$$

(The public sector)

$$g = t + b \tag{15}$$

$$t = t_p + t_c \tag{16}$$

$$t_p = r_{tp}\, d_f. \tag{17}$$

From the above equation system, we could derive all the equilibrium amounts and rates, including the equilibrium level of output (y), price level (P) and interest rate(i), if all the relations and functions are specified and if the following exogenous variables and constants are given outside of the model: i.e., the quantity of money existing in the economy ($\overline{M}_e$), the 'propensity to consume' (p_c) (or 'disposition to produce' (d_p)), the three money-balance constants (k_1, k_2 and k_3), and three of the four optional policy variables of public finance (g, r_{tp}, t_c and b).[42]

As we did for the initial situation of the economy with no public finance, we may reduce all these equations to a few, to show particularly the relation between the level of output, price level and the rate of interest in the economy where the government runs its public finance as a means of regulating the economic activities of the private sector. First of all, from the equilibrium condition of the money market, we could obtain the following relation between the amount of 'effectual demand', price level and the rate of interest. That is,

$$M_s = M_d \tag*{(from 6)}$$

[42] With 4 additional equations and unknowns (15 - 18; three out of g, t, b, t_p, t_c and r_{tp}, and l_t), we have altogether 16 equations and unknowns, respectively, in the whole system. As far as the optional policy variables of public finance are concerned, for example, if we assume the amount of public spending (g) and two of the three alternative sources of revenue, i.e., the rate of 'proportional' tax (r_{tp}), the amount of lump-sum 'cumulative' tax (t_c) and the amount of public borrowing (b), to be given, *ceteris paribus*, the remaining one would be determined endogenously.

$$\overline{M}_e - P\,h(i) = P\,(l_c + l_y + l_t) \qquad \text{(from 1, 4 and 5)}$$
$$= P\,(k_1\,c + k_2\,u + k_3\,t_c) \qquad \text{(from 2, 3 and 18)}$$
$$= P\,\{k\,(d_f - g) + k_3\,t_c\},\ k = k_1\,p_c + k_2\,d_p \qquad \text{(from 10' and 11')}$$
$$= P\,k\,(d_f - g + t_c),\ k = k_3.$$ [43]

Therefore, in the demand side of the economy,

$$d_f(P, i) = 1/k\,((\overline{M}_e/P - h(i)) + g - t_c,\ \partial d_f/\partial P < 0,\ \partial d_f/\partial i > 0. \qquad (13)'$$

Second, we have a production function as follows:

$$y = y(u) = y(u(r(P) - i)). \qquad \text{(from 7, 8 and 9)}$$

Therefore, in the supply side of the economy,

$$y(P, i) = y(u(r(P) - i)),\ \partial y/\partial P > 0,\ \partial y/\partial i < 0. \qquad (14)$$

Third, for the equilibrium of demand and supply in the economy,

$$y = d_f. \qquad (12)$$

Finally, for the equilibrium of revenue and expenditure in the public sector,

$$g = t + b = r_{tp}\,d_f + t_c + b. \qquad \text{(from 15, 16 and 17)} \qquad (19)$$

From these 4 equations (12, 13′, 14 and 19), we could now draw the equilibrium level of output ($y = d_f$), price level (P), interest rate (i) and one of the policy variables of public finance (g, r_{tp}, t_c or b), in the economy under the active finance of government, as soon as the other three policy variables of public finance are decided exogenously.[44]

Let us first depict the above equilibrium situation in Figure 8.2, and then observe the consequences of certain changes in the exogenously given policy variables of pubic finance to see how the government's active finance works. Using equation (13)′, we could describe the demand side of the economy with the public sector in terms of curve d_f^1, which resembles the one for the economy without the public sector (curve d_f^0), except shifting outward by ($g - t_c$).[45] On the other hand, with equation (14), we could describe the supply side

---

[43] For what is meant by the constant *k*, see section 4 in Ch.6 above. Meanwhile, for the simplicity of the model, we assume $k = k_3$. This implies that money circulates at the same velocity, regardless of sectors, private or public.

[44] In comparison with the previous summarizing equations (12, 13 and 14) for the economy without public finance, we may note that, apart from the additional one for the public sector (equation 19), it is only the equation for the demand side of the economy (equation 13′) which is modified, the rest being unchanged, in the summarizing equations for the economy with public finance.

[45] Alternatively, we may say that curve d_f^1 shifts outward from curve d_f^0 by $1/(1 - r_{tp})$ times plus $b/(1 - r_{tp})$, as

$$d_f = 1/k\,(\overline{M}_e/P - h(i)) + g - t_c$$
$$= 1/k\,(\overline{M}_e/P - h(i)) + r_{tp}\,d_f + b \qquad \text{(from equation 19)}$$

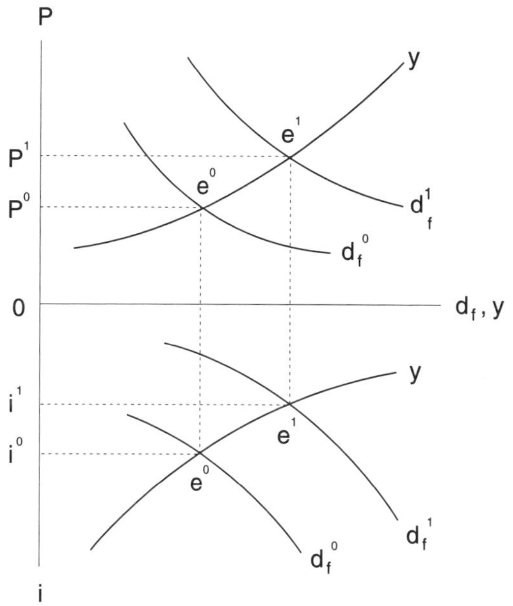

Figure 8.2 The simultaneous determination of price, output and the rate of interest in the economy with public finance

of the economy in terms of curve y, which is actually the same as the one for the economy without the public sector. The intersection of these two curves, d_f^1 and y, represents the equilibrium of demand and supply in the economy (e^1); hence, the simultaneous determination of the level of output ($d_f^1 = y$), price level (P^1) and interest rate (i^1). In addition, as soon as we get the equilibrium level of output, we could find out the equilibrium amount or rate of one of the four optional policy variables of public finance, which is left to be determined endogenously, from equation (19).

What would happen if the government changes any of the policy variables of its public finance, i.e., the amount of public spending (g), the rate of 'proportional' tax (r_{tp}), the amount of lump-sum 'cumulative' tax (t_c) or the amount of public borrowing (b), except the one which is to be determined endogenously? For example, if the government increases the amount of public spending with both the rate of 'proportional' tax and the amount of 'cumulative' tax being unchanged, then will the level of output in the economy increase? What about price level? Must the amount of public borrowing increase by the same amount as the increase in the amount of

---

$= \{1/k\,(\overline{M}_e/P - h(i)) + b\}/(1 - r_{tp})$.

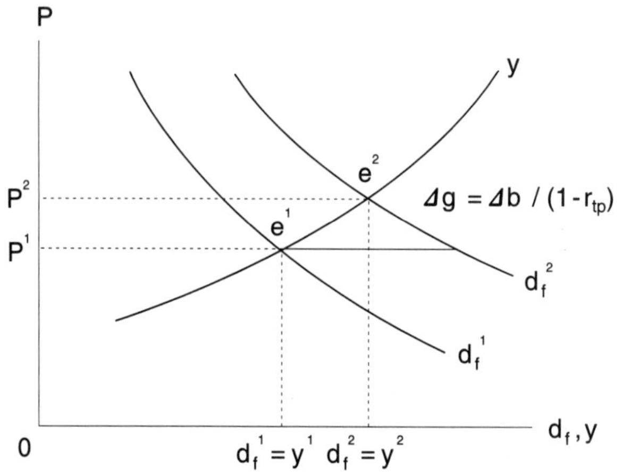

Figure 8.3 The consequences of the expansion of public spending by means of public credit

public spending? On the other hand, among the alternative sources of revenue, i.e., the imposition of 'proportional' tax, that of 'cumulative' tax or the application of public credit, which is the most preferable to the economy in terms of its functional role? Utilizing the above model of Steuart's monetary explanation of the workings of the economy, and Figure 8.2 in particular, we shall answer all these questions concerning the operations of the active finance of government.[46]

First (see Figure 8.3), if the government increases its spending ($g + \Delta g$) with a given rate of 'proportional' tax (r_{tp}) and a given amount of 'cumulative' tax (t_c), both the level of output and the price level in the economy would also increase ($e^1 \rightarrow e^2$); whereas the amount of public borrowing to defray the difference between the whole expenditure of the government and its tax revenue would increase less than the amount of public spending, as the amount of 'proportional' tax would also increase as a result of the higher level of output in the economy ($\Delta b = \Delta g - r_{tp}\, \Delta d_f$).[47] To put it another way, if the

[46] From now on, we will not draw the lower half of the diagram simply to save our labour; in fact, as d_f and y in that half must shift whenever the price level changes in the upper half, the ups and downs of the rate of interest could not be decided unless obvious.

[47] From equation (19),

$$g = r_{tp}\, d_f + t_c + b$$

$$\Delta g = d_f\, \Delta r_{tp} + r_{tp}\, \Delta d_f + \Delta t_c + \Delta b;$$

as $\Delta r_{tp} = 0$ and $\Delta t_c = 0$,

$$\Delta g = r_{tp}\, \Delta d_f + \Delta b$$

$$\Delta b = \Delta g - r_{tp}\, \Delta d_f.$$

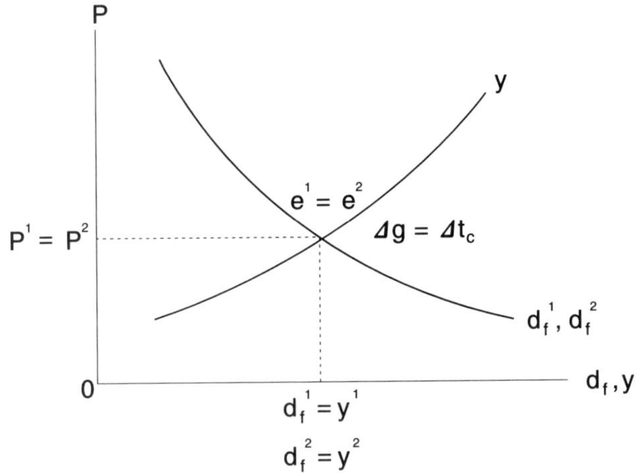

Figure 8.4 The consequences of the expansion of public spending by means of 'cumulative' tax

government expands public credit with a view to spending more, not only it does boost the economy as the increment of public spending would increase the level of output, but also it does not have to increase the borrowing in proportion to the spending as the tax revenue would increase in consequence of the very increase in the level of output.[48]

Next (see Figure 8.4), if the government opts to augment the amount of 'cumulative' tax ($t_c + \Delta t_c$) for the purpose of raising its revenue to defray its increasing expenditure ($g + \Delta g$), there would be no increase in the level of output. In this case, the increase of 'effectual demand' in the public sector is offset by its decrease in the private sector, as part of the 'effectual demand' is simply transferred from one sector to the other. Hence, there is no change in price level and interest rate as well as in the level of output.

Finally (see Figure 8.5), if the government decides to raise the rate of 'proportional' tax ($r_{tp} + \Delta r_{tp}$) in order to procure the revenue for extending its expenditure ($g + \Delta g$) without augmenting either the public borrowing (b) or the amount of 'cumulative' tax (t_c), then it would still enhance the level of output in the economy. From the initial equilibrium situation (e^1), the price level would rise, as the public spending increases by the exogenously given amount ($\Delta g = \Delta r_{tp}\, d_f^1/(1 - r_{tp})$). As a result, while the amount of production would increase, the amount of 'effectual demand' would be diminishing in the economy. Then, eventually, the economy would settle down in a new

48 For a detailed discussion of Steuart's macroeconomic analysis of public credit and debts, see sub-section 2.4 above.

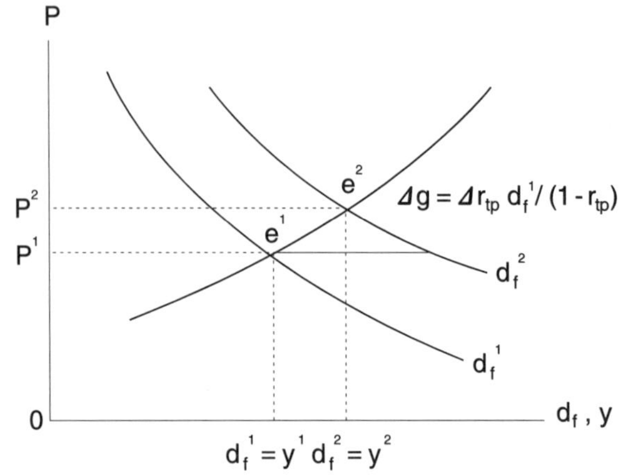

Figure 8.5 The consequences of the expansion of public spending by means of 'proportional' tax

equilibrium situation with a higher level of output and a higher price level than before (e^2).[49]

From all the above comparative statics of the alternative policy options of public finance, we could draw some conclusions as follows. First, the expansion of public spending may or may not enhance the level of output in the economy, depending on which source of revenue is to be chosen by the government to defray the expenditure, among the three alternatives, i.e., 'proportional' taxation', 'cumulative' taxation' or public credit. That is, if the government opts either for 'proportional' taxation or public credit, the augmentation of public expenditure would increase the level of output in the economy; whereas if it opts for 'cumulative' taxation, the augmentation would not increase the level. Second, whenever the expansion of public spending enhances the level of output, it would also raises the price level in the economy. Third, when the government relies on public credit to spend more without altering the present tax system, it does not need to borrow the same amount of money from the private sector as the increment of its expenditure. Fourth, nevertheless, the increase of public borrowing would inevitably result in the increase of public debts, which must be paid off in due course of time, as, otherwise, the public credit itself would break down.[50] Last, therefore, as far as the active finance of government for enhancing the level of output in the economy is concerned, the combination of increasing public spending and

---

49 For a close comparison between the two taxes, 'cumulative' and 'proportional', in terms of their impact of the economy as a whole, see sub-section 1.4 above.

50 For Steuart's discussions of various methods of contracting and paying off public debts, and the public bankruptcy of a state, see sub-section 2.3 above.

enlarging the 'proportional' taxation is the most preferable option, according to Steuart's analysis of public finance.

9. Human Beings, Society and the Body Politic

In the previous chapters, we have mainly concentrated on Steuart's analysis of the workings of an exchange economy, as such, i.e., its mechanics. Needless to say, this presupposes certain social, political and even cultural institutions as its analytical background, along with some assumptions of human nature. In our interpretative discussions so far, we have tried to strain them out, as far as possible, in pursuit only of its economic logic. However, to have a complete picture of Steuart's political economy, we must bring them up and articulate them clearly. To this effect, in this final chapter of our analytical interpretation of his *Inquiry*, we shall discuss Steuart's understanding of some fundamental elements of the subject matter: i.e., human beings, society and the body politic. To be specific, we will examine, first, what he thought of human nature, which ultimately underlies the whole of his economic analysis; second, how he conceived of society, particularly in association with economic development; and, finally, what relation he observed between the economy and the body politic. In addition, we will append a short methodological note focusing on some affiliations between Steuart, Montesquieu and Hume.

1. HUMAN NATURE AND THE 'SPIRIT OF THE TIMES'

In his *Inquiry*, Steuart made, explicitly or implicitly, some important presumptions on human nature, which typified the behavioural motivations in various economic activities of individual human beings. In what follows, we shall scrutinize them, one after another, in conjunction with some important issues related to them. This will eventually lead us to a certain self-contained image of human beings. Beyond this image, however, Steuart also understood human nature in its sociological and historical context. We shall, therefore, also discuss in the present section, this aspect of his conception of human nature, i.e., what he called the 'spirit of the people' or the 'spirit of the times'.

1.1 Self-interest and 'Public Good'

First of all, Steuart assumed from first to last in his *Inquiry* that human beings are basically self-interested. He explicitly declared,

> The principle of self-interest will serve as a general key to this inquiry; and it may, in one sense, be considered as the ruling principle of my subject, and may therefore be traced throughout the whole. ... From this principle, men are engaged to act in a thousand different ways, every action draws after it certain necessary consequences. The question therefore constantly under consideration comes to be, what will mankind find it their interest to do, under such and such circumstances? (*Works*, vol.1, pp.218-9.)

Thus, Steuart regarded self-interest as a primary cause of human conduct for all the economic activities with which he was dealing.[1] While this assumption of self-interested human nature is the most fundamental and inclusive of all in his political economy, the question is how Steuart saw the relation of 'private interest' and 'public good'.

> I expect, therefore, that every man is to act for his own interest in what regards the public; and, politically speaking, every one ought to do so. *It is the combination of every private interest which forms the public good, and of this the public, that is, the statesman only, can judge.* (*Works*, vol.1, p.221; italics added.)

A glance at the above passage might lead us to believe that Steuart was convinced of the resulting 'public virtue' from 'private selfishness'.[2] However, he actually did not mean by this that those economic and political activities carried out individually according to one's own interest would always be beneficent to the society as a whole. On the contrary, it just elucidates the supposition that everyone will, or must, act from a motive of private interest, and rather points to the role of the state or 'statesman'. Let us explore further on this.

For Steuart, above all, it is most natural to suppose that every private individual would pursue his own interest.

> Were miracles wrought every day, the laws of nature would no longer be laws: and were every one to act for the public, and neglect himself, the statesman would be bewildered, and the supposition is ridiculous. (*Works*, vol.1, pp.220-1.)

Then, it follows that both the object and the means of administration of the state must be subject to the individual's pursuit of self-interest. That is to say, the object of 'statesman' is to enhance 'public good', which is none other than the harmonious integration of every 'private interest'.

---

[1] When he was explaining the multiplication of population in terms of the enhancement of industry, Steuart remarked,

> Whether, in all cases, this principle of christianity [charity] advances the prosperity of a modern society, is a question which lies out of my road to examine. (*Works*, vol.1, p.119; bracket added.)

Thus, as far as his economic analysis was concerned, self-interest was the general motive for human action.

[2] The passage, quoted above, looks like an exact anticipation of Smith's optimistic view of the relation between 'private interest' and 'public good'.

> The *union of every private interest* makes the common good: this consequently ought to be the motive of all his [statesman's] action; because the goodness of an action depends on the conformity between the motive and the duty of the agent. (*Works*, vol.2, pp.212-3; italics added.)

In other words, while 'public good' ultimately consists of individual 'private interest', how the latter is integrated into the former solely depends on the state or 'statesman'. Meanwhile, the means by which the 'statesman' could achieve his object must be compatible with the 'main spring of human action', i.e., self-interest.

> The best way to govern a society, and to engage every one to conduct himself according to a plan, is for the statesman to form a system of administration, *the most consistent possible with the interest of every individual*, and never to flatter himself that his people will be brought to act in general, and in matters which purely regard the public, from any principle than private interest. (*Works*, vol.1, p.220; italics added.)

As far as Steuart was concerned, therefore, upon the supposition that all human activities – economic and political – are motivated by individuals' self-interest, the question of the relation between 'private interest' and 'public good' inevitably involved yet another one of the role of the state, its object and its means.[3] Generally speaking, Steuart was no less stressing the *need* of 'public spirit' for the 'statesman', than the *nature* of 'self-interest' for private individuals.

> The less attentive any government is to do their duty, the more essential it is that every individual be animated by that spirit, which then languishes in the very part where it ought to flourish with the greatest strength and vigour; and on the other hand, the more public spirit is shewn in the administration of public affairs, the less occasion has the state for assistance from individuals. (*Works*, vol.1, p.222.)

While the assumption of self-interest as the first principle of human activities runs all through Steuart's political economy, it becomes more specific and concrete when joining another, which we shall discuss next.

1.2 Materialistic Nature and 'Luxury'

Steuart also perceived human nature as epicurean, i.e., pleasure-seeking through material things.[4] Although it was lurking in the whole of his

---

[3] We have already seen, on various occasions, Steuart's interventionist view on the role of the state in an exchange economy. For the details of when or how (or why) it intervenes in the market or private sector, see the particular cases we have discussed in the previous chapters above; whereas for its general discussion, see Ch.10 below.

[4] In the present context, we consider not only tangible goods but also intangible services as material, so far as they both could be regarded as commodities. Meanwhile, in a chapter of his *Inquiry* (ch.XIV 'Security, Ease and Happiness, no inseparable Concomitants of Trade and Industry', book II), Steuart noted, by taking an example of a Spartan republic, that 'trade and industry' are not essential to the 'security and happiness' of people. It appears, then, that as an exception he admitted that human pleasure might not always depend on material things. However, later, he continued that, on the

economic analysis, the characterization of human nature as materialistic was less explicitly expressed than the one we have already discussed above, i.e., egoistic individualism. Nevertheless, it was most palpably exposed in his discussions of 'luxury'.

From Steuart's distinction between 'luxury' and 'necessary [necessity]', we could observe that they just represent different levels of consumption or enjoyment of material things, rather than those material things themselves, classified in any arbitrary way.[5]

> It is ample subsistence where no degree of superfluity is implied, which communicates an idea of the physical-necessary. ... A man enjoys the physical-necessary as to food, when he is fully fed; if he is likewise sufficiently clothed, and well defended against every thing which may hurt him, he enjoys his full physical-necessary. The moment he begins to add to this, he may be considered as moving upwards into another class, to wit, that of the luxurious, or consumers of superfluity; of which there are to be found, in most countries, as many stages upward, as there are stages downwards, from where he stood before. ... and yet upon the whole, it would be hard to determine, which are those who enjoy superfluity; which are those who possess the pure physical-necessary; and which are those who fall below it. (*Works*, vol.1, pp.412-3.)

Given that the two categories of consumption, 'luxury' and 'necessary [necessity]', are different in degree, rather than in nature, the distinction between them must still be subjective. In other words, it depends on

---

introduction of 'luxury' to the inhabitants, the system of well-planned economy would necessarily collapse in that republic.

> Lycurgus [the dictator of the Spartan republic] had penetration enough to perceive the weak side of his institution. He was no stranger to the seducing influence of luxury; and plainly foresaw, that the consequence of industry, which procures to mankind a great variety of new objects of desire, and a wonderful facility in satisfying them, would easily root out the principles he had endeavoured to instil into his countrymen, if the state of simplicity should ever come to be corrupted by foreign communications. (*Works*, vol.1, p.341; brackets added.)

Thus, his argument was intended to show that under the 'perfect plan of political economy', such as the policy of seclusion by a despot', people might satisfy themselves with the simplest way of living in a material sense, rather than to disprove the materialistic side of human nature. Cf. *op.cit.*, vol.1, pp.332-46.

[5] Steuart clearly pointed out the arbitrariness of the classification of material things themselves into 'luxury', 'necessary [necessity]' or whatever. To quote,

> The same thing which appears superfluity to a peasant, appears necessary to a citizen; and the utmost luxury of this class frequently does not come up to what is thought the mere necessary for one in a high rank. (*Works*, vol.1, p.343.)

Meanwhile, in our previous discussion of Steuart's basic conception of an exchange economy (Ch.2 above), we simply assumed that agricultural products are 'necessaries [necessities]' and manufactured goods are 'luxuries'. However, whatever they might be called, it would not affect our analysis, as every class was supposed to consume both of them to some extent anyway. In other words, as long as the distinction between 'luxury' and 'necessary [necessity]' had to do with consumption, rather than production, and as long as all the people in the economy were to consume both of them, it would not give rise to any qualitative change in the relation between sectors and classes. Indeed, in Steuart's analysis of the 'political effects of luxury', what was meant by 'luxury' could be regarded generally as some 'extraordinary consumption', rather than that of any particular sorts of commodities. Cf. section 2, Ch.4 above. Also see *Works*, vol.1, p.350 and p.406.

individuals and sociological context. Steuart ascribed this to the existence of 'political necessary [necessity]'.[6]

> The nature of man furnishes him with some desires relative to his wants, which do not proceed from his animal oeconomy, but which are entirely similar to them in their effects. These proceed from the affections of his mind, are formed by habit and education, and when once regularly established, create another kind of necessary, which, for the sake of distinction, we shall call political. The similitude between these two species of necessary, is therefore the cause of ambiguity. ... The measure of this last species of necessary, is determined by general opinion only, and therefore can never be justly ascertained. (*Works*, vol.1, pp.413-4.)

That is to say, as there exists 'political necessary [necessity]', which is purely subject to individual and social background, between the two broad categories of consumption, it is impossible to distinguish one from the other exactly in any objective sense.

Despite the difficulty in distinguishing it from 'necessary [necessity]', the notion of 'luxury' played an important part in Steuart's analysis of the determination of the level of output in an exchange economy. That is, as we have already discussed in a previous chapter, the 'taste for luxury or superfluity' constitutes one of main pillars of his argument of the 'political effects of luxury'.[7]

> In the ancient times, money was not wanting; but the taste for superfluities not being in proportion to it, the species was locked up. This was the case in Europe four hundred years ago. A new taste for superfluity has drawn, perhaps, more money into circulation, from our own treasures, than from the mines of the new world. ... It is more, therefore, through the taste for superfluity, than in consequence of the quantity of coin, that trade comes to be established; and it is in consequence of trade only that we see industry carry things in our days to so high a pitch of refinement and delicacy. (*Works*, vol.1, pp.237-8.)

Thus, Steuart saw the 'taste for luxury or superfluity' as the prime mover of trade and industry in the economy.[8] In any case, all these notions of 'luxury', 'political' and 'physical necessary [necessity]', and the 'taste of superfluity' reflect the materialistic conception of human nature in his political economy.

---

[6] Describing 'luxury' as the 'providing of superfluity with view to consumption', Steuart further distinguished it from 'excess'. That is, they are different in that the one and the other, respectively, imply the 'moderate' and 'immoderate gratification of our natural or rational desires'. But, according to him, 'what appears an excess to one man, may appear moderation to another'. Cf. *Works*, vol.1, pp.405-11.

[7] Cf. section 2, Ch.4 above. As a matter of fact, in Steuart's analysis of the 'political effects of luxury', what was meant by 'luxury' could be regarded as some 'extraordinary consumption' in general, rather than that of any particular sorts of commodities. Also see *Works*, vol.1, p.350 and p.406.

[8] As we shall soon see in the next section, Steuart even explained the transition of society from one stage to another in terms of his notion of the 'taste for luxury or superfluity'.

1.3 The Desire for Gain and 'Double Competition'

In line with those aspects of human nature, discussed above, there is another presumed in Steuart's *Inquiry*: that is, avarice. (Human beings are not only selfish and materialistic but also greedy!) This aspect of human nature was most plainly expressed in his notion of 'double competition', among others.

Steuart illustrated the process of determination of the market price of a commodity through the competition both among buyers and among sellers, as follows:

> You may come to a fair where you find a great variety of every kind of merchandise, in the possession of different merchants. These, by offering their goods to sale, constitute a tacit competition; every one of them wishes to sell in preference to another, and at the same time with the best advantage to himself. The buyers begin, by cheapening at every shop. The first price asked marks the covetousness of the seller; the first price offered, that of the buyer. From this operation, I say, competition begins to work its effects on both sides, and so becomes double. (*Works*, vol.1, p.265.)

Thus, it must be presupposed, in order to explain the 'current price' of commodity in terms of 'double competition', that both buyers and sellers are acquisitive.[9] This is merely an instance. In fact, Steuart made sense of a wide range of economic activities of human beings in terms of the desire for gain. Not only his discussions of the price of commodities but also those of the 'profit upon alienation', the wages of labour, the rent of land and the interest of money, are indeed based on the assumption of the human desire for gain, in so far as all these relate to some sorts of gains or other and can be seen in the competition among those who seek for the same sort. According to Steuart, if the competition among those seeking more gain is 'double-sided', it would ultimately constrain all the above price and rates to fluctuate within some reasonable limits, even though there might be no end to their avarice. The limits could be reasonable, in that the 'double competition' would bring about a sort of 'harmony' among them.

So far in our discussion of what Steuart presumed of human nature in his economic analysis, we have examined just three characteristic aspects of it. There are some others which propped up particular facets of his analysis.[10]

---

[9] For detailed discussions of his notions of 'current price of commodity' and 'double competition', see sub-section 1.2 and section 2 in Ch.3 above.

[10] For instance, when Steuart was searching for the natural cause of the multiplication of mankind, he called attention to its generative instinct.

> ... the principle of generation is inherent in man, and prompts him to multiply. (*Works*, vol.1, p.28.)

And when he was explaining the gradual introduction of luxuries and refinements in an infant stage of trade and industry, he mentioned the self-motivated human ingenuity.

> ... these refinements seem more generally owing to the industry and invention of the manufacturers (who by their ingenuity daily contrive means of softening or relieving

Nevertheless, it is beyond the scope of the present discussion to enumerate all the psychological and sociological aspects of human behaviour dealt with in his *Inquiry*. Those three aspects, treated here, seem to be enough to re-create a self-contained image of what Steuart conceived or assumed of human nature. It could be epitomized in so-called 'economic man', who is always self-interested, materialistic and acquisitive. While the typification of human nature in this way, *per se*, constitutes one of basics of Steuart's political economy, his economic theory indeed rests on the supposition that all human beings are of this type of 'economic man'.

1.4 The 'Spirit of the Times'

In conjunction with the previous discussion of Steuart's conception of human nature, we should not fail to mention a point, which is actually one of most significant characters of his political economy – that is, he understood human nature in its sociological and historical context. The human nature epitomized in 'economic man' must be still subject to its social and historical background. The point presents itself most expressively in his frequent references to the 'spirit of the times' or the 'spirit of the people'. At the very outset of his *Inquiry*, Steuart remarked,

> ... there is no treating any point which regards the political oeconomy of a nation, without accompanying the example with some supposition relative to the spirit of people. (*Works*, vol.1, p.12.)

That is to say, the 'spirit of the times or the people' exerts such great influence upon every branch of human activity, economic and political, that it would be quite impossible to understand any country or economy without taking it into consideration. Let us further explore this point with a typical instance in Steuart's actual analysis.

When Steuart explained the growth of population in a country in terms of the increment of 'effectual demand' in its economy, he clearly showed that the 'spirit of the times' would directly affect the 'taste of luxury or superfluity' in the people, which is one of the important factors in the creation of 'effectual demand'.[11]

> ... the human species will multiply pretty much in proportion to their industry; their industry will increase according to their wants, and these again will be diversified according to the spirit of the times. (*Works*, vol.1, p.47.)

---

inconveniences, which mankind seldom perceive to be such, till the way of removing them be contrived) than to the taste for luxury in the rich, who, to indulge their ease, engage the poor to become industrious. (*Works*, vol.1, P.240; original parentheses.)

[11] For Steuart's 'effectual demand' theory of population, see section 4, Ch.4 above. Also cf. our earlier discussion of Steuart's presumption of materialistic human nature and the notion of the 'taste of luxury or superfluity'.

> The spirit therefore of the principle people of a county determines the employment of the lower classes; the employment of these determines their usefulness to the state, and their usefulness, their multiplication. The more they are useful, the more they gain, according to our definition of the contract of society; the more they gain, the more they can feed; and consequently, the more they will marry and divide with their children. (*Op.cit.*, vol.1, p.138.)

> ... no destruction of inhabitants by expulsion, captivity, war, pestilence or famine, is so permanently hurtful to population, as a revolution in that spirit which is necessary for the increase and support of numbers. Let that spirit be kept up, and let mankind be well governed, numbers will quickly increase to their former standard, after the greatest reduction possible, (*Op.cit.*, vol.1, pp.142-3.)

In this case, the 'spirit of the times or the people' relates to the sociological and historical context of the 'taste of luxury or superfluity' in the people.[12] Not only in his analysis of population but in almost every part of his political economy, Steuart took account of the 'spirit of the times or the people'. It seems then that, while his constant consideration of the 'spirit of the times or the people' came from his conception of human nature in its sociological and historical context, it reflected a characteristic feature of his method, i.e., an empirico-historical relativism.[13]

2. ECONOMIC DEVELOPMENT AND SOCIETY: THREE STAGES

We have just seen how Steuart conceived of human nature, or, more precisely, what he presumed of it in his political economy. In this section, we shall proceed to discuss how he thought the society composed of those human beings is organized. The main point here is that Steuart approached this question in terms of its history, as he did the rest of his political economy. While this historical approach is really characteristic of his political economy, in general, it is quite notable in his analysis of the origin and the structure of society, in particular.[14] Meanwhile, Steuart explained the process of the historical advancement of society in economic terms.[15] He categorized it in terms of the modes or forms of procuring subsistence for the members of

---

[12] See section 4, Ch.4, for Steuart's distinction between 'moral' and 'physical incapacity of multiplication' of population. Also see *op.cit.*, vol.2, pp.53-66, for his discussion of the 'spirit of the times' in relation to government policies.

[13] In the appendix to this chapter, we shall discuss Steuart's method in political economy separately and generally.

[14] This seems to present a striking contrast to the approaches of the philosophers of natural law and social contract in the 17th and 18th centuries, who presupposed certain *a priori* views of society. Cf. our methodological appendix below.

[15] Skinner (1962) claimed that 'Steuart's historical materialism discloses a remarkable parallel with the work of the Scottish Historical School' (p.17). Also cf. Skinner (1965a) and Meek (1954b).

society.[16] That is to say, according to him, society has advanced along with its economic development, or with the changes of its economic conditions, in three stages: the stage of gathering and hunting, that of agriculture and barter, and that of trade and industry. While each of these denotes a dominant mode or form of subsistence in the corresponding stage of society, the modes or forms themselves might coexist at the same stage. Let us examine them in order.

2.1 The Stage of Gathering and Hunting

At this stage of society, according to Steuart, men subsisted mainly on the 'spontaneous fruits of the earth'.

> Did the earth produce of itself the proper nourishment for man with unlimited abundance, we should find no occasion to labour in order to procure it. (*Works*, vol.1, p.23.)

However, as the earth would not be able to maintain any considerable number of people without their labour, there must have been a certain limit in the multiplication of population,.[17]

> Were the earth therefore uncultivated, the number of mankind would not exceed the proportion of the spontaneous fruits which she offers for their immediate use, or for that of the animals which might be the proper nourishment of man. (*Works*, vol.1, p.24.)

There were two things immanent in human nature which drove the society of this stage to move, according to Steuart. On the one hand, the 'generative faculty' of human beings prompted them to multiply further; on the other hand, their 'self-love' led to the appropriation of the means of subsistence by a few of them.

> ... the principle of generation is inherent in man, and prompts him to multiply. Another principle, as naturally inherent in the mind, as the first is in the body, is self-love, or a desire of ease and happiness, which prompts those who find in themselves any superiority, whether personal or political, to make use of every natural advantage. Consequently, such will multiply proportionably: because by appropriating to themselves the fruits of the earth, they have means of subsisting their offspring. The others, I think, will very naturally become their servants; as this method is, of all others, the most easy to procure subsistence. ... This seems a consequence not unnatural in the infancy of the world. (*Works*, vol.1, p.28.)

[16] In contrast, R. Cantillon classified human society, both historically and typologically, in terms of the 'ownership' or appropriation of land: that is, 'wandering' and 'settled' societies. Cf. ch.1 'of Wealth' and ch.2 'of Human Societies' in his *Essai*.

[17] Cf. Steuart's theory of population in section 4, Ch.4 above. Basically, according to Steuart, 'the numbers of mankind must depend upon the quantity of food produced by the earth for their nourishment' (*Works*, vol.1. p.31).

In consequence, there ensued two results. In the first place, as mankind was gradually obliged to work the soil, agriculture became the most essential requisite for the procurement of their subsistence.

> I now suppose man to add his labour and industry to the natural activity of soil: so far, as by this he produces an additional quantity of food, so far he lays a foundation for the maintenance of an additional number. (*Works*, vol.1, p.127.)

In the second place, the appropriation of the means of subsistence by a few directly brought into existence the society of 'subordination' of 'slaves' or the 'labourers of the ground' to their 'masters' or 'feudal lords'.

> Those who become servants for the sake of food, will soon become slaves: for slavery is but the abuse of service, established by a civil institution; and men who find no possibility of subsisting otherwise, will be obliged to serve upon the conditions prescribed to them. ... The subordination of children to their parents, and of servants to their masters, seems to be the most rational origin of society and government. The first of these is natural, and follows as the unavoidable consequence of an entire dependence: the second is political, and may very naturally take place as to those who cannot otherwise procure subsistence. This last species of subordination may, I think, have taken place, the moment man became obliged to labour for subsistence, but no sooner. (*Works*, vol.1., pp.28-9.)

As soon as agriculture became extensive in its economic sphere and subordination was prevailing in its political sphere, the society moved from one stage to another.

2.2 The Stage of Agriculture and Barter

In the society of the second stage, there seemed to be another characteristic aspect in its economic sphere, apart from extensive agriculture: 'bartering' or 'trade in its infancy'. Steuart explained the emergence of 'bartering' in terms of the 'taste for luxury or superfluity' in human nature, i.e., the desire for consuming things other than subsistence requirements.[18]

> The wants of man are not confined to food, merely. When food is to be produced from the rude surface of the earth, a great part of his time must be taken up this object, even supposing him to be provided with every utensil proper for the exercise of his industry: he must therefore be in a worse condition to provide for his other wants: consequently, he may be willing to serve any one who will do it for him. (*Works*, vol.1, p.29.)

Thus, there began to appear another group of people, besides 'slaves' or the 'labourers of the ground' and 'masters' or 'feudal lord': that is, the 'industrious free hands' who supplied wants other than subsistence for the others, in exchange for their own subsistence. In fact, according to Steuart, the appearance of the 'industrious free hands', as well as that of 'slaves' or the

---

[18] Indeed, according to him, this 'taste for luxury or superfluity' would further urge the society to move from this to the next stage.

'labourers of ground', was essentially due to the appropriation of land by a small number of people in the society.

> When the earth is not in common to those who live upon her spontaneous fruits, but is appropriated by a few, there either slavery or industry must be introduced among those who consume the surplus of the proprietors; because these will expect either their service or work in return for their superfluity. (*Works*, vol.1, p.60.)

In any case, as long as the society was founded, economically, on agriculture and barter, and, politically, on 'slavery' or 'feudal system', it still stood at the second stage.[19] Yet, within this stage, there were some covert symptoms and signs of movement into another stage. That is to say, there seemed to already exist some elements of 'trade and industry' in their germinal forms: barter might develop into trade as its scale grew fast, and not only the 'industrious free hands' but also 'slaves' or the 'labourers of the ground' would become politically more free, as the economic relation between different groups of people came to dominate the political one.

The transition from the stage of agriculture and barter to that of trade and industry came complete gradually in both the economic and political spheres of society, as the dominant features of each sphere were changing by degrees. In the economic sphere, as a result of the enhancement of productivity in agriculture, more subsistence became available for the 'industrious free hands'; whereas wants other than subsistence increasingly prevailed among the 'proprietors of land' on account of their 'taste for superfluity'. As these two things went hand in hand with each other, trade and industry became far-reaching in the society. Some significant economic factors in the process of transition could be enumerated, as follows. First, the production of 'surplus' in agriculture was the essential requisite for the transition. Steuart concisely expressed,

> The more the necessities of man increase, *caeteris paribus*, the more free hands are require to supply them; and the more free hands are required, the more surplus food must be produced by additional labour, to supply their demand. (*Works*, vol.1, p.236.)

Second, the 'taste for superfluity' among people was also important for the acceleration of 'reciprocal wants' and thus of production in both agriculture and other industries.

> A free man who by his industry can procure all the comforts of a simple life, will enjoy his rest, and work no more: And, in general, all increase of work will cease, so soon as the demand for the purposes mentioned come to be satisfied. There is a plain reason for this. When the free hands have procured, by their labour, wherewithal to supply their wants, their ambition is satisfied: so soon as the husbandmen have produced the necessary surplus for relieving theirs, they work no more. (*Works*, vol.1, p.237.)

[19] In his discussion of the three stages of society, Steuart did not make any exact distinction between 'slavery' and 'feudal system'.

Third, in connection with the above point, Steuart laid great emphasis on the introduction of money in the process of transition.[20]

> When wants are multiplied, bartering becomes (for obvious reasons) more difficult; upon this money is introduced. This is the common price of all things: it is a proper equivalent in the hands of those who feel want, perfectly calculated to supply the occasions of those who, by industry, can relieve it. ... So soon as money is introduced into a country it becomes, as we have said above, an universal object of want to all the inhabitants. The consequence is, that the free hands of the state, who before stopped working, because all their wants were provided for, having this new object of ambition before their eyes, endeavour, by refinements upon their labour, to remove the smaller inconveniences which result from a simplicity of manners. (*Works*, vol.1, pp.238-9.)

On the other hand, in the political sphere, as the 'voluntary subordination' based on the social division of labour began to dominate the 'involuntary subordination' originated from the appropriation of land, so-called 'free society' replaced the 'slavery' or 'feudal system'. Steuart pointed out,

> ... the failure of the slavish form of feudal government, and the extension thereby given to civil and domestic liberty, were the source from which the whole system of modern policy has sprung. Under the feudal form, the higher classes were perhaps more free than at present, but the lower classes were either slaves, or under a most servile dependence, which, as to the consequence of interrupting the progress of private industry, is entirely the same thing. (*Works*, vol.1, p.227-8.)

No sooner have the 'trade and industry' in the economic sphere and the 'free men' in the political sphere become dominant features of the society, than it enters the final stage.

2.3 The Stage of Trade and Industry

At this stage, basically, the 'reciprocal wants' between different sectors of the economy are to account for the 'band' or 'bond' of society.

> ... a farmer will not labour to produce a superfluity of grain relatively to his consumption, unless he finds some want which may be supplied by means of that superfluity; neither will other industrious persons work to supply the wants of the farmers for any other reason than to procure subsistence, which they cannot otherwise so easily obtain. (*Works*, vol.1, p.36.)

In fact, according to Steuart, there are two broad groups of people in the society: that is, 'farmers' and 'free hands'. The former are those engaged in agriculture; whereas the latter are composed of the 'industrious free hands' engaged in the other industries, and those who receive rents from the 'farmers' and spend them mainly on what the 'industrious free hands' produce.[21]

---

[20] Cf. *Works*, vol., pp.41-6. Steuart sometimes called money 'imaginary wealth'. For a discussion of the functions of money, assumed in his *Inquiry*, see section 1, Ch.6 above.

[21] For a detailed discussion of Steuart's conception of the class structure of the society at this stage and the sectoral division of its economy, see section 1, Ch.2 above.

Not only 'industry' but also agriculture come to be exercised for exchange through 'trade' to their full extent, as the society at this juncture takes on the complete phase of an exchange economy.[22]

> ... when I employ the term agriculture in treating of modern policy, I always consider it to be exercised as a trade, and producing a surplus, and not as the direct means of subsisting, where all is consumed by the husbandman. (*Works*, vol.1, p.153.)

Meanwhile, though 'trade' and 'industry' might exist independently of each other, they actually 'facilitate and support' each other.[23]

> To ask, whether trade owes its beginning to industry, or industry to trade, is like asking, whether the motion of heart is owing to the blood, or the motion of the blood to the heart. Both the one and the other, I suppose, are formed by such insensible degrees, that it is impossible to determine where the motion begins. But so soon as the body comes to be perfectly formed, I have little doubt of the heart's being the principle of circulation. ... We cannot therefore say, that trade will force industry, or that industry will force trade; but we may, that trade will facilitate industry, and that industry will support trade. (*Works*, vol.1, pp.229-31.)

While trade and industry are carried out on the basis of their mutual dependence, they represent a most distinctive feature of the society at this stage. In the previous chapters, in fact, we have already discussed Steuart's analysis of the economic sphere of the society quite thoroughly. Thus, let us here move on to examine particularly the relationship between the economic and the political sphere of the society at the stage of trade and industry, in a broad context of his three-stage theory of the development of society.

3. THE ECONOMY AND THE BODY POLITIC

In the last section, we saw that, in Steuart's conception of society, there has always been what he called 'subordination', of some kind or other, between its

---

[22] According to Steuart, only when agriculture is exercised as a 'trade', rather than as a 'direct means of subsisting', and only when land is appropriated by a few, could the 'surplus' or 'what answers to the land-rent' be produced. Cf. *Works*, vol.1, pp.114-7. To put it another way, if everyone in the economy had his own bit of land which he could cultivate by way of directly procuring his subsistence, then there would be no surplus, whatsoever, produced in the economy as a whole. Steuart considered this case as an 'abuse' resulting from an 'over-extension of agriculture and subdivision of lands' (*loc.cit.*). While this point reflects Steuart's general idea of society as being organized by the mutual dependence among its members in the economic sense, it seems to be based on his own concept of surplus, i.e., as a social concept. He conceived of surplus in terms of the social relation between different classes of people in the economy. Cf. section 2, Ch.2 and section 3, Ch.3, above.

[23] Steuart observed,

> ... trade may exist without industry, because things produced partly by nature may be exchanged between men; industry may be exercised without trade, because a man may be very ingenious in working to supply his own consumption, and where there is exchange, there can be no trade. (*Works*, vol.1, p.224.)

For the formal definitions of 'trade' and 'industry', see *op.cit.*, vol.1, p.223.

members since land was appropriated by a minority of them. In the agrarian society, it was more or less 'involuntary', as the society was built upon either 'slavery' or the 'feudal system', in which 'slaves' or the 'labourers of the ground' entirely and almost unilaterally depended on their 'masters' or 'feudal lords' for their subsistence. By contrast, in the industrial society, it becomes by and large 'voluntary', with the society based on the 'reciprocal demand' of 'free individuals' in different economic sectors. 'Farmers' and the 'industrious free hands' depend on each other for what the others produce. Steuart illustrated the comparison between the two societies at different stages, as follows:

> Men were then forced to labour because they were slaves to other; men are now forced to labour because they are slaves of their own wants. (*Works*, vol.1, p.52.)

In this way, Steuart related the economic sphere of each society to its political sphere in terms of the nature of 'subordination and dependence' among different groups of people in the society. In this section, we shall further discuss Steuart's analysis of the relation between the economic and the political sphere of society at the two different stages.

To be specific, the questions under consideration are, on the one hand, whether the relation between the economic and the political sphere of each stage of society is separable; and, if separable, how the body politic would fit in with the economy, on the other hand. We shall answer the first question by examining Steuart's discussion of the nature of the social relations among people at each stage; whereas, for the second question, we shall focus on his discussion of the effects of the different forms of government on the workings of the economy. Meanwhile, the basic tool-kits of Steuart's analysis of these questions were the notions of 'subordination' and 'dependence' among people in a society. Following at his heels, let us move on to the first question.

Above all, Steuart understood the notions of 'subordination' and 'dependence' in the following way:

> ... by subordination is implied an authority which superiors have over inferiors; and by dependence, is implied certain advantages which the inferiors draw from their subordination. (*Works*, vol.1, p.316.)

Thus, according to him, they are relative to each other: that is, 'subordination' is what is paid for 'dependence'. Steuart regarded the relation of 'subordination and dependence' as a 'general principle' of all sorts of human relations.[24] He divided it into three categories, according to the ground on which it is founded: i.e., 'natural', 'political' and 'commercial', the last of which might rather be called 'economic'.

---

[24] Once, he called it even the 'law of nature'. Cf. *Works*, vol.1, p.317.

> The first natural, between parents and children; the second political, between masters and servants, lord and vassals, Princes and subjects; the third commercial, between the rich and the industrious. (*Works*, vol.1, p.317.)

And Steuart further observed that the 'subordination' ought to be proportional to 'dependence', or *vice versa*.[25]

> In proportion, therefore, as certain classes, or certain individuals become more dependent than formerly, in the same proportion ought their just subordination to increase: and in proportion as they become less dependent than formerly, in the same proportion ought this just subordination to diminish. (*Works*, vol.1, p.318.)

Now, the relations between 'masters' and 'slaves', and between 'feudal lords' and the 'labourers of the ground' – both in the society of 'agriculture and barter' – were not only political but also economic; though in the respective cases showing different degrees of 'subordination and dependence'.

> Dependence is the only bond of society. ... the dependence of one man upon another for food, is a very natural introduction of slavery. This was the first contrivance mankind fell upon, in order to become useful to one another. (*Works*, vol.1, pp.316-7.)
>
> I deduce the origin of the great subordination under the feudal government, from the necessary dependence of the lower classes for their subsistence. They consumed the produce of the land, as the price of their subordination, not as the reward of their industry in making it produce. (*Op.cit.*, vol.1, p.319.)

On the other hand, the relation between 'farmers' and 'free hands' in the society of 'trade and industry' is only an economic one, with the lowest degree of 'subordination and dependence'.[26]

> The last refinement, and that which has brought liberty to be generally extended to the lowest denominations of a people, without destroying that dependence necessary to serve as a band of society, was the introduction of industry: by this is implied, the circulation of an adequate equivalent for every service, which procures to the rich every advantage they expect to reap, either from the servitude or dependence of the poor; and to these again, every comfort they could wish to enjoy under the mildest slavery, or most gentle subordination. (*Works*, vol.1, p.317.)

Therefore, it follows that, as far as the social relations among people are concerned, at the stage of 'agriculture and barter', the economic and political spheres were inseparable; whereas, at the stage of 'trade and industry', they become separable from each other. According to Steuart, it is particularly what he called 'free commerce', based on the social division of labour

---

[25] In fact, Steuart graded the relation of 'subordination and dependence' according to its degree: i.e., the one between 'masters' and 'slaves' the highest; the one between parents and children and the one between 'feudal lords' and the 'labourers of the ground in the middle; and the one between 'tradesmen and manufacturers' and their 'employers' the lowest. Cf. *Works*, vol.1, p.318.

[26] In the present context, Steuart did not explicitly consider the presence of the landlord class who get rent revenue from the 'farmers' for their ownership of land to be a feature of the society at the stage of 'trade and industry'; though their spending on 'luxury' was supposed to play a great part in the creation of 'effectual demand' in the economy, in his analysis of output. Cf. section 2, Ch.4.

between 'farmers' and 'free hands', that has eventually brought 'political liberty' to all the members of the society at the stage of 'trade and industry'.

Then, while the 'free commerce' confines itself to being an economic system, is it compatible with any form of government? In what follows, we shall further explore Steuart's discussion of this particular aspect of the relation between the economy and the body politic in the society at the stage of 'trade and industry'. First of all, to the above question, we may immediately answer that 'free commerce' is only compatible with those forms of government which allow 'political liberty' for individuals in the society. The reason for this is rather obvious from Steuart's discussion of its nature, examined so far: that is to say, not only is it accompanied by the 'political liberty' of individuals, it is actually founded on it. It is this characteristic of the society of 'trade and industry' which circumscribes its form of government within certain bounds.[27] Meanwhile, according to Steuart, there are some 'boundaries of subordination' among people in the 'free society'. They are due to the laws in the society.

> A people who depend upon nothing but their own industry for their subsistence, ought to be under no further subordination than what is necessary for their protection. And as the protection of the whole body of such a people implies the protection of every individual, so every political subordination should there be general and equal: no person, no class should be under a greater subordination than another. This is the subordination of law: and whenever laws establish a subordination more than what is proportionate to the dependence of those who are subordinate, so far such laws may be considered as contrary to natural equity, and arbitrary. (*Works*, vol.1, pp.321-2.)

In the 'free society', though it is confined to the economic sphere only, the relation of 'subordination and dependence' among people is still subject to the content and application of the laws. Thus, as far as the enactment of laws and their administration are part of the political process of the body politic, the latter yet exerts influence on the economic mechanism of the society. Then, after all, it could be observed that, despite the apparent independent relation between the economy and the body politic of the 'free society', the one actually circumscribes the other in regard to its fundamental character whereas

---

[27] As a matter of fact, Steuart gave detailed accounts on 'how the feudal form of government must be unfavourable both to trade and industry' and how it was subsequently replaced by other forms of government based on 'public liberty'. (Cf. *Works*, vol.1, pp.326-31.) A part of them reads,

> Some kingdoms have been quit for a bloody rebellion or a long civil war. Other countries have likewise demonstrated the force of the principle here laid down: a wealthy populace has broken their chains to pieces, and overturned the very foundation of the feudal system. ... and an attentive spectator may find amusement in viewing the progress of it in many states of Europe. Trade and industry are in vogue; and their establishment is occasioning a wonderful fermentation with the remaining fierceness of the feudal constitution. (*Works*, vol.1, pp.328-9.)

Thus, Steuart later concentrated on discussing the two alternative forms of government, 'republican' and 'monarchical', founded on the 'liberty and independence of individuals', for the society at the stage of 'trade and industry'. We shall shortly come back to this point.

the other in its turn affects the one in regard to its working. In this context, we shall briefly introduce Steuart's comparative account of the two alternative forms of government, republic and monarchy, in the rest of this section.

Steuart talked about some merits and demerits of each form of government in terms of its effects on the workings of the economy in the 'free society'. As soon as the relation of 'subordination and dependence' among people becomes purely economic after the establishment of 'trade and 'industry', every individual in the society acquires political 'liberty and independence'. On the other hand, there still exists 'inequality', both economic and political, between 'higher class' and 'lower classes', i.e., between those who own some property, land in particular, and those who do not.[28] Steuart supposed that the 'republican' form tends to remove this 'inequality' between the classes whereas the 'monarchical' preserve it.

> If we reason, from facts, and from experience, we shall find, that trade and industry have been found to flourish best under the republican form, and under those which have come the nearest to it. May I be allowed to say, that, perhaps, one principal reason for this has been, that under these forms the administration of the laws has been the most uniform, and consequently, that most liberty has *actually* been there enjoyed: I say actually, because I have said above, that in my acceptation of the term, liberty is equally compatible with monarchy as with democracy: I do not say the enjoyment of it is equally secure under both; because under the first it is much more liable to be destroyed. The life of the democratical system is equality, Monarchy conveys the idea of the greatest inequality possible. Now if, on one side, the equality of democracy secures liberty; on the other, the moderation in expence [expense] discourages industry; and if, on one side, the inequality of the monarchy endangers liberty, the progress of luxury encourages industry on the other. (*Works*, vol.1, p.322; original italics.)

Thus, according to Steuart, 'trade and industry' might flourish more in a republic than in a monarchy, as long as the 'equality' between classes, ensured under the former, would enhance the 'liberty and independence' of individuals, which would eventually promote 'trade and industry' in the economy. However, as the very 'inequality' between classes, aggravated under the monarchy, would foster the consumption of 'luxury' in the economy (whereas the 'equality' under the republic would moderate it), the 'trade and industry' might be well sustained in the monarchy.[29] Therefore, Steuart observed that the 'republican' form of government would be good for the

[28] Steuart called 'higher class' 'those to whom the surplus of the farmers directly belongs or who, with a revenue in money already acquired, can purchase it'; whereas 'lower classes' both 'farmers' and 'those who purchase it [the surplus of the farmers] with their daily labour or personal service'. Cf. *Works*, vol.1, pp.61-2. Also see section 1, Ch.2 above, for Steuart's conception of the social classes and the economic sectors in the stage of 'trade and industry'.

[29] For Steuart's discussion of the 'political effects of luxury', see section 2, Ch.4 above.

economy engaged in 'foreign trade'; whereas the 'monarchical' form would be good for the one engaged in either 'infant trade' or 'inland commerce'.[30]

> From whence we may conclude, that the democratical system is naturally the best for giving birth to foreign trade; the monarchical, for the refinement of luxurious arts, and for promoting a rapid circulation of inland commerce. (*Works*, vol.1, pp.322-3.)

In addition, Steuart emphasized that each government should make possible efforts to remove or lessen some adverse side-effects of it own form.[31] After all, from his comparative discussion of the two alternative forms of government, it becomes clear that the nature of the body politic would definitely affect the workings of the economy in the 'free society'.

In summary, we have seen in this chapter how Steuart understood human nature, society and the body politic in his *Inquiry*. While it constitutes an essential part of his political economy, it serves as the background of his economic analysis discussed in the previous chapters.[32]

---

[30] According to Steuart, there are three kinds of trade which the modern exchange economy sometimes passes through in stages or sometimes carries on at the same time: 'infant', 'foreign' and 'inland' trade (commerce). When the economy is engaged in either 'infant' or 'inland' trade, he argued, it should encourage 'luxury' at home so as to increase its level of output; whereas when in 'foreign' trade, it should discourage it. For a detailed discussion of his analysis of the three stages or categories of trade and the respective economic strategies for them, see section 2, Ch.5 above.

[31] According to Steuart,

> The danger which liberty is exposed to under monarchy, and the discouragement to industry, from the frugality of the democracy, are only the natural and immediate effects of the two forms of government; and these inconveniences will take place only, while statesmen neglect the interest of commerce, so far as not to make it an object of administration. (*Works*, vol.1, p.323.)

Nevertheless, Steuart warned that each form of government should not exercise an 'arbitrary' power in enacting and executing the laws; otherwise, it would hurt itself and even endanger its own existence.

> The disadvantages, therefore, of the monarchical form, in point of trade and industry, does not proceed from the inequality it establishes among the citizens, but from the consequence of this inequality, which is very often accompanied with an arbitrary and undeterminate [indeterminate] subordination between the individuals of the higher classes, and those of the lower; or between those vested with the execution of the laws, and the body of the people. The moment it is found that any subordination within the monarchy, between subject and subject, is left without proper bounds prescribed, liberty is so far at an end. Nay monarchy itself is hereby hurt, as this undeterminate [indeterminate] subordination implies an arbitrary power in the state, not vested in the monarch. *Arbitrary* power never can be delegated; for if it be *arbitrary*, it may be turned against the monarch, as well as against the subject. (*Works*, vol.1. p.323; original italics but brackets added.)

In fact, Steuart distinguished an 'abuse' of power from a 'tyranny': that is, the one refers to the exercise of such an arbitrary power by the government, contrary to its own 'constitution'; whereas the other refers to the government whose very 'constitution' allows it to exercise such an arbitrary power, contrary to the 'general principle of subordination and dependence'. Cf. *Works*, vol.1, pp.323-6.

[32] After having worked through both the background and the actual analysis of Steuart's political economy, one thing we have to further note is the method he adopted. We shall discuss it in the appendix below.

APPENDIX: Steuart's Method

> While our belief is implicit we are beyond conviction; not because we do not perceive the force of arguments brought against our opinion; but because we are ignorant of the forces of those which can be brought to support it. And as no body will sell what belongs to him, without previously being informed of its value, so nobody will give up their opinion without knowing all that can be said for it.
>
> Sir James Steuart,
> *Dedication to Lady Mary Wortley Montagu*
> (Chamley (1965), p.136)

The time when Sir James Steuart (1713-80) lived and wrote, belongs to the era of the Enlightenment in the Western hemisphere. It appears that the 'spirit of the times' partly accounts for the kind of method which he adopted in making his *Inquiry into the Principles of Political Oeconomy*. Indeed, in that respect, he was greatly influenced by such prominent thinkers of his day as Montesquieu (1689-1755) and Hume (1711-76);[1] or, at least, they all three shared a common ground in their methods: that is, empirico-historical relativism. In what follows, we shall substantiate this proposition by contrasting Steuart's general views on society and the body politic with those of the philosophers of natural law and social contract, whose ideas had been predominant ever since the preceding century but were seriously doubted by the two contemporary thinkers. And, to go a step further, we shall discuss what amounts to Steuart's own credit for adapting the method in question in economic analysis.[2]

I

According to the philosophers of natural law and social contract, broadly speaking, society has been established from the 'state of nature' through what

[1] Meanwhile, in economic thought in particular, Cantillon (1680?-1734), Quesnay (1694-1774) and Smith (1723-90) were also active at that time. For the interchange of their economic ideas and some affinities and disparities between them, see the previous appendices to Chs. 2, 3 and 5 above.

[2] Though not many commentators have discussed Steuart's method seriously, as is the case with his analysis itself, somewhat different aspects of it were emphasized among those who did. Among others, Grossman (1943, part II) put emphasis on the socio-evolutionary approach; Sen (1957, ch.IV) on the balance between induction and deduction; Vickers (1959) on the 'piecemeal approach'; Skinner (1963, 1965b, analytical introduction to 1966, and 1981) on the empiricism; and Davie (1967) even on the political motivation. The present discussion would not much deviate from all these aspects. Here, they are synthesized in what may be called empirico-historical relativism. Also cf. Chamley (1963) and Macfie (1955).

is called 'contract' between its members. The actual contents of 'social contract' vary among the individual philosophers, depending on their descriptions of the 'state of nature', e.g., Hobbes's 'state of war' or Locke's 'state of peace'. Nevertheless, there is one thing in common among these philosophers: they all presupposed, one way or another, the direction in which the society would move. In other words, they all had in their minds certain *a priori* views of the ideal state, to which society ought to proceed. In any case, the final goal seems to be described as the achievement of or progress toward 'freedom' and 'equality' for every member of society. By contrast, Steuart's outlook on society was based on an economico-historical approach. According to him, society came into existence basically for economic reasons, i.e., as a result of human efforts to secure subsistence, and that it still moves blindly as its economic conditions change. Meanwhile, how the economic conditions of a particular society determine the way it moves still depends on its political and other social backgrounds. While the former point is obvious from Steuart's three-stage theory of society in terms of economic development, the latter becomes clear from his discussions of the relation between the economy and the body politic within each stage.[3] On the whole, this view of social formation reflects the empirico-historical relativism in Steuart's method.

The distinctive feature of Steuart's method would become plainer, if we make a comparison between his view and that of the philosophers of natural law and social contract on the 'origin of supreme authority' of the body politic in conjunction with social formation. As to the question of 'how far subordination among men is authorised', Steuart observed,

> ... so far as the subordination is in proportion to the dependence, so far it is reasonable and just. This represents an even balance. If the scale of subordination is found too weighty, tyranny ensues; and licentiousness is implied, in proportion as it rises above the level. (*Works*, vol.1, pp.317-8.)

That is to say, all authority of 'subordination' must be in proportion to 'dependence'.[4] Therefore, it must vary according to circumstances.

> I think it is as rational to say, that the fatherly power proceeded originally from the act of the children, as to say, that the great body of the people who were fed, and protected by a few great lords, was the foundation of power, and creator of subordination. Those who have no other equivalent to give for their food and protection, must pay in personal service, respect and submission; and so soon as they came to be in a situation to pay a proper equivalent for these dependences, so far they acquire a title to liberty and independence. (*Works*, vol.1, p.319.)

---

[3] For Steuart's three-stage theory of society and his discussion of the relation between the economy and the body politic, see sections 2 and 3, respectively, in the chapter above.

[4] See section 3 in the chapter above, for Steuart's discussion of the 'general principle of subordination and dependence'.

While the 'supreme authority' of the body politic comes from the relation of 'subordination and dependence' between the body politic and the people, it must be subject to various circumstances regarding its economic, political and social backgrounds. This is a striking contrast with the views of the philosophers of natural law and social contract. According to them, the 'supreme authority' originates from the 'contract' between the ruler and the ruled, and must be the same all the time everywhere, unless the 'contract' itself changes. But, as far as the 'freedom and equality' of individuals are concerned, the 'contract' ought to be the same. Steuart himself pointed out the difference between his view and that of these philosophers, as follows:

> The rights of Kings, therefore, are to be sought for in history; not founded upon the supposition of tacit contracts between them and their people, inferred from the principles of an imaginary law of nature, which makes all mankind equal: nature can never be in opposition to common reason. The general principle I have laid down, appears, in my humble opinion, more rational than this imaginary contract; and as consonant to the full with the spirit of free government. If the original tacit contract of government between Prince and people is admitted universally, then all governments ought to be similar; and every subordination, which appears contrary to the entire liberty and independence of lower classes, ought to be construed as tyrannical: whereas, according to my principle, the subordination of classes may, in different countries, be vastly different; the prerogative of one sovereign may, from different circumstances, be far more extended than that of another. (*Works*, vol.1, p.320.)

It seems, then, that the difference in their political views stems from their different starting points, i.e., their methods. One emphasized the induction from empirical and historical evidence, whereas the other emphasized the deduction from an *a priori* supposition based on reason.[5] We may note also that Steuart's coherent and unifying explanations of the origin and development of society and the relation between the economy and the body politic were firmly built upon his empirico-historical relativism in method. In this regard, he was quite distinct from the philosophers of natural law and social contract and more akin to Montesquieu and Hume.

II

When Steuart got down to the economic analysis, he adopted again a method based on empirico-historical relativism. His *Inquiry* starts with the following modest preface:

[5] In connection with his political view, Steuart explicitly noted,

> Matter of fact, which is stronger than all reasoning, demonstrates the force of the principle here laid down. Do we not see how subordination rises and falls under different reigns, under a rich Elizabeth, and a necessitous Charles, under a powerful Austrian, and a distressed Bavarian Emperor? (*Works*, vol.1, p.321.)

> It is with the greatest diffidence that I present to the public this attempt towards reducing to principles, and forming into a regular science, the complicated interests of domestic policy. (*Works*, vol.1, p.v.)

Above all, we may note from this that the object of his *Inquiry* is the 'complicated interests of domestic policy'. Thus, the subject in itself is empirical and relative to a particular economy, which must be understood in its social, political, cultural and even environmental backgrounds. He himself clarified it, as follows:

> If one considers the variety which is found in different countries, in the distribution of property, subordination of classes, genius of people, proceeding from the variety of forms of government, laws, climate, and manners, one may conclude, that the political oeconomy in each must necessarily be different, and that principles, however universally true, may become quite in effectual in practice, without a sufficient preparation of the spirit of a people. (*Works*, vol.1, pp.3-4.)

On the other hand, the method of his *Inquiry* is 'reducing to principles and forming into a regular science' the object of study. In other words, the discipline itself is established through both generalization and logical reasoning. Thus, being firmly based on empiricism, the method must be not only inductive but also deductive. Steuart also made this point clear at the outset of his *Inquiry*, as follows:

> It goes little further than to collect and arrange some elements relating to the most interesting branches of modern policy, such as population, agriculture, trade, industry, money, coin interest, circulation, banks, exchange, public credit, and taxes. The principle deduced from all these topics, appear tolerably consistent; and the whole is a train of reasoning, through which I have adhered to the connection of subjects as faithfully as I could: but the nature of the work being a deduction of principles, not a collection of institutions, I seized the opportunities which my reasoning threw in my way, to connect every principle, as I went along, with every part of the inquiry to which it could refer; and when I found the connexion sufficiently shewn, I broke off such disquisitions as would have led me from the object then present. (*Works*, vol.1, pp.x-xi.)

Nevertheless, as he deduced certain corollaries and conclusions from general observations on empirical and historical facts, he tried to specify under what circumstances they were logically inferred. In this light, Steuart accused what was called French *systemes* of its impracticability, as follows:[6]

> The great danger of running into error upon particular points relating to this subject, proceeds from our viewing them in a light too confined, and to our not attending to the influence of concomitant circumstances, which render general rules of little use. Men of parts and knowledge seldom fail to reason consequentially on every subject; but when enquiries are made concerning the complicated interests of society, the vivacity of an author's genius is apt to prevent him from attending to the variety of circumstances which render uncertain every consequence, almost, which he can draw

---

[6] Campbell (1947) observed that 'Steuart, with his abhorrence of *systemes*, was anything but doctrinaire' (p.38).

> from his reasoning. To this I ascribe the habit of running into what the French call *Systemes*. These are no more than a chain of contingent consequences, drawn from a few fundamental maxims, adopted, perhaps, rashly. Such systems are mere conceits; they mislead the understanding, and efface the path to truth. An induction is formed, from whence a conclusion, called a principle, is drawn and defined; but this is no sooner done, than the author extends its influence far beyond the limits of the ideas present to his understanding, when he made his definition. The best method, therefore, to detect a pretended system, is always to substitute the definition in place of the term. (*Works*, vol.1, p.xii.)

Thus, we may call how Steuart conducted his analysis an induction-oriented method, whereas the French *systemes* could be regarded as deduction-oriented.[7]

Steuart's induction-oriented method explains why he constantly took account of the general circumstances, or the stages of development, of the things concerned.[8] As a matter of fact, he did this so scrupulously that sometimes one part of his analysis, particularly its conclusion, seemed to contradict another. For example, the 'political effects of luxury' in a closed economy, such as one engaged in either 'infant trade' or 'inland commerce', must be quite opposite to those in an open economy, such as one in 'foreign trade';[9] depending on the state of the balance of payments, the imposition of coinage would have different effects on the relative price of coin and bullion;[10] and, according to the demand and supply conditions of the money market, the two alternative taxes, 'proportional' and 'cumulative', would have their own uses.[11] Although all these must have come through some deductive process or other, the comprehensive scope of Steuart's analysis demonstratively shows how painstaking he was with his induction-oriented method. As regards the categorization of different stages of trade, for instance, Steuart himself confessed,

> I hope, from this short recapitulation and exposition of principles, I have sufficiently communicated to my reader the distinctions I want to establish, between what I have called infant, foreign, and inland trade. Such distinctions are very necessary to be retained, because it is proper they should be applied in many places of this treatise, in order to qualify general propositions: these cannot be avoided, without a perpetual

---

[7] In any economic analysis, some logical deduction is inevitable, as long as it contains certain theoretical elements. In fact, it might be said that the proportion of induction to deduction varies among different economic analyses. In this context, Sen (1957) observed,

> He [Steuart] is one of the few outstanding economists who have tried to maintain an even balance between inductive and deductive studies and have taken as much care to explain their methodology as the content of their theories. (p.26.)

For a general discussion of Steuart's methodology, Sen (1957), pp.26-31.

[8] Let us leave out those purely descriptive parts of his analysis. As far as his economic analysis is concerned, its kernel consists of the theoretical elements in it.

[9] Cf. section 2, Ch.4 and section 2, Ch.5, above.

[10] Cf. sub-section 2.5, Ch.6 and sub-section 2.1, Ch.7, above.

[11] Cf. sub-section 1.4, Ch.8 above.

> repetition of such restrictions, which would tire the reader, appear frivolous to him, and divert his attention. (*Works*, vol.1, p.405.)

Despite his induction-oriented method, there is still some strong normative aspect in Steuart's analysis. This is apparent in his definition of political economy as an art.

> The great art therefore of political oeconomy is first to adapt the different operations of it to the spirit, manners, habits, and customs of the people; and afterwards to model these circumstances so, as to be able to introduce a set of new and more useful institutions. (*Works*, vol.1, p.3.)

Thus, combined with his empirico-historically relativistic views of society and the body politic, the induction-oriented method ultimately pointed to the role of the state.[12] Is this a fundamental assumption of his economic analysis or its conclusive message? The question must be answered on the basis of a thorough examination of the whole of his political economy.

---

[12] In the previous chapters, in fact, we have already seen some particulars of his interventionist view of the role of the state throughout his economic analysis.

10. CONCLUSION

> It is of governments as of machines, the more they are simple, the more they are solid and lasting; the more they are artfully composed, the more they become useful; but the more apt they are to be out of order.
>
> Sir James Steuart,
> *An Inquiry into the Principles of Political Oeconomy* (*Works*, vol.1, p.331.)

From the foregoing interpretation of Steuart's *Inquiry*, what could we say about his political economy as a whole? Or rather what did *he* ultimately try to say through that? To conclude the present analysis, we will draw our attention to two things about Steuart's political economy: its central theme and its ultimate message. To find the former, we shall take an overview of what has been said so far, focusing particularly on the analytical structure of his economic theory. For the latter, we will seek it in conjunction with the way how he unfolded the former. As we concentrate on theoretical aspects of Steuart's political economy, we may only hope that the present interpretation of his *Inquiry* would provide a basis for some serious evaluation of his contribution to the development of economics. Thus, we will leave behind the actual re-assessment of his place in the history of economic thought.

I

Given the discussions of the analytical and methodological background of Steuart's *Inquiry* (Ch.9), we may first take up his basic conception of an exchange economy (Ch.2). Firmly based on the recognition of the interdependence of economic sectors and social classes, he clearly grasped the circular system of production, distribution and consumption in the exchange economy. From this, some basic ideas and notions of his economic analysis, such as 'effectual demand', 'luxuries' and 'necessaries [necessities]', were derived. His theory of value and distribution (Ch.3) further clarifies in what terms and how the circular system of production, distribution and consumption completes itself in the exchange economy. While his notion of the 'real value' of commodities denotes merely their prime cost of production, that of 'current price' determined by the supply and demand in their markets is fully compatible with the circular system of economic activities and processes. The difference between the 'current price' and the 'real value' of commodities accrues to the producers, including merchants, as their 'profit upon alienation' or what he sometimes called the 'profit of trade and industry'. In Steuart, the determination of the value of commodities and that of the distribution of income represent simply the different sides of the same coin. While the income of the whole economy is categorized into the 'profit upon alienation', the wages of labour and the rent of land, the first two categories of income depend on the valuation of commodities and the last is determined as a residual. In other words, once the 'current price' is determined in the commodity market, the wages of heterogeneous labour, as its price, would be determined in the labour market; and subsequently, the 'profit upon alienation' and the rent of land would be discerned, given the state of technology in the economy. What then about the scale of income or the composition of output in the economy?

This question leads us to Steuart's theory of output, employment and population (Ch.4). He explained the determination of the level of output in an exchange economy in terms of the 'political effects of luxury'. Bringing the interdependence of economic sectors and social classes into focus, Steuart utilized the notion of 'effectual demand'. As soon as the level of output is determined by the 'effectual demand' for 'luxuries' in the economy, both the amount of employment and the size of population would be known correspondingly. While the former depends on the scale and the composition of output in the economy as a whole, the latter depends mainly on those in the agricultural sector. Thus, unless the other economic sectors grow in proportion to the agricultural sector, there must be either unemployment or a general stagnation in the economy. Apart from the problem of imbalance between sectors, there are some immanent limitations to the growth of output in a closed economy. (We now move on to Steuart's theory of economic growth and foreign trade (Ch.5).) These limitations are represented by what Steuart called 'physical' and 'moral incapacity'. The one relates to the state of technology and the endowment of resources in the economy whereas the other to a lack of demand. In either case, the introduction of foreign trade might help. It depends on general circumstances of the economy concerned. Steuart grouped them into three categories or stages of trade: 'infant trade', 'foreign trade' and 'inland commerce'. A country in the first stage must store up its economic potential in preparation for the next stage, in which foreign trade would greatly help to ease or remove the limitations of its economic growth. After being drained of relative advantages over other countries in foreign trade, the country would come to the last stage, in which the domestic creation of 'effectual demand' becomes again the key to economic growth. According to Steuart, however, the growth of the level of output does not necessarily mean the growth of the wealth of a country. In his conception, wealth is potential consumption rather than potential production. On the basis of this stock concept of wealth, Steuart built up his argument for the favourable balance of trade. He *did not* dispute the benefits of international trade for both trading parties, but he *did* qualify when and how a country should enter into foreign trade.

Money is not neutral in Steuart's analysis. According to his consumption-production theory of money (Ch.6), it is demanded not only for consumption but also for production. A change in the supply of money affects both the demand and the supply side of the commodity market. The rate of interest, determined in the money market, has some proportional relation to the rate of profit, determined in the commodity market. Both money and commodity markets are so inseparably interrelated that they should be equilibrated concurrently. Thus, Steuart's monetary analysis of a closed economy represents a simultaneous determination of the rate of interest, price level and the level of output. His theory of international money could be understood in a similar way (Ch.7). Steuart explained the determination of both the rate of exchange and the balance of payments in a general equilibrium context. The balance of payments, as the difference between domestic production and absorption in the economy, is to be determined simultaneously with the rate of exchange (as the ratio between foreign and domestic price level) and those other variables mentioned above. Steuart's monetary analysis also encompasses the theory of public finance (Ch.8). At a macroeconomic level, his theory of public finance would well fit in with his monetary general equilibrium model. He emphasized the functional role of public finance in the workings of the modern exchange economy. In fact, according to Steuart, taxation, public spending and public borrowing constitute optional policy instruments for the government to regulate price level and the level of output in the economy.

From the above overview of Steuart's economic analysis, could we assume any particular theme under which all its different parts and pieces are systematically organized? Upon the present interpretation of his *Inquiry*, at least, we may observe that he put some different emphasis on each part of his economic analysis. For instance, his theory of distribution could be seen as a by-product of his theory of value and that of output. We may also note some analytical hierarchy between the different subjects. His theory of public finance cannot be properly understood without premising his theory of money. It seems then that the central theme of Steuart's political economy is the macroeconomic analysis of trade and growth.[1] For this theme, his theory of value and distribution furnishes some microeconomic foundations, while both his theory of output, employment and population and that of economic growth

[1] In this context, the 'trade' implies in a broad sense what Steuart called 'alienation', i.e., the production of commodities for exchange and the exchange process itself, and it covers both domestic and foreign trade.

and foreign trade constitute the main body of his argument. Meanwhile, his theory of national and international money provides some links between real and monetary phenomena, and thereupon his theory of public finance endorses the active fiscal policy of government. As a matter of fact, his discussions of the 'current price' of commodities and the 'profit upon alienation', the 'balance of work and demand', 'effectual demand', the 'political effects of luxury', employment and unemployment, the growth of population, gains from foreign trade, the three stages of trade, and the analogy between the 'balance of wealth' and the 'balance of trade', national and international money, taxation, public credit and debts, are all among the major topics in his *Inquiry* and represent the logical steps of his argument under the central theme of trade and growth.

II

Let us finally discuss what Steuart ultimately told us in relation to the central theme of his political economy. To state the conclusion first, the message is neither *laissez-faire* nor central planning. While he was constantly emphatic on the role of the state in guiding and adjusting the workings of the market economy, he was far from advocating any sort of totalitarian command economy. The point is obvious from the following remark in his *Inquiry*.[2]

> As modern oeconomy, therefore, is the most effectual bridle ever was invented against the folly of despotism; so the wisdom of so great a power never shines with greater lustre, than when we see it exerted in planning and establishing this oeconomy, as a bridle against the wanton exercise of itself in succeeding generations. (*Works*, vol.1, p.427.)

---

[2] Misquoting part of the above passage, Anderson and Tollison (1984) asserted,

> The author of the *Principles* can be accused of offering statist planning as only a vague panacea, but his overall prescription – in effect, the rejection of the liberal order of free trade, both domestic and foreign – is completely unambiguous. (p.462.)

They misrepresented Steuart as an advocate of 'totalitarian mercantilism' (p.465). In fact, Steuart was sometimes regarded as an anachronistic state interventionist by his contemporaries (e.g., *Critical Review* (1767; p.411 – quoted by Vickers (1970; p.1190)), and mistaken for a 'naive' economic planner in later literature (e.g., Johnson (1937), p.234). Basically, Steuart saw the relation between the economy and the state in a 'free society', as follows:

> When once a state begins to subsist by the consequences of industry, there is less danger to be apprehended from the power of the sovereign. The mechanism of his administration becomes more complex, and ... he finds himself so bound up by the laws of his political oeconomy, that every transgression of them runs him into new difficulties. (*Works*, vol.1, pp.330-1.)

In other words, as 'trade and industry' take their firm root in the society, its economy and the state naturally go their own ways; and *vice versa*. Cf. the quotation at the beginning of this chapter. Also cf. section 3, Ch.9 above.

Nevertheless, Steuart's state interventionism is not a mere presupposition or assumption of his economic analysis, but its logical conclusion. We can ascertain this from every quarter of his political economy.[3]

After showing how the 'current price' of commodities, determined in the markets, serves as a signal for the efficient allocation of resources in the economy, Steuart emphasized the role of the state in promoting 'double competition' to ensure the 'balance of work and demand'. According to him, the self-adjusting market mechanism or what is called market force driven by profit-seeking capitalist entrepreneurs, might not prevent the 'subversion' of the 'balance of work and demand' in a dynamic sense. Unless the state guides the market economy by means of its industrial policy, some possible imbalance between economic sectors or industries would impede the growth of the economy as a whole, directly or indirectly through the decline of foreign trade. This point indicates expressly where the analytical focus of Steuart's political economy is. It is on the interdependence of economic sectors and the dynamic process of balanced growth between them, rather than on any static criterion for the efficiency of the allocation of economic resources in terms of *Pareto* optimality.

While Steuart's case for the state interventionism is based on his dynamic view of an exchange economy, it further points to a particular sphere of the workings of the economy. Having grasped the interdependence of different economic sectors and social classes, Steuart explained the determination of the level of output, the amount of employment and the size of population in the economy, in terms of the notion of 'effectual demand'. The creation of 'effectual demand' among different sectors and classes in the economy is directly related to his state interventionism. According to Steuart,

> The political oeconomy of government is brought to perfection, when every class in general, and every individual in particular, is made to be aiding and assisting the community, in proportion to the assistance he receives from it. (*Works*, vol.1, p.109.)

As to the question of how the state intervenes in the market, or how it creates 'effectual demand' in the economy, Steuart's theory of economic growth and foreign trade answers it. While the amount of 'effectual demand' in the economy is basically determined by two factors, i.e., the productivity of economic sectors and the luxury spending of social classes, both factors set limits to the growth of output in a closed economy with a given endowment of natural resources. Foreign trade might be a breakthrough, as it adds some

[3] Vickers (1970) suggested that the interventionism in Steuart's *Inquiry* must be understood in terms of the 'internal coherence and theoretical acumen of work itself' (p.1190). Indeed, Eltis (1986) succinctly dealt with Steuart's state interventionism to this effect. After clarifying the basic assumptions of Steuart's economic analysis, he examined how they led him to the interventionist conclusions, including the actual policy proposals, and articulated some different analytical grounds for Steuart's interventionism and Smith's *laissez-faire*. Also cf. Sen (1957; ch.IX) and Meek (1958).

extra 'effective demand'. In his analysis of the three stages of trade, Steuart prescribed in detail different growth strategies for respective stages. The competitiveness of export prices decides whether or not a country could open the door to foreign trade. It is in this discussion of growth strategies that Steuart's interventionism is revealed most explicitly.

Apparently, Steuart's argument against the legal rate of interest produces counterevidence of his state interventionism. Nevertheless, in fact, the former attests to the nature of the latter: that is, his interventionism is a corollary of his economic analysis rather than its presupposition. On the basis of his theory of money, Steuart maintained that the state's stipulation of a legal rate of interest lower than the market rate would result in a lower level of output in the economy than otherwise. Apart from this, his arguments for fixing the money-unit in a mean proportion of metals, using paper money and facilitating banking, all reflect the interventionist view based on his monetary analysis. His macroeconomic analysis of public finance represents another systematic exposition of the major part played by the state in the monetary economy.

III

Under the theme of trade and growth, Steuart left in his *Inquiry* a clear message of the role of the state in the modern exchange economy. Since it first appeared in 1767, there have been many ups and downs of different economic ideas and doctrines. Depending on the trend of the times, his work, as a 'prophet of the mixed economy',[4] has drawn more or less attention; far less than what it deserves, however. It is still our job to shed ever new light upon it. We can never exhaust a forest by taking out bits of dead wood.

[4] Hutchison (1967), p.646.

References

Akhtar, M.A. (1978), 'Sir James Steuart on Economic Growth', *Scottish Journal of Political Economy*, Vol.25, No.1, February, pp.57-74.

Akhtar, M.A. (1979), 'An Analytical Outline of Sir James Steuart's Macroeconomic Model', *Oxford Economic Papers*, (New Series) Vol.31, July, pp.283-302.

Alexander, S.S. (1952), 'Effects of a Devaluation on a Trade Balance', *IMF Staff Papers*, pp.263-78.

Anderson, G.M. and Tollison, R.D. (1984), 'Sir James Steuart as the Apotheosis of Mercantilism and His Relation to Adam Smith', *Southern Economic Journal*, Vol.51, No.1, July, pp.456-68.

Beer, M. (1938), *Early British Economics: from the XIIIth to the Middle of the XVIIIth Century*, London: Allen & Unwin.

Bell, J.F. (1953), *A History of Economic Thought*, New York: Ronald Press.

Blaug, M. (1985), *Economic Theory in Retrospect*, 4th ed., Cambridge: Cambridge University Press.

Bowley, M. (1973), *Studies in the History of Economic Theory before 1870*, London: Macmillan.

Bowley, M. (1979), 'Some Aspects of the Treatment of Capital in *The Wealth of Nations*', in *Essays on Adam Smith*, ed. Andrew S. Skinner and T. Wilson, Oxford: Clarendon Press.

Campbell, R. (1947), *Sir James Steuart: A Study in the Development of Economic Thought*, Dissertation, University of California.

Cantillon, R. (1775), *Essai sur la Nature du Commerce en Général (Essay on the Nature of Trade in General)*, ed. and tr. in English, Henry Higgs, Macmillan and Co., 1931; reissued, London: Frank Cass and Co., 1959.

Chamley, P. (1962), 'Sir James Steuart Inspirateur de la Théorie Générale de Lord Keynes?', *Revue d'Économie Politique*, No.3, pp.303-13.

Chamley, P. (1963), *Economie Politique et Philosophie chez Steuart et Hegel*, Paris: Librairie Dalloz.

Chamley, P. (1965), *Documents Relatifs à Sir James Steuart*. Paris: Librairie Dalloz.

The Critical Review, Vols.23 and 24, 1767.

Davidson. P. (1978), *Money and the Real World*, London: Macmillan.

Davie, G.E. (1967), 'Anglophobe and Anglophile', *Scottish Journal of Political Economy*, Vol.14, November, pp.291-304.

Eagly, R.V. (1961), 'Sir James Steuart and the "Aspiration Effect"', *Economica*, February, pp.53-61.

Eatwell, J. (1979), 'Theories of Value, Output and Employment', first published in *Thames Papers in Political Economy*; revised version in Eatwell and Milgate (1983).

Eatwell, J. and Milgate, M. (1983), eds., *Keynes's Economics and the Theory of Value and Distribution*, London: Duckworth.

Ekelund, R.B., Jr. and Hébert, R.F. (1990), *A History of Economic Theory and Method*, 3rd ed., McGraw-Hill.

Eltis, W. (1975a), 'François Quesnay: a Reinterpretation 1, the *Tableau Economique*', *Oxford Economic Papers*, Vol.XXVII, 2; revised in Ch.1 of Eltis (1984).

Eltis, W. (1975b), 'François Quesnay: a Reinterpretation 2, the Theory of Economic Growth', *Oxford Economic Papers*, Vol.XXVII, 3; revised in Ch.2 of Eltis (1984).

Eltis, W. (1984), *The Classical Theory of Economic Growth*, London: Macmillan Press.

Eltis, W. (1986), ' Sir James Steuart's Corporate State', *Ideas in Economics* (Proceedings of Section F (Economics) of the British Association for the Advancement of Science, Strathclyde, 1985), ed. R.D. Collison Black, London: Macmillan.

Eltis, W. (1987), 'Steuart, Sir James (1713-1780)', *The New Palgrave: A Dictionary of Economics*, Vol.III, pp.494-97.

Erskine, D. Steuart (11th Earl of Buchan) (1792), 'Memoir of the Life of Sir James Steuart Denham, Bart.', in *Transactions* of the Society of Antiquaries of Scotland, Vol.I.

Feilbogen, S. (1889), 'James Steuart und Adam Smith', *Zeitschrift für die gesamte Staatswissenschaft*, Vol.xlv, pp.218-60.

Fraser, L.M. (1937), 'Steuart, Sir James Denham (1712-80)', *Encyclopaedia of the Social Sciences*, Vol.14.

Gordon, B. (1975), *Economic Analysis before Adam Smith: Hesiod to Lessius*, London: Macmillan.

Groenewegen, P.D. (1977), tr. and ed. with an introduction, *The Economics of A.R.J. Turgot*, Hague: Martinus Nijhoff.

Groenewegen, P.D. (1983), tr. and ed., *Quesnay: Farmers 1756 and Turgot: Sur la Grande et la Petite Culture 1766*, Reprints of Economic Classics, Series 2, No.2, University of Sydney.

Grossman, H. (1943), 'The Evolutionary Revolt Against Classical Economics', *Journal of Political Economy*; Part I. 'In France – Condorcet, Saint-Simon, Sismonde de Sismondi', October, pp. 381-96; Part II. 'In England – James Steuart, Richard Jones, Karl Marx', December, pp.506-22.

Haney, L.H. (1949), *History of Economic Thought*, London: Macmillan.

Hasbach, W. (1891), *Untersuchungen über Adam Smith und die Entwicklung der Politschen Oekonomie*, Leipzig: Berlag von Dunder & Humblot.

Heaton, H. (1936), Economic History of Europe, revised ed., New York: Harper & Brothers.

Hicks, J.R. (1937), 'Mr. Keynes and the "Classics"; A Suggested Interpretation', *Econometrica,* 5, April, pp.147-59.

Higgs H. (1931), ed. and tr. in English with other material, *Essai sur la Nature du Commerce en Général* by Richard Cantillon, Macmillan & Co.; reissued, London: Frank Cass and Co., 1959.

Hollander, S. (1973), *The Economics of Adam Smith*, London: Heinemann.

Hull, C.H. (1900), 'Petty's Place in the History of Economic Theory', *Quarterly Journal of Economics*, Vol.XIV.

Hume, D. (1752), *Political Discourses*; 9 of 12 essays ('Of Commerce', 'Of Refinement in the Arts', 'Of Money', 'Of Interest', 'Of the Balance of Trade', 'Of the Jealousy of Trade', 'Of Taxes', 'Of Public Credit', and 'Of the Populousness of Ancient Nations') reprinted in *David Hume: Writings on Economics*, ed. and intro. Eugene Rotwein, Thomas Nelson and Sons, 1955.

Hutchison, T.W. (1967), Review of the Skinner edition of Steuart's *Inquiry*, *Economic Journal*, September, pp.645-7.

Hutchison, T.W. (1977), 'Keynes *versus* the Keynesians', published as a Hobart Paper by IEA; revised version in Hutchison (1981).

Hutchison, T.W. (1981), *The Politics and Philosophy of Economics: Marxians, Keynesians and Austrians*, Oxford: Basil Blackwell.

Hutchison, T.W. (1988), *Before Adam Smith: The Emergence of Political Economy, 1662-1776*, Oxford: Basil Blackwell.

Ingram, J.K. (1888), *A History of Political Economy*, London: A. & C. Black.

Jevons, W.S. (1881), 'Richard Cantillon and the Nationality of Political Economy', in Higgs (1931).

Johnson, E.A.J. (1937), *Predecessors of Adam Smith: The Growth of British Economic Thought*, London: P.S. King & Son (New York: Prentice-Hall).

Johnson, H.G. (1958), *International Trade and Economic Growth*, Cambridge: Harvard University Press.

Keynes, J.M. (1936), *The General Theory of Employment, Interest, and Money*, Macmillan; reprinted as Vol.VII of *The Collected Writings of John Maynard Keynes*, London: Macmillan St. Martin's Press for the Royal Economic Society, 1973.

Kobayashi, N. (1967), *James Steuart, Adam Smith, and Friedrich List*, Tokyo: The Science Council of Japan, Division of Economics, Commerce and Business Administration.

Kuczynski, M. and Meek, R.L. (1972), *Quesnay's Tableau Economique*, London: Macmillan.

Law, J. (1705), *Money and Trade Considered, With a Proposal for Supplying the Nation With Money*, Edinburgh; Andrew Anderson; reprinted ed., New York: Augustus M. Kelly, 1966.

Lerner, A.P. (1943), 'Functional Finance and the Federal Debt', *Social Research*, 10, February, pp.38-51.

Lerner, A.P. (1944), *The Economics of Control: Principles of Welfare Economics*, New York: Macmillan.

Letwin, W. (1963), *The Origins of Scientific Economics: English Economic Thought 1660-1776*, Methuen & Co. Ltd.

Locke, J. (1691), *Some Considerations of Consequences of the Lowering of Interest and Raising the Value of Money*; reprinted in Locke (1696).

Locke, J (1695), *Further Considerations Concerning Raising the Value of Money*; reprinted in Locke (1696).

Locke, J. (1696), *Several Papers Relating to Money, Interest and Trade, etcetera*; reprinted ed., New York: Augustus M. Kelly, 1968.

Macfie, A. L.(1955), 'The Scottish Tradition in Economic Thought', *Scottish Journal of Political Economy*, Vol.2.

Mandeville, B. de (1714-29), *The Fable of the Bees: or Private Vices, Public Benefits*, ed. with a commentary, by F.B. Kaye, 2 vols., Oxford: Clarendon, 1924.

Marshall, A. (1923), *Money Credit and Commerce*, London: Macmillan.

Marx, K. (1859), *A Contribution to the Critique of Political Economy*; tr. S.W. Ryazanskaya, ed. Maurice Dobb, London: Lawrence & Wishart, 1970.

Marx, K. (1862-3), *The Theories of Surplus Value*; Part I, tr. Emile Burns, ed. S. Ryazanskay, London: Lawrence & Wishart, 1969; Part II, tr. Renate Simpson, ed. S. Ryazanskaya, London: Lawrence & Wishart, 1969; Part III, tr. Jack Cohen and S.W. Ryazanskaya, ed. S.W. Ryazanskaya and Richard Dixon, London: Lawrence & Wishart, 1972.

Marx, K. (1867), *Capital: A Critique of Political Economy*, Vol.1; tr. Ben Fowkes, Harmondsworth: Penguin Books, 1976.

Meek, R.L. (1954b), 'The Scottish Contribution to Marxist Sociology', in *Democracy and the Labour Movement*, ed. John Saville, London: Lawrence and Wishart; amended in *Economics and Ideology and Other Essays: Studies in the Development of Economic Thought*, London: Chapman & Hall, 1967.

Meek, R.L. (1958), 'The Economics of Control Prefigured by Sir James Steuart', *Science and Society* 22, Fall, pp.289-305; amended in 'The Rehabilitation of Sir James Steuart', *Economics and Ideology and Other Essays: Studies in the Development of Economic Thought*, London: Chapman & Hall, 1967.

Meek, R.L. (1959), 'The Physiocratic Concept of Profit', *Economica*, February; amended version in Meek (1962).

Meek, R.L. (1960), 'Problems of *Tableau Economique*', *Economica*, November; amended and enlarged version in Meek (1962).

Meek, R.L. (1962), *The Economics of Physiocracy: Essays and Translations*, George Allen and Unwin; reprinted, Cambridge, Massachusetts: Harvard University Press.

Meek, R.L. (1973a), tr. and ed. with an introduction, *Turgot on Progress, Sociology and Economics*, Cambridge: Cambridge University Press.

Meek, R.L. (1973b), *Studies in the Labour Theory of Value*, 1st ed., 1956; 2nd ed., London: Lawrence & Wishart.

Monroe, A.E. (1923), *Monetary Theory before Adam Smith*; reprinted, New York: Augustus M. Kelley, 1966.

Montesquieu, Baron de (Charles de Secondat) (1748), *L'Esprit des Lois (The Spirit of the Laws)*; tr. Thomas Nugent, intro. Franz Neumann, 2 vols. in one, New York: Hafner Press, 1949.

The Monthly Review, Vol.XXXVI and Vol.XXXVII, 1767; Vol.L, Series II, 1806.

Murphy, A. (1986), *Richard Cantillon: Entrepreneur and Economist*, Oxford: Clarendon Press.

The New Palgrave: A Dictionary of Economics (1987), 4 vols., eds. J. Eatwell, M. Milgate and P. Newman, London: Macmillan.

O'Brien, G. (1920), *An Essay on Mediaeval Economic Teaching*, London: Longmans, Green & Co.; reprinted, New York: Augustus M. Kelly Publishers, 1967.

Perelman, M. (1983), *Classical Political Economy: Primitive Accumulation and the Social Division of Labour*, London: Rowman & Allanhead.

Perlman, M. (1990), 'Sir James Steuart's Absorption and Wealth Approach to the Balance of Trade', *History of Political Economy*, 22:1, pp.125-36.

Perrotta, C. (1991), 'Is the Mercantilist Theory of the Favourable Balance of Trade Really Erroneous?', *History of Political Economy*, 23:2, PP.301-36.

Petty, Sir W. (1662), *A Treatise of Taxes and Contributions*, written and published anonymously in 1662; in Petty (1899).

Petty, Sir W. (1665), *Verbum Sapienti*, written in 1665; in Petty (1899).

Petty, Sir W. (1671-2), *The Political Anatomy of Ireland*, written in 1671-2; in Petty (1899).

Petty, Sir W. (1672-6), *Political Arithmetic*, written in 1672-6; in Petty (1899).

Petty, Sir W. (1682), *Quantulumcunque concerning Money*, written in 1682; in Petty (1899).

Petty, Sir W. (1899), *Economic Writings of Sir William Petty*, ed. Charles Henry Hull, 2 vols., Cambridge: Cambridge University Press.

Petty, Sir W. (1927), *The Petty Papers: Some Unpublished Writings of Sir William Petty*, Vol.1, ed. Marquis of Lansdowne, 2 vols.; reprinted in 1 vol., New York: Augustus M. Kelly Publishers, 1967.

Postlethwayt, M. (1757), *Britain's Commercial Interest Explained and Improved*; reprinted ed., New York: Augustus M. Kelly, 1968.

Quesnay, F. (1757a), *Farmers*; extracts in Groenewegen (1983).

Quesnay, F. (1757b), *Corn*; extracts in Meek (1962).

Quesnay, F. (1757c), *Men*, published in 1908; extracts in Meek (1962).

Quesnay, F. (1757d), *Taxation*, appearing 1902; extracts in Meek (1962).

Quesnay, F. (1758), *Tableau Economique*, 1st ed.; 2nd and 3rd ed., 1759; in Meek (1962) and in Kuczynski and Meek (1972).

Quesnay, F.(1763), *Rural Philosophy*, written together with Mirabeau; extracts in Meek (1962).

Quesnay, F.(1766a), *Analysis*; extracts in Meek (1962).

Quesnay, F.(1766b), *First Economic Problem*; extracts in Meek (1962).

Quesnay, F.(1767), *Second Economic Problem*; extracts in Meek (1962).

Ricardo, D. (1951-73), *The Works and Correspondence of David Ricardo*, ed. Piero Sraffa with M.H. Dobb, 11 vols., Cambridge: Cambridge University Press.

Roll, E. (1942), *A History of Economic Thought*, London; revised and enlarged ed., London: Faber and Faber, 1961.

Roncaglia, A. (1985), *Petty: The Origin of Political Economy*, University College Cardiff Press.

Schumpeter, J.A. (1954), *History of Economic Analysis*, New York: Oxford University Press.

Sen, S.R. (1947), 'Sir James Steuart's General Theory of Employment, Interest and Money', *Economica*, 14, February, pp.19-36.

Sen, S.R. (1957), *The Economics of Sir James Steuart*, London: G. Bell & Sons.

Skinner, A.S. (1962), 'Sir James Steuart: Economics and Politics', *Scottish Journal of Political Economy*, Vol.9, pp.17-37.

Skinner, A.S. (1963), 'Sir James Steuart: International Relations', *Economic History Review*, Vol.15, pp.438-50.

Skinner, A.S. (1965a), 'Economics and History – The Scottish Enlightenment', *Scottish Journal of Political Economy,* Vol.12, February, pp.1-22.

Skinner, A.S. (1965b), 'Economics and the Problem of Method: An Eighteenth Century View', *Scottish Journal of Political Economy*, Vol.12, pp.267-80.

Skinner, A.S. (1966), *Sir James Steuart: An Inquiry into the Principles of Political Oeconomy*, abridged ed. of Steuart (1767) with a biographical sketch, an analytical introduction and appendices, Edinburgh and London: Oliver & Boyd.

Skinner, A.S. (1967), 'Money and Prices: A Critique of the Quantity Theory', *Scottish Journal of Political Economy*, Vol.14, November, pp.275-90.

Skinner, A.S. (1981), 'Sir James Steuart: Author of a System', *Scottish Journal of Political Economy*, Vol.28, No.1, February, pp.20-42.
Smith, A. (1776), *An Inquiry into the Nature and Causes of the Wealth of Nations*, ed. Edward Cannan, The University of Chicago Press, 1976.
Smith, A. (1977), *The Correspondence of Adam Smith*, ed. E.C. Mossner and I.S. Ross, Oxford: Clarendon Press.
Sraffa, P. (1951), 'Introduction' to Ricardo (1951-73), *op.cit.*, Vol.1, pp.xiii-lxii.
Sraffa, P. (1960), *Production of Commodities by Means of Commodities: Prelude to a Critique of Economic Theory*, Cambridge University Press.
Stephen, L. (1876), *A History of English Thought in the 18th Century*, 2 vols.; 2nd ed., London: Smith, Elder & Co., 1881.
Stettner, W.F. (1945), 'Sir James Steuart on the Public Debt', *Quarterly Journal of Economics*, Vol.LIX, pp.451-76.
Steuart, Sir J. (1759), *A Dissertation on the Policy of Grain, with a view to a Plan for preventing scarcity or exorbitant prices, in the Common Markets of England*; reprinted in Steuart (1805), Vol.5.
Steuart, Sir J. (1761), *A Dissertation upon the Doctrine and Principles of Money Applied to the German Coin*, Tubingen; reprinted in Steuart (1805), Vol.5.
Steuart, Sir J. (1767), *An Inquiry into the Principles of Political Oeconomy: Being an Essay on the Science of Domestic Policy in Free Nations. In which are particularly considered Population, Agriculture, Trade, Industry, Money, Coin, Interest, Circulation, Banks, Exchange, Public Credit, and Taxes*, 2 quarto vols., London: A. Miller and T. Cadell; reprinted, 3 vols., Dublin, 1770; translated into German by J. Von Pauli, Hamburg, 1769-70, and by C.F. Schott, Tubingen, 1769-72; translated into French by M. de Senovert, Paris, 1789; a revised version was published in the first 4 vols. of Steuart (1805); a reduced edition in Skinner (1966).
Steuart, Sir J. (1769), *Considerations on the Interest of the County of Lanark in Scotland; which (in several respects) may be applied to that of Great Britain in General*; reprinted in Steuart (1805), Vol.5.
Steuart, Sir J. (1772), *The Principles of Money Applied to the Present State of the Coin in Bengal*; reprinted in Steuart (1805), Vol.5.
Steuart, Sir J. (1805), *The Works, Political Metaphysical, and Chronological, of the late Sir James Steuart of Coltness, Bart. now first collected by General Sir James Steuart, Bart. his Son, from his Father's Corrected Copies. To which are Subjoined Anecdotes of the Author*, 6 vols., London: T. Cadell & W. Davies, Strand; reprinted, New York: Augustus M. Kelly Publishers, 1967.
Steuart, General Sir James (1805), 'Anecdotes of the Life of Sir James Steuart, Baronet', in Steuart (1805), Vol.6.

Taylor, W.L. (1957), 'A Short Life of Sir James Steuart: Political Economist', *South African Journal of Economics*, Vol.25, pp.290-302.

Thiers, A. (1859), *The Mississippi Bubble: A Memoir of John Law, to which are added, Authentic Accounts of the Darien Expedition, and the South Sea Scheme*, tr. and ed. Frank S. Fiske, New York: Greenwood Press, 1969.

Turgot, A.R.J. (1766), *Réflexions sur la Formation et la Distribution des Richesses (Reflections on the Formation and the Distribution of Wealth)*, published 1769; in Meek (1973a) and Groenewegen (1977).

Vaggi, G. (1983), 'The Physiocratic Theory of Prices', *Contributions to Political Economy*, 2.

Vaggi, G. (1985), 'A Physiocratic Model of Relative Prices and Income Distribution', *Economic Journal*, Vol.95, December.

Vaggi, G. (1987), *The Economics of François Quesnay*, Durham (U.S.A.): Duke University Press.

Vickers, D. (1959), *Studies in the Theory of Money, 1690-1776*, London: Peter Owen Ltd.

Vickers, D. (1970), 'The Works, Political, Metaphysical, and Chronological, of Sir James Steuart', Review, *Journal of Economic Literature*, 8, December, pp.1190-5.

Viner, J. (1937), *Studies in the Theory of International Trade*, London: George Allen & Unwin Ltd.

Woloch, I. (1982), *Eighteenth-Century Europe: Tradition and Progress 1715-1789*, W.W. Norton & Company.

Woog, H. (1950), The Tableau Economique of François Quesnay: An Essay in the Explanation of its Mechanism and a Critical Review of the Interpretations of Marx, Bilimovic and Oncken, Bern: A. Francke A.G. Verlag.

Zaller, R. (1984), *Europe in Transition, 1660-1815*, New York: Harper & Row.

Index